TM

References for the Rest of Us! ®

BESTSELLING BOOK SERIES

Are you intimidated and confused by computers? Do you find that traditional manuals are overloaded with technical details you'll never use? Do your friends and family always call you to fix simple problems on their PCs? Then the For Dummies® computer book series from Wiley Publishing, Inc. is for you.

For Dummies books are written for those frustrated computer users who know they aren't really dumb but find that PC hardware, software, and indeed the unique vocabulary of computing make them feel helpless. For Dummies books use a lighthearted approach, a down-to-earth style, and even cartoons and humorous icons to dispel computer novices' fears and build their confidence. Lighthearted but not lightweight, these books are a perfect survival guide for anyone forced to use a computer.

> *"I like my copy so much I told friends; now they bought copies."*
> — Irene C., Orwell, Ohio

> *"Quick, concise, nontechnical, and humorous."*
> — Jay A., Elburn, Illinois

> *"Thanks, I needed this book. Now I can sleep at night."*
> — Robin F., British Columbia, Canada

Already, millions of satisfied readers agree. They have made For Dummies books the #1 introductory level computer book series and have written asking for more. So, if you're looking for the most fun and easy way to learn about computers, look to For Dummies books to give you a helping hand.

Wiley Publishing, Inc.

5/09

ACCESS 2000 PROGRAMMING FOR DUMMIES®

ACCESS 2000 PROGRAMMING FOR DUMMIES®

by Rob Krumm

WILEY

Wiley Publishing, Inc.

Access 2000 Programming For Dummies®

Published by
Wiley Publishing, Inc.
909 Third Avenue
New York, NY 10022
www.wiley.com

Copyright © 1999 Wiley Publishing, Inc., Indianapolis, Indiana

Published simultaneously in Canada

For general information on our other products and services or to obtain technical support, please contact our Customer Care Department within the U.S. at 800-762-2974, outside the U.S. at 317-572-3993, or fax 317-572-4002.

Wiley also publishes its books in a variety of electronic formats. Some content that appears in print may not be available in electronic books.

Library of Congress Cataloging-in-Publication Data:

Library of Congress Control Number: 99-63213

ISBN: 0-7645-0565-3

Manufactured in the United States of America

10 9 8 7 6

1B/SQ/QW/QT/IN

About the Author

Rob Krumm has been using personal computers since 1979, when he was working as a teacher in Philadelphia. In 1981 he founded his own school to teach people how to use personal computers. In 1983, he published *Understanding and Using dBase II,* the first of 49 books he has written on computers and software. In 1997 Rob worked with the OSCE in Bosnia building databases for the municipal elections. He is the owner of Enotech software, which produces Winebase II software for California wineries and other e-commerce clients. Rob teaches MCSE courses at Diablo Valley Community College in Concord, California.

Rob can be reached at robkrumm@pacbell.net or through the Web site www.wbase2.com.

Dedication

We must learn to reawaken and keep ourselves awake, not by mechanical aids, but by an infinite expectation of the dawn, which does not forsake us in our soundest sleep. I know of no more encouraging fact than the unquestionable ability of man to elevate his life by a conscious endeavor. *Henry Thoreau*

For Eric, Amber, Nicholas and Alexander Robert — the next generation.

Publisher's Acknowledgments

We're proud of this book; please send us your comments through our online registration form located at `www.dummies.com/register/`.

Some of the people who helped bring this book to market include the following:

Acquisitions, Editorial, and Media Development

Project Editor: Pat O'Brien

Acquisitions Editor: Greg Croy

Copy Editor: Darren Meiss

Technical Editor: Sally Neuman

Media Development Editor: Marita Ellixson

Associate Permissions Editor: Carmen Krikorian

Media Development Coordinator: Megan Roney

Editorial Manager: Rev Mengle

Media Development Manager: Heather Heath Dismore

Editorial Assistant: Jamila Pree

Production

Associate Project Coordinator: Maridee Ennis

Layout and Graphics: Angela F. Hunckler, David McKelvey, Barry Offringa, Brent Savage, Jacque Schneider, Michael A. Sullivan, Brian Torwelle, Dan Whetstine

Proofreaders: Chris Collins, Stephanie Koutek, Nancy Price, Marianne Santy, Rebecca Senninger

Indexer: Sharon Hilgenberg

Publishing and Editorial for Technology Dummies

Richard Swadley, Vice President and Executive Group Publisher

Andy Cummings, Vice President and Publisher

Mary C. Corder, Editorial Director

Publishing for Consumer Dummies

Diane Graves Steele, Vice President and Publisher

Joyce Pepple, Acquisitions Director

Composition Services

Gerry Fahey, Vice President of Production Services

Debbie Stailey, Director of Composition Services

Contents at a Glance

Cartoons at a Glance

By Rich Tennant

page 9

page 123

page 399

page 241

page 387

page 319

Fax: 978-546-7747
E-mail: richtennant@the5thwave.com
World Wide Web: www.the5thwave.com

Table of Contents

Introduction

*E*verything is a database!" That is the remark I make the first evening of each course I teach. I have always believed that if you want to understand anything about computers, from spreadsheets to the Internet, look for the database within and you will find the key to the technology. And, if you want to control and customize the technology, the key is understanding how to modify your own database programs.

Sounds pretty intimidating. But what I like about Access 2000 is that it provides all of the tools needed to learn both databases and database programming in a single package. Even though you may never have composed anything more elaborate than a formula that adds two numbers together, you will be well on your way to transforming Access 2000 into your own custom-designed database application by the time you finish this book.

Who Needs This Book

Databases are different. Most PC applications (word processing, spreadsheet, graphics) are stand-alone applications designed for personal productivity. When you accumulate data into a database, it's only natural to share that information with a group of people who work together in harmony (more or less) toward a common goal (despite appearances to the contrary). In fact, the real value of the data surfaces when many different people apply the data in different ways.

Access 2000 provides Windows users with a powerful, simple-to-use tool for storing and sharing that data. This book explains how you can use the programming language built right into Access to make Access fit the needs and preferences of your organization, how to avoid tedious repetitive tasks, and how to make Access more intelligent.

There are two big reasons why you should take advantage of Access programming:

- It is easier to teach Access about your business than it is to teach your colleagues about Access.
- Since you have already paid for the programming language when you bought Access, you may as well get your money's worth.

Another reason is that you will get quite a kick out of watching other people use the programs you created. Take my word for it.

About This Book

The purpose of this book is to get you to exercise the power of Access programming as quickly as possible. If you've never done any programming, you can approach the subject in two ways:

- ✔ **Scholarly.** This approach begins with a chapter or two explaining the theory, terminology, philosophy, and conceptual framework of the programming language before you go on to actually doing something.
- ✔ **Total Immersion.** The other approach is to just jump in and start doing things and watch how the program reacts to your instructions. You pick up the theory, terminology, philosophy, and concepts along the way.

No big shock to say that in a ...*For Dummies* book the winner is Total Immersion. By the second chapter, you will have already written your first program, and it will do a lot more than say "Hello World." The examples in this book deal with the same type of everyday information you find in any business, and the CD programs provide practical tools to process and organize that data. More about the CD later in this Introduction.

How This Book Is Organized

This book is organized into six parts. Feel free to begin at Chapter 1 and then progress sequentially through the chapters, or just skip around and look for the juiciest tidbits. (Hey, it's *your* book.)

Part I: Building Blocks

Instead of an overview of Access or programming, the three chapters in this section get right to the heart of all Access programming — that is, the three building blocks: Objects, Statements, and SQL. This section provides all of the fundamental tools and techniques you need to use and understand Access programming.

Part II: Educating Access

Computers are very good at doing certain things — such as adding lots of numbers very quickly and very accurately. However, they don't know much about life on the planet Earth. What makes a good application is that it include some understanding of the work people are actually trying to do with the computer. The three chapters in this section look at how you can educate Access by programming intelligent user interfaces. An intelligent interface combines standard Access forms and controls with Access programming code. The results are forms that are easy to use and intuitive to work with because the Access programming code logically connects the individual elements into a more intelligent whole.

Part III: Controlling the Dialog

This section expands on the concepts involved in making intelligent interfaces by explaining how to use forms and Access programming to create custom-designed applications. The three chapters in this section will show you how to create custom-designed dialog boxes, linking reports to specific data sets and how to work with multiple databases, including Microsoft SQL Server databases.

Part IV: Active Controls and Objects

Access 2000 is not just a stand-alone product. It is designed to integrate with the other components of Microsoft Office, such as Word, Excel, Outlook, and Internet Explorer. This section deals with integrating Access into the Office suite and using Access as a basis for Web-based applications.

Part V: The Part of Tens

Here is a quick tour through my favorite programming tricks. If you find them half as handy as I do, they'll be worth the price of this book by themselves.

Part VI: Appendix

I've dedicated a few precious pages to showing how the CD works.

Conventions Used in This Book

In any technical book (and let's face it — computers are nothing if not technical) there is a need to distinguish different types of text or write about computer stuff, such as shortcut keys or menu commands. Here's what you need to know about those special items:

Programming code

This book is full of text that represents programs written in the Access Visual Basic language. Programmers refer to this text as *code*. This is the stuff you actually type into Access in order to create programs. You find code examples in this book styled as follows:

```
For k = 1 To 10
    Debug.Print "Number = " & k
Next
```

Syntax examples

A syntax example is a special type of code example used to illustrate the general form of a statement rather than a specific example. In the following code line, the words *somenumber, start,* and *end* are in italics to indicate the location where you would enter some number, a start value, and an end value. I don't ask you to type in these examples. They are for reference purposes.

```
For somenumber = start To end
```

Sometimes I draw your attention to a particular segment of code by formatting the segment in boldface. This formatting has no purpose other than to grab your attention.

Literals

Programming languages allow you to insert words and phrases that don't mean anything to the program but are useful for humans who need to read the output of your programs. These phrases are called *literals*. Literals are always enclosed in punctuation marks called *delimiters*. In Access, text items can be enclosed in either double quotes (" ") or single quotes (' ') so long as you use the same punctuation at the beginning and the end of the literal.

```
"Walter Lafish" or 'Walter Lafish'
```

Access also supports literal dates. Dates are delimited with # characters as the following line of code shows.

```
#1/1/2000#
```

Upper and lower

Access Visual Basic is not case-sensitive. This means that when you enter code, it doesn't matter which of the letters is in upper- or lowercase. The three following lines have exactly the same meaning:

```
Orders.RecordCount
Orders.Recordcount
orders.recordcount
```

Note, however, that the code in this book uses the upper- and lowercase conventions that appear in the official Access Visual Basic language guide from Microsoft. The guide uses uppercase letters in the middle of some words to make their meaning clear. For example, the term RecordCount is shown with an uppercase C to indicate that it has something to do with the number of records.

```
Orders.RecordCount
```

If you type code, you really don't have to bother with uppercase letters at all if you don't want to. Access automatically changes the text to uppercase letters for you.

Line continuation

When you enter programming code into Access, you can type lines that are much wider than the width of the text that can be printed in this book. In order to write code that fits the pages of this book, I have inserted line-continuation characters. The following two lines actually represent one line of code because the end of the first line has a space followed by an _. This tells Access that the statement continues on the next line.

```
StandardListPrice = Cost * CustomerDiscount _
   * TaxRate
```

If you retype the code, you are free to skip the line-continuation characters and enter the statement on a single line. If you choose to enter the line-continuation characters, remember that you must include a space followed by a _#. Don't forget the space!

Shortcut keys

When you need to enter a special key combination (such as pressing and holding down Ctrl and then pressing G), I write it as Ctrl+G.

Menu command

When you need to use a command on a menu, such as choosing the Open Database command from the File menu, I write it as File⇨Open Database.

Foolish Assumptions

Any book written in the _...For Dummies_ style should avoid assuming too much about the potential reader. However, it's not possible to cover everything about Access in a single book. I assume that anyone reading about programming Access will be familiar with (not a master of) the following concepts:

- ✔ How to use the Database window
- ✔ How to create a table and define fields
- ✔ How to create a form or a report
- ✔ How to create a simple query using the Query form

Note that you don't need to know anything about macros in order to write programs. My own preference is to forget about macros altogether and simply work with Access Visual Basic.

Icons Used in This Book

This icon flags useful information or suggestions that, while maybe not part of the current example, might come in handy later on.

I have made my share of mistakes writing programs. A word to the wise will (hopefully) keep you out of some of these programming potholes.

This data is included for those of you who wonder about why some odd-looking thing works or where some strange-sounding term got its name. You can program perfectly well without this information but some people find it comforting.

This icon marks information that I may have given to you already, but I want to be sure that you remember (hence the name, right?).

This icon marks a new feature added to Access 2000 that wasn't included in earlier versions.

This icon shows you where to find a table, query, form, report, or module on the CD. In general, each heading in this book contains one or more examples. The text tells you about the problem or task and the Access 2000 technique you need to use. The explanation ends with the result followed by one of these icons which tells you where on the CD you can find the example.

Where to Go from Here

Now that you've got all of this preliminary stuff out of the way, you're ready to get started. Remember to check out the CD attached to the back cover of this book because it contains the files you need to duplicate the examples in the chapters.

Time to get started. Fire up Access and get started programming right now!

Part I
Building Blocks

The 5th Wave   By Rich Tennant

"DO YOU WANT ME TO CALL THE COMPANY AND HAVE THEM SEND ANOTHER REVIEW COPY OF THEIR DATABASE SOFTWARE SYSTEM, OR DO YOU KNOW WHAT YOU'RE GOING TO WRITE?"

In this part . . .

Even the Great Wall of China was built one brick at a time. As it turns out, programming is a lot like that. No matter how fancy the computer or hot or cool the language, the program is built one line at a time.

Access programming has basic building blocks that you use to create all of the other programming parts. Part I explains these basic building blocks.

Chapter 1

Objects and Names

● ●

In This Chapter

▶ Me? A programmer?

▶ A name for everything

▶ Using CD databases

▶ Displaying object properties and methods

▶ Setting properties

▶ The DoCmd object

● ●

The purpose of this book, to put things as simply as possible, is to help Access users become Access programmers. In this spirit of simplicity, the term *programmer* doesn't refer to someone who necessarily makes a living writing computer applications. Here the term refers to anyone who wants to move beyond merely clicking and typing through the Access interface and tap into the full power of Access. The real power of Access programming is that it allows you to shape and mold Access into a system custom-designed for your needs and the needs of your coworkers.

Me? A Programmer?

Programming is often thought of as a highly technical skill that is as tedious and frustrating as building a model of the Space Shuttle out of toothpicks. I don't agree.

Programming is really about building *intelligence* into your computer. You provide the intelligence. As you write a program, you teach the computer what you know so that the computer can help you more.

Opening your toolkit

When the program comes out of the box (or should I say *off the CD?*), Access consists of a generic set of information management tools. Almost any business or organization can use Access because, after all, *everyone* accumulates data — usually lots of it! Programming can add features to Access that fit the way *you* work with your databases.

With programming, you can place a button on a form that writes 2,500 invoices, charges credit cards, and electronically sends out 2,500 orders with a single click! (I know such buttons are possible because I wrote a program in Access that performs these functions.)

A specialized button like the one I describe isn't useful to everyone. That's why Access doesn't come with a built-in button like that one. However, Access includes the *Visual Basic for Applications* programming language that allows you to build that button or other features just as powerful.

When you build intelligence into a form, a report, or a button, you accomplish several important goals:

- **Make the machine do the work.** While working with a program, you often find that you need to repeat the same series of actions over and over again to accomplish your goal — that is, you're trying to work like a *machine*.

  All appearances to the contrary, you're not a machine. Attempts to behave like one always lead to errors because humans simply don't do well with mechanically repeating a long series of operations. Such repetition also takes a lot of time that you can use for tasks that actually require human intelligence!

  Learning to program enables you to shift the burden of this mechanical work to the computer — where such work should have gone in the first place. You reduce errors and save time.

- **Ensure reliability if you go on vacation.** Suppose, for the moment, that you don't mind performing a lot of mindless mechanical work and you seldom make any errors — at least none that get you into trouble. You're still left with the problem that if you're not present all the time, who's left at work who knows what to do to get your work done?

  If you program your tasks into an Access 2000 application, someone else at the office can keep things going, even if you're not there to tell that person exactly what to do. In this case, you transfer your *business knowledge* into a form that other people can work with fairly easily. So you don't need to wallpaper your cube with notes every time you want to take an afternoon off.

✔ **Make things work as they should.** One of the most important, but seldom appreciated, advantages of writing programs is that doing so forces you to think logically and in great detail about how a given job needs to be done. This process often yields insight about your task and eliminates a lot of problems that may currently fall through the cracks. As you write a program, you actually try to explain how to do a job to a very stupid machine — that is, the computer.

Although a computer can do many things very quickly, computers have an abysmal lack of knowledge about the planet Earth. Luckily, you've probably spent a good portion of your life on such a planet. If you gain an understanding of the computer's language, you can fill your computer in on how you do stuff around here.

To put it another way, I see a lot of people working with computers but I don't see all that much computing. *Computing* means the computer is doing the work. The way most people use PC's reminds me of the guy who had so much trouble with his car that every Sunday he took his family out for a push. It's about time you stop pushing your computer around and start riding.

Well, that's the story about programming in a nutshell — less than a page! The rest of this book describes how to explain to the computer what you want it to do. The programming language in this book is called *Visual Basic*. As you discover how to express ideas in Visual Basic, you discover programming. Programming enables you to shape an Access 2000 application into performing the tasks that you need your computer to do.

Another reason for knowing Visual Basic is that Access isn't the only program that speaks this language. All the programs in Office 2000 (Word 2000, Excel 2000, PowerPoint 2000, Outlook, and the Binder) also speak Visual Basic. If you want to advance to a more professional style of programming, Visual Basic is a good place to start because Visual Basic 6.0 (a software development system) and Visual Basic within Access 2000 have a great deal in common.

A Name for Everything

You may wonder how a single language such as Visual Basic can enable you to program in a wide variety of applications, from Word 2000 to Excel 2000 to Access 2000. The trick is to separate the programming language into the following two parts:

✔ **Standard programming.** In any programming language, you must have commands to perform a core set of actions that all programs have in common. Because VBA is designed for Windows 95/98 (and its sister networking environment, Windows NT 4.0), the language includes basic operations common to all Windows programs. This core set of tasks doesn't change much from one application to another. Actions such as creating *variables,* evaluating *conditional expressions,* and executing *loops* are the stuff of which all programs consist. (In Chapter 2, you find out how to create and use these elements.)

✔ **Application-specific programming.** The other part of programming in Access 2000 (or other Office 2000 applications) is using the *objects* that the program provides for you. In Access 2000, for example, objects include tables, queries, forms, and reports. If you program in Access 2000, you don't need to create these objects. They're already there for you to use. The same is true in Excel 2000, except the objects consist of worksheets, cells, and charts. Your programming manipulates Access 2000 objects according to lists of instructions that you enter into special structures called *modules.* A module is a text document into which you type the instructions that you want Access to follow at a later time when you execute your program. Each Office 2000 application provides a set of built-in objects that form the basic building blocks on which you build your programs.

The goal of this chapter is to familiarize you with the set of objects that Access 2000 provides and to show you the conventions Access uses to refer to these objects. Understanding that every element in Access 2000 has a *name* is the first step towards learning Access 2000 programming. If you select from menus, click on buttons, or fill in dialog boxes to use Access, you don't need to know the actual names of the objects they represent. You can simply point and click on different areas of the screen to indicate what table, record, field, form, or control you want to use.

But if you want to write a program, you no longer have the luxury of simply pointing at something to tell Access 2000 that you want to use it. You must instead *write out* the name of the item in your program, as well as write out what you want Access to do with the object. Therefore, it is helpful to know the names of actions and procedures that Access can do. The text that tells Access what to do and what tools to use to perform the functions is a *statement.* One or more statements compose a program.

Before you can get comfortable with writing out lists of program statements, you may want to take some time to explore the way Access 2000 assigns names to all of its elements. Access assigns random names to its elements. The elements are organized into a hierarchy that contains some objects within other objects. This *hierarchy* is known as an *object model* because it represents all the elements contained within Access 2000.

The object model reflects the fact that each element in an application has a specific relationship to all the other elements. Access 2000, for example, contains *database objects*. Within each database, one or more table objects exist.

Within each table, one or more field objects exist. This series of interconnected relationships among the objects forms a sort of outline in which the objects are arranged in sections and subsections. Figure 1-1 illustrates a portion of the Access 2000 object model.

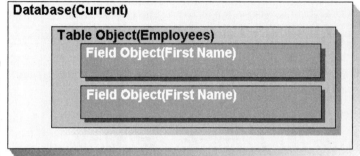

Figure 1-1:
Application objects are organized in a hierarchy.

Using the CD Databases

The CD-ROM at the back of this book contains MDB files for each chapter. These files provide all the tables, queries, forms, and other Access elements that I discuss in each chapter. For this chapter, you need to open the following database:

> *Database Folder: Access Prog Dummies\Chapter 1*
> *Database File: OBJECTS.MDB*
> *Module: Object Examples*

For the purposes of this chapter, you don't do much more than enter one-line commands with the Objects Database. However, I include all the commands shown in this chapter on the CD for your convenience.

If you want to use the CD examples for this chapter, do the following:

1. **Open the database file OBJECT.MDB.**

2. **Click the Modules tab.**

   You see a module named *Object Examples* displayed in the window.

3. **Click the Design button to open the Object Examples module.**

   This module contains the 34 examples, named `Example1()` through `Example34()`, that appear in this chapter.

4. **To run an example, scroll down the screen until you position the cursor over the command that you want to execute.**

5. Press F5.

The command executes. If the command begins with DebugPrint, switch to the Debug window (press Ctrl+G) to see the results. They appear only in the Debug window.

The following tip breaks one of my personal rules: I suggest that if you are new to Access programming, you take the trouble to actually type this chapter's commands instead of using the CD module. The commands are very long but the experience helps you learn the program.

Once you open the OBJECT.MDB database, you are ready to start using Visual Basic.

Using the Immediate window

Programming usually results in delayed gratification. In order to get anything done, you have to write down a bunch of statements first and then see the results later.

But Access 2000 includes a cool feature that allows you to receive an *immediate* response from Access after you enter a statement. This feature is the *Immediate window*. The Immediate window executes any statement that you type and displays the results underneath the command you typed. You can't build a program in the Immediate window but it is a great place to experiment with Access.

When you start Access, you never see the Immediate window right away. But you can press Ctrl+G at any time to access the Immediate window. Give it a try.

Oops? What happened to Access? What am I looking at?

Pressing Ctrl+G does more than display the Immediate window (see Figure 1-2). In addition to displaying the Immediate window, you also activate the Visual Basic portion of Access 2000. In certain respects, Visual Basic functions as if it were another application. It has its own window, a different menu, and an icon bar that differs from Access 2000. Visual Basic also displays other windows like the Project and Properties windows that you will learn more about later in this book.

Properties window

Project window   Immediate window

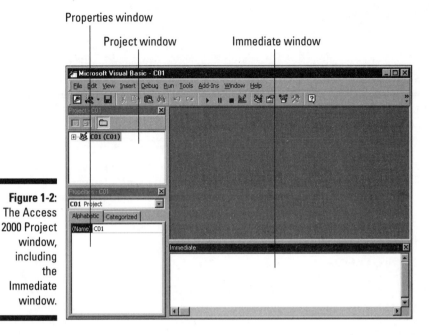

You can use the Immediate window without knowing much about the Visual Basic window or other windows.

You can enter the `Print` command into the Immediate window. This command is one of the oldest in Visual Basic, as well as one of the handiest. (The `Print` command works in Visual Basic now about the same way it did in versions of the BASIC language that were written in the 1970s.) The `Print` command outputs information to the Immediate window. To try it out, follow these steps:

1. **Type** `Print 1` **in the Immediate window.**

2. **Press Enter.**

In reaction to your instructions, Access prints 1 in the window directly below your instructions. Now try something more complicated:

1. **Type** `Print 1+1`.

2. **Press Enter.**

Smart computer! Instead of printing a literal copy of what you entered, Access evaluates 1+1 and prints the answer, 2. In Visual Basic 1+1, is called an *expression*. An *expression* is a logical statement that contains items (such as numbers) and operators (such as the math operators + or –). Whenever you use an expression in a Visual Basic statement, the data Access returns is the result of the evaluated expression. Enter the following:

1. **Type** `Print Hello.`
2. **Press Enter.**

Nothing? What's wrong? In fact nothing is wrong. When you use any sort of text like *Hello* in a statement, Visual Basic assumes that it's the name of some object that's already defined in Access or some other part of Visual Basic. In this case, Visual Basic can't find anything called *Hello* so it prints a blank line. Searching for values related to names like *Hello* is part of Visual Basic's expression evaluation process.

What if you actually wanted to print the word *Hello*? Easy for Visual Basic to do — but you need to be very specific about giving your instructions. When you want to print something literally, you need to enclose the word or phrase in quotation marks. Try this command:

1. **Type** `Print "Hello".`
2. **Press Enter.**

Because you enclose the text in quotation marks, Visual Basic doesn't try to evaluate the text. Instead, the program prints what you enclose in quotes exactly as you type it. In fact, anything you enclose in quotations is a *literal* in Visual Basic.

So far, you haven't probed deeply into Access 2000. What do you think happens when you enter the following statement? Give it a try:

1. **Type** `Print Name.`
2. **Press Enter.**

Interesting. Visual Basic prints *Microsoft Access* rather than a blank line. *Name* actually means something in Access. The truth is that you've stumbled onto part of the object model. In this case, Name represents the name of the program in which you are working, *Microsoft Access.* Enter another name.

1. **Type** `Print currentuser.`
2. **Press Enter.**

Access returns `Admin` because Access assigns the name *Admin* to the user when you open an unsecured Access database, by default. Enter the following:

1. **Type** `Print assistant.`
2. **Press Enter.**

What does Access return this time? Clippit appears. What in the world is Clippit? Clippit is the name of that annoying cartoon that pops up all the time offering you help when you don't even want it.

If you want to get rid of happy little Clippit, point the mouse at the cartoon and right-click. Select Options from the drop-down menu and a dialog box appears. Uncheck the Office Assistant box to disable Clippit.

Object lists

It's all well and good that I tell you the correct magical words to type so that Access 2000 responds with information. But Access doesn't require you to memorize all of these names. All you need to do is type the name of the object you want to work with; Access supplies a list of items you can explore.

If you want to get information about the Access application, enter the application. The *application* is the name of the object that represents the currently running function of Access.

1. Type `Print application.`

2. Type `.`

When you type the period, a drop-down list box appears (Figure 1-3), listing all the items in Access that relate to the Application object. `AccessError` and `AddToFavorites` begin the alphabetical list.

AutoList Members drop-down list

Figure 1-3:
Access 2000
displays a
list of items
associated
with the
Application
object.

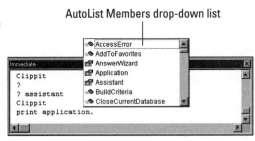

Use the arrow keys or the mouse to scroll down this list. You can also type an item to perform a speed search.

3. Type `c`.

The highlight moves to the first item in the list that begins with the letter you typed — in this case, `CloseCurrentDatabase`.

4. Type `u`.

The highlight moves to `CurrentData`, which is the first item that matches `cu`. You can now see the item `CurrentUser` displayed near the bottom of the list.

5. **Double-click on** `CurrentUser.`

   Access inserts the remaining characters, `CurrentUser,` to complete
   your entry. This feature helps you quickly and accurately enter the correct spelling into your Visual Basic program. This feature is called
   Auto-complete. Auto-complete is active whenever you are typing in
   Visual Basic statements in Access. Complete the entry of the statement.

6. **Press Enter.**

   Access displays the name of the current user, `Admin`. Now that you see
   how Auto-complete works, use it to save yourself time when you type
   the statements shown in this book. To save space, I simply show the
   command in its complete state. When you type the command, you find
   that Access pops the list up each time you type in a period. Use the lists
   to avoid entering the command's full text. That is how you are supposed
   to write programming statements.

Another shortcut that saves some typing is the ? command. All versions of
Visual Basic recognize ? as an abbreviation for the Print command. Type **?
Application.CurrentUser** and then press Enter. The results are the same as
when you use the full word **Print**.

Object properties and methods

When Access displays the Auto-complete lists (see Figure 1-3), it displays
icons in front item names on the list.

 Property. A *property* is some characteristic of the object. Use a property to
display or change a numeric or text value associated with some aspect of the
object. The example that you work with in this chapter is the Application
object's `CurrentUser` property. Since properties are always numeric or text
values, you can always print a property. Note that not all properties always
have values. If there is no value for a property at the current time, Access
prints a blank line.

 Method. *Methods* serve two functions: They specify some action or operation
that you can perform on the current object, or they link the current object to
another object that the specified object contains. Common methods are
operations like Delete or Count.

The meanings of properties and methods sound quite abstract but working
with a few examples makes them easier to understand. Follow these steps:

1. **Type** ? `Application.Currentdb.`

   If you look at the Auto-complete list you notice that a property icon
   marks `CurrentUser`, but a method icon marks `CurrentDB`. See what
   happens when you work with a method instead of a property.

2. **Press Enter.**

   Access displays an error message box, as shown in Figure 1-4.

Figure 1-4:
Access 2000
displays an
error mes-
sage box.

   Why? The CurrentDb method represents a link between the Application object and the CurrentDb object. Remember that when you open an Access database, you open the Access application (the Application object) and a database (the CurrentDb object). This is similar to the way Word behaves when it is first loaded. Word has an application object (Word) and a document object (Document1). In order to make a complete statement, you must specify what property of the CurrentDb object you want to print.

3. **Press Enter. The error message box disappears.**

4. **Type** ? application.currentdb.

   Visual Basic now displays another list of properties and methods. This list of properties and methods relates specifically to the CurrentDb object. Specify the Name property of the CurrentDb object.

5. **Type** name.

6. **Press Enter.**

Access prints something like C:\Access Programming\C01\C01.MDB. Note that the exact drive and folder names depend on where you stored the C01.MDB file in your system. Type **? Application.CurrentDb.Version** to display the Version property of the CurrentDb object.

Access indicates that the current database is version 4.0 of Access. The statement that you entered shows how Visual Basic represents the relationship between objects in Access 2000. The period operators chain objects together in a logical set of relationships. You can read the statement to see that the Application object contains the CurrentDb object. Put another way, the Application object is the CurrentDb object's *container*. Learning Access 2000 programming requires you to understand the relationships among the objects that Access works with.

Access is one part of a complicated set of interrelated tools that integrate database functions within Windows 9x and Microsoft Office 2000. The part of Access that actually deals with tables and queries is the Jet Database Engine. The *Jet Database Engine* is an SQL-based database system that can function independently from Access. You use it to connect Excel, Word, and PowerPoint to databases without using the Access interface. I discuss SQL (Structured Query Language) in Chapter 3.

Table and field collections

It's time to move deeper into the Access 2000 object model and deal with the most important set objects you find in a database — tables and fields.

If you have used Access before, you know that one or more tables store all the data in the database. One or more fields (also referred to as *columns*) make up these tables. Use the properties and methods of the `CurrentDb` object to access and manipulate these very important elements (that are part of the object model) through Visual Basic. In Access 2000, there is always a `CurrentDB` object that refers to the database you are currently working with.

The *TableDefs* (short for table definitions) collection contains all the tables in an Access database. What is a collection? A *collection* is special type of property that represents a group of objects. For example, the Name property of an object is not a collection. Why? Because any object can have one, and only one, name. In contrast, the number of tables in a database can vary from 0 to 1,024. You can usually spot a collection because the collection's name ends with the letter *s* (`TableDefs`, for example).

One property that every collection has is the `Count` property. The `Count` property tells you the number of objects in a collection. The command below gives you the number of tables in the open database.

```
? Application.Currentdb.TableDefs.Count
```

The value 15 returns because that's the number of tables.

The `QueryDefs` collection is also part of any Access 2000 database. The `QueryDefs` object is created when you create a Query form using the Access interface to display the number of queries in the current database.

```
? Currentdb.QueryDefs.Count
```

The program responds with 5. Notice that I didn't bother to start with the Application object. In order to save time and effort, Access 2000 recognizes `CurrentDb` as the default database object in the Application. You don't have to enter Application each time you want to refer to `CurrentDb`.

Object within a collection

The `TableDefs` and `QueryDefs` objects refer to the entire collection of tables or queries as a whole. You can, however, use these objects to refer to individual objects (tables, queries, and so on) within the collection in either of the following two ways:

✔ **By name.** If you use Access 2000 manually to create objects such as tables or queries, you must assign a unique name to each object. If you want to refer to a specific table or query within the `TableDefs` or `QueryDefs` collections, use the name of the object, as shown in the following example. The name of the collection member is always enclosed in parentheses.

```
container.collection(name)
```

Suppose, for example, that you want to display the creation date of the Employees table in the current database. First, you use the phrase shown in the following line of code to refer to that table. Remember that you must enclose the name of the table (Employees) in quotation marks because it is a user-given name, and that it's not case-sensitive:

```
Currentdb.TableDefs("employees")
```

You can also put this phrase into a command, as shown in the following example. When you press Enter at the end of the command, Access displays the value of the Employee table's `DateCreated` property on the next line of the Immediate window.

```
? Currentdb.TableDefs("employees").DateCreated
2/26/99 12:27:26 PM
```

✔ **By index.** Access 2000 assigns every object in a collection an *index number*. Zero is the first object's index number. Note that the index number is enclosed in parentheses, but not in quotation marks, because it's a numeric value and not a user-given name. The phrase shown in the following example refers to the table in the current database, which has an assigned index number of one.

```
Currentdb.TableDefs(1)
```

The following command displays the creation date of the table in the current database that Access 2000 assigns the index number 1.

```
? Currentdb.TableDefs(1).DateCreated
```

Collections in Access are *zero-based* — that is, the first item in the collection receives the index number zero, not the number one. The number of the last item in a collection is always one less than the total number of items in the collection. If, for example, the `Count` property of the `TableDefs` collection returns 15, the index numbers of the `TableDefs` range from 0 to 14. In Access

2000 programming, you frequently refer to the last item in a collection by using the expression *Count –1*. This expression should remind you that collection index numbers are zero-based.

The *name style* of reference is useful if you know the name of a specific table with which you want to work. The *index style* of reference is useful if you're not sure about the names of the tables in a database. In such a case, refer to the table's index numbers to check out the properties.

Interestingly, you can use the Name property to retrieve the name of a table if you refer to the table by index number.

```
? Currentdb.TableDefs(1).Name
Employees
```

The index numbers that Access 2000 assigns to objects aren't permanent assignments but *dynamic,* which means that as soon as you delete or add an object to a collection, the program reassigns the index numbers accordingly. So never write a program that relies on the index number of an object as a means of identification, that index number may change. Always use the name of the object instead.

Another useful property of TableDefs objects is the RecordCount property. This property returns the number of records in each table. The following example causes Access 2000 to display the number of records (5) in the Employees table:

```
? Currentdb.TableDefs("employees").RecordCount
  5
```

Collections within objects

In the preceding section, I discuss how to refer to individual objects that a collection contains — for example, tables within the TableDefs collection. Individual objects such as tables, however, may themselves contain other objects — or even entire collections. Every Access user knows, for example, that tables contain one or more fields.

In terms of the object model, the relationship between tables and fields means that any object in the TableDefs collection also contains a Fields collection. The Fields collection consists of all the fields a given table defines. You may recall from the discussion earlier in this chapter about properties and methods that every collection supports the Count property. You can, therefore, string together a series of objects and collections to determine values, such as the number of fields in the Employees table. See the following example:

```
? Currentdb.TableDefs("employees").Fields.Count
6
```

What are the names of the six fields in the Employees table? Select elements of the `Fields` collection for the Employees table to obtain that information. The first field in a table would be `Fields(0)` — that nasty zero-based mentality again. The `Name` property returns the name of the field. If you put these elements together with the `TableDefs` object, use the following command to find out the name of the field:

```
? Currentdb.TableDefs("employees").Fields(0).Name
EmployeeID
```

Change the index value to one to get the name of the second field in the Employees table.

```
? Currentdb.TableDefs("employees").Fields(1).Name
FirstName
```

Nesting object references

In some ways, programmers resemble detectives. In order to get the answer you seek, you need to start with one clue and then use that clue to find the next clue. You put all the pieces together to arrive at the puzzle's answer. In computer programming, *nesting* refers to a process by which you use one result or value to fill in a value that is used as part of another expression.

To understand nesting and its usefulness, imagine that your task is to display the name of the *last* field in the Employees table. Displaying the name of the *first* field is easy, because it's always item zero in the collection. But how do you know the index number of the last field?

To retrieve the name of the last field in the collection, break the problem down into two steps. For Step 1, use a statement similar to the following one to determine the total number of fields in the table.

```
? Currentdb.TableDefs("employees").Fields.Count '#1
```

You can add plain-English comments or notes to a command. Insert an apostrophe at the end of the command, and then add your notes after the apostrophe. Access stops reading the command when it encounters the apostrophe. The apostrophe is used in the above statement is used in the following to label the command as Step 1.

After you know the total number of fields, you can use that value in Step 2 to calculate the index number of the last field in the collection. For example, if the total number of fields is 6, the index number of the last field in the collection is 5 (because the first element in an object collection is 0, not 1). The following example uses the number you obtained in Step 1 to retrieve the name of the last field in the collection.

```
? Currentdb.TableDefs("employees").Fields(5).Name '#2
```

The two-step approach contains a significant weakness: It requires that you read the result of Step 1 and then insert the appropriate value into the command used in Step 2. For a better approach, combine the commands used in Step 1 and Step 2 into a single command in which the entire object phrase from Step 1 becomes part of a larger command. In the following example, you see that the object name used in Step 1 is inserted where the index number of the field appeared in Step 2. Note that Count -1 is used because collection index numbers begin with zero, not 1. `WorkPhone`, the name of the last field in the Employees table, is the result; the result requires one, not two, commands.

If you enter long commands, you can use the *line continuation character* (a space followed by an underscore) at the end of each line that you want to continue, to break the entry up into multiple lines. The following example uses the line continuation character to break the command into two lines. Remember that you must enter a space *and* an underscore to create such a line continuation.

```
? Currentdb.TableDefs("employees").Fields( _
Currentdb.TableDefs("employees").Fields.Count-1).Name
WorkPhone
```

Placing a command inside another command refers to the *nesting* technique. When Access encounters a statement that contains one or more nested commands, it first calculates the values of the nested items, and then uses those values to figure out the value of the entire command. A command with nested commands is a sort of mini-program that includes a number of separate calculations written as a single command.

Nesting's primary value is that it allows you to write more generalized commands. A *generalized command* isn't limited to a specific object; you can apply it to any object of the same type. This example uses the Employees table. However, the statement above would work exactly the same way for any table in any Access database. As an illustration, the following statement is identical to the preceding example, except the following command replaces the name of the table ("`employees`") with index number 0. The command displays the name of the last field in the first table of the current database.

```
? Currentdb.TableDefs(0).Fields( _
Currentdb.TableDefs(0).Fields.Count-1).Name
CategoryName
```

Properties that return codes

Some object properties, such as `Name` or `DateCreated`, return information in the form of text or dates that you can immediately understand as you see them. Many properties, however, return numeric codes that correspond to various settings or attributes.

The following command, for example, returns the `Type` property of the first field in the Employees table:

```
? Currentdb.TableDefs("employees").Fields(0).Type
 4
```

The property returns the value 4. The 4 is not an actual field type — for example, Text or Yes/No — but a numeric code that *stands for* the field type. What type of field does 4 stand for? You can find the answer in the Access 2000 VBA Help files. To access Help for the `Type` property, for example, perform the following steps:

1. **Double-click** `Type` **on the Immediate window.**

   This action highlights the word.

2. **Press F1.**

   Access automatically performs a search of the help files for a topic that matches the highlighted word or phrase. This technique works in the Debug window and in any code module window in Access.

   The Help screen explains how the coding system for field types operates in Access 2000. Access 2000 recognizes 20 field types. The Help screen, however, does not show the number codes for the field types. Instead, the screen lists a series of names, such as `dbBigInt` or `dbBinary`, next to the field types.

   The names represent a built-in set of special names (called *constants*) that Access 2000 recognizes as numeric values. The program uses these names because names are easier to remember than numbers.

   When you finish looking at the Help screen, you need to return to Access 2000 to continue working. Remember that in Windows, the Help screen displays are not part of the application (such as Access 2000) but a separate program running in its own application window.

3. Press Alt+F4.

You are now back in Access, where you can continue exploring the Access 2000 object model.

Recall from the Type Property Help that the `Type` property uses names such as `dbText`. What happens if you use this name in a command without any reference to the `Type` property? Enter the following to find out.

```
? dbText
   10
```

Access 2000 returns the number `10`, which is the value assigned to the constant `dbText`. Any field-type property, therefore, that returns a value of `10` is a Text type field. `dbText` is simply a term that Access 2000 uses to represent the number `10`. The idea is that it is easier to remember the name `dbText` than it is to remember that the code number for text is 10. The use of names to represent numbers is a standard part of all forms of Visual Basic, including VBA in Access, Word, Excel, and PowerPoint.

But what about a field that returns a `Type` value of 4? Unfortunately, the Access 2000 Help screen information doesn't answer this question; the screen lists only the constants' names, not their actual numeric values. Printing out the values of each constant to find their numeric equivalents, as done in the previous command, is the only way to find the answer to this question. After you perform this task, you end up with the information that I've summarized in Table 1-1, which lists both the constant name and the numeric code value for each of the possible values that the `Type` property returns. You can see, for example, that 4 indicates a *Long* (integer) field type.

Table 1-1	Field Type Values	
Type	*Constant*	*Value*
Boolean	dbBoolean	1
Byte	dbByte	2
Integer	dbInteger	3
Long	dbLong	4
Currency	dbCurrency	5
Single	dbSingle	6
Double	dbDouble	7
Date/Time	dbDate	8
Binary	dbBinary	9

Type	Constant	Value
Text	dbText	10
Long Binary (OLE Object)	dbLongBinary	11
Memo	dbMemo	12
GUID	dbGUID	15
VarBinary	dbVarBinary	17
Char	dbChar	18
Numeric	dbNumeric	19
Decimal	dbDecimal	20
Float	dbFloat	21
Time	dbTime	22
Time Stamp	dbTimeStamp	23

ON THE CD

The OBJECTS.MDB file contains a simple Visual Basic program that prints to the Debug window, using the information shown in Table 1-1. To run this program, type **ListTypeConstants** and then press Enter. You can then copy and paste the text into a word-processing document if you want a printed copy of the information.

Using the information in Table 1-1, you can determine the field type for the second field in the Employees table. You don't need to enter the entire command if you simply edit the last entry you made. Change `Fields(0)` to `Fields(1)`, as in the following example, and then press Enter.

```
? Currentdb.TableDefs("employees").Fields(1).Type
10
```

Access returns 10, indicating that the second field in the table — `Fields(1)` — is a *Text* field type.

Properties that return numeric codes can prove rather inconvenient to work with because you have no obvious, simple way to figure out the meaning of the numeric code. Unfortunately, even with the use of the Access 2000 Help screen, you can't determine the meaning of the numbers that the `Type` property returned without looking at the data in Table 1-1. In Chapter 4, you discover how to use Visual Basic to solve this problem.

Setting Properties

Object commands aren't limited to displaying information. You can also use object commands to change the value of object properties. For example, the following command displays the name of the first table in the current database:

```
? Currentdb.TableDefs(0).Name
Categories
```

Issue a command that uses the form shown in the following example to set the value of a property. In this form, the name of the object property entered is equal to the new value for that object. Notice that you don't use the ? to set a property.

```
object.property = newvalue
```

The following statement changes the Name property of the first table in the current database from its current name (Categories) to *Table 1*. The statement is the Visual Basic equivalent of using the Edit⇨Rename menu command to rename a table. Figure 1-4 shows how the database window looks before you change the name of the table. Note that this statement, unlike most of the previous examples, doesn't begin with a ?. Statements that change the value of a property always begin with the name of the object whose property you want to change.

```
Currentdb.TableDefs("categories").Name = "Table 1"
```

Selecting the object and pressing F2 also renames objects listed in the database window.

You can check the effect of the statement:

```
? Currentdb.TableDefs(0).Name
```

What did Access 2000 return? Is it what you expected? Hardly! The program displays the name employees for TableDefs(0). What is going on here?

The answer lies in the fact that the index numbers assigned to objects in a collection are *dynamic*. When you change the name of the Categories table to Table 1, you change its position in the collection because, by default, Access 2000 arranges tables in the TableDefs collection alphabetically by name. If you change the name of a table, you may also be changing its position in the collection. Change the table's name back to categories to reverse the process as follows:

```
Currentdb.TableDefs("Table 1").Name = "Categories"
```

In addition to changing the name, you should also change the position of the object in the collection so the table is back to position 0 in the collection. Test this theory with the following statement.

```
? Currentdb.TableDefs(0).Name
```

Access 2000 returns the name `categories,` confirming the relationship between `TableDef` names and numbers.

Methods that Require Arguments

One method that supports all collections is the Delete method — which permanently removes an object from a collection. Note that deletions can't be undone in Access 2000. Once deletions are made, your data is permanently lost.

As an example, execute the following statement that removes the My Company Information table from the `TableDefs` collection.

1. **Enter** `CurrentDb.TableDefs.Delete`.

2. **Press the Spacebar once.**

   The Quick Info box appears and shows `Delete(Name As String),` as shown in Figure 1-5. The Quick Info box displays information about any *arguments* that the specified method may use. An argument is a value that provides required or optional details related to the operation carried out by a method. In this example, Delete is the method used and the required argument is the name of the object you want to delete. The Quick Info box indicates that you need to supply the Name in the form of *string* information — another word for text.

   In the Quick Info box, optional arguments are enclosed in square brackets ([ ]). Arguments not enclosed in square brackets are required.

Figure 1-5:
Access 2000
displays the
Quick Info
box, indicat-
ing the
arguments
the selected
method
uses.

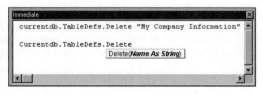

Provide the required argument to complete the statement. Make sure you enter the quotation marks because they are part of the statement.

3. **Type** "My Company Information".

4. **Press Enter.**

Access 2000 removes the table from the current database. Remember, once deleted you can't recover a table with Undo.

The DoCmd Object

Almost all the operations you can perform in Access 2000 manually — using menus, toolbars, and dialog boxes — you can also carry out using the DoCmd object in Visual Basic. The DoCmd object provides Visual Basic with command equivalents for all the actions you can perform using Access 2000 macros. Your Visual Basic programs, therefore, can include operations that range from maximizing windows to importing and exporting tables to and from other file formats.

Each type of macro action is a *method* of the DoCmd object. The Access 2000 macro command Maximize, for example, maximizes the windows inside the Access application window. The Visual Basic equivalent of the Maximize macro action appears in the following example, where Maximize is a method of the DoCmd object. You can use the DoCmd object and its methods to directly enter the equivalent of macro actions into the Debug window. Enter the following command:

```
DoCmd.Maximize
```

Access responds to this command in the same way, whether you manually maximize the Access 2000 Application window (with a mouse click or menu selection) or use a macro to perform the maximizing action. Note that the Access 2000 window is maximized, not the Visual Basic window in which you're working. Depending on how the windows are arranged on your screen, you may or may not be able to see that your window has been maximized.

Use DoCmd to execute the Restore method to return the window to its normal size. To restore the window to its previous size, type the object and dot connector, as shown in the following example:

```
DoCmd.Restore
```

The Access 2000 window returns to its normal size.

Use the DoCmd object to perform other types of operations directly from the Debug window. You can, for example, use the OpenTable method with DoCmd to open a table window. Enter the following command in the Debug window:

1. **Type** `DoCmd.OpenTable`.

2. **Press the Spacebar.**

Access 2000 automatically displays the Quick Info box that lists the arguments related to the `OpenTable` method, shown in Figure 1-6.

Figure 1-6:
The Quick
Info box can
contain
information
about a
number of
arguments.

Access 2000 (as do other Microsoft Office 2000 programs) uses a set of conventions to display the syntax of a method.

Like spoken and written languages, computer languages have a set of grammatical rules that apply to the way you write statements (sentences). Computer language *syntax* refers to the rules that tell you the proper way to write and punctuate programming statements.

- ✔ The names of the arguments appear in *italics*. In Figure 1-6, for example, the box that appears lists three arguments for the `OpenTable` method: `TableName, View As,` and `DataMode`.

- ✔ Brackets [ ] enclose any optional arguments. Required arguments for the method aren't enclosed in brackets.

- ✔ Many of the arguments that Access 2000 Visual Basic methods use require numeric codes. To simplify the entry of these codes, Access 2000 supports the use of *constants.*

  A constant is a special name that represents a value that stays the same no matter where you use it in Access 2000. For example, if you want to open a table you can open the table in a normal window, in Design mode, or in Print Preview mode. The `OpenTable` method supports an argument called `View As` that enables you to specify exactly how you open the table. The following table lists both the numeric codes and the Access constant names that you can use as arguments for the OpenTable method. Because the constant names indicate their meaning, they are easier to understand and remember than numeric codes.

✔ The syntax display shows the constant name of the default value for any arguments that require a numeric code. In Figure 1-6, for example, the syntax box shows *View As* AcView=acViewNormal. AcView **is the name** of the family of constants that you can use for this argument; =acView Normal indicates the default value for this argument. If you want to omit the optional argument, the OpenTable method uses the default value.

Table 1-2	View Arguments for the OpenTable Method	
View Type	*Numeric Code*	*Constant Name*
Normal	0	acViewNormal
Design	1	acViewDesign
Print Preview	2	acViewPreview

If you move the mouse or cursor to another part of the screen, Access removes the Quick Info box from the screen. Return the cursor to the previous position and then press Ctrl+I to make the box reappear.

You can continue to fill in the name of the table as the first argument in the command you are entering, as follows:

```
"employees",
```

After you type the comma (after "employees") in this example, Access 2000 moves the highlight (bold type) in the syntax box to the next argument (View), and displays a list of the relevant constant names, as shown in Figure 1-7.

Figure 1-7:
Access 2000 automatically lists constants for the current argument.

Use the lists of constants that Access 2000 provides, as described in the following steps, to complete the entry.

1. **To select the Normal view, double-click** `acViewNormal` **in the constant list.**

   Access inserts the selected name into your command and removes the list from the screen.

2. **Type another comma to add the next argument.**

   Access 2000 displays a new list of constants (`acAdd`, `acEdit`, and `acReadOnly`) that are appropriate for `DataMode`, the current argument.

3. **Double-click** `acReadOnly` **in the second list of constants and press Enter.**

   `acReadOnly` ensures that, in this example, the data can be read but not changed. `acEdit` allows editing and `acAdd` allows you to enter only new records (the equivalent of the Data Entry mode).

Did the statement actually open the table? Yes, but you can't see it right now because you opened it in the Access 2000 program window and you're currently in the Visual Basic window. Switch to the Access 2000 window by clicking on the Access 2000 icon on the Windows taskbar to see your results.

After you switch to the Access 2000 Application window, the Employees table is open, as shown in Figure 1-8. The `OpenTable` method of the `DoCmd` object produced the same result as opening the table from the database window. Of course, you can't tell by looking at the window which method was used, and there is no functional difference between opening it manually or opening it through Visual Basic. Notice that because you selected `acReadOnly` as the `DataMode` argument, you can't edit the table.

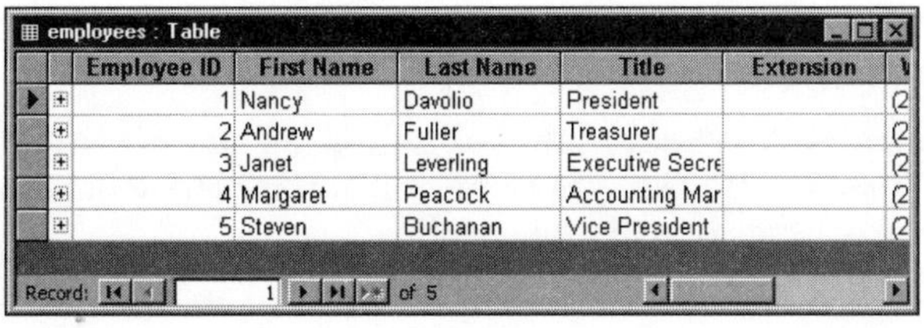

Figure 1-8:
The Employees table opened by means of a Visual Basic statement.

Click on the Visual Basic icon on the toolbar to return to Visual Basic.

You can open and close the table window with Visual Basic. Enter the command in the following example to close the window with the Close method. If you pause momentarily as you enter each argument, Access presents you with syntax help.

```
DoCmd.Close acTable,"employees"
```

Requesting syntax help

By default, Access 2000 displays lists of properties, methods, and syntax information as you enter a command into the Debug window (or any module window). After you type the period that follows an object's name (such as DoCmd, for example), Access displays a list of properties and methods associated with that object.

As you manually edit a command, however, you may want Access to redisplay a list of the syntax information at a point where the program doesn't do so automatically. Table 1-3 lists the menu commands and shortcuts that you can use to display the language aids available in Access 2000.

Table 1-3 Commands that Display Visual Basic Lists and Syntax

Information	*Menu Command*	*Shortcut Key*
Properties and methods	Edit⇨List Properties/Methods	Ctrl+J
Constants	Edit⇨List Constants	Ctrl+Shift+J
Argument syntax	Edit⇨Quick Info	Ctrl+I

If you want to stop Access 2000 from automatically displaying the lists and syntax information, change the options that Access 2000 uses for Visual Basic modules. To do so, follow these steps:

1. **Choose Tools⇨Options from the menu bar to open the Options dialog box.**

   Access displays the Editor tab. The Editor tab shows settings that affect the way Visual Basic behaves when you enter statements into the Immediate window or a Module window.

2. **Remove the checkmarks from any features (Auto List Members, Auto Quick Info, Auto Data Tips, etc.) that you want to disable.**

3. **Click OK to close the dialog box and save the new options.**

Keep in mind that even after you turn off the automatic displays of the lists and syntax information, you can use the menu commands or shortcut keys listed in Table 1-3 to view these displays.

Using objects as arguments

If you work with the `DoCmd` object, many of its methods, such as `OpenTable` or `Close`, require additional items of information, such as the name and type of object that you want to use. Type this additional information in a list following the method's name. In computer languages, any items listed after a command or method are *arguments*. In the following command, `"employees"` is the argument for the `OpenTable` method.

```
DoCmd.OpenTable "employees"
```

In the preceding example, I entered the argument for the method *literally;* that is, I specified the exact name of the table that I want to open as a name enclosed in quotation marks. You're not limited, however, to using just *literals* for arguments. You can use an object reference as an argument. Suppose, for example, that you want to open the first query in the `QueryDefs` collection of the current database. You can use an object reference to return the name, even though you don't know the actual name of that query.

The object name in the following example returns the name of the first query (index number zero) in the current database:

```
Currentdb.QueryDefs(0).Name
```

You can insert this object reference as the argument for the `OpenQuery` method of the `DoCmd` object. The following command opens the query window.

```
DoCmd.OpenQuery Currentdb.QueryDefs(0).Name
```

You can use a similar command to close the query window. Switch back to the Debug window. Instead of writing a new command, change the method from `OpenQuery` to `Close` and add the object type argument, `acQuery`, as shown in the following example to edit the previous command:

```
DoCmd.Close acQuery, Currentdb.QueryDefs(0).Name
```

Temporary storage of values

The previous two statements are important because they show that the values used to supply arguments for various methods don't have to be literal values — they can be any valid Visual Basic expression. A statement is acceptable to Visual Basic as long as the expression used as an argument ultimately evaluates it as a value that is valid for the specified method.

In the previous `DoCmd.OpenQuery` example, you used the Name property of a `QueryDefs` object to supply the name an `OpenQuery` or `Close` method requires. Visual Basic also supports the creation of *temporary objects* that you can name and assign values. Temporary objects are handy when you want to use the same value several time but you don't want to have to type in a long text item, such as `Parks By Region`, over and over again.

You can create a temporary object using the Let statement. Enter the following:

```
Let QName = "Parks By Region"
```

In Visual Basic, temporary object names are not case sensitive. `QName`, `qname`, `qName`, or any other upper- or lower-case combination all refer to the same thing.

You've just created a temporary object called `QName` and assigned `Parks By Region` as a text value. `QName` is temporary because Access discards it when you exit the program. Also, temporary objects you create with the `Let` statement have only one property, their value. Use Print to see the value of temporary objects. Enter the following:

```
? QName
```

Visual Basic prints the text that you assigned to `QName`.

If you've had experience with other programming languages, you recognize temporary objects by their traditional name variables. I avoid using "traditional name variables" in this chapter because I think that readers with no previous programming experience see the natural connection between permanent objects and temporary value storage. On the other hand, I want to let more experienced readers know that I do know what a variable is, and that I get around to using the more traditional term a bit later in this book.

You can now use `QName` in any statement that requires the text you assigned to `QName`. Enter the following:

```
DoCmd.OpenQuery QName
```

If you switch to the Access 2000 Application window, you see that you've just opened the `Parks By Region` query window. Return to Visual Basic and use the temporary object to close the window using the following command.

```
Docmd.Close acQuery, QName
```

You can also assign permanent object values to temporary objects to save you the trouble of writing out a long expression each time you want to refer to an object property. Enter the following:

```
Let QName = Currentdb.QueryDefs(2).Name
```

Next enter:

```
? QName
```

The value of QName changes to Parks By State. The value of a temporary object changes each time you use the Let statement to assign a value. The temporary object's new value replaces its old value. You can change the value of a temporary object as many times as you like. Enter the following:

```
DoCmd.OpenQuery QName
```

Switch to the Access 2000 Application window to see the open Parks By State query window. Return to Visual Basic and use the temporary object to close the window.

```
Docmd.Close acQuery, QName
```

Temporary objects prove very useful. In fact, temporary objects are the heart of Visual Basic. They provide a means by which you can write a program and not link the statements to a specific table, query, or other permanent object.

Look at the two previous statements and notice that the statements you used to open the two different query windows are identical. Although identical, the different query windows open two different windows because the value of the temporary object, QName, was altered prior to the execution of each statement.

It's possible to create a series of statements that manipulate an object (open, print, and then close a query window, for example) without actually specifying the name of the query. Instead of specifying the name of the query, use the temporary object name as a placeholder for the name of some permanent query. Just be sure to assign a valid name to the temporary object before you execute the statements.

Using temporary objects to write statements allows you to compose a single set of instructions that manipulate any number of different objects. In fact, you can write statements that anticipate the creation of new objects that don't currently exist.

Named arguments

Earlier in this book, I show you how to use methods that require one or more arguments, such as those associated with the DoCmd object. Traditionally, you enter arguments as a list of items separated by commas, as shown in the following example. The ellipses (. . .) at the end of the list indicate that you can add unlimited arguments to the list.

```
object.method argument1,argument2,argument3 . . .
```

Entering arguments as a series separated by commas has several drawbacks:

- ✔ Argument meanings are unclear because the commands that indicate or label the purpose of each argument do not contain information.

- ✔ The order of the arguments determines their meaning. The two OpenQuery commands that follow, for example, contain the same information. One of the commands, however, doesn't work, because its arguments, although valid, appear in the wrong order. (Which one is incorrect? The first command. The query name is always the first argument following the OpenQuery method.)

```
DoCmd.OpenQuery acViewDesign, "Parks By Region
DoCmd.OpenQuery "Parks By Region", acViewDesign
```

Beginning with Excel version 5.0, new versions of Visual Basic in other Office applications can support the use of *named arguments*. A named argument begins with an *identifier*. Named argument identifiers always end with :=, and then the argument, as shown in the following example:

```
object.method name1:= argument1, name2:= argument2
```

Named arguments that you enter use := as the operator. No space exists between the : and the =. If you forget to enter the := and enter a =, the meaning of the statement completely changes and typically results in an error when you try to execute the statement.

Named arguments solve both problems that characterize traditional argument lists, as I describe in the following list:

- ✔ Each argument has a label that indicates its purpose and meaning in the command. This eliminates the confusion that can occur when you read a list of unlabeled arguments.

- ✔ Because each argument has a label, you can enter arguments in any order. You no longer need to enter the arguments in a specific sequence, which is especially useful if you want to skip over optional arguments.

The following command uses a named argument to specify the name of the query that you want to open:

```
DoCmd.OpenQuery QueryName:= "Parks By Region"
```

In response to this command, a window opens that displays the data set that the `Parks By Region` query defines. You need to switch back to the Access 2000 Application window to see the opened query window.

Use the `Close` method of the `DoCmd` object to close document windows. Remember that you must switch to the Visual basic window to issue another Visual Basic command.

The following command takes advantage of the fact that you can enter named arguments in any order. Normally, the object-type argument precedes the object name. However, using named arguments enables you to begin with the object name if you like. Beginning with the object name may seem more natural because the `OpenQuery` method, used in the statement that opened the query starts with the object name. The named arguments give the two statements a similar construction. The named arguments also avoid the fact that Access doesn't place the object name argument first in the `Close` method.

```
DoCmd.Close ObjectName:= "Parks By Region", _
    ObjectType:= acQuery
```

If you want to open the query in Design mode, you can use either of the following commands, because the order of the named arguments is not significant. Notice that the use of the `acViewDesign` constant selects the Design mode display of the specified query. Figure 1-9 shows the opened query in the design window. Remember that in order to see the query, you must switch to the application window.

```
DoCmd.OpenQuery View:= acViewDesign, _
    QueryName:= "Parks By Region"
DoCmd.OpenQuery QueryName:= "Parks By Region" _
    , View:= acViewDesign
```

Figure 1-9:
An open query in the Design mode.

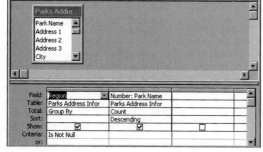

Use a command without named arguments to close the query window:

```
DoCmd.Close acQuery, "Parks By Region"
```

The RunCommand method

The RunCommand method provides Access Visual Basic a means of executing the equivalent 336 commands that Access 2000 includes in various menus and toolbars. The RunCommand method associates with the DoCmd object.

The RunCommand method and its corresponding constants replace the DoMenuItem method that previous versions of Access used. (Access 2000 still recognizes the DoMenuItem method, however, to ensure compatibility with previous versions of Access.)

The following command performs the operation that occurs after you choose the menu command Window⇨Cascade (it arranges all open windows in cascade style):

```
DoCmd.RunCommand acCmdWindowCascade
```

Keep in mind that the RunCommand method executes commands from the Access 2000 menu structure. Some of the method's operations, therefore, are open dialog boxes that you must manually manipulate. The following command is the equivalent of the menu command Tools⇨Options. After you execute the command, the Options dialog box opens.

```
DoCmd.RunCommand acCmdOptions
```

After the dialog box opens, you must manually close the dialog box.

You can find a full list of all the constants that the RunCommand method uses in the *Run Command Constants* table in the OBJECTS.MDB database. The OBJECTS.MDB also contains the examples for this chapter.

Chapter 2

Your First Program

● ●

In This Chapter

▶ What's a program?

▶ Defining procedures

▶ Displaying a message

▶ Getting user input

▶ Interacting with database objects

▶ The Debug mode

▶ Handling errors

▶ Enumerating collections

▶ If conditions

▶ Using DoCmd in a procedure

● ●

*C*hapter 1 illustrates how Visual Basic can interact with a program such as Access 2000, which consists of many elements. From Visual Basic's point of view, everything that makes up Access — the menus, tables, queries, fields, and so on — are all *objects,* each of which has a unique name. You can use the *properties* and *methods,* which you apply to specific objects, to manipulate these objects. As a result, you can write out a single Visual Basic statement that, for example, counts the number of fields in a table or opens a query window without the use of Access menus, toolbars, or shortcut keys. In this chapter, you move beyond one-line statements and begin writing some simple (but useful) Visual Basic programs.

> *Database Folder: ACCPROG\Chapter 2*
> *Database File: BASIC.MDB*
> *Module: Basic*

If you don't feel like typing all the code shown in this chapter, don't worry. You can avoid all of the typing by loading copies of the examples stored on the CD-ROM. To use these examples, perform the following steps:

1. **Open the database file BASIC.MDB.**

2. **Click the Modules tab.**

   You see a module named *BasicExamples.*

3. **Click the Design button to open this module.**

   This module contains all the examples discussed in this chapter. The names in the module match the names of the examples in this chapter.

4. **To run an example, scroll down until you position the cursor in any part of the code that you want to execute.**

5. **Press the F5 key.**

   Access runs the code.

What's a Program?

In Chapter 1, you discovered how to enter Visual Basic statements into the Immediate window, where the result of the statement was immediate — that is, the statement was executed as soon as you pressed Enter at the end of each line.

Writing a computer *program* is different from working in the Immediate window in that Visual Basic does not attempt to execute the statements as you enter them. Instead, Visual Basic allows you to enter as many statements as you desire — without making any attempt to perform the tasks indicated by the statements.

When you finally get to a point where you want to execute the statement, you tell Visual Basic to *run* the program. (Another term for run is *execute.*) When you run a program, Visual Basic executes all of the statements you have entered up to that point, as quickly as it possibly can. As soon as it executes one statement, Visual Basic goes on and does the next and the next, without stopping until it reaches the end of your list of statements. The effect of the program is the cumulative effect of all the statements contained within it.

Why bother to write a program? The primary reason is that many tasks are too complicated to express in a single statement. Writing a program allows you to bundle together a lot of small operations that add up to a bigger, complex result.

Because all programs consist of *text,* writing programs is actually just a specialized form of word processing. Access provides *module windows* that are specifically designed to facilitate the entry of programming text. In a word processor, you have a spelling checker to help you eliminate misspellings. In a module window, you have a *syntax checker* to help eliminate incorrectly entered Visual Basic statements.

Module windows in Access provide a number of special features, such as Auto Property/Method Lists you encounter in the Immediate window, designed to expedite writing programs. Each time you enter a property or method for an object such as DoCmd, Access displays information about the syntax and constants in order to help you write a valid statement.

If you're new to programming, take a look at the following list, which describes a few key terms that you often use in programming:

- ✔ **Code.** In programming, you call the instruction text that you enter in a module *code*. The name *code* reflects the fact that the programmer designs the syntax of the instructions so that the computer, not a person, understands the instructions. In order for Access to correctly carry out your instructions, you must learn to express your ideas within the limits of Visual Basic language.

- ✔ **Statement.** A *statement* is one complete line of code that completes a single instruction. Statements are also known as *commands*. The term *command,* however, is considered a bit obsolete in languages such as Visual Basic that encompass sophisticated programming concepts such as objects, properties, and methods.

- ✔ **Structure.** A *structure* is a set of statements that work together to perform a single action. Sub and End Sub, for example, are separate statements that work together to define the start and the end of a Visual Basic procedure.

- ✔ **Procedure.** A *procedure* is a set of statements that form the smallest unit of code that Visual Basic can execute. In Visual Basic, the smallest possible procedure must contain three statements. Each procedure must have a unique name within the database. Names don't have to be fancy. They can be as simple as a single letter such as Q. In general, try to give your programs names that suggest what they do or what their purpose is, for example, FindCustomerAddress or CalcSalesTax.

- ✔ **Run.** If you *run* a procedure, Access reads the first statement in the procedure and carries out the operation specified by that statement. Access then reads the next statement in the procedure, if any, and performs the specified action. This process continues until Access reaches the last statement in the procedure. Procedures automatically terminate if Access cannot perform their instructions.

- ✔ **Error.** An *error* occurs if Access cannot perform the operation that a given statement describes. Access displays a message box that indicates the reason why the program can't carry out the instruction.

- ✔ **Debugging.** *Debugging* is the process of eliminating errors from your program. Access provides special tools to help you analyze errors when it can't carry out your instructions. For example, you can execute a program in a step-by-step mode, in which Visual Basic pauses after each statement so that you can track down which statements in a program are causing a problem.

In Access, you enter and store Visual Basic instructions in *modules*. The first step in writing a Visual Basic program is to open a *module window*. To open a module window, follow these steps:

1. **If you have not already done so, open the BASIC.MDB file supplied on the CD.**
2. **When the database window appears, click the Modules tab.**
3. **Click the New button to open this module window inside the Visual Basic editor window.**

After the module window opens, you see the following a line of text already entered in the module:

```
Option Compare Database
```

At this point, the meaning of the preceding text is obscure, rather technical, and not very significant for what you're about to explore in this chapter. If you're like most people, however, you hate to let anything go by without explanation as you're picking up something new, so here's a brief comment:

✔ **Option Compare Database.** This statement ensures that any comparisons the program performs in this module use the same set of comparison rules that Access uses in its database operations. Essentially, Compare Database means that sorting is not sensitive to the case of the characters. Table 2-1 shows that, if this command is missing, Access views the upper- and lowercase versions of the same word — for example, *Zebra* and *zebra* — as different terms. If `Database` comparison is active, Access treats the two versions of the word as logically equivalent.

Note that the examples used in Table 2-1 are enclosed in quotations. Visual Basic requires text items to be marked with quotations so that they can be distinguished from other parts of the Visual Basic language.

Table 2-1	How Option Compare Affects Access	
Option Compare	*Example*	*True or False*
None	"ZEBRA" = "zebra"	False
Database	"ZEBRA" = "zebra"	True

Another statement that is often used at the beginning of a module is `Option Explicit`. The purpose of this statement is to act as a kind of spell checker for programmers. The most common source of errors in programs turns out to be misspellings of various user-defined names. To avoid such errors, the `Explicit` option requires that you register each user-defined name using a

Dim statement. The Dim statements create a dictionary of valid names and Visual Basic automatically flags any unregistered names as errors while you are entering your statements. Although the Explicit option adds a few more steps to writing programs, this option can help ensure that your program doesn't fail because of misspelled names. You will find out more about using Option Explicit later in the book.

Defining Procedures

After you open a module window (as described in the preceding section), you're ready to take the next step in writing a program — defining a *procedure*. A procedure is a single list of one or more Visual Basic statements. Unlike the Immediate window, where one statement at a time is executed, all statements in a procedure are executed one after the other, as quickly as your computer is capable.

A procedure is the smallest unit of programming instruction that Access can execute. A module window can hold one or more procedures, and an Access database can contain one or more modules.

Each procedure must have a distinct starting and ending point. The procedure always begins with a statement that indicates the start of a procedure and the name of the procedure. All procedures end with a statement that marks the end of the procedure so Visual Basic knows when the procedure is complete.

When you want to execute the procedure, you refer to it by the name given in the first statement of the procedure. You can enter the name of the procedure in the Immediate window or inside of another procedure. Visual Basic stops when it reaches the ending statement of the procedure.

Visual Basic uses the following three types of procedures:

- **Sub.** Sub stands for *subroutine.* Traditionally, subroutines were used to break up large, complex programs into smaller, more manageable segments. A Sub procedure is the simplest type of procedure in Visual Basic. The only requirements are the starting and ending statements.

- **Function.** A Function is similar to a Sub procedure with the addition that it can return a value. Many applications, such Microsoft Excel, support the use of functions — such as the Sum( ) function in Excel that calculates the total value of a range of cells. In Visual Basic, you can create your own user-defined functions based on your own design.

✔ **Property.** Property procedures are the newest and most complex type of Visual Basic procedure. Property procedures are stored in special types of modules called Class modules. Property procedures enable you to define a set of properties and methods related to a specific object. The object can be part of Access — for example, a form or a report — or an entirely new type of object that you define on your own.

If all these definitions seem obscure, don't be alarmed. You'll be surprised how everything becomes clearer with a little time and experience. In Chapter 1, you enter individual statements in the Immediate window. To begin getting experience with actual programming, you can start by writing a Sub type procedure.

You create a new procedure by typing **Sub** or **Function**, followed by the name of the procedure, in any part of the module. Here, I name the procedure Sub Basic1. Keep in mind that all the procedures in a database (regardless of the module) must have unique names:

To create a new Sub procedure, follow these steps:

1. **Type Sub Basic1 on the first available blank line.**

2. **Press Enter.**

   Access reacts to your entry by creating a new procedure. The program creates the procedure by adding two statements to the module, as shown in the following example:

   • The Sub statement does two things: First, the statement marks the starting location of the procedure, and second, this statement registers the name (for example, Basic1) as a procedure.

   • The End Sub statement marks the end of the procedure. After Access encounters the End Sub statement, the program stops executing instructions and ends the procedure.

In addition, Access adds ( ) following the name of the procedure. The ( ) are a standard part of every procedure name. What you see in the following example is what appears on-screen:

```
Sub Basic1()

End Sub
```

Notice that you entered a blank line between the Sub and End Sub statements. The blank line indicates that you enter the instructions that make up the procedure there, between Sub and End Sub.

If you look carefully at the text in the Module window, you notice that some of the text, such as the words Sub and End Sub appear in blue. Others, such as Basic1, appear as black text. The folks at Microsoft designed Access to alter the color of the text in the module to help identify the meaning of the text. Visual Basic keywords such as Sub and End Sub, for example, appear in blue, and identifiers such as Basic1 appear as black text. You can customize the color scheme for Visual Basic code by using the Code Colors settings on the Module tab of the Tools⇨Options dialog box.

Displaying a Message

One of the most versatile statements in Visual Basic is the MsgBox (or *message box*) statement. The statement displays a simple dialog box in the center of the screen. You can control the appearance of the message box by using any of the following three arguments. The arguments shown in brackets ([]) are optional.

✔ Prompt determines the text that appears within the message box.

✔ [Buttons] determines the number and type of button that appears. If you omit this argument, an OK button appears in the box.

✔ [Title] determines the text of the title bar at the top of the message window. If you omit this argument, the title bar contains the name of the current application — for example, Microsoft Access.

In the Basic1 procedure, insert the following MsgBox statement. This statement displays the text Hello in a message box. Notice that, in the following example, I indent the statement one tab inward from the Sub and End Sub statements. Indenting has no meaning to Visual Basic or Access. Indenting does, however, make your programs easier for people (including you) to read.

```
Sub Basic1()
   MsgBox "Hello"
End Sub
```

You now have a simple but complete procedure. You can have Access execute the code in either of the following two ways:

✔ If your cursor is positioned anywhere within the procedure in the module window, you can run the program by choosing Run⇨Go/Continue or by pressing F5.

✔ In the Immediate window, type the name of the Sub procedure — for example, **Basic1** — and press Enter. (You can display the Debug window at any time by pressing Ctrl+G.)

Begin with the Run method.

1. Make sure that the cursor is positioned inside the procedure Basic1. Press F5.

When the procedure executes, the MsgBox statement causes Access to display a small, message box window, as shown in Figure 2-1. This message box displays the text Hello because you specified that text in the MsgBox statement.

Figure 2-1:
The
MsgBox
Statement
displays a
simple mes-
sage box.

The window that the MsgBox statement displays is the type of window that doesn't enable you to select anything outside that window while it's open. To continue, you must select one of the buttons in the box or press Alt+F4. Access calls this type of window a *modal* window. In fact, you can define any dialog box as being a modal window because you must complete your dialog with the window before the program allows you to continue.

2. Close the message box by clicking on OK.

You now return to the Visual Basic module because the Basic1() procedure doesn't have any more statements to execute.

Next, try executing the same procedure by referring to it by name.

1. Press Ctrl+G to open the Immediate window.

2. Type basic1 and press Enter.

3. Click OK to close the message box.

4. Press Alt+F4 to close the Immediate window.

In both cases, Access executes the same Visual Basic statement and produces the identical result on the screen: the display of a message box with the word Hello inside. Executing a procedure by entering its name is known as *calling* the procedure.

Built-in functions

Although you can build your own functions with Visual Basic, Access and Visual Basic provide a number of *built-in functions*. These functions are actually procedures built directly into the Access program. You can use functions in Access tables, queries, forms, and reports, as well as in Visual Basic. These built-in functions perform calculations, obtain or manipulate information. Most Access users are familiar with the Date function. This function returns the current date as maintained by the computer's internal clock. The following procedure displays the current date, as shown in Figure 2-2:

```
Sub Basic2()
   MsgBox Date
End Sub
```

Figure 2-2:
The current
date
appears in a
message
box.

Almost all functions in Access require parentheses — ( ) — following the function name. Exceptions are the Date (today's date) and Now (today's time and date) functions. If you enter **Date( )** anywhere in Access, Access automatically removes the ( ).

Another source of information in any Access database is the information that various object properties return. Chapter 1 notes that you can obtain the name of the open database by using the Name property of the CurrentDB object. The following code example displays the full path name of the current database, as shown in Figure 2-3:

```
Sub Basic3()
   MsgBox CurrentDb.Name
End Sub
```

Figure 2-3:
The full path
name of the
current
database
appears.

So far, the items appearing in the message box are all the results of simple arguments. You're not limited, however, to simple items. The following example uses the `Pmt()` function to calculate the monthly payment of a $10,000 loan for 36 months at 8.5 percent interest. The result appears in Figure 2-4.

In using functions such as `Pmt()` that use interest rates, remember that people usually express interest rates as APRs (annual percentage rates) but usually calculate payments on a monthly basis. Remember to divide the APR by 12 to get the correct monthly interest rate.

```
Sub Basic4()
  MsgBox Pmt(0.085 / 12, 36, -10000)
End Sub
```

Figure 2-4:
The mes-
sage box
returns the
result of a
calculation.

In Access (and in Excel, too), functions that make calculations about loans, such as `Pmt` (monthly payment), `Ppmt` (the principal portion of a monthly payment), and `IPmt` (the interest portion of a monthly payment), express the amount of the loan as a negative number. These functions view the amount as the initial cash flow from the lender's point of view. (The *initial cash flow* in a loan is one in which the lender gives up a lump sum to the borrower and then, in return, receives a series of positive cash flows, usually in the form of monthly payments.) If you're more familiar with the `Pmt` function in products such as Lotus 1-2-3 or even Microsoft Works (which express the loan amount as a positive number), the Access approach may seem odd but it is mathematically correct.

Using the Format function

In the previous example, the data obtained by the Pmt() function was displayed as 315.675374235574. Although this number may be accurate, it may be a bit awkward to display to a user as the monthly payment amount. In a spreadsheet program such as Excel, you control the appearance of numbers like 315.675374235574 by using the Format Number command to apply a formatting style to the raw data.

In Visual Basic, the Format () function provides methods for controlling the appearance of the values calculated during a procedure. Format plays roughly the same role in Visual Basic that Format Number does in Excel.

> ✔ Value. This is the text, number, or date value to format.
>
> ✔ Format. This is the name of a standard format — for example, Currency, Standard, Percent, or a custom-designed format template, such as 0.000%.

The following example uses the Format() function to convert the raw output of the Pmt() function to a currency style value, as shown in Figure 2-5. Notice that I insert the entire Pmt() function as the value argument for the Format() function. As described in Chapter 1, this technique is called *nesting*. In this case, the Pmt() function nests inside the Format() function, which in turn forms the argument for the MsgBox statement.

```
Sub Basic5()
MsgBox Format(Pmt(0.085 / 12, 36, _
-10000), "currency")
End Sub
```

Figure 2-5:
The Format
() function
controls the
appearance
of the
number.

The previous example appears on two lines but is actually a single statement. Placing a space followed by an underscore at the end of a line allows you to continue the same statement on another line. This technique is used in this book because the page width limits the width of the statements that can be displayed. In a Visual Basic module, you are free to type long statements on a single line, or to break up a statement into two or more lines, using the space and underscore to indicate line continuation.

You can also apply the Format () function to dates as well as numbers. The following example uses the Long Date format to display the current system date — for example *Tuesday, March 9, 1999* — in the message box:

```
Sub Basic6()
  MsgBox Format(Date, "Long Date")
End Sub
```

String expressions

So far in this chapter, the information appearing in the message box is the result of a single item, such as a function or an object property. You can improve the informational value of the message box display if you add a label or text explaining the meaning of the number or date that appears in the box.

You add a label or text to the message box by creating a *string expression*. You create string expressions by chaining together literal text, numbers, dates, functions, and/or calculations to form a single output. Suppose, for example, that you want to display a message box that reads Today is Monday, March 8, 1999 (where 3/8/99 is today's date).

Text strings consist of two parts, as shown in the following example. The first part is a *text literal*. A *literal* is a value that looks the same in the code as it does after you run the program. Quotation marks always enclose text literals. The second part of the string involves the functions that generate the desired date.

```
"Today is "
Format(Date, "Long Date")
```

Remember that if you want to have a space between items when they are combined you have to add a space inside the quotation marks. For example, if you type **"Today is"** (without the extra space at the end) you might get something like Today isMarch 8, 1999 on the screen.

You can connect two or more different data items by using the & operator (also called the *concatenation operator*). Procedure Basic7 uses the & operator to combine text and date information into a single output, as shown in Figure 2-6.

The word *concatenation* comes from the Latin word *concate,* which means to forge into a chain. When you use a concatenation operator you are chaining together two or more items into a single block of text. The result of concatenation is always text.

Figure 2-6:
The message box displays the result of the string expression.

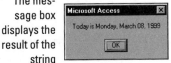

The following example demonstrates how this text string appears in the `Basic7` procedure:

```
Sub Basic7()
MsgBox "Today is " & _
Format(Date, "Long Date")
End Sub
```

You can apply the same technique to combinations of text and numbers. `Basic8` (the procedure shown in the following example) combines text with the `Pmt()` calculation to produce the message box shown in Figure 2-7. Notice in the following example that `Basic8` uses the & twice. The second & inserts a period at the end of the expression to make the output a grammatically correct sentence.

```
Sub Basic8()
  MsgBox "The Monthly Payment is " _
  & Format(Pmt(0.085 / 12, 36, -10000), "currency") _
  & "."
End Sub
```

Figure 2-7:
Add punctuation to the end of the message by using the & operator.

Multiple-line text expressions

Sometimes, the information you want to appear in the message box may look better as several lines of text rather than as a single, long line of text stretching across the box. If you are typing text in a word processor, you start a new line by pressing Enter. But how do you insert a new line into a string expression?

The answer comes in the form of the Chr() function. Keyboards communicate with the computer through numeric codes. This procedure is true not only for the visible characters (A, z, 1, 2, $, and so on), but also for the invisible characters that you produce by pressing keys such as Enter or Esc. The letter *A,* for example, is equivalent to a numeric code of 65. The Chr() function enables you to specify a character by its code number. If, for example, you enter the following command in the Debug window, the result is the letter A:

```
? Chr(65)
```

The best-known coding system for the standard U.S. keyboard is the *American Standard Code for Information Interchange (ASCII).* ASCII, which was the standard for teletype machines, contains 128 characters. Most PCs are and have long been capable of supporting more than 128 characters. The *American National Standards Institute (ANSI)* code, for example, expands the coding system to 256 characters. Many Windows fonts support the full 256-character ANSI code set.

You can create a multiple-line display in a message box by taking advantage of the character codes for the invisible characters, specifically the code produced by the Enter key, *13.* You can use Chr(13) to insert a new line into a string expression. Basic9 employs this technique in the following example to create the multiple-line display shown in Figure 2-8:

```
Sub Basic9()
  MsgBox "Date: " & Date & _
  Chr(13) & "Time: " & Time
End Sub
```

Figure 2-8:
The Chr( )
function
enables you
to create a
multiple-line
string
expression.

Basic10 shows how you can combine the concept of a string expression with the Access object model to create an expression that provides specific information about a database object — here, a table. The expression inserts the name of a table with the Name property and then uses the Fields.Count property to return the number of fields in that table, as shown in the following example:

```
Sub Basic10()
  MsgBox "The " & CurrentDb.TableDefs(0).Name _
  & " table contains " & _
  CurrentDb.TableDefs(0).Fields.Count _
  & " fields."
End Sub
```

What's interesting about Basic10 (the previous example) is the way that you can alter the object model reference to yield information about a different object. What do you need to change to create a procedure that displays the name and field count for the second table in the current database? The answer is only two characters — change the 0s to 1s, as in the following example, and you get the result shown in Figure 2-9.

```
Sub Basic11()
MsgBox "The " & CurrentDb.TableDefs(1).Name _
& " table" & Chr(13) & "contains " & _
CurrentDb.TableDefs(1).Fields.Count _
& " fields."
End Sub
```

Figure 2-9:
The message box displays information about table definition number 1.

Using built-in constants

While using Chr(13) to insert a carriage return is a useful tool, it is not very easy to remember or intuitive that Chr(13) is the number that relates to starting a new line. As you will find, many statements exist that require specific values to indicate how the statement should operate. In order to make it easier to write and later read Visual Basic code, the program includes several hundred *constants*. A constant is a special type of object that you can use to represent some value. The key difference is that a constant has the same value no matter what statement or procedure it appears in. Constants also conserve memory since it takes less memory to insert a constant value than it does to perform a function like Chr( ).

For example, the constant vbCr has the value of Chr(13), but it is probably a lot easier to remember. You can insert vbCr in place of Chr(13) in any statement in Access.

```
Sub Basic11withConstant()
MsgBox "The " & CurrentDb.TableDefs(1).Name _
& " table" & vbCr & "contains " & _
CurrentDb.TableDefs(1).Fields.Count _
& " fields."
End Sub
```

This version of the Basic11withConstant () procedure uses the constant vbCr in place of Chr(13) producing the same result as Basic11().

When you send text to the printer or a text file, you usually need a Carriage Return/Line Feed combination to start a new line. The constant vbCrLf inserts both characters. You can also use vbCrLf in the message box in place of vbCr. That way you only have to remember one constant name for both functions.

Getting User Input

All the examples discussed so far in this chapter consist of statements that produce the same essential results each time they are executed. For example, Basic10 and Basic11 use specific index numbers, for example 0 or 1, to refer to the table object used in the procedure. They always refer to that particular table unless you edit the statement to refer to a different table. Typing the specific number or name of an object is called *hardwiring* your code. Hardwired code works, but only for the exact set of objects you specified when you wrote the code.

A better way to build procedures is to create *dynamic* procedures. A dynamic procedure uses statements in a such a way that the specific objects manipulated by the procedure can change each time the procedure is executed.

For example, suppose you wanted to create a procedure that can display the number of fields in any table in the database not merely table 0 or table 1. In contrast to the hardwired approach, this technique results in a generalized procedure that you can use to retrieve information about any table without having to rewrite your code each time.

To create this type of code, add the following two elements to your procedures:

- ✔ **Input.** You need a way to pause the execution of your code, enabling the user to enter a value, such as the index number of the table, into the procedure.

- ✔ **Temporary Object.** When the user enters information during the execution of a procedure you need a way to temporarily store the user's input so that it can then be inserted into other statements. If the user enters **2** (for the third table in the collection) you must insert that value into the expression `CurrentDB.TableDefs(???)` where I have typed `(???)`.

Both of these needs involve the use of temporary storage area into which you can insert data and then later retrieve it. In Chapter 1, I call these temporary objects. The more traditional name for these objects is *variables*. To be consistent, I refer to these temporary storage objects as variables throughout the remainder of the book.

The concept of a variable is one of the harder ones to grasp mainly because you can never see a visual representation of a variable the way you can see a table displayed as a datasheet. Variables are used to store single text, numeric, or date values, which you can retrieve from the variable at a later point in the procedure. This definition sounds very much like the definition of a field in a table. The difference is that field data is permanently stored in a file on the disk. Data stored in a variable is temporary and is not saved permanently. The only way to tell what value a variable contains is to refer to it by name within a Visual Basic statement.

Objects that are stored on the disk, such as tables and forms, are called persistent objects.

You create variables using the `Dim` statement. The following example defines a variable called `TableNumber`:

```
Dim TableNumber
```

Dim is short for dimension. The name has very little to do with its function as shown here. `Dim` was originally used in BASIC to set the number of elements in a subscripted array such as x(1), x(2), x(3), and so on. In Visual Basic, `Dim` is used to define variable names, and it still retains its old usage for arrays.

Variables have roughly the same function in Visual Basic as the clipboard has in Windows. The main difference is that while Windows only has one clipboard (you can only copy and paste one item at a time), Visual Basic allows you to have as many variables as your computer's memory can hold. In order to distinguish one memory box from another, you must give each variable a unique name.

Visual Basic gives you wide latitude in creating variable names. The only limitations are that names must begin with an alphabetical character; can't be longer than 255 characters; and can't contain a period, a space, or the symbols *$, %, &,* or *!.* Variables aren't case-sensitive.

The goal in this example is to enable the user to input a value and then insert that value into a `MsgBox` statement, such as the one in examples `Basic10` and `Basic11`. The simplest way to get user input is by using the `Input` statement. The simplest form of this statement uses `InputBox` to assign whatever the user entered to a variable name, as shown in the following example:

```
VariableName = InputBox(prompt)
```

`Basic12` shows how you would use `InputBox` in a program. First, the `Dim` statement is used to create the variable `DateOfBirth`. This means that you have created a box in memory, labeled `DateOfBirth`, into which you can place some text, a date, or a number. `InputBox` is then used to insert whatever the user entered into the `DateOfBirth` box. Then, the `MsgBox` statement extracts the value stored in `DateOfBirth` and uses that value to calculate the age of the person whose date of birth was entered using the `DateDiff` function.

The `DateDiff()` function calculates the difference in time between two dates. The first argument in the function is a text code (`yyyy` = year, `q` = quarter, `m` = month, `y` = day of year, `d` = day, `w` = weekday, `ww` = week, `h` = hour, `n` = minute, `s` = second) that sets the unit of time calculated. In `Basic12` the code "`yyyy`", as displayed in the following example, expresses the date difference in years:

```
Sub Basic12()
   Dim DateOfBirth
   DateOfBirth = InputBox("Enter your date of birth")
   MsgBox "You are " & DateDiff("yyyy", DateOfBirth, _
   Date)& " years old."
End Sub
```

After the `Basic12` procedure runs, it displays a message box that pauses the execution of the procedure (see Figure 2-10). This pause enables the user to enter an appropriate value in the box — for example, **9/13/51**.

After the user makes this entry, a second message box appears, as shown in Figure 2-11. This time, the message box shows the person's age based on the entry made in the previous message box.

Figure 2-10:
The InputBox enables the user to enter a value that other statements in the program can use.

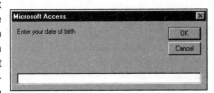

Figure 2-11:
The user's input determines the content of the message box.

The key to how `Basic12` works is the use of the variable `DateOfBirth`. Think of the variable as a kind of storage box. `InputBox` deposits information into the storage box. The `MsgBox` statement then looks in the storage box to see what the user left and uses that date to perform the `DateDiff()` calculation.

What happens to the storage box after the procedure ends? Access destroys it. The next time the procedure is run, Access creates a new storage box for `DateOfBirth` when it executes the `Dim` statement again. It may seem wasteful to destroy the storage boxes each time. However, destroying the variables at the end of each procedure prevents data from one run affecting the next run of the same procedure. Each time the procedure is run, it starts with a clean slate.

To summarize, `Basic12` illustrates the three steps involved in writing an interactive procedure:

✔ Create a variable for each item of data the user needs to enter.

✔ Use `InputBox` to fill the variables with the user's input.

✔ Use the data stored in the variables to produce new information and display that information within a message box.

Interacting with Database Objects

The procedure Basic12 illustrated the basic approach to interactive programming. Interactive programming creates procedures that require the user to make an entry. More importantly, the entry they make actually determines the result of the procedure.

Of course, the simple message displayed by Basic12 doesn't accomplish much. The next task is to apply the interactive programming to the database objects found in Access. The structure of Basic13 is identical to the structure of Basic12 in that it contains the three basic steps of interactive programming: Create variables, fill with user input, and obtain and display the specified data.

Figure 2-12 shows the dialog boxes that generate this procedure. The input box asks the user to enter the index number of the table that the user wants analyzed. Access stores the value the user enters in the variable TableName. The program then inserts the variable into the object expression where the index number normally appears. Thus, whatever number the user enters determines which table Access summarizes. You now have a single procedure that you can use to find the field count of any table in the open database, as shown in the following example:

```
Sub Basic13()
   Dim TableName As Integer
   TableName = InputBox("Enter the table index number")

   MsgBox "The " & CurrentDb.TableDefs(TableName).Name _
   & " table contains " & _
   CurrentDb.TableDefs(TableName).Fields.Count _
   & " fields."
End Sub
```

Figure 2-12:
User input
determines
which
TableDef
object
Access
analyzes.

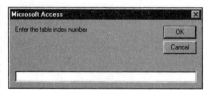

One technical change appears in `Basic13` that did not appear in `Basic12`. The difference occurs in the `Dim` statement. In `Basic12`, the variable was not assigned a specific data type (text, number, date, and so on). If you mention no specific data type, Visual Basic creates a generic type of variable called a *variant*. Variants can store text, numbers, or dates. You don't need to decide in advance which type of variable to use.

On the other hand, as the programmer, you know in advance that the entry made by the user is going to be the index of an object in a collection. Access requires that the index number be an integer-type (a whole number). Adding the `As Integer` keywords to the `Dim` statement, as shown in the following example, ensures that Access converts any user input into a whole number value which is compatible with the rest of the statements in the procedure:

```
Dim DateOfBirth          'Basic12
Dim TableName As Integer  'Basic13
```

One problem with `Basic13` is that the users don't know the maximum index number for the current database. The possibility exists that they could enter a value that is greater than the actual number of tables in the database and cause an error to occur.

In Chapter 1, I explain how entering an index number that exceeds the actual number of tables (minus one) causes an error. The object reference shown in the following example returns the maximum index value possible for tables in the current database:

```
CurrentDb.TableDefs.Count - 1
```

You can alert the users to the range of valid entries by inserting that object reference into the `InputBox` prompt to form a phrase such as `Enter a number from 0 to 17` in the box, as shown in the following example:

```
TableName = InputBox("Enter a number from 0 to " & _
CurrentDb.TableDefs.Count - 1)
```

`Basic14`, as shown in the following example, displays a message that alerts the user to the range of valid index numbers for the current database.

```
Sub Basic14()
  Dim TableName As Integer
  TableName = InputBox("Enter a number from 0 to " & _
  CurrentDb.TableDefs.Count - 1)
  MsgBox "The " & CurrentDb.TableDefs(TableName).Name _
  & " table contains " & _
  CurrentDb.TableDefs(TableName).Fields.Count _
  & " fields."
End Sub
```

One problem with `Basic14` is that for most users, the index numbers of the tables aren't very meaningful. The program would be more user-friendly if the user could enter the name of the table instead of its index number.

`Basic15` enables the user to enter the name of the table for which the program can count fields. Notice that, in the following example, the `Dim` statement you use to define the variable drops the `As Integer` keywords. This change enables the variable to store text data, such as the name of a table. Run `Basic15()` and enter the name **products** into the input box. Keep in mind that the entry is not case-sensitive. The procedure returns the field count for the *Products* table.

```
Sub Basic15()
    Dim TName
    TName = InputBox("Enter the table name")
    MsgBox "The " & CurrentDb.TableDefs(TName).Name _
    & " table contains " & _
    CurrentDb.TableDefs(TName).Fields.Count _
    & " fields."
End Sub
```

Procedures `Basic13`, `Basic14`, and `Basic15` illustrate how you can include user input in a simple Visual Basic program. The input box pauses program execution and allows the user to interact with the application before Visual Basic executes the remaining statements in the procedure. The result of this technique is a single procedure that can return a variety of results based on input the user enters each time the procedure is executed.

The Debug Mode

A flaw in `Basic15()` is that the user has no guidance as to the actual table names contained in this database. They are free to enter anything.

1. **Run `Basic15()` again.**

2. **When the input box appears, type** `orders`.

   What happened? Why? Access generated an error because none of the tables in the current database has a name that matches *orders* (see Figure 2-13). Any statement in `Basic15()` that refers to the table *orders* is a statement that Access cannot resolve. The result is an error message that reads `Item not found in this collection`. Item refers to the *orders* table and collection refers to the collection of table definitions in the current database.

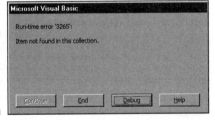

Figure 2-13:
User input
can result in
errors.

The Access error message offers you three options:

- **End.** Selecting this button terminates the current Visual Basic program.

- **Debug.** By far the most useful option. Selecting this button places Access into the Visual Basic debug mode. In the debug mode, execution of the program is paused and you can view your programming code. The statement that caused the error is highlighted in yellow.

- **Help.** This button launches Help and tries to locate an entry that corresponds to the error. This option seldom produces any help that tells you anything useful about the cause of the error.

3. **Click on the Debug button.**

   Access displays the module window that contains the procedure that contains the statement that caused the error. The specific statement is highlighted in yellow (see Figure 2-14). In this case, the Msgbox statement is the culprit.

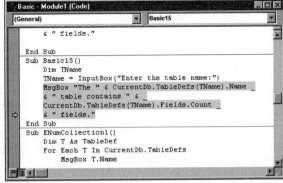

Figure 2-14:
The state-
ment that
caused the
error is
highlighted
in yellow in
the Debug
mode.

The cause of the error is the value assigned to the variable TName by means of the previous Inputbox statement. You can check the value of a variable by pointing the mouse at the name of the variable anywhere in the current procedure.

4. **Point the mouse at the name** `TName` **anywhere in the procedure code and keep it in place for a few seconds.**

   A tip box, shown in Figure 2-15, appears showing the current value assigned to the variable `TName`. In this case, the value is `orders`, which isn't a valid table name in the current database.

Figure 2-15:
Pointing at names causes Visual Basic to display tip text showing the current value.

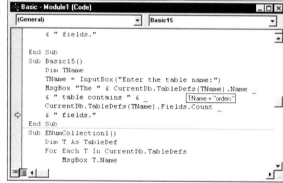

The debug mode is very important because it provides a means by which you can see the actual state of the variables in your program as specific places in your code. Your goal is to see if the values you thought or hoped the program would assign to the variables are the values that were assigned. In this case the problem occurred because the user made an invalid entry.

The ultimate solution to this error is to create a program that does not rely on the users to enter valid names. Instead, you create a form that displays a list of valid names from which the user can make a selection. You are then assured that whatever selection they make is a valid one

In the debug mode, you have several options as to what to do next.

- **Reset**. Choose Run⬎Reset to terminate execution of the program.

- **Retry the highlighted statement**. Press F8 to have Access retry executing the highlighted statement. Typically you would do this after you have edited the highlighted command to correct any mistakes. You can also use F5 to retry the highlighted statement and then continue with the rest of the program assuming there are more statements in the procedure.

- **Start at Cursor**. You can tell Visual Basic to skip the statement which caused the error and continue at some other location in the procedure by placing the cursor on the statement you want to start with and pressing Ctrl+F8.

In this case, stop execution.

5. **Choose Run⬎Reset to terminate execution of the program.**

Handling Errors

No matter how careful you are about writing programs, some expected or unexpected combination of factors can result in an error. Under normal use, errors that occur in Visual Basic programs cause Access to display the error message box shown back in Figure 2-13.

This error message box is fine when you are creating or testing a new program. But when other users use your program, they may find that the standard error message is more confusing than helpful. Visual Basic allows you to add custom designed error-handling routines to your programs. When you add one of these to a procedure, it takes the place of the standard error message box.

To add custom-designed error-handling to a procedure, you must include three new elements:

✔ **On Error Goto.** This statement serves two functions. First, it turns off the normal error-handling process for the procedure. It specifies the location of the error-handling code within the procedure by including the name of the *label* that marks the error-handling code.

✔ **Label.** A *label* is a place holder added to a procedure to mark a section of the code. Labels are always typed at the left margin of the code window and end with a colon. Labels are normally ignored by Visual Basic unless they are referenced in a statement such as On Error Goto. The actual name of the label has no significance. Its only purpose is to act as a place marker within the procedure.

✔ **End.** Procedures that have error-handling code included actually have two end points. One end point represents the end of the procedure if no error has occurred and the other is the end point of the procedure when an error occurs. Typically, the End Sub statement marks the end of the procedure when an error occurs. In order to create a second end point, you must insert an End statement to separate the error-handling portion of the procedure from the normal code.

The following example is an outline of a procedure that contains a custom-designed error-handler. The On Error Goto statement appears at the very beginning of the procedure to activate custom error handling. It also indicates the location of the code that should execute if, and only if, an error occurs. This is accomplished by the label ErrorHandler. When an error occurs, Visual Basic stops executing the statements in consecutive order and jumps to the label specified in the On Error Goto statement.

```
Sub Example()
  On Error Goto ErrorHandler
  statements...
  statements...
  End   'end program if not error

ErrorHandler:
  statements...
  statements...
End Sub 'end of the program if error
```

Take special notice of the location of the End statement. It is inserted into the procedure to separate the error handler code, which is always at the bottom of the procedure, from the non-error statements.

The ErrorExample procedure shown in the next example applies the concept of error handling to the problem raised by Basic15(). I added an error-handling routine to the procedure by inserting an On Error Goto statement, an End statement, and label. If no error occurs, the procedure behaves exactly like Basic15().

But if the user enters an invalid table name, Visual Basic jumps from the Msgbox statement that causes the error to the statement following the label Problem. In this case, the error-handling consists of a message box that informs the user of cause of the problem.

```
Sub ErrorExample()
    On Error GoTo Problem
    Dim TName

    TName = InputBox("Enter the table name")

    MsgBox "The " & CurrentDb.TableDefs(TName).Name _
    & " table contains " & _
    CurrentDb.TableDefs(TName).Fields.Count _
    & " fields."
    End

Problem:
    MsgBox TName & " is not a valid table name."
End Sub
```

1. **Run** ErrorExample().

2. **Type** products **in the Inputbox.**

   The procedure runs normally because *Products* is a valid table name.

3. **Run** ErrorExample().

4. Type orders in the Inputbox.

This time the procedure displays the message that *Orders* is not a valid table name. Because the procedure contains error-handling code, the standard error message, shown back in Figure 2-13, is suppressed. In its place, the error handler in the ErrorExample() code is activated displaying the message box specified within the procedure.

The example shown here is a very simple error-handler. It assumes that only one reason can cause an error to occur. This is not usually the case. As programs become more complex, error handlers usually include code to handle unexpected errors as well as the errors that you can anticipate.

Enumerating Collections

In all the procedures you've worked with in this chapter, you've dealt with one member of a collection at a time. You selected that member either by using its index number within the collection or by referring to the name of the object — for example, the name of a table. But what about the collections themselves? How would you deal with all of the members of a collection?

The process of dealing with all of the members of a collection is called *enumerating* the collection. Enumerating is a programming technique that deals with all the members of a collection, starting with the first member (index number 0) and continuing through to the last member.

Visual Basic provides a structure that's specifically designed to help you enumerate all the members of a collection. The For Each and Next statements create a structure that repeats one or more operations for each element in a collection.

```
For Each object In collection
...
Next
```

The procedure shown in the following example, ENumCollection1, illustrates how you can use a For Each structure to perform the same action once for every member of a collection. As an example, suppose the collection is the set of tables contained in the TableDefs collection. You could use this structure to display the name of every table that is a member of the collection.

To make this work, you use the `Dim` statement to create a variable that the `For Each` statement uses as a temporary container for each member of the collection. Remember that to assign an object such as a table, query, field, form, or report to a variable, you must specify the object type in the `Dim` statement (for example, `TableDef` or `QueryDef`). Because `ENumCollection1` processes table definitions, the variable `T` is defined as a `TableDef` type variable.

```
Sub ENumCollection1()
   Dim T As TableDef
   For Each T In CurrentDb.TableDefs
     MsgBox T.Name
   Next
End Sub
```

The selection of `T` as the name for the object variable has no special significance. The variable could be anything — for example, `TName`, `TableName`, or `NameOfTable`. I use `T` here because it is the simplest possible name (a single character), and the simplicity makes the code a bit easier to understand. On the other hand, a longer, more descriptive name might be easier to understand when you haven't looked at the code in a long time. If a procedure is using only a single variable of a given type, my own preference is to use simple names like `T` for `TableDef`, `R` for a `Recordset`, and `Q` for a `QueryDef`. Professional programmers often add prefixes to their variable names that identify their meaning such as `tbl` for a `Table`, `rs` for a `Recordset` and `qry` for a `QueryDef`. For example, `tblCompany` would refer to a `TableDef`, `rsCompany` would refer to a `Recordset`, and so on. These prefixes are useful when your code contains several different variables of the same type.

After this procedure runs, the result is a series of message boxes. Each message box displays the name of one of the members of the collection. You need to click the OK button 15 times (once for each message box that is displayed) to work your way through the entire collection.

In `ENumCollection1`, the keywords `TableDef` and `TableDefs` both appear. Is this a mistake? What's the difference? If you have a collection of objects such as tables, the name that ends with `s` refers to the entire collection. The name without the `s` refers to a single member of the collection. `TableDefs` refers to the entire collection of tables. `TableDef` refers to a single table within the collection.

Building a text string

Although `ENumCollection1` does succeed in displaying the name of each table in the database, the procedure does so in a rather inconvenient way. Clicking through a long series of boxes, each of which carries only a single item of information about the collection, can quickly become annoying. Creating a single box that lists all the tables in the database is a much better idea.

You can accomplish this by using the same techniques (the & operator and variables) that I introduced earlier in this chapter. The difference is that you will put them together in a slightly different way.

The trick involves using a variable to store not just one name, but all of the table names. If all of the names are stored in one variable, you can display all of the names in one message box at the end instead of a series of message boxes with one name in each.

Because this technique is a bit unintuitive, you may find it useful to play around with some variables in the Debug window before you try to use this technique in a procedure. Perform the following steps:

1. **Activate the Debug window by pressing Ctrl+G.**

2. **Move the cursor to the first blank line at the bottom of the Debug window.**

3. **Create a variable by entering** people = "John".

   Remember to press Enter after each entry.

4. **Enter** ? people **to display the value of the variable.**

   Access displays John on-screen. This response confirms that the variable people contains the name John. What happens if you assigned a different name to the same variable?

5. **Type** people = "Mary".

6. **Type** ? people.

   Not surprisingly, Access replaces the old contents of the variable (John) with the newly assigned value, Mary. Each time you assign a new value to a variable, Access erases the old value. But suppose that you actually want to *add* a value to an existing variable *without* erasing the old value. How? The solution appears following Step 8. Enter the commands in Steps 7 and 8 and see what happens.

7. **Type** people = people & "John".

8. **Type** ? people.

   The screen displays MaryJohn. Access added John to Mary instead of replacing one with the other. The statement people = people & "John" means that people can contain whatever is currently stored in people — plus the characters John. Because the variable name people appears on both the left and the right side of the =, Access adds the new text to the existing text.

Of course, the variable's result would look more like a list if each name appeared on a separate line. Remember, to create multiple-lined text displays, insert the constant `vbCrLf` into the text whenever you want to start a new line. Try Steps 9 and 10.

9. **Type** `people = people & vbCrLf & "Sue"`.

10. **Type** `? people`.

The display shows that the new name, `Sue`, appears on a line separate from the previous text, as in the following example:

```
MaryJohn
Sue
```

With this technique in hand, you can return to the problem of listing the table names. You may want to close the Debug window if it covers your view of the module window.

`ENumCollection2` applies this technique to the `TableDefs` collection. You use a variable called `TableList` to accumulate a list of the table names that the `TableDefs` collection contains. Keep in mind that nothing appears on-screen until all the names are stuffed into the `TableList` variable. Notice the use of `vbCrLf` in the following example to add a new line after each name. The result is shown in Figure 2-16, where the message box contains a full list of the tables contained in the current database.

```
Sub ENumCollection2()
   Dim T As TableDef, TableList
   For Each T In CurrentDb.TableDefs
      TableList = TableList & T.Name & vbCrLf
   Next
   MsgBox TableList
End Sub
```

Figure 2-16:
The message box shows a list of all the tables in the current database, each on its own separate line.

You can expand the amount of information gathered about the members of the collection to include the number of fields as well as the table names. In the following example, ENumCollection3 adds T.Fields.Count to the text stored for each table to produce a list of tables with the number of fields in each one, as shown in Figure 2-17.

```
Sub ENumCollection3()
  Dim T As TableDef, TableList
  For Each T In CurrentDb.TableDefs
    TableList = TableList & T.Name _
      & " - " & T.Fields.Count & VbCrLf
  Next
  MsgBox TableList
End Sub
```

You can use the same logic to show a variety of information. In the following example, ENumCollection4 replaces the Fields. Count property with the RecordCount property to list the number of records in each table.

```
Sub ENumCollection4()
  Dim T As TableDef, TableList
  For Each T In CurrentDb.TableDefs
    TableList = TableList & T.Name _
      & " - Records " & T.RecordCount & VbCrLf
  Next
  MsgBox TableList
End Sub
```

You can also apply the concept of nesting — that is, of putting one program-ming structure inside another — to For Each loops. Tables and fields, for example, represent nested collections. This means that inside the TableDefs collection are individual tables, each of which contains a collection of fields.

ENumCollection5 uses two For Each structures, one nested inside the other, to process all the fields in all the tables, as shown in Figure 2-18.

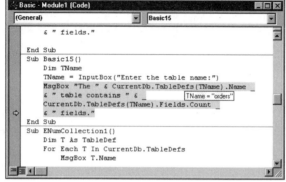

Figure 2-18:
The Fields collection nests inside the TableDefs collection.

Specifically, ENumCollection5 generates one message box for each table in the current database. Included in each message, however, is a complete list of all the fields in that table.

Notice that the program contains two statements that affect the content of the TableInfo variable, as shown in Figure 2-19.

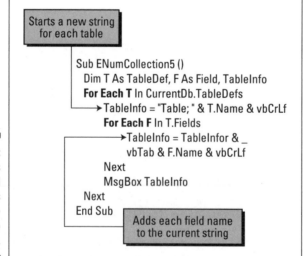

Figure 2-19:
Statements that control the contents of the TableInfo variable.

✔ Access executes the first statement each time you select a new TableDef. This statement erases the previous contents of the variable, if any, and inserts the name of the current table in the collection.

✔ The second statement that deals with TableInfo uses the string-building technique to combine the names of all the fields in the current table into a single variable.

The result of the procedure is a series of message boxes, similar to the one shown in Figure 2-20, which lists all the fields in each table. When you execute `ENumCollection5`, you are presented with a series of message boxes that display the field list for each of the tables in the current database.

If Conditions

Chapter 1 notes that, among the tables in the `TableDefs` collection of any database, one set of eight tables normally doesn't appear in the database window. These tables are special *system tables* that Access uses internally to keep track of the user-defined objects (tables, queries, forms, reports, and modules). These tables are not meant to be altered by the user, because incorrect changes can corrupt data. For this reason, the tables are hidden from the user. However, when you enumerate the `TableDefs` collection, as is done in `EnumCollection5()`, they are included. In most cases, you want to avoid using the system tables in your programs.

Suppose, however, that you could limit the enumerated tables to only those tables that appear in the database window. You need a way to select some, but not all, of the tables included in the `TableDefs` collection.

The first step in creating such a procedure is to find a means by which you can logically differentiate between user tables and system tables. Access provides just such a means in the form of the table `Attributes` property. The `Attributes` property identifies the special characteristics of database objects such as tables and fields. The procedure `ENumCollection6()` generates a message box that shows the value of the attributes property for each table in the database.

When you execute `ENumCollection6()`, you get a list of tables and their `Attributes`, as shown in Figure 2-21.

Figure 2-21:
The
Attributes
property
value for
each table
appears in
the mes-
sage box.

```
Sub ENumCollection6()
   Dim T As TableDef, TableInfo
   For Each T In CurrentDb.TableDefs
     TableInfo = TableInfo & T.Name & " = " _
     & T.Attributes & VbCrLf
   Next
   MsgBox TableInfo
End Sub
```

If you look at the list of attributes shown in Figure 2-21, you may notice a pattern. All the user-defined tables — that is, those tables having names that appear in the database window list of tables — have an attribute of 0. This means that if you limit the tables included in a procedure to those with an Attribute value of 0, you limit the list to only the user-defined table.

The solution to this and a whole range of similar problems is to use an If...Then...End If structure. Note that I use the term *structure* not *statement*. A structure consists of two or more statements that work together to control the flow of program execution.

The If...Then...End If structure consists of two separate statements. The If...Then portion of the structure always contains a *logical expression*. A logical expression is one that is either true or false, as shown in Figure 2-22. If the expression evaluates as true, Access executes any statements that follow the If...Then statement. On the other hand, if the expression evaluates as false, the procedure skips all the statements following the If statement and resumes execution with the first statement following the End If statement. The purpose of the If...Then...End If structure is to create sections in a procedure that can be skipped or executed, depending on the truth or falsity of some logically expressed condition.

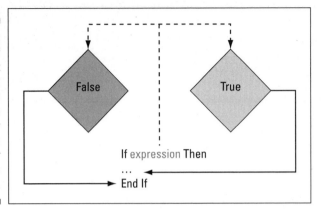

In this case, the task is to include information about a table only if the
Attributes property is zero. This idea is expressed in Visual Basic code as
shown in the following example of code. The If statement is true if the current table definition is a user-defined table and false in all other cases.

```
If T.Attributes = 0 Then
```

The procedure ENumCollection7 shows how an If...Then...End If can
be applied to the current problem. The If structure is placed inside a For
Each structure. As each member of the TableDefs collection is processed,
the Attributes property of the TableDef is tested by the If statement.
When the value of the Attributes property is zero, the name and record
count of the table are added to the TableList variable. Conversely, when the
value is not zero, the procedure skips the statement that adds information to
TableList. See Figure 2-23.

```
Sub ENumCollection7()
   Dim T As TableDef, TableList
   For Each T In CurrentDb.TableDefs
     If T.Attributes = 0 Then
        TableList = TableList & T.Name _
        & " - " & T.RecordCount & " records" _
        & VbCrLf
     End If
   Next
   MsgBox TableList
End Sub
```

Figure 2-23:
The table
information
now
includes
only the
user-
defined
tables in the
current
database.

The basic `If...Then...End If` structure can be expanded by adding a third statement to the structure: `Else`. The `Else` is inserted between `If` and `Endif` to create alternative sets of statements. Those statements entered between `If` and `Else` are executed when the condition is true. When the condition is false, the statements between `Else` and `Endif` are executed.

This principle is applied in `ENumCollection8()`. This procedure generates a line of text for all tables. However, the style of text displayed varies according to the `Attributes` of each table. If the `Attribute` is not zero, the words `System Table` are printed next to the table name, taking the place of the record count.

```
Sub ENumCollection8()
  Dim T As TableDef, TableList
  For Each T In CurrentDb.TableDefs
    If T.Attributes = 0 Then
      TableList = TableList & T.Name _
      & " - " & T.RecordCount & " records" _
      & VbCrLf
    Else
      TableList = TableList & T.Name _
      & " System Table" _
      & VbCrLf
    End If
  Next
  MsgBox TableList
End Sub
```

Using DoCmd in a Procedure

In Chapter 1, I describe how the `DoCmd` object enables you to execute Access macro actions and menu commands. In Chapter 1, you entered the Visual

Basic code equivalents of these actions directly into the Debug window. You can also use these same commands within a procedure in which you want to execute a macro command or a menu operation.

Suppose, for example, that you want to open a table (such as the Employees table) and sort it according to its `LastName` field. You can accomplish this task by using the Visual Basic equivalents of the macro and menu operations you would use if you were performing the task manually.

The following example uses three `DoCmd` object methods to open and sort the table. First, the example uses `OpenTable` to open a window containing the contents of the specified table. Then, the example uses `GoToControl` to select the sort field. In an open table or query window, this command moves the cursor to a specific field column. In this case, the cursor moves to the `LastName` field. The `RunCommand` method of the third example executes the equivalent of the Records⇨Sort⇨Sort Ascending menu command by using the constant `acCmdSortAscending` as its argument. The resulting display is shown in Figure 2-24.

Note that when you execute the `DoCmd` procedure, Access returns to the Visual Basic window. In order to see the table that was opened, you need to switch back to the Access window.

```
Sub DoCmd1()
   DoCmd.OpenTable "Employees"
   DoCmd.GoToControl "LastName"
   DoCmd.RunCommand acCmdSortAscending
End Sub
```

Figure 2-24: Access 2000 sorts the table by the LastName field.

Employee ID	FirstName	LastName	Title	Extension	Work Phone
5	Steven	Buchanan	Vice President		(212) 555-1189
1	Nancy	Davolio	President		(212) 555-9857
2	Andrew	Fuller	Treasurer		(212) 555-9482
3	Janet	Leverling	Executive Secre		(212) 555-3412
4	Margaret	Peacock	Accounting Mar		(212) 555-8122
*	(AutoNumber)				

Record: 14 ◀ 1 ▶ ▶I ▶* of 5

Editing macro actions in Visual Basic code is usually quite simple. To change the sort order of the records from `LastName` to `Title`, for example, all you need to do is edit the name of the field that you use as an argument for the `GoToControl` method, as shown in the following example:

```
Sub DoCmd2()
   DoCmd.OpenTable "Employees"
   DoCmd.GoToControl "Title"
   DoCmd.RunCommand acCmdSortAscending
End Sub
```

You can easily use Visual Basic code to express such operations as applying a filter to a table. In the following example, DoCmd3 shows the use of the ApplyFilter method to select only those records from the Parks Address Information table that have a State value of PA.

```
Sub DoCmd3()
   DoCmd.OpenTable "Parks Address Information"
   DoCmd.ApplyFilter WhereCondition:="State = 'PA'"
End Sub
```

If you want to insert a text literal as part of a text item, you can use apostrophes (' ') around the text literal, as is the case in DoCmd3, where you use the expression "State = 'PA'" to filter records.

Chapter 3

The SQL Story

*O*ne of the most powerful tools available in database management software is *SQL (Structured Query Language)*, typically pronounced *sequel* — you know, like a newer (usually worse) version of a movie. This chapter explains what SQL is, why it's important in Access 2000, and how you can use SQL to manipulate the data stored in Access tables.

> **Database Folder: Chapter 3 Database**
> **File: SQL.MDB**
> **Module: Object Example**

Before you begin, do the following:

1. **Open the database for Chapter 3, SQL.MDB.**

2. **Click on the Queries tab.**

   This tab lists the queries that correspond to those named in this chapter.

3. **Open the specified query form in the design mode.**

   This, of course, is optional. You can choose to enter the commands as they appear in the book, if you'd rather.

While running the previously entered queries saves time, some people feel that actually doing the typing helps them to understand what they are entering.

Why SQL?

SQL? Isn't this a book about Access 2000 programming? Why am I introducing another language in Chapter 3?

It turns out that you can't do much Access programming without encountering SQL. SQL was originally designed back in the Neolithic age of computers to help average human beings access data stored on their mainframe computers. The goal was to allow people to request sets of data by writing sentences like "select these fields from that table."

While it may be possible to write Access programs and not directly use SQL, you will find that the most efficient way to write Access programs is to combine the objects discussed in Chapters 1 and 2 with SQL operations explained in this chapter.

Using the SQL View

Unlike most desktop applications (such as Word or Excel), Access is actually a collection of several different applications bundled together in a single user interface. Table 3-1 lists the six basic parts of the Access interface that correspond to the six tabs in the database window (Tables, Queries, Forms, Reports, Macros, and Modules).

What's interesting about this list is that only three of the six components (Forms, Reports, and Macros) are designed specifically for Access and only Access. The other three (Tables, Queries, and Modules) are components that Access uses and can also function outside of Access as part of other applications. For example, the tables used in Access conform to the Microsoft DAO (Data Access Objects) and ADO (Active Data Objects) models. Other applications such as Word and Excel — and even full development environments such as Visual Basic 6.0 — also support DAO and ADO models. This means that data-related code written to run in Access can, with little or no modification, run in other applications that support the same data models.

Table 3-1	Component Parts of the Access System		
Access Name	*Other Name*	*Acronym*	*Function*
Tables	Data Access Objects	DAO	Defines the structures in which data is entered and stored.

Access Name	Other Name	Acronym	Function
Queries	Structured Query Language	SQL	Provides a standard method for retrieving sets of data.
Forms	Access Form Objects	none	Provides screen windows in which data can be viewed and edited.
Reports	Access Report Objects	none	Provides paginated output forms for printing sets of data.
Macros	Access Macros	none	Provides a macro language to customize Access Forms and Reports.
Modules	Visual Basic for Applications	VISUAL BASIC	Provides a standard programming language that can be used to manipulate all of the elements in Access and the Microsoft Office suite.

The subject of this chapter is SQL — a component behind the Access Query feature (as listed in Table 3-1). Access uses SQL in a variety of ways to select sets of data based on logical criteria. The data sets can then be displayed in forms, printed on reports, or used to calculate summary information.

FAQs about SQL

Before you dig into the details of SQL, it may be useful to clarify a few points about the Access/SQL personality split.

Where did SQL come from?

SQL is not new. The language was developed over a decade ago to make it simpler for users to retrieve information from mainframe databases. At that time, users needed to learn a different set of commands for retrieving data from each database they wanted to access.

The goal of SQL is to provide a single set of commands that you can use to retrieve data from any database. As a result, SQL eliminates the need to learn a variety of database commands or languages and allows a user or programmer to apply his knowledge of SQL to a wide array of data resources. For example, Microsoft sells two different database products: Access and SQL Server. However, because both products support SQL, each of the products can process the same commands. In this book, you discover how to access SQL Server data as well as Access data by using SQL statements.

What is a query language?

Table 3-1 lists two types of languages in Access: SQL and Visual Basic (Visual Basic for Applications). SQL is called a *query language* because its set of commands is limited to entering, updating, and retrieving sets of data — or *querying*. While this is an important function, languages such as Visual Basic provide the user with a broader set of functions. These functions can control all aspects of an application, including the user interface, data security, and printed reports.

If SQL is so important, why don't I see it when I use Access?

While SQL is not a difficult language to learn, it's still a computer language. Languages, no matter how simple, require the user to write out structured commands that include specific terms placed in the correct order, and with the correct punctuation. To make Access data easy to retrieve, Access hides SQL behind its query grid interface.

As an example, look at Figure 3-1 which shows the Access query grid. The grid contains a visual representation of a query that will retrieve two fields (`LastName` and `City`) from the `Customers` table.

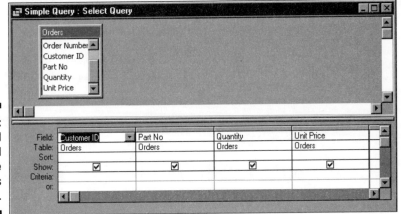

Figure 3-1:
A typical
query laid
out in the
Access
query grid.

Query: Simple Query

However, behind every Access query grid is an equivalent SQL command, also called a *statement*. You can change the display of the query window to reveal the SQL statement that corresponds to the query you've designed.

Do this by selecting SQL View, using the View icon on the Design toolbar (shown in Figure 3-2), or by choosing View⇨SQL View.

Figure 3-2:
The SQL
View
command
as found on
the Design
toolbar.

When you select either of these commands, the contents of the query window change to reveal the SQL statement (see Figure 3-3) that is equivalent to the query you created in the design grid.

While the query grid may be a useful and easy way to specify the data you want to retrieve, it's actually the text of the SQL statement itself that Access processes.

```
Query1 : Select Query                                    _ □ ×
SELECT Customers.LastName, Customers.City
FROM Customers;
```

Why would I need to use SQL instead of the query grid?

Here are a few reasons for using SQL instead of the query grid:

- You may find, in some cases, that it's easier to create or modify a query by editing the SQL statement instead of manipulating the objects in the query grid.

- As you become more expert with SQL, you may find that Access cannot graphically represent the query in the grid, even though it is capable of executing the statement.

- The query grid is only one of the ways that you can use SQL in Access. As you'll find out, you can integrate SQL statements into Visual Basic code in a number of ways that greatly enhance the power and flexibility of the forms and reports you create.

Defining a Data Set with SQL

The key concept behind SQL is the concept of a *data set*. A data set is a set of rows and fields. Access displays data sets in Datasheets. The SQL statement is a definition of the type and amount of data that should be included in a data set. When a SQL statement becomes processed, the result is a set of rows and columns that matches the details specified in the SQL statement.

The simplest possible SQL statement consists of two parts:

- SELECT. The section begins with the keyword SELECT, followed by a list of fields that you want to include in the data set. Commas separate the names in a field list. If you want to include all the fields in a table, you can type an asterisk (*) instead of a field list.

- FROM. This portion begins with the keyword FROM. It specifies the table or tables from which the fields are to be drawn.

The following SQL statement shows how to generate a data set that consists of the names and cities for all the records in the Customers table. The results of this statement appear in Figure 3-4.

```
SELECT lastname,city
FROM customers;
```

Figure 3-4:
The data set
resulting
from a
simple SQL
statement.

Last Name	City
Estabrook	Stamford
Talman	San Francisco
Bensky	Belmont
Ditto	Champaign
Bremseth	Stamford
Hsi	Stamford
Schwartz	Miami Beach
Meyer	San Diego
Baldwin	Wayne
Finchum	Toronto
Rost	Algona
Chana	Kitchener

SQL Example 01 : Select Query

Record: 1 of 1151

Query: SQL Example 01

By default, Access opens new queries in the grid display mode. When you create a query and save it, Access reopens the query in the display mode in which you last saved it. If you want to reopen a query in the SQL display mode, switch the mode to SQL before you save it. The next time you open the query, it appears in the SQL display.

You should make note of a few points about the way you write a SQL statement.

- ✔ SQL statements processed in Access always end with a semicolon (;).

  The semicolon is characteristic only of SQL in Access. Other forms of SQL — such as Transact SQL, supported by Microsoft SQL Server — do not use the semicolon at the end of the SQL statement.

- ✔ SQL is not case-sensitive. You can write a SQL statement in any combination of upper- or lowercase characters.

- ✔ While it's true that SQL statements are not case-sensitive, it's a widely followed convention that SQL keywords are written in uppercase, and field and table names are written in lowercase. Another traditional element is that the SELECT and FROM keywords are typed on separate lines. The following example shows the traditional style of writing SQL statements.

```
SELECT lastname, city
FROM customers;
```

✔ You can write SQL statements on one or more lines within the query window. As shown in the following code, you have the option to combine the SELECT and FROM keywords on a single line. Or you can go the other direction and add more lines to spread out the statement onto three, four, or more lines. SQL also ignores additional white space such as tabs or extra blank spaces. This allows you the freedom to arrange the elements in a SQL statement in any way you like, without affecting the meaning of the statement. The second example in the following query places the keywords on lines by themselves. The semicolon also is placed on a separate line. This style clearly differentiates the keywords (which are always the same) from the table-specific names (which will vary).

```
SELECT lastname, city FROM customers;

SELECT
lastname, city
FROM
customers
;
```

✔ If you want to include all the fields from a table within a SQL data set, you can avoid typing in all the names by typing an asterisk (*) in place of the field list.

```
SELECT *
FROM customers;
```

Query: SQL Example 02

Using the WHERE keyword

The simplest SQL statements require only the SELECT and FROM keywords. However, this type of query will always include all the records in the specified table. In order to select records based on logical criteria, you need to add the WHERE keyword followed by a *logical expression*. A logical expression is one that compares two or more values and yields either a True or False value. For example, state = "CA" can either be True or False, depending upon the actual value of the state field.

The following SQL statement returns the name and city fields from the Customers table when the value for the state field is TX. The WHERE keyword, plus the logical expression (for example, WHERE state = "TX"), is often called a *WHERE clause*. You can see the data set resulting from the query in Figure 3-5.

```
SELECT lastname, city
FROM customers
WHERE state = "TX";
```

Figure 3-5:
Customer
records
selected by
a WHERE
clause.

Last Name	City
Sheppard	Odessa
Harry	Rockwall
Bunch	Houston
Colo	Lubbock
Paley	Coppell
Hall	Conroe
Johnson	Palestine
Stanford	Rowlett
O'brien	Cleburne
Lang	Dallas
Edmundson	Lewisville

SQL Example 03 : Select Query

Record: 1 of 65

Access SQL, like most forms of SQL, allows the use of single-quotation marks
('') or apostrophes to enclose text items, as shown in the following example.
The characters used to enclose literal text items are called *delimiters*.

```
SELECT name, city
FROM customers
WHERE state = 'TX';
```

Query: SQL Example 03

Using expressions with SELECT

In addition to lists of fields, the SELECT keyword can operate with any valid
Access *expression*. Expressions can include arithmetic operations and built-in
functions, as well as string operations. For example, the following statement
retrieves data stored in the city, state, and zip fields. The result is a record
set that contains separate columns, as shown in previous examples.

```
SELECT city, state, zip
FROM customers;
```

On the other hand, you often see this information expressed as a single item
in which city, state, and zip, are combined with punctuation to form a
single phrase. The technical term for combining two strings is *concatenate*.
The following statement uses the & (concatenation) operator to combine the
contents of the fields with text literals (the items enclosed in quotation
marks). This combination creates a data set consisting of a single column
based on the concatenation expression, as shown in Figure 3-6.

```
SELECT city & ", " & state & " " & zip
FROM customers;
```

Query: SQL Example 04

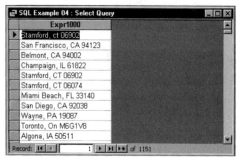

Figure 3-6:
The data set
contains the
single-
column
result of an
expression.

Another common expression is one that displays *lastname, firstname* as a single column. See SQL Example 04a on the CD.

Setting column names

As you may have noticed when Access processes a SQL statement, it uses the field names as the column headings in the resulting data set. If you use an expression to generate a column, as is the case in Figure 3-6, Access generates a generic name, Expr1000, as the column heading.

SQL allows you to specify a different name for a column by using the AS keyword with either a field name or an expression. The following example uses the AS keyword to assign Customer Name to the name field and Location to the expression city & ", " & state & " " & zip as shown in Figure 3-7.

```
SELECT lastname & ", " & firstname AS [Customer Name],
city & ", " & state & " " & zip AS Location
FROM customers;
```

Note that you can use the AS keyword to assign a multiword name to a column as long as brackets enclose the name, for example, [Customer Name]. Keep in mind that the case of the characters used with the AS keyword affect the names appearing as column headings.

Figure 3-7:
Column
names
defined
using the AS
keyword.

Customer Name	Location
Estabrook, Mike	Stamford, ct 06902
Talman, Ron	San Francisco, CA 94123
Bensky, Tony	Belmont, CA 94002
Ditto, Irene	Champaign, IL 61822
Bremseth, Ben	Stamford, CT 06902
Hsi, Richard	Stamford, CT 06074
Schwartz, Ronald	Miami Beach, FL 33140
Meyer, Michael	San Diego, CA 92038
Baldwin, Bill	Wayne, PA 19087
Finchum, Marc	Toronto, On M6G1V8
Rost, DALE	Algona, IA 50511

Query: SQL Example 05

Sorting records

You can control the order of the records returned in the data set by using the
ORDER BY keyword to specify which field, fields, or expression to use to
determine the order of the records. The following example uses the ORDER
BY keyword to sort the records in the resulting data set alphabetically by city.
You can see the sorted data set in Figure 3-8.

Figure 3-8:
The ORDER
BY keyword
used to sort
data by city.

Last Name	First Name	address1	city
Del Duke	Jerome	310 E. 44th Stre	Acampo
Soberman	Thomas	26318 Hendrie E	Agana
Shaia	Keith	12301 Tiverton L	Aiea
Forbet	Andy	242 Link Lane	Akron
Chen	Sandra	6f, 5, Alley 20, l	Albany
Bures	James	1853 South Hav	Albany
Grove	Bev	41000 Montelen	Albany
Hoffman	James	2743 Moores V	Albany
Spillane	Denis	4209 Ewell Roa	Albert Lea
Foster	Denis	P.o. Box 296 10	Albert Lea
Foster	David	P.o. Box 296 10	Albion
Stedwill	Paul	132 Cardinal Cr	Albuquerque
Intanjudin	sol	5, Jalan Rata 8/	Albuquerque

```
SELECT lastname, firstname, address1, city
FROM customers
ORDER BY city;
```

Query: SQL Example 06

When a SQL statement contains both a WHERE and an ORDER BY keyword, the
WHERE clause must precede the ORDER BY keyword. The following example
limits the records to state = "CA" while sorting the records by city.

```
SELECT lastname, firstname, address1, city
FROM customers
WHERE state = "CA"
ORDER BY city;
```

| Query: SQL Example 07 |

By default, the ORDER BY keyword assumes an ascending (low-to-high) order. You can specify a descending (high-to-low) order by adding DESC to the statement following the sort fields. The following example sorts the records in descending order by ZIP code.

```
SELECT lastname, firstname, address1, city
FROM customers
WHERE state = "CA"
ORDER BY zip DESC;
```

| Query: SQL Example 08 |

Sorting on multiple keys

In some cases, you may need to sort records by several key fields in order to arrange the records in the desired sequence. U.S. addresses offer a common example of this kind of sorting because locations in the United States are sorted first by state, and then within state by city.

In a SQL ORDER BY clause, multiple sort keys are listed in the order of their priority. In the following example, records are sorted first by state, and then within state by city when you use the phrase ORDER BY state, city, as shown in Figure 3-9. Keep in mind that the order of the field names is important. The phrase ORDER BY city, state would produce a recordset sorted first by city and then by state.

```
SELECT lastname, firstname, address1, city
FROM customers
ORDER BY state, city;
```

Last Name	First Name	city	state
Ditto	Joanta	Sausalito	
Robertson	John	Lami	00
▶ Lin	Michael	Apo	AE
Frank	Michael	Apo	AE
Horwood	Justin	Fpo	AE
Anderson	mark	Anchorage	AK
Smith	Glenn	Fairbanks	AK
5805 Oak Fores	david	Fairbanks	AK
Drossis	Glenn	Fairbanks	AK
Prud'homme	Keith	Wasilla	AK
Felsheim	Bob	Anniston	AL
Inbar	susan	Ashford	AL

SQL Example 09 : Select Query
Record: 3 of 1144

Figure 3-9:
Locations
sorted by
state and
then by city.

Query: SQL Example 09

Dealing with null values

A special type of criterion concerns whether a field contains data or is blank. In SQL, blank fields are called *null values,* or simply *nulls.* SQL supports special keywords for dealing with nulls.

✔ IS NULL. Use this phrase to select records that have blank values in a specific field.

✔ IS NOT NULL. Use this phrase to select records that have an entry other than a blank value in a specific field.

Nulls occur in text, memo, and date fields. In a number or currency field, a blank entry is treated as a value of zero. In Yes/No fields, a blank is always a No (False) value.

The following statement selects records with a blank value in the contact field. When you execute this query, you find that there is one record in the table that has a null value in the State column. This type of query is often important in an application where you want to make sure that you have data in certain key fields. For example, if you were printing address labels, you would want to make sure that you did not print labels that had no state.

```
SELECT lastname,firstname
FROM customers
WHERE state IS NULL;
```

Query: SQL Example 10

Conversely, you can exclude records based on a blank value in a specific field. The following example inverts the logic of the previous statement by adding NOT to the IS NULL phrase. The result is that records with an entry other than a blank are included in the resulting data set.

```
SELECT lastname,firstname
FROM customers
WHERE state IS NOT NULL;
```

| Query: SQL Example 11 |

Blanks and nulls

In most cases, a blank entry requires no special treatment or interpretation. For example, say you encounter a blank field for a ZIP code or a Social Security number. If you live in the United States, you can assume the field is blank because you were missing the necessary information for the field when you entered the data — a safe assumption, because every U.S. location has a ZIP code, and most U.S. citizens (over the age of 2) have Social Security numbers.

On the other hand, some blanks in some fields may suggest other meanings. In the previous example, the `contact` field in some records is blank. The blank could mean missing data — you didn't know the name of the contact for that company at the time you entered the data. However, it may also mean that no contact exists for this company. In this case, the blank doesn't mean *unknown at the time of entry* but *not applicable to this company*. In some cases, the difference between unknown and not applicable may be significant. Access and Access SQL support the ability to distinguish between two types of blank fields: (1) a *null* value that means unknown at the time of entry, and (2) a *zero-length string* that means the value is known and its value is blank (not applicable) for that record.

Enter a zero-length string by typing `""`, in a field — a pair of double-quotation marks with no space between them. Follow that by a press of the Enter key.

Keep in mind that when you enter a zero-length string in a field, the `""` appear only for a moment while you make the entry. As soon as you move to another field, the `""` disappear and the cell appears blank. You have no way to determine visually whether or not a field contains a null or a zero-length string. However, SQL statements can distinguish between the two types of entries.

By default, Access *does not permit* you to enter zero-length strings into database fields. If you want to allow zero-length strings, you must alter the property sheet of the field.

1. **Open the table in the Design mode.**

2. **Select the field where you want to enter the zero-length strings.**

3. **On the General tab of the field properties sheets (in the lower-half of the screen), you see the Allow Zero-Length property; change this from No to Yes.**

4. Save the changes to the table's design.

You can now enter zero-length strings.

Zero-length strings can cause problems when you import tables stored in certain non-Access files. In some cases, the programs that originally created the data will designate empty fields as "". Access treats these values as zero-length fields. If the table into which you are importing does not permit zero-length strings, you may get an error message during the import process telling you that Access does not allow zero-length strings. If you encounter this type of error while importing, change the structure of the table you're importing into to allow zero-length strings. You can then re-import the data without error.

An example of a table that contains both nulls and zero-length strings is the Customers with Zero Length Fields table in SQL. This table includes records that don't have a null value but do appear to be blank because the Customers with Zero Length Fields table includes records that have zero-length strings in the State column. The following query selects six records that have null values in the State column.

```
SELECT lastname, firstname
FROM [Customers with Zero Length Fields]
WHERE state IS  NULL;
```

Query: Nulls 01

On the other hand, the next query seeks to locate records that have a zero-length string in the state field. The SQL statement uses "" (two quotes with nothing in-between) to specify a match for a zero-length string rather than a null value. This query retrieves two records that were not included in the previous set of records.

```
SELECT lastname, firstname
FROM [Customers with Zero Length Fields]
WHERE state="";
```

Query: Nulls 02

Another way to locate zero-length strings is to use the Visual Basic Len() function. The Len() function counts the number of characters in a field or string variable. By definition, zero-length strings have a length of zero. The expression Len(state)=0 is logically the same as state-"". Check Nulls 03 for an example that uses Len().

If you want to locate all of the records with a missing value in a table that allows zero-length strings, you need to create a SQL statement that checks for both Nulls and zero-length strings as shown in the following query. This query retrieves eight records — the six nulls and two zero-length strings — that have no visible value in the State column.

```
SELECT lastname, firstname
FROM [Customers with Zero Length Fields]
WHERE state="" Or state Is Null;
```

Query: Nulls 03

The query Nulls 03a shows how to exclude all null or zero-length string values from a key field such as state. The resulting record set excludes any records that do not have a visible value in the state field.

SQL Comparison Operators

SQL statements support the use of the common logical operators (for example, =, <>, >, <, <= and >=). In addition, SQL supports three special operators that simplify the syntax required to perform selections based on multiple possible matches.

- ✔ LIKE. Use this operator to select records based on a pattern match rather than an exact match.
- ✔ IN. Use this operator to match one item from a list of items.
- ✔ BETWEEN...AND. Use this operator to select records based on an inclusive range of values.

The LIKE operator

The LIKE operator provides a number of simple ways to match text items based on patterns rather than exact matches. The LIKE operator permits the use of *wildcard* logic in expressions. Wildcards are symbols that define patterns used to select fields containing text that matches the pattern. If you have used file-specification wildcards in DOS, for example, *dir *.doc,* you find that the LIKE operator functions similarly.

The pattern can contain any sequence of characters, plus the wildcards *, ?, and #. The * lets you match any group of characters. The ? matches any one character, and # matches any one digit.

The LIKE operator is useful when you want to match a part of the data in a given column. For example, it is often useful to search for part of a last name when you are not sure of the exact spelling.

The following example uses the expression `lastname LIKE "ben*"` to select any record that has a *lastname* that begins with *ben*, regardless of what other characters, if any, are in the rest of the field. You can see the resulting data set in Figure 3-10.

Figure 3-10: Using LIKE with a wildcard to mark partial matches.

Like 01 : Select Query	Sort Descending
Last Name	**First Name**
Benenson	Dennis
Benenson	Mark
Benenson	Tom
Bennett	HENRY
Bennett	Jack
Bensky	Frank
Bensky	h.c.
Bensky	JOHN
Bensky	Ralph
Bensky	Richard
Bensky	Stacey

Record: 1 of 13

ON THE CD

```
SELECT lastname, firstname
FROM customers
WHERE lastname LIKE "ben*";
```

Query: Like 01

If you place the * at the beginning of the pattern, it signifies a match for the characters at the end of a field. The following statement matches last names that end with *berg*. Figure 3-11 shows the result.

```
SELECT lastname, firstname
FROM customers
WHERE lastname LIKE "*berg";
```

Figure 3-11: LIKE used to select by the text at the end of a field.

Like 02 : Select Query	
Last Name	**First Name**
Mandelberg	Elizabeth
Goldberg	amy
Rosenberg	jason
Kornberg	Cheryl
Mandelberg	Hidenori
Goldberg	Barry
Rosenberg	kelli
Trakhtenberg	Jim
Mandelberg	JO
Rosenberg	Lo
Trakhtenberg	mike

Record: 1 of 23

> ### Query: Like 02

An * before and after a group of characters causes a *substring search*. A substring search is one that locates the character or characters at any position within the field. The following statement locates any item that contains the letters *man* in any part of the Lastname field (see the result in Figure 3-12).

Figure 3-12:
LIKE used to
select the
text in any
part of a
field.

Quantity	Price	Total
1	$12.95	12.95
1	$13.95	13.95
1	$10.95	10.95
3	$13.95	41.85
1	$11.95	11.95
3	$12.95	38.85
1	$12.95	12.95
1	$13.95	13.95
1	$15.95	15.95
1	$13.95	13.95
1	$12.95	12.95

Calc 01 : Select Query

Record: 1 of 2228

```
SELECT lastname, firstname
FROM customers
WHERE lastname LIKE "*man*";
```

> ### Query: Like 03

You can also use pattern matching with date fields. The following example selects records for a specific month, for example, March 1999, by using the * as a wildcard for the day portion of a formatted m/d/yy:

```
SELECT orderid, orderdate
FROM orders
WHERE orderdate LIKE "3/*/99";
```

> ### Query: Like 04

The technique shown in Like 04 for selecting dates by month assumes that the dates have been entered without time information. Access allows you to enter date/time values — such as 3/7/99 12:32:29 PM — into Date fields. Such dates would be ignored by Like 04. In addition, systems using international date formats instead of American date formats would be a problem for Like 04. A more verbose but more accurate approach is to use the Month() and Year() functions to extract the numeric values of the date parts. The following example, on the CD as Like 04a, shows a query that correctly selects March, 1999 dates in all cases.

```
SELECT orderid, orderdate
FROM orders
WHERE Month(orderdate) = 3
AND Year(orderdate)=1999;
```

Another useful form of pattern matching is the use of ranges within a pattern. You can specify a range by enclosing the characters in [ ]. Suppose that you were looking for a customer whose name could be either Carp or Karp. The entry [ck] matches either a *c* or a *k* in the first position in a pattern search.

```
SELECT LastName, FirstName
FROM customers
WHERE LastName Like "[ck]ar*";
```

Query: Like 05

You can specify a specific range of characters. For example, [a-m] selects all of the items that begin with letters *a* through *m*.

```
SELECT lastname, firstname, city
FROM customers
WHERE city LIKE "[a-m]*";
```

Query: Like 06

The next example uses a list of characters, [a-m,w], to select cities that begin with *a, m* or *w*.

```
SELECT lastname, firstname, city
FROM customers
WHERE city LIKE "[a,m,w]*";
```

Query: Like 07

The IN operator

Use the IN operator to determine whether or not an item is in a list of values. The following statement compares the contents of the city field to the contents of a list of items, for example, "San Francisco" , "San Jose", "Sacramento". The resulting data set contains only records whose cities match one of the items in the list.

```
SELECT lastname, city, state
FROM customers
WHERE city IN("San Francisco","San Jose","Sacramento");
```

Query: IN 01

The BETWEEN...AND operator

The BETWEEN...AND operator is useful when you want to specify a range of
values as a criterion for selecting records for a data set. The following statement selects records by the Price field. Records are included if the Price is
between 5 and 10. Note that such a *between range* includes the values (for
example, 5 and 10) that set the scope of the range.

```
SELECT item, quantity
FROM orderdetails
WHERE price BETWEEN 5 AND 10;
```

Query: BETWEEN 01

You can also use the BETWEEN...AND operator to select a range of dates as
shown in the following code where the Order Date field is used to select
records from 3/1/99 to 3/15/99.

```
SELECT orderid,ordertotal
FROM orders
WHERE orderdate BETWEEN #3/1/99# AND #3/15/99#;
```

Query: BETWEEN 02

Distinct values

Normally, a query returns all the records and fields that fit the specifications
that you enter in the SQL statement. Often this means that the same value
appears in more than one record.

In some cases, you want to limit the items returned to a list of *distinct* values
so that the data set includes only one occurrence of each unique value. For
example, suppose you want to get a list of the cities from which your customer base is derived. The following statement lists the names of the cities.

```
SELECT city
FROM customers;
```

However, this list may contain duplicates because several customers may
reside in the same city. Adding the DISTINCT keyword eliminates the duplicates from the data set.

```
SELECT DISTINCT city
FROM customers;
```

Query: Distinct 01

If one or more records have a blank (null) value, the blank is included at the top of the data set. In most cases, you want to eliminate the blank from the list by adding a WHERE clause:

```
SELECT DISTINCT city
FROM customers
WHERE city IS NOT NULL;
```

Query: Distinct 02

The DISTINCT keyword can also function with a list of fields. The following statement produces a data set that contains a list of the unique combinations of city and state. When you run this query, you now get two records for Chico, one for California and one for Oregon: Chico CA, Chico OR.

```
SELECT DISTINCT city, state
FROM customers;
```

Query: Distinct 03

An added benefit of using the DISTINCT keyword is that the items are automatically sorted in ascending order. This occurs because Access must sort the items in order to eliminate the duplicate items from the listing. Thus, all DISTINCT data sets are also sorted data sets.

Calculated Columns

SQL allows you to generate columns in a data set by using expressions to define the contents of the column. In Access, SQL expressions can include any operator or function that Access supports. You can use these functions to manipulate text, dates, or make special match calculations such as the Pmt() function that calculates loan payments.

Access SQL supports built-in Access functions such as Month(), Left(), Pmt(), and so on. Standard SQL (for example, SQL supported by Microsoft SQL Server) has very limited sets of functions.

You can find a typical example using the Orders table, which contains fields for Quantity and Price but not a field for the total for the order. This probably is a good strategy for minimizing the size of that table. Because you can easily calculate the total by multiplying the quantity times the price, you don't need to explicitly store the total.

The following SQL statement generates a new column named *Total* (by means of the `AS` keyword) that performs the calculation for each record in the data set, as you can see in Figure 3-13.

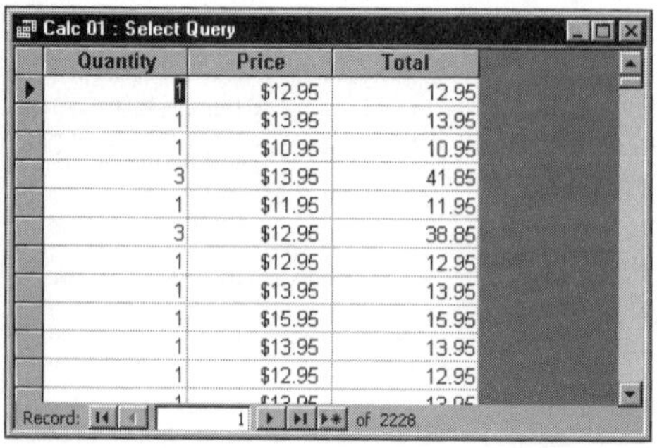

Quantity	Price	Total
1	$12.95	12.95
1	$13.95	13.95
1	$10.95	10.95
3	$13.95	41.85
1	$11.95	11.95
3	$12.95	38.85
1	$12.95	12.95
1	$13.95	13.95
1	$15.95	15.95
1	$13.95	13.95
1	$12.95	12.95

Figure 3-13: An expression generates a calculated column.

```
SELECT Quantity, Price,
Quantity* Price AS Total
FROM orderdetails;
```

ON THE CD

Query: Calc 01

In addition to basic arithmetic, calculated columns are often handy for manipulating date information. For example, suppose you want to display a column with the month and year rather than the full date of each order. The following example uses the built-in functions `Year` and `Month` to manipulate the `OrderDate` field to display a month designation (in the form mm/yyyy) in the data set as shown in Figure 3-14.

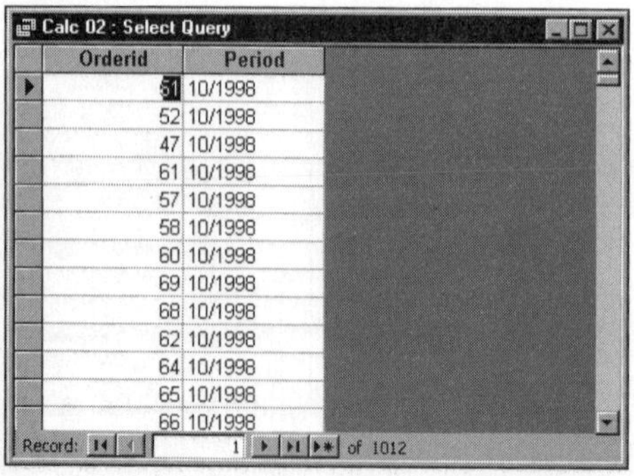

Orderid	Period
51	10/1998
52	10/1998
47	10/1998
61	10/1998
57	10/1998
58	10/1998
60	10/1998
69	10/1998
68	10/1998
62	10/1998
64	10/1998
65	10/1998
66	10/1998

Figure 3-14: The date function manipulates date information.

```
SELECT Orderid,
Month(orderdate) & "/" & Year(orderdate) AS Period
FROM orders
ORDER BY orderdate;
```

Query: Calc 02

In looking at the data set represented in Figure 3-14, you may wonder why the `Unit Price` column is formatted as currency while the `Total` column is displayed without currency formatting. `Unit Price` appears as currency because the data was entered into a field defined as a currency type field in the table design. On the other hand, `Total`, which is a calculated field, is automatically treated as a number with no special formatting.

In most cases, you needn't be concerned about the difference in formatting because a form or a report often displays the result of the query. In such cases, you have the opportunity to select the formatting style for the calculated field from the property sheet of the control used to display the field. On the other hand, to simply print the results of the query — without having to build a form or a report — apply a format to the calculation using the `Format` function described next.

```
Format (value, format-spec)
```

- ✔ `value` is the field or calculation that supplies the value to be formatted.

- ✔ `format-spec` is the name of a predefined format, for example, `currency`, or a format string, for example, `###,###.00`.

The following example applies the currency format to the calculated column Total.

```
SELECT Quantity,
Price,
Format(Quantity* Price,"currency") AS Total
FROM orderdetails;
```

Query: Calc 03

One oddity that occurs when you use `Format` in a query is that the formatted numbers are left-aligned, not right-aligned in the column. This is because the `Format` function always returns a text value. Since Access automatically left-aligns text columns, the formatted numbers end up left-aligned.

You should avoid using `Format` in a query that you will use later as the record source for a form or a report. Use `Format` only when you want to output the results of the query directly without using a form or report.

You can also use `Format` to manipulate dates. For example, in many cases when you summarize data, you want to summarize on the month and year but not on each specific date. The `Format()` function provides a way to convert full dates to other formats. The following example lists only the month and year from each order date — for example, 2/1999 — instead of the full date as entered into the `OrderDate` field.

```
SELECT OrderID,
Format(orderdate,"m/yyyy") AS Period
FROM orders
ORDER BY orderdate;
```

Query: Calc 04

SQL Aggregate Functions

In SQL, the term *aggregate* refers to all data included in the resulting record data set generated by a query. The SQL aggregate functions listed in Table 3-2 summarize values in a data set.

Table 3-2	SQL Aggregate Functions
Function Name	*Operation*
Avg()	Arithmetic average of the values
Count()	Number of records
First()	Value of the first record in the set
Last()	Value of the last record in the set
Min()	Smallest value in the set
Max()	Largest value in the set
Sum()	Total of all records
STDev()	Standard deviation (nonbiased)
StDevP()	Standard deviation (biased)
Var()	Variance (nonbiased)
VarP()	Variance deviation (biased)

You can use aggregate functions in two ways:

✔ Summarize All. This type of query returns a single row of information. Each column displays a summary value used on all of the records that qualify for the data set by meeting the criteria established by the WHERE clause. If you don't use a WHERE clause, then the entire table is summarized.

> ✔ Summarize By Group. This type of query returns one row of summary values for each unique member of a group. For example, you may want to calculate the totals for each customer. You can accomplish this by using the GROUP BY keyword with aggregate functions.

Summarizing all records

The simplest type of aggregate query is one that summarizes the value in all the records in a table for a specific field. The following statement summarizes the Items field. The result is a data set with a single column and a single row with the value 2078, which is the sum of all of the items in all of the orders.

```
SELECT Sum(Items) AS Total
FROM orders;
```

Query: Agg 01

You can also summarize the result of a calculation with the aggregate functions. For example, in the OrderDetails table you need to multiply Quantity by Price to calculate the total for each detail. The following statement calculates the totals for each record and then produces a single row containing the total for all orders: 33585.47.

```
SELECT sum(quantity * price) AS Total
FROM orderdetails;
```

Query: Agg 02

You can use the WHERE clause to limit the records included in the aggregate. The following example totals only those records with an Order Date in February, 1999.

```
SELECT Sum(items) AS TotalUnits,
Sum(ordertotal) AS TotalDollars
FROM orders
WHERE Month(orderdate)=2
AND Year(orderdate)=1999;
```

Query: Agg 03

The Min() and Max() functions locate the smallest and largest values in field. When used with date fields, they locate the earliest and latest dates entered into a field. The following statement produces two dates, 10/22/98 6:44:31 AM and 3/10/99, representing the range of dates found in the Orders table.

```
SELECT Min(orderdate) AS Start,
Max(orderdate) AS Finish
FROM orders;
```

ON THE CD

| Query: Agg 04 |

Summarizing by group

You can generate a data set that summarizes information by group by adding a GROUP BY keyword to the query statement. The following example generates a total for each item included in the Orders table, as shown in Figure 3-15.

```
SELECT Item, Sum(quantity*Price) AS TotalSales
FROM OrderDetails
GROUP BY Item
```

Figure 3-15: Summary values produced by group.

Item	TotalSales
Kenya - Gaturiri AA	4830.35
Kona Mountain Estate	3116.95
Kenya Nyaithee AA	2926.3
Brazil Fancy Bourbon Santos	1858.8
Sumatra Mandheling	1825.95
Napoli Blend	1393.55
Jamaica Blue Mtn. - Old Tavern #1	1327.25
Ethiopia Yirgacheffe	1262.65
Estate-roasted Grade No. 1 - 1998	1194
Perugia Blend	1155.95
Costa Rica - La Minita Tarrazu	1107.7
Owner's Reserve	1089.05
Kenya AA	911.300000000
Kona, Hawaii - Bayview Farms	829.000000000

Agg 06 : Select Query

Record: 1 of 64

ON THE CD

| Query: Agg 05 |

When you construct a group aggregate query, you need to keep in mind that if a field name (which is not part of an aggregate function) appears in the SELECT portion of the statement, that field name must also be included in the GROUP BY list.

You can also use the aggregate functions to determine the order of the records. The following statement produces the same set of data shown in Figure 3-15, but orders the records so that the items are ranked according to which have the largest volume of sales. In order to produce the required results, Access must first calculate each group total and then rank the records by the calculated total. The fact that a SQL statement can express these requirements in a single statement is an illustration of the power of SQL as a query language.

```
SELECT Item, Sum(quantity* Price) AS TotalSales
FROM orderdetails
GROUP BY Item
ORDER BY  Sum(quantity* Price) DESC;
```

> **Query: Agg 06**

Adding a WHERE clause restricts the summary to specific sets of records. The following example limits the summary to the month of February, 1999 by CustomerID. The resulting recordset ranks the customers by who purchased the greatest amount of products.

```
SELECT CustomerID, Sum(OrderTotal) AS TotalSales
FROM orders
WHERE Month(orderdate) = 2
AND Year(orderdate) = 1999
GROUP BY CustomerID
ORDER BY Sum(OrderTotal)  DESC;
```

> **Query: Agg 07**

It's often useful to perform more than one summary calculation on the same record set. For example, you may want to calculate the total dollar amount of sales for each item, and also count the number of sales for that item. The following statement adds a second aggregate function, Count( ), to the query in order to produce the data shown in Figure 3-16. Note that when you count records, the field specified is not important because Count( ) is merely counting the number of records in each grouping. You can simply use * as the field name to simplify the query.

```
SELECT CustomerID,
Count(OrderID) As Orders,
Sum(Items) AS TotalUnits,
Sum(OrderTotal) AS TotalSales
FROM orders
WHERE Month(orderdate) = 2
AND Year(orderdate) = 1999
GROUP BY CustomerID
ORDER BY Sum(OrderTotal)DESC;
```

Joins

One of the key characteristics of *relational* databases is the ability to create *virtual* data sets by joining data stored in separate tables. The term *virtual* is applied to this type of data set because it is not permanently stored in any table or file. The data set is composed on the fly when the SQL statement that contains a JOIN clause is executed. The data set is assembled for temporary use and then is discarded. All that needs to be stored is the SQL statement, which can be used again later to regenerate the data set at some later point.

CustomerID	Orders	TotalUnits	TotalSales
136	1	12	$324.45
60	1	1	$211.95
1560	1	12	$172.35
1000	1	12	$163.35
1516	1	15	$151.14
786	1	9	$116.50
1172	2	9	$104.50
876	1	6	$77.70
1505	1	5	$77.70
1318	1	8	$76.95
1014	1	3	$75.80
296	3	5	$73.60
803	1	4	$62.75
473	1	1	$60.90

Record: 1 of 187

Figure 3-16: Multiple summary calculations performed on a data set.

The SQL.MDB database contains three tables: customers, orders, and order details. Up to this point in the chapter, all of the queries have selected, sorted, grouped, and summarized data stored in just one of these tables at a time. However, some questions cannot be answered by any one table. For example, suppose you wanted to count the number of orders for each customer and then sort by customer name. The customer names and the order are in two different tables. The tables however have a common data field, CustomerID. By performing a JOIN on the CustomerID fields, you can generate a data set that combines and summarizes data contained in two tables. Figure 3-17 shows the fields that relate the three tables in the SQL.MDB database.

Figure 3-17: Relational databases use joins to relate data stored in separate tables.

SQL statements that include a JOIN are a bit more verbose than those that work with a single table. When there is only one table involved, a FROM clause is all that you need to identify the source of the data. The simplest form of joins is an `INNER JOIN`. In an `INNER JOIN`, the only records included in the data set are those which have a matching value in the key field in each table. The general form of an `INNER JOIN` is as follows:

```
FROM tablename1
INNER JOIN tablename2
ON tablename1.Field = tablename2.Field
```

In the current example, the two tables are Customers and Orders. The key field in each table is `CustomerID`. Indicate the name of the table in which a field is located by adding the table name as a prefix to the field name. Use a period to connect the table name to the field name.

```
FROM Customers
INNER JOIN Orders
ON Customers.CustomerID = Orders.CustomerID
```

The following example shows a SQL statement that uses `JOIN` to connect the Customers and Orders Tables. When you run the query, you see a result set, shown in Figure 3-18, that lists the names of the customers and the order numbers for each customer.

```
SELECT LastName, FirstName, OrderID
FROM Customers
INNER JOIN Orders
ON Customers.CustomerID=Orders.CustomerID
ORDER BY LastName, FirstName;
```

Query: Join 01

Last Name	First Name	OrderID
Adams	Ellen	1046
Adams	Ronald	865
Adler	Daniel	137
Adler	timothy	51
Adler	timothy	1030
Adler	timothy	220
Allan	Carole	524
Amerise	Thomas	567
Amerise	Thomas	811
Anderson	DENNIS J.	468
Anderson	DENNIS J.	955
Anderson	Julianne	851
Anthony	James	962

Record: 1 of 778

Figure 3-18:
The results of an INNER JOIN lists the orders next to the customer name.

The records displayed in Figure 3-18 simply list the order numbers. The goal is to get a count of the orders. You can accomplish this by performing a `GROUP BY` operation on the name fields and using `COUNT()` on the `OrderID` field, as shown in Figure 3-19.

```
SELECT Customers.LastName,
Customers.FirstName,
Count(Orders.OrderID) AS Orders
FROM Customers
INNER JOIN Orders
ON Customers.CustomerID = Orders.CustomerID
GROUP BY Customers.LastName, Customers.FirstName
ORDER BY Customers.LastName, Customers.FirstName;
```

Figure 3-19:
The results
of an INNER
JOIN lists
the number
of orders
next to the
customer
names.

Last Name	First Name	Orders
Adams	Ellen	1
Adams	Ronald	1
Adler	Daniel	1
Adler	timothy	3
Allan	Carole	1
Amerise	Thomas	2
Anderson	DENNIS J.	2
Anderson	Julianne	1
Anthony	James	1
Anthony	Jim	1
Arapian	Jami	3
Arapian	Philip	1
Arata	Baseball	1

Record: 1 of 567

Query: Join 02

Take note that when you have a GROUP BY and an ORDER BY clause in the same statement, as in Join 02, the GROUP BY always precedes the ORDER BY. Access returns an error if ORDER BY comes before GROUP BY.

Joins are not limited to two tables but can link as many tables as are needed to produce the desired data. As an example, suppose that you wanted to list the specific items purchased by each customer. The names of the items appear not in the Orders table but the OrdersDetails table. In order to show customer names and product names, you must join Customers to Orders and Orders to OrderDetails.

The way that Access SQL approaches this task is to join the third table to the join that defines the relationship between the first two tables. This is indicated by enclosing the first join in parentheses. The following code fragment shows the general outline of a three table join where T1, T2, and T3 represent the tables involved.

```
FROM(T1 INNER JOIN T2 ON T1.F = T2.F)
INNER JOIN T3 ON T2.F = T3.F
```

When this approach is applied to the tables in this example, you end up with the following SQL statement. When you execute this statement, it returns the data set shown in Figure 3-20, which lists customers and the items that were included in their orders. Note that none of the columns in the data set are drawn from the Orders table. In this SQL statement, the Orders table serves as a means of connecting records in the Customers table with data in the OrderDetails table.

```
SELECT LastName, FirstName, Item
FROM
(Customers INNER JOIN Orders
ON Customers.CustomerID=Orders.CustomerID)
INNER JOIN OrderDetails
ON Orders.OrderID = OrderDetails.OrderLink
GROUP BY Lastname, Firstname,Item
ORDER BY LastName,FirstName;
```

Query: Join 03

Last Name	First Name	Item
Adams	Ellen	Kenya Nyaithee AA
Adams	Ellen	Kona Mountain Estate
Adams	Ronald	Sumatra Mandheling
Adler	Daniel	Costa Rica - La Minita Tarrazu
Adler	Daniel	Kenya Nyaithee AA
Adler	Daniel	Nicaraguan Segovia
Adler	timothy	Brazil Fancy Bourbon Santos
Adler	timothy	Costa Rica - Tierre Madre Organic
Adler	timothy	Guatemala - Finca Bella Carmona
Adler	timothy	Kenya Nyaithee AA
Adler	timothy	-Kona Extra Fancy (Bay View Farm
Adler	timothy	New Orleans Organic Decaf
Adler	timothy	Nicaraguan Segovia

Record: 1 of 1281

Figure 3-20: A three table joins display customers and products ordered.

As you can see, the syntax for multiple table joins gets a bit complex. However, when you are building Access programs you will probably find that joins are not as daunting as they might first appear to be.

✔ You can take advantage of the graphical interface of the Access query grid and create joins by dragging the key field name from one table onto the corresponding field in another table. When you have created the joins graphically, you can view the query as a SQL statement and simply copy and paste the SQL into your program.

✔ Unlike most elements in a SQL statement, the joins tend not to change very much among the SQL queries used in a given application. The reason is that the relationships among tables within an application don't usually change. For example, when you have Customers, Orders, and

OrderDetails, all of the SQL queries performed on those tables will differ in their SELECT, WHERE, GROUP BY, and ORDER BY specifications, but they will probably all use the same join structure. Once you have worked out the basic join syntax for the database, you can use it over and over again.

Subqueries

In all the query examples in this chapter that use WHERE clauses to select records, the criterion used is a known value. The following statement specifies a specific, literal value, in this case TX as the state name, to which the contents of the state field will be compared.

```
SELECT lastname,firstname, city
FROM customers
WHERE state = "TX";
```

But suppose you don't know in advance the exact item you want to use as a criterion. For example, suppose you have a customer whose name is Brian Minkow, and you want to know if you have any other customers in the same city. Getting the answer to that would require two steps: Find the city for Brian Minkow and then perform a second query to locate other customers in that city. The query statement to use for part two would look like the following one. But the statement isn't complete because you haven't performed the first step to locate the name of the city needed for step two.

```
SELECT name
FROM customers
WHERE city = ????;
```

SQL offers a shortcut. Instead of performing two separate queries, you can insert the first query in this section in place of the ???? in the previous query statement. When you combine the two, you get a statement that looks like the following one in which the criterion used in the first WHERE clause is a complete SQL statement. When you enclose a SQL statement inside another statement, it's called a *subquery*. When the statement is processed, the subquery first returns its data — here, the name of the city — which in turn is used as the primary query to select the list of companies, shown in Figure 3-21.

```
SELECT lastname, firstname, city
FROM customers
WHERE city =
(SELECT city
FROM customers
WHERE firstname = "Brian"
AND lastname ="Minkow");
```

Figure 3-21:
A data set
generated
by a query
that con-
tains a
subquery.

Last Name	First Name	city
Russell	Kevin	New York
Prud'homme	Eli	New York
Prud'homme	Peter	New York
Saunders	Darrell	New York
Barker	Marilyn	New York
Johnson	Jeremy	New York
Eastburn	John	New York
Tarter	Gail	New York
Menapace	Gail	New York
Terng	Peter	New York
Smith	Alice	New York
Ealy	Gail	New York

Record: 1 of 20

Query: Sub 01

Using Parameters in Queries

In the SQL query statements discussed so far, the values used as criteria have been entered as part of the SQL statement in the form of text, date, or numeric literals. The following statement is typical of this approach. It selects records that match the text literal, CA.

```
SELECT Lastname, Firstname, city
FROM customers
WHERE state = "CA";
```

Parameters allow you to create a query where you do not directly enter the criteria into the SQL statement, but can enter the criteria in a dialog box prior to the execution of the statement. In the following statement, the literal criterion for the state, for example, CA, was replaced with a placeholder that consists of a ? enclosed in [ ].

```
SELECT Lastname, Firstname, city
FROM customers
WHERE state = [?];
```

When Access executes this query, it finds that there is no field in the Customers table named ?. This causes Access to assume that [?] is a placeholder for a parameter. Access then displays a dialog box, shown in Figure 3-22, that allows you to type in a value.

Query: Param 01

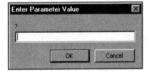

Figure 3-22:
Access
displays a
box for
entering the
value of a
parameter.

The value you enter passes through to the query, where it's used to replace the placeholder identifier — for example, [?] — with an actual value. If you typed **co** into the dialog box shown in Figure 3-22, the query returns the data for customers in Colorado.

Each time you execute the query, you are asked to enter the parameter. The resulting data set will vary depending upon what value you enter each time. Parameters are significant because they provide a way to create a single query statement that you can use with a number of different criteria.

You should keep in mind the following points when dealing with SQL parameter queries:

 ✔ The name of the parameter placeholder appears in the dialog box as the prompt text. In order to aid users in filling in parameters, you can add placeholder names that read like sentences or questions. The following example uses `Please enter the 2 letter state code:` as the name of the parameter identifier. When you execute this statement, the dialog box displays a prompt that actually explains what data the user should enter.

```
SELECT Lastname, Firstname, city
FROM customers
WHERE state = [Please enter the 2 letter state code:]
```

Query: Param 02

 ✔ If you want to provide the user the option of selecting all the records rather than entering a specific criterion, you can modify the query to use a `LIKE` operator instead of an = operator, as shown in the following example. If the user does not want to select a particular state, then she can type *****. Because * is a wildcard recognized by the `LIKE` operator, the statement retrieves all the states.

```
SELECT name, city, contact
FROM customers
WHERE state
LIKE [Enter the 2 letter state code or * for all:];
```

Query: Param 03

✔ You can enter as many placeholders as you desire in a statement. The following example uses a parameter for Start Date: and one for End Date:. When the query executes, Access displays a separate dialog box for each parameter. This example requires a dialog box for Start Date: and one for End Date:. The boxes appear in the order in which the placeholders are encountered in the SQL statement. Because Start Date: is the first placeholder, its dialog box is the first displayed.

```
SELECT OrderID, OrderDate
FROM orders
WHERE OrderDate Between [Start Date:]
AND [End Date:];
```

Query: Param 04

✔ You *cannot* use parameters to insert field names into the SQL statement. The following statement seems to allow a parameter to determine the name of the second field in the SELECT list. However, if you enter a field name, for example, Street, Access does not insert the Street field name in the statement. Rather, the text **"Street"** is entered, resulting in a column that lists the word Street on each row.

```
SELECT Lastname. firstname. [?]
FROM customers;
```

✔ Spelling mistakes are often interpreted as parameters. For example, suppose you enter contract instead of contact as a field name. Access reacts to the misspelling by assuming that contract is a parameter and displays a dialog box asking you to type in the value for that parameter. The problem goes away when you correctly enter the field name.

In the previous examples, simply adding placeholders to the query established parameters. Access tries to automatically resolve problems in SQL statements by treating any identifier that cannot be matched with a field or column as a parameter. This is a handy feature in Access, but it's not a standard SQL feature. Other programs that also process SQL statements, such as Microsoft SQL Server, cannot resolve this type of statement.

The standard SQL approach to using parameters is to add a *parameters* section to the SQL statement. The parameters section begins with the PARAMETERS keyword followed by a list of one or more parameter identifiers. Each identifier must be assigned a specific data *type* such as text, DateTime, integer, or double.

The following statement follows the standard SQL format for a parameter query by adding a parameters section that defines the parameter `Please enter the 2 letter state code:` as a text parameter. Note that the name of the parameter must be identical each time it's used in the statement. In this example, the parameter name includes a punctuation character, a colon. The words must include that character each time the parameter is referenced, or else Access treats the two as different parameters.

```
PARAMETERS [Please enter the 2 letter state code:] text;
SELECT lastname, firstname , city
FROM customers
WHERE state = [Please enter the 2 letter state code:];
```

Query: Param 05

If you want to use multiple parameters in a statement, each parameter must be listed following the `PARAMETERS` keyword in the parameters section of the statement. The following example allows for entry of two parameters, `Start Date` and `End Date`, each of which is defined as `DateTime` type values.

```
PARAMETERS [Start Date:] DateTime, [End date:] DateTime;
SELECT OrderID, OrderDate
FROM orders
WHERE OrderDate Between [Start Date:]
AND [End Date:];
```

Query: Param 06

The order in which the parameters are listed in the parameters section determines the order of the dialog boxes displayed for the parameters. However, you may insert the parameter names into the `SELECT` section of the statement in any order.

Updates

A good percentage of the changes made to a database are made by direct editing in datasheets or in forms. When you build programs in Access, you will also make changes to data using your programming tools. SQL provides the ability to update one or more records with a single statement by using `UPDATE` queries. Unlike the `SELECT` queries you have used so far, updates do not display any data. Instead, they modify the data stored in the tables.

The `UPDATE` statement has the following form:

```
UPDATE tablename
SET field = value, field = value, etc.
```

An update query can change the value of a field throughout an entire table. For example, the RecordCreated field in the Customers table is currently blank. You can fill that field throughout the table by executing the following SQL statement. Note that when you execute this query, Access warns you that you are about to alter a number of records. If you select Yes, the data in the table will be changed. Because the data in SQL.MDB is set up for practice, you can feel free to perform the update.

```
UPDATE Customers
SET RecordCreated = date();
```

Query: Update 01

You can also use updates to modify the data in a column that already contains data. You may have noticed in some of the previous queries that some of the entries in the Lastname and Firstname fields are not entered with the proper upper- and lowercase letters. In some cases, names are all lowercase while others are all uppercase. Access includes a function called StrConv() that can convert text to the Proper format (first letter of each word uppercase and the rest lowercase). You can clean up the Customers table with the following query.

Observe that in the update statement you can use the data currently in a field as part of the formula. For example, StrConv(firstname,3) determines the new value.

```
UPDATE customers
SET firstname = strconv(firstname,3),
lastname = strconv(lastname,3)
```

Query: Update 02

The value 3 specifies Proper case in the StrConv() function. If you were using the function inside of a Visual Basic module rather than a SQL query, you could use the Visual Basic constant vbProperCase instead of the number 3. However, Visual Basic constants such as vbProperCase or vbCrLf are not available inside a SQL query. Note that all Visual Basic constants represent numeric values. You can figure out the value of a constant by printing is value in the immediate window, for example, ? vbProperCase.

You can perform updates selectively by adding a WHERE clause to an UPDATE query. For example, the Country field in the Customers table contains entries for US and USA. Suppose that you wanted to standardize on USA. In that case, you want to update only the records containing US to read USA.

```
UPDATE customers
SET country = "USA"
WHERE country = "US"
```

Query: Update 03

Remember that updates performed with SQL cannot be undone. Changes made with update statements are permanent.

Deletions

You can also delete records using SQL statements. The DELETE statement is usually used with a WHERE clause to select the records to remove. For example, suppose that any record with a blank last name field is a bad record and should be removed from the table. The following statement removes those records from the Customers with Zero Length Fields table. Because deletions can't be recovered, you receive a warning message before the records are removed.

```
DELETE
FROM [Customers with Zero Length Fields]
WHERE lastname is null
```

Query: Delete 01

Domain Aggregate Functions

All the examples presented so far in this chapter have shown the use of SQL within Access query forms. However, Access allows SQL statements to be used in a variety of ways within forms, reports, and Visual Basic modules. One of the simplest and most powerful ways to integrate SQL data retrieval operations in forms, reports, macros, or modules, is through the use of *domain aggregate functions*.

Domain aggregate functions are a special form of a SQL statement that is embedded within the standard Access function format. Domain aggregate functions allow you to execute a SQL summary query. The function performs a SQL operation on the specified table and returns the summary value as the value of the function. Table 3-3 lists the domain aggregate functions available in Access.

Table 3-3	Domain Aggregate Functions
Function Name	*Operation*
DAvg()	Arithmetic average of the values
DCount()	Number of records
DFirst()	Value of the first record in the set
DLast()	Value of the last record in the set
DMin()	Smallest value in the set
DMax()	Largest value in the set
DSum()	Total of all records
DSTDev()	Standard deviation (nonbiased)
DStDevP()	Standard deviation (biased)
DVar()	Variance (nonbiased)
DVarP()	Variance deviation (biased)

All of the domain aggregate functions share the same structure and syntax.

```
DFunction(expression, domain criteria)
```

The argument actually corresponds to the elements in a SQL query. The first argument corresponds to the field name or expression that follows the SELECT keyword. The second argument is called the *domain* in the name of the table from which the records will be retrieved, which corresponds to the FROM keyword. The last argument, which is optional, corresponds to the expression used with the WHERE clause to select records to be included in the summary.

```
DFunction (SELECT..., FROM... WHERE...)
```

If you understand SQL, you can translate any SQL statement as it might appear in a query form and write it as a domain function. For example, take the SQL statement used earlier in this chapter to show the use of an aggregate function. The query calculates the sum of the Items field in the Orders table.

```
SELECT Sum(items) AS Total
FROM Orders;
```

ON THE CD

> **Query: Agg 01**

Instead of using a query form to execute the calculation, you can enter the equivalent domain aggregate function, DSum( ), in any part of Access (Form, Report, Macro, or Module) that allows Access functions.

If you remove all the standard SQL keywords and syntax, what you have left are the expression and domain arguments for the DSum( ) function.

The function would be written like this:

```
DSum("items" ,"orders")
```

Note that each of the arguments is entered as a *text literal* — that is, they are enclosed in quotation marks.

You can use the DSum( ) function in almost any part of Access where calculations can be performed. In this case, you can use the Debug window to execute the statements, just as I explain in Chapter 1.

Access displays the number 2078 in the Debug window, which represents that sum of the Items field in the Orders table. You may recall that this is exactly the number that was returned by the SQL statement discussed earlier in this chapter under SQL aggregate functions.

You can summarize calculated columns with the domain aggregate functions. The SQL statement shown next sums the quantity times unit price value for each record in Orders.

```
SELECT Sum(quantity*Price)
FROM orderdetails;
```

ON THE CD

> **Query: Agg 02**

Enter the equivalent domain aggregate function (shown next) in the Debug window.

```
? DSum("quantity*price","orderdetails")
```

The function returns the value 33585.47, which is identical to the result achieved with the SQL statement used earlier in this chapter.

If you want to apply a domain aggregate function to a specific set of records, you can add the optional third argument, which is equivalent to the expressions used with the SQL WHERE keyword. Eliminating the SQL keywords from the following statement shows the items that should be used as the arguments for the DSum( ) function.

```
SELECT Sum(ordertotal)
FROM orders
WHERE Month(OrderDate) = 2
AND Year(OrderDate) = 1999;
```

Enter the following in the Debug window:

```
? DSum("ordertotal" "orders", "Month(OrderDate) = 2" & _
" AND Year(OrderDate) = 1999 ")
```

If you are using the `Dcount()` function, you can simply type * for the first argument because the field name in a count operation is not significant. The statement returns the number of records, `217`, that have order dates in February, 1999.

```
? DCount("*", "orders", "Month(OrderDate) = 2" & _
" AND Year(OrderDate) = 1999")
```

> ### *Module: Domain Examples: Sub: DomainSamples*

Part II
Educating Access

The 5th Wave · By Rich Tennant

Re'al Pro'gram·mers:
Real Programmers have trouble supressing homicidal tendencies when asked, "Are you sure?".

In this part . . .

Only a small percentage of Access users ever get around to taking advantage of the built-in Access programming language. That's a shame. Access programming takes the plain, old, vanilla, Access program straight out of the box (off the CD, actually) and educates Access about how you and your colleagues actually work.

Part II illustrates how Access programming educates your computer to respond to your requests for information, reports, and calculations.

Chapter 4

Making Forms Smarter

● ●

In This Chapter

▶ Smart calculations

▶ Storing calculated values

▶ Isolating business rules

▶ Using select case

▶ Using local variables

▶ Using lookup tables with Visual Basic

▶ Time-stamping entries

▶ Entering percentages

▶ Controlling appearance with Visual Basic

▶ Using color

▶ Lookups

● ●

*F*orms are the basic structure by which users interact with database information. You can use Access Visual Basic to go beyond simple data-entry forms and create *smart forms* that can carry out many of the required tasks automatically.

> ***Database Folder: Chapter 4 Database File: SmartForms.MDB***

If you want to use the examples on the CD, open the database for Chapter 4, SMTFRM.MDB. Then, click the Forms tab to see the list of forms that I use in this chapter. On the CD icons indicate which form goes with which example.

Smart Calculations

Among the most useful features of Access forms is their ability to perform calculations automatically for each record you display. You typically accomplish this by creating a *calculated field*. A calculated field is an unbound control that contains an expression as its `Control Source` property. On an Access form, a *control* is a text box, list box, label, or button.

An *unbound control* is a control on a form that's not linked directly to a field in the underlying table or query. The value of the control isn't directly related to the data in any table. A *bound control* is one that's directly linked to a field in the underlying table. The contents of the field and table to which it's bound determine the contents of a bound control.

Figure 4-1, for example, shows a format that displays information from the Parts table. The table contains the following three fields that concern the pricing of parts:

- ✔ `List Price`. This field contains the suggested retail price of the part that the manufacturer supplies.

- ✔ `Discount`. This field contains the dealer discount that the manufacturer offers. The discount can be expressed as a percentage or as a decimal value depending on how the users choose to enter it into the field.

- ✔ `Cost`. The manufacturer doesn't supply the `Cost`, as he does the values for the `ListPrice` and `Discount` fields. Instead, you calculate `Cost` by applying the `Discount` percentage against the `ListPrice`.

Figure 4-1 shows the property sheet for the `Cost` control. The `Control Source` property contains the expression `=[ListPrice]*(1-[Discount])`, which automatically calculates the cost each time a new record appears in the form.

Figure 4-1:
Calculated
controls dis-
play their
results on
forms.

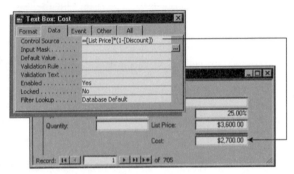

Form: Calc 01

A simple way to calculate the discounted price of an item is to multiply the item by 1 minus the discount percentage. In this case, the number 1 is the equivalent of 100 percent. Multiplying by 1 – 30 percent, for example, is the same as multiplying by 70 percent, which calculates the final cost of the item.

This approach, however, has one drawback. The value for the cost that appears on the form isn't actually a part of the table. The expression that the unbound control uses does display the calculated value for Cost on-screen but doesn't actually store that calculated value in the table, as shown in Figure 4-2. This figure demonstrates that the Cost field in the Parts table doesn't display any calculated costs.

Calculated controls do not fill fields with data

Figure 4-2:
Calculated
controls
don't store
their results
in the table's
Cost field.

Part No	Description	Type	Discount	Cost	List Price
ACC:5FX111046	SUN SPARC 110 T	Server Part	25.00%		$3,600.00
ACC:A11-UBA1-9S-064	Sun Ultra 1,167MH	Router	33.00%		$10,381.00
ACC:A14-UCB2-1E-25E	Sun Ultra 2, 2x200l	Router	33.00%		$33,831.65
ACC:FIR-1GW-ALA	Server Part	Server Part	33.00%		$5,120.00
ACC:NS-91-01009	Netscape Commer	Server	33.00%		$796.00
ACC:NZ-11102415	NZ-11102415 Maint	Server	33.00%		$313.00
ACC:S20FX1-151-32-P9	Sparc20, 150Mhz,	Server Part	28.00%		$12,391.65
ACC:S20S-151-32-P97	Sparc 20,150Mhz,3	Router	28.00%		$11,721.65
ACC:S5F24-110-32-P98	Sparc5, 110Mhz, 3	Router	33.00%		$5,691.65
ACC:S5S-110-32-P98	Sparc5, 110Mhz, 3	Router	28.00%		$6,026.65
ACC:SF2411095	Sparc5 110MHZ 32	Router	33.00%		$5,691.65

Record: 14 ◀ 1 ▶ ▶I ▶* of 705

Table: Parts

Why is this a problem? In theory, you have no absolute necessity to store a value such as the Cost, which you can always instruct Access to calculate from other stored values (for example, List Price and Discount). In practice, however, you may find that storing the value in the Cost field is useful, because, that way, the value is immediately available if you use the table in other forms, reports, queries, and so on. Calculating a value only when you need it (the cost, for example) is usually feasible, but you can save a lot of time and effort if you just store the value in the table at the time you enter the original data.

If you plan to export or link data from an Access 2000 table for use with some other application (for example, Word to create form letters), your best bet is usually to store these calculated values in the tables; making calculations in word-processing programs is *much* more cumbersome than doing so in Access 2000.

Storing Calculated Values

How can you get Access to actually write the result of the calculation into the field instead of just showing it on the form? The answer lies in *event procedures*. An event procedure is an Access Visual Basic procedure that automatically executes every time a specific *event* takes place.

By interacting with Access — that is, by pressing a key, clicking the mouse, or performing a combination of the two — a user triggers one or more events. The two most important events for most of the tasks you perform on Access 2000 forms are as follows:

- ✔ OnCurrent. This event takes place just before a new record appears on a form. Each time you click the navigation buttons to move to the next or previous record, for example, the OnCurrent event takes place.

- ✔ AfterUpdate. The AfterUpdate event takes place after you enter and save new information. Two types of AfterUpdate events actually take place on a form. Each control generates an AfterUpdate event after you enter a new or modified item of information. If, for example, you enter a new value into the Discount control and then move to another control on the form, the Discount control triggers an AfterUpdate event.

  In addition to the AfterUpdate event for each control, Access registers an AfterUpdate event for each record. This event occurs before you move to a new record after making any changes to one or more of the controls on the current record.

What good are these events, anyway? The purpose of an event is to provide an opportunity for you to instruct Access 2000 to perform some action automatically every time the user interacts with the form in a specific way. You implement this automatic action by linking the execution of a Visual Basic procedure with the occurrence of a specific event.

To return to the example of the Cost calculation, what events require the recalculation of the Cost? The events in the following list relate to Cost because they affect the values Access 2000 uses to calculate the cost. If either of these changes takes place, you need to instruct Access to recalculate the cost value and then update the value stored in the field.

- ✔ The user changes the value in the Discount control (field).
- ✔ The user changes the value in the List Price control (field).

For the sake of simplicity, you can assume that each of the fields involved is bound to a text box control that has the same name. In this case, you can think of the terms *field* and *control* interchangeably.

Assuming that you have already opened the database for Chapter 4, follow these steps to edit the event procedure for the first event you want to control, that is, a change value in the Discount control:

> **Form: Calc 02**

1. **Open the form you want to change.**

   In this example, open the form Calc 02 in the Design mode.

2. **Click the Discount control.**

3. **Display the property sheet (if not already open) by choosing View⇨Properties.**

4. **Click the Event tab.**

   The Event tab, as shown in Figure 4-3, lists all the events that can occur as a user interacts with the selected control. In this case, you're interested in the event that occurs after you make a change to the Discount control — that is, the AfterUpdate event.

Figure 4-3:
The Event tab on a control's property sheet.

5. **Click the After Update property box.**

6. **Click the drop-down list arrow to the right of this property box and select [Event Procedure] from the drop-down list.**

7. **Click the Build button (...), located to the right of the drop-down list.**

If you select the listing to create an Event Procedure as the value of an event property, Access 2000 automatically opens Visual Basic and a module window for the current form. It also generates a new procedure within that module, as shown in Figure 4-4, when you click the Build button. If the property is blank, Access 2000 allows you to choose to create an expression, a macro, or a procedure for the event property.

The module created for the form is a special module designed to hold Access Visual Basic procedures that relate to this specific form. The program stores the code for these procedures along with the form. The module that Access 2000 stores with the form isn't listed on the Modules tab of the database. You can access the module only through the form after you open the form in Design mode.

Event procedure

Control name   Event name

Figure 4-4:
Access gen-
erates an
event pro-
cedure in
the form's
Visual Basic
module.

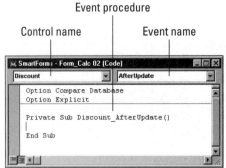

You need to understand the following three points about the automatically generated procedure shown in Figure 4-4:

- ✔ `Private`. The keyword `Private` means that only other procedures in the module can access this procedure — that is, the current form. The event procedures created for a form are meant only for that form and aren't recognized outside of that form. Access automatically defines all the event procedures in a form module as Private.

- ✔ `Sub`. All event procedures are Sub type procedures. You can add Function procedures to a Form module but are directly linked only to Sub procedures.

- ✔ `Name`. The program automatically creates the name of the procedure by combining the name of the event with the name of the control — for example, `Discount_AfterUpdate`.

Notice the two drop-down list boxes at the top of the module window (refer to Figure 4-4). The list box on the left shows the name of the control, and the list box on the right shows the name of the event. You can use these drop-down lists to navigate around the module to view or create additional procedures without returning to the form window. Simply select the name of a control from the left box and the name of the event from the right box and Access displays the procedure for that control/event combination. If there isn't already a procedure for that control/event combination, Access 2000 creates one.

After you create the procedure, you can add one or more Visual Basic statements that you want to execute whenever the event occurs (here, updating
the Discount control). In this case, you want to calculate the Cost and store
that value in the Cost control. The statement I've inserted into the following
procedure makes that calculation and places the results in the Cost field.
The Cost, therefore, is a permanent part of the table — not just a value
appearing on the form.

```
Private Sub Discount_AfterUpdate()
   [Cost] = [List Price] * (1 - [Discount])
End Sub
```

Access 2000 supports an alternative syntax for entering the names of controls within a form module. This approach takes advantage of the Me object.
In a form, the Me object refers to the form in which you are working. This is
useful because Access automatically includes the names of all the controls on
the form as properties of the Me object. In practical terms, this means that
you can avoid typing (and potential typos) by selecting control names from
the property list instead of entering then manually.

To take advantage of the Me object, type **Me.** A list appears that contains all
the form's properties, including all the control names listed alphabetically.
Because this is a *speed search* list, you can locate a name by typing the first
few letters and then selecting the name from the list. If the control name contains a space, Access automatically inserts an underscore in the property
name, for example [List Price] becomes List_Price. Note: You must
type the period after Me in order to display the list. Here's the alternative
syntax for the discount calculation:

```
Me.Cost = Me.List_Price * (1 - Me.Discount)
```

In addition to executing the calculation whenever the Discount changes, you
also need to perform the same operation whenever you update the List
Price control.

However, you do not have to return to the form in order to add another event
procedure. You can generate an After Update procedure for the List
Price control from within the module window by selecting the event and
control names from the drop-down list boxes at the top of the window. The
box on the left lists all the controls on the form. The box on the right lists all
the events associated with the displayed control. To generate the procedure,
follow these steps:

1. **Click the arrow of the left drop-down list box and select List Price
   from the list that appears.**

   Access automatically generates a new procedure, shown in the following
   example, for the Before Update event of the List Price control.
   Before Update is the default event for a Text Box control type.

```
Private Sub List_Price_BeforeUpdate(Cancel As Integer)

End Sub
```

However, you want to work with the After Update event of the List Price control.

2. **Click the arrow of the right drop-down list box and select AfterUpdate from the list.**

You might notice that the List_Price_BeforeUpdate is still part of the module. What should you do about the List_Price_BeforeUpdate procedure? Nothing! The empty procedure has no effect because it does not contain any code.

Enter the same statement into the following procedure as you did in the Discount_AfterUpdate procedure so that each time an update is made to the List Price box, the Discount is recalculated. You can save some typing by simply using Copy and Paste to insert a copy of the statement already in the Discount_AfterUpdate procedure.

```
Private Sub List_Price_AfterUpdate()
    [Cost] = [List Price] * (1 - [Discount])
End Sub
```

Access actually creates an empty List Price_BeforeUpdate procedure that remains part of the form module. Because the procedure is empty, however, it has no effect on how the form operates. If you're a compulsive sort, you may want to find these empty procedures and delete them. To remove a procedure, simply highlight the Sub through End Sub statements and press the Delete key.

You've now set up the form to automatically calculate the cost whenever you make any change to either the Discount or List Price controls. To see how this works, open the form and then change the value of the Discount control — from 25 percent on the first record, for example, to 33 percent. Remember that, to activate the After Update event, you must save the new value. You can do so by tabbing to the next control.

> **Form: Calc 02 and Calc 02 No Code(do it yourself)**

If you were to open the table window for the table (Parts) associated with the form, you'd see that the calculated cost actually appears in the Cost field of the table.

Isolating Business Rules

In the example described in the preceding section, you created two event procedures that use the same basic calculation to determine the cost of an item based on its list price and manufacturer discount. The following example illustrates these two event procedures:

```
Private Sub Discount_AfterUpdate()
   [Cost] = [List Price] * (1 - [Discount])
End Sub

Private Sub List_Price_AfterUpdate()
   [Cost] = [List Price] * (1 - [Discount])
End Sub
```

In these procedures, the statement that actually calculates the cost plays the role of a *business rule*. A business rule is a calculation, procedure, or other action that a business defines as the standard of conduct for the organization. In this example, the business rule is a simple calculation that defines the meaning of *cost* by using an arithmetic formula. In other cases, the business rule may be a complex set of related calculations that determine credit limits for customers or estimated taxes.

Regardless of the complexity or simplicity of the rule, all business rules share something in common — you're supposed to apply them consistently. In the current example, several events require you to apply the *cost business rule*. The rule itself (the formula for cost), however, is always the same.

To ensure that you apply a business-rule calculation consistently, no matter how many different events trigger that rule, you want to isolate the business rule from the event procedures. The following example demonstrates a simple procedure called `CalcDiscount` that encapsulates the business rule you use to calculate the cost of an inventory item.

```
Sub CalcDiscount()
   [Cost] = [List Price] * (1 - [Discount])
End Sub
```

After you create the business-rule procedure, you can *call* that rule from any of the event procedures that require the calculation of the cost. The term *call* refers to a statement that you enter into one procedure that itself executes another procedure. The following example shows an event procedure that doesn't contain a specific business-rule calculation. Instead, this event procedure contains a `Call` statement that executes the procedure `CalcDiscount`.

```
Private Sub Discount_AfterUpdate()
   Call CalcDiscount
End Sub
```

You can call only Sub type procedures. Function and Property procedures execute by using different methods.

In Visual Basic, the keyword Call is optional, and most programmers don't bother to use it. With or without Call, the procedure behaves in exactly the same way.

You can transform the logic of the code used in the form Calc 02 so that each event procedure contains a call to the business rule procedure CalcDiscount, as shown in the following example:

```
Option Compare Database
Option Explicit
Sub CalcDiscount()
    [Cost] = [List Price] * (1 - [Discount])
End Sub

Private Sub Discount_AfterUpdate()
    CalcDiscount
End Sub

Private Sub List_Price_AfterUpdate()
    CalcDiscount
End Sub
```

Form: Calc 03

Why is it important to isolate the business rules portion of a procedure from the rest of the event procedures? For three reasons:

- ✔ **Apply rules consistently.** Using a single business-rule procedure and then calling that procedure in each event that requires that rule ensures that you're applying the same rule in all cases. If you attempt to write code for each event requiring the calculation, you run the risk of making mistakes or changes in one instance that aren't the same as another. This inconsistency may cause variations in results.

- ✔ **Make changes easily.** If you need to change the way a business rule carries out its calculation or analysis, you need only go to a single procedure to make the change.

- ✔ **Add new events.** If you isolate the business-rule from the event procedures, you can easily include another event in the set of event procedures that triggers the business-rule calculation.

All the code stored in all the modules in a database consists of a single Visual Basic project in Access 2000. After you open the Visual Basic editor, you can display a window that contains all the modules in an Windows Explorer-like structure. This window is called the Project Explorer. If the window is not visible, you can open it by pressing Ctrl+R. To open any module, double-click the name of the module in the explorer tree. Note that all form modules are assigned the prefix Form_.

Using On Current to update records

You may already have guessed that the example requires performing CalcDiscount on a third event. You may recall that, after you opened the form, you saw only blanks in all the Cost boxes in existing records. These boxes remain blank because Access triggers the After Update procedures for Discount and List Price only if you actually change the value in one of those controls.

Because the table contains more than 700 records, forcing the calculation of the cost by editing each of the Discount or List Price controls for each record would prove awfully cumbersome. An easier method is to take advantage of the On Current event. This event takes place every time a new record appears. Typically, you use this event to evaluate the current state of the records and perform any updates required before the record appears on-screen.

You could, for example, use the On Current event to check to see whether the Cost field is empty. If the field is empty, the event calls the CalcDiscount procedure to calculate the cost. The effect is that every displayed record appears with a calculated cost.

The On Current event is an event linked to the Form object. To create an OnCurrent procedure, follow these steps:

1. **Open the form in the Design mode.**

2. **Press Ctrl+R to select the** Form **object.**

3. **Display the property sheet, if not already open, by choosing View⇨Properties from the menu bar.**

4. **Click the Event tab of the property sheet.**

5. **Click the On Current property box.**

6. **Click the drop-down list's arrow and select** [Event Procedure] **from the list.**

7. **Click the Build button (...).**

In this example, the procedure you need to write must check the contents of the Cost control to see whether the control is empty — that is, whether the control contains a null value.

How do you check for nulls? The correct way to evaluate null values in Access is through the use of the IsNull() function. The Form_Current procedure in the following example uses the IsNull() function to determine whether to call the CalcDiscount procedure.

```
Private Sub Form_Current()
    If IsNull([Cost]) Then
        CalcDiscount
    End If
End Sub
```

| Form: Calc 04 |

More business rules

The business rule implemented in the CalcDiscount procedure is the simplest possible rule — that is, a simple arithmetic calculation that you can apply across the board to all the records in the table. In most cases, you can implement very simple business rules just as well by using expressions in unbound fields.

Other business rules are more complex, requiring additional types of programming logic that you can implement only by using event procedures that call business-rule procedures. Figure 4-5, for example, shows three new fields added to the parts inventory form: *Installation, 1 Year Maintain,* and *3 Year Maintain.* Although you can price these additional service items many different ways, many businesses establish rules or formulas for calculating the cost of these items if sold in conjunction with a specific piece of equipment.

As an example, suppose that the following business rules apply if you calculate the service-item prices for one type of products (for example, Internet routers):

- ✔ *Installation* equals 17.5 percent of margin — that is, *List Price – Cost.*

- ✔ One-year maintenance contract (*1 Year Maintain*) equals *Installation* + 38 percent of the *Installation.*

- ✔ Three-year maintenance contract (*3 Year Maintain*) equals *Installation* + 10 percent of the installation price each year.

Figure 4-5:
Additional
business
calculations
now appear
on the
inventory
form.

Calc 05 : Form		
Part No:	ACC-5FX111046	
Description:	SUN SPARC 110 TGX	
Type:	Server Part	Discount: 33.00%
Quantity:		List Price: $3,600.00
		Cost: $2,412.00
Installation:		
1 Year Maintain:		
3 Year Maintain:		

Record: 1 of 705

You can express these rules in Visual Basic code, as shown in the CalcService procedure in the following example:

```
Sub CalcService()
    If [Type] = "Router" Then
        [Installation] = 0.175 * ([List Price] - [Cost])
        [1 Year Maintain] = [Installation] * 1.38
        [3 Year Maintain] = [Installation] * 1.1 * 3
    End If
End Sub
```

After you add this business-rule procedure to the form's module, the next task is to call the procedure from the appropriate event procedures. You could execute a call for the CalcService procedure, for example, from the Form_Current procedure if the Installation control on the current form is null. The following example shows how different procedures can be called based on null values in specific controls (fields).

```
Private Sub Form_Current()
    If IsNull([Cost]) Or [Cost] = 0 Then
        CalcDiscount
    End If
    If IsNull([Installation]) Then
        CalcService
    End If
End Sub
```

Additionally, because the service calculations depend on the value of the Cost field, which in turn depends on Discount and List Price, any change you make to Cost requires that CalcService execute. To ensure the accuracy of the data, you need to find every place in the program that calls CalcDiscount and then add a call to CalcService, as shown in the following code sample. The program now calls two procedures each time a change is made to either the discount amount or the list price.

```
Private Sub Discount_AfterUpdate()
    CalcDiscount
    CalcService
End Sub
Private Sub List_Price_AfterUpdate()
    CalcDiscount
    CalcService
End Sub
```

You have, however, a simpler and more reliable way to ensure that any change in Cost ripples through to the service values: Insert a call for the CalcService procedure in the CalcDiscount procedure, as shown in the following example. Here, one business rule calls another business rule. This structure establishes a relationship between various business rules that interact with one or more common values.

```
Private Sub Discount_AfterUpdate()
    CalcDiscount
End Sub
Private Sub List_Price_AfterUpdate()
    CalcDiscount
End Sub
Sub CalcDiscount()
    [Cost] = [List Price] * (1 - [Discount])
    CalcService
End Sub
```

Figure 4-6 shows how effective these simple code examples can be in generating information based on the business rules embedded in the Visual Basic module of a form. When the user displays the record shown in the figure, the procedures automatically evaluate the contents of the record and fill in the required installation and maintenance values.

Figure 4-6:
After you
display a
router
record,
Access 2000
calculates
the values
for service
products.

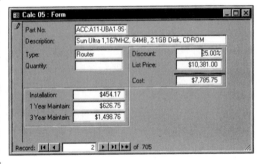

Form: Calc 05

Using Select Case

In the preceding section, the business rule in the CalcService procedure accounts for a single product type — *router* — by using an If statement to determine the type of product appearing in the current record. The following statement tests the value of the Type control (field) to see whether it contains Router.

```
If [Type] = "Router" Then
```

Suppose that additional business rules apply to different product types — for example, DSU, Server, and others. Table 4-1 shows a sample table of values that your program will use to calculate the cost of the service products for each type of product.

Table 4-1	Values for the Business Rules for Calculating Service Prices		
Type	*Installation*	*1 Year Maintain*	*3 Year Maintain*
Router	17.5%	38%	10%
DSU	15%	40%	25%
Server	22.5%	35%	20%
All others	none	none	none

Just to show how with-it I really am, I have chosen as my example database a company that sells networking technology. Of course it really doesn't matter what type of products are used as examples — widgets are widgets. However, some readers won't rest unless they know what all these parts are. A *router* is the device that makes the Internet possible. Routers are intelligent devices that can determine the best path for sending data from a computer on one network to a computer on another network. A *DSU* (digital service unit) is a device that connects network devices like bridges and routers to a digital-quality transmission line. A *server* is a computer that provides data to other computers on a network.

One way to accommodate a series of options — in this example, based on the type of product — is to use a `Select Case...End Case` structure. The diagram in Figure 4-7 shows how this structure works.

Figure 4-7:
A Select
Case
structure
evaluates
any number
of specific
cases.

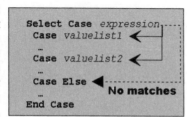

```
Select Case expression
   Case valuelist1
   ...
   Case valuelist2
   ...
   Case Else
   ...            No matches
End Case
```

In the first statement in the structure, the Select Case statement is assigned a value from a field, control, or an expression. The Select Case statement is followed by a series of one or more Case statements. Each Case statement is assigned one or more values that represent a possible match for the value assigned to the Select Case statement.

If Access finds that the value assigned to a Case statement matches the value that Access has assigned to the Select Case statement, then Access will execute any additional statements that are grouped under that Case.

You can also add an optional Case Else statement. If none of the specific cases turn out to be a match for the expression, Access 2000 selects Case Else and executes the statements in that group.

The order in which you list the cases is significant. In a Select Case structure, Visual Basic always selects the *first* matching case if more than one of the cases can be true at the same time. The program ignores all other cases that follow the first match, even if they also match the expression.

The following example is a revised version of the CalcService business-rule procedure. This example uses the values shown in Table 4-1 to calculate the service-product prices for specific product types. Notice that the Case Else inserts Null values into the fields of all products that aren't of the specified types — that is, router, DSN, or server.

```
Sub CalcService()
    Select Case [Type]
        Case "Router"
            [Installation]=0.175 * ([List Price] - [Cost])
            [1 Year Maintain]=[Installation] * 1.38
            [3 Year Maintain]=[Installation] * 1.1 * 3
        Case "DSU"
            [Installation]=0.15 * ([List Price] - [Cost])
            [1 Year Maintain]=[Installation] * 1.4
            [3 Year Maintain]=[Installation] * 1.25 * 3
        Case "Server"
            [Installation]=0.225 * ([List Price] - [Cost])
            [1 Year Maintain]=[Installation] * 1.35
            [3 Year Maintain]=[Installation] * 1.2 * 3
        Case Else
            [Installation]=Null
            [1 Year Maintain]=Null
            [3 Year Maintain]=Null
    End Select
End Sub
```

Form: Calc 06

The revised `CalcService` procedure now automatically fills in values for the additional product types as you enter the product types or as they appear on-screen, because the event procedures that monitor user interaction with the form call this procedure.

This is a good example of isolating business rules in procedures separated from the event procedures that may call them. Making changes to a single business-rule procedure causes those changes to automatically flow through to all the event procedures that call `CalcService`.

Using Local Variables

If you look at the code that the `Select Case` structure uses in the preceding section, you may notice that a great deal of the code is repetitious. You must repeat the basic formula for calculations, for example, in each example. If you look carefully at the code, you can see that each calculation is identical to the other, with the exception of the specific percentage you use. If you remove the percentages, however, and replace them with ???? as a placeholder, you get a general pattern for the calculations, as shown in the following example:

```
[Installation]= ???? * ([List Price] - [Cost])
[1 Year Maintain]=[Installation] * (1 + ???? )
[3 Year Maintain]=[Installation] * (1 + ???? ) * 3
```

You can greatly simplify the code required to perform the `CalcService` business-rule procedure by using local variables to insert the required percentages into the formulas instead of repeating the entire formula for each case. A *local variable* is a temporary object that you define within a procedure and then discard after the procedure finishes. You can assign any variable a value throughout the procedure. You can then use the variable name to insert the value assigned to that variable into other statements.

The code fragment in the following example shows the basic way that you use local variables. First you use the `Dim` statement to define a local variable name. Then you assign to that variable name (`RateInstall`, in this example) a value — for example, **.175**. Then you insert the variable name into a calculation where the variable supplies its current value to the formula.

```
Dim RateInstall
RateInstall = .175
[Installation]= RateInstall * ([List Price] - [Cost])
```

The abbreviation *Dim* is short for *dimension*. The designers of BASIC originally used the `Dim` statement to create arrays of values. An *array* is a set of
variables that share the same name but are differentiated by number — for
example, x(1), x(2), x(3), and so on. The *dimension* of an array is the
total number of numbered elements in the array.

Using local variables, you can rewrite the code for the `CalcService` procedure as shown in the following example. In this example, you assign three
local variables (`RateInstall, Rate1Year, and Rate3Year`) different
rates, depending on the type of product in the `Select Case` structure. At the
end of the procedure, a single instance of the formulas used to calculate the
installation and maintenance prices can calculate those values using the
rates supplied by the local variables. Using this approach you don't have
to include a formula under each case.

Using local variables greatly reduces the amount and complexity of the code.
This example states the actual formulas only once in the procedure instead
of repeating the formulas after each `Case` statement. This method improves
the code by eliminating the possibility of anyone incorrectly or inconsistently
entering the formula in some of the cases. This method also isolates the specific rates from the formula that uses the rates, which makes changing the
business rules easier and reduces the possibility of introducing errors
because of typing mistakes.

```
Sub CalcService()
    Dim RateInstall, Rate1Year, Rate3Year
    Select Case [Type]
        Case "Router"
            RateInstall = 0.175
            Rate1Year = 0.38
            Rate3Year = 0.1
        Case "DSU"
            RateInstall = 0.15
            Rate1Year = 0.4
            Rate3Year = 0.25
        Case "Server"
            RateInstall = 0.225
            Rate1Year = 0.35
            Rate3Year = 0.2
        Case Else
            RateInstall = Null
            Rate1Year = Null
            Rate3Year = Null
    End Select
    Installation]=RateInstall * ([List Price] - [Cost])
    [1 Year Maintain]=[Installation] * (1 + Rate1Year)
    [3 Year Maintain]=[Installation] * (1 + Rate3Year) * 3
End Sub
```

Form: Calc 07

Look at the two statements that follow. Suppose that your task is to change the rate the statement uses from 25 percent to 30 percent. You can see that editing the second statement is much simpler than changing the first statement. More significantly, the second statement doesn't actually contain the formula, so you don't run the risk that you may accidentally delete some part of the formula while entering a new value.

```
[3 Year Maintain]=[Installation] * 1.25 * 3 'hard to edit
Rate3Year = 0.25 'easy to change
```

The revised `CalcService` procedure produces exactly the same results, but the code is much easier to read and maintain.

Using Lookup Tables with Visual Basic

The two previous versions of the `CalcService` procedure are based on the data listed in Table 4-1. That table appears in this book because it displays, in a simple and straightforward manner, the essential values that define the business rules that `CalcService` implements.

This is a clue! If that table works well in this book, perhaps an Access table may prove useful in the database as a source for the values you need so you can implement the business rule. At this point, Access 2000 stores the specific values (the percentages the program uses to calculate the prices) in the actual Visual Basic code of the `CalcService` procedure. Suppose that your company decides to change its servicing pricing values. Which course do you think is easier — to edit the Visual Basic code module or to edit values in a table?

The obvious answer is that anyone familiar with Access can edit the table, but you can expect or trust only someone who understands programming to edit the Visual Basic code. Putting the values in an Access 2000 table enables anyone to change the percentages without needing to touch the procedure code at all.

But how can you accomplish this? One way is to take advantage of the Domain Aggregate functions I discuss in Chapter 3. These functions enable you to perform the equivalent of a full SQL query as part of some expression or formula. The Domain Aggregate functions make combining table-based operations, such as queries with Visual Basic statements, simple.

Figure 4-8 shows the data from Table 4-1 entered into an Access table called `Rates`, with fields called `ID`, `Type`, `Install`, `1 Year`, and `3 Year`.

Figure 4-8:
The Rates
table con-
tains the
values that
the
CalcService
procedure
uses.

ID	Type	Install	1 Year	3 Year
1	Router	17.50%	38.00%	10.00%
2	DSU	15.00%	40.00%	25.00%
3	Server	25.00%	35.00%	20.00%
(AutoNumber)				

Record: 1 of 3

You can use the DLookUp() function to extract specific values from the table.
The following example, which you can enter into the Debug window, extracts
the *Install* percentage for the router product type.

```
? DLookup("Install","Rates" ,"Type ='Router'")
  0.175
```

The arguments of the DLookUp() function correspond to the SELECT, FROM,
and WHERE keywords in a SQL statement. The SQL statement in the following
example is the equivalent of the DLookUp() function in the preceding example.

```
SELECT [Install]
FROM Rates
WHERE Type = 'Router'
```

If you use the DLookUp() function inside the CalcService procedure, the
procedure looks a bit different from the version shown in the preceding
example, because the WHERE clause expression isn't a literal entry — such as
router — but instead is the text you stored in the Type field. The expressions
in the following examples show how you can insert the value of the Type field
into the DLookUp() function. The first example uses the apostrophe (') to
insert the quotation inside the double quotation marks (" "). The second
example uses the Chr() function to perform the same task. You can use
either style. In this book, I use the apostrophe (') in most cases, because this
character is the simplest to enter — although the apostrophe is sometimes
hard to pick out if you're reading the text off the screen.

Look out for the Irish! In most cases, it doesn't matter functionally whether
you use Chr(34) or an embedded apostrophe in an expression with one very
important exception: when the variable, control, or field enclosed in quotations contains an apostrophe. This is a rare event, in most cases — with the
exception of company-name and last-name fields because of names like
O'Conner, O'Brien, and so on. If you are working with any table where you
may run into the possibility of a name with an apostrophe, take care to use
the Chr(34) syntax.

```
"Type = '" & [Type] & "'"
"Type = " & Chr(34) & [Type] & Chr(34)
```

Using the DLookUp() function to query the Rates table for the required values results in a CalcService procedure such as the one shown in the following example.

Notice that this example lists three values ("Router", "DSU", "Server") for the first Case statement. Items separated by commas are called a *list*. When you use a list with a Case statement the program selects the case if any one of the listed names matches the value of the Type field.

The DLookUp() function then queries the Rates table to acquire the appropriate percentages for the installation and maintenance calculations. The remainder of the procedure is unchanged from the previous example shown in the section titled "Using Local Variables."

```
Sub CalcService()
    Dim RateInstall, Rate1Year, Rate3Year
    Select Case [Type]
        Case "Router", "DSU", "Server"
            RateInstall = DLookup("Install", "rates", _
            "Type = '" & [Type] & "'")
            Rate1Year = DLookup("[1 Year]", "rates", _
            "Type = '" & [Type] & "'")
            Rate3Year = DLookup("[3 Year]", "rates", _
            "Type = '" & [Type] & "'")
        Case Else
            RateInstall = Null
            Rate1Year = Null
            Rate3Year = Null
    End Select
    [Installation]=RateInstall * ([List Price] - [Cost])
    [1 Year Maintain]=[Installation] * (1 + Rate1Year)
    [3 Year Maintain]=[Installation] * (1 + Rate3Year) * 3
End Sub
```

Form: Calc 08

Time-Stamping Entries

The use of a separate table to contain the rates that the business-rule procedure CalcService uses raises an important issue: Suppose that someone edits the Rates table and changes the installation percentage for routers from 17.5 percent to 20 percent. What effect does or should this change have on the inventory form?

The answer is that any change to the Rates table potentially invalidates some of or all the values stored in the Parts table. However, the program you originally created assumed that updates would only be triggered by users making changes to the data when it was displayed in a form. Now you have the possibility that updates may need to be triggered by events that take place outside the context of a form. How can you account for this type of event?

One answer is to *time-stamp* the records in both tables. If you time-stamp a record, you store the date and time that you make a change to that record. You can then compare the time-stamps of two records to determine whether one is out of sync with the other.

Because time-stamping involves two tables, Rates and Parts, you must add a field to each table in which you intend to store the time-stamp for each record. Table 4-2 lists the time-stamp fields you need to add to each table.

Table 4-2	Time-Stamp Fields
Table	*Time-Stamp Field*
Rates	EnteredOn
Parts	ServiceUpdate

How do you make sure that records receive a time-stamp showing a date each time you change those records? The only way to make sure that time-stamping occurs is to create a form that you can use for editing the Rates table and then use an event procedure to automatically enter the time-stamp value whenever you make any changes to a record. Figure 4-9 shows the form I used for editing the percentages in the Rates table.

Figure 4-9:
A form you can use for editing the Rates table.

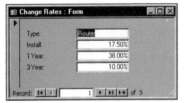

Form: Change Rates

To time-stamp each record, you must create an event procedure for the BeforeUpdate event of the Form object. This procedure, as shown in the following example, contains a single statement that inserts the current time and date into the EnteredOn field (by using the Now keyword).

```
Private Sub Form_BeforeUpdate(Cancel As Integer)
   [EnteredOn] = Now
End Sub
```

The reason I chose the `Before Update` event for the preceding example, instead of the `After Update` event, is subtle but important. First, review the timing of the two events, as described in the following paragraphs:

- `Form_BeforeUpdate` **event.** This event takes place after the user performs any action, such as moving to a new record or pressing Shift+Enter, that saves the data in the form to the underlying tables.

- `Form_AfterUpdate` **event.** This event takes place after the user saves the data in the form to the tables linked to the form.

What happens if the `Form_AfterUpdate` event executes the statement `[EnteredOn] = Now`? The `Form_AfterUpdate` takes place after you save the data. But here, as soon as you save the data, the statements in the `AfterUpdate` procedure change the record. The result is that a new value is inserted into the record just as it's supposed to have been saved. Ironically, this means that the record has changes that weren't saved.

This is a bit of a contradiction, because the `Form_AfterUpdate` event assumes that all the edits in the form are saved. Access 2000 reacts to this situation by preventing you from moving to the next record — by *"freezing"* the current record. The reason for this freeze is that, each time Access 2000 attempts to close out the record by saving any pending changes, the `Form_AfterUpdate` procedure edits the record, something it by definition should not be allowed to do because it negates its function of saving all the changes to the record.

As a general rule, *never* put a statement into the `Form_AfterUpdate` event procedure that changes any of the controls on the form or any of the fields in the underlying table.

Using the `Form_BeforeUpdate` event works because the procedure inserts the time-stamp prior to saving the change to the record. The value that the procedure inserts is simply lumped together with any changes the user enters. Then Access saves the entire record with both the user-made and procedure-made changes.

You've now completed half the time-stamp solution for ensuring accurate updates. The second part is to change the `OnCurrent` event procedure of the inventory form to check the time-stamp field in the `Parts` table so you can see whether you need to update the record.

The procedure shown in the following example adds an Else structure that contains another If. The If statement checks the time-stamp field, ServiceUpdated, to see whether it needs to adjust the values in the service price field to match any new rates in the Rates table. The procedure employs a Dlookup() function to extract the time-stamp from the Rates table to determine whether the record is out of sync. If the time-stamp field is a null, Access 2000 automatically updates the record.

Notice in the example, too, the use of the variable WhereClause, which inserts the WHERE clause expression into the Dlookup() function. Because the expression "Type = '" & [Type] & '" is a bit awkward to read, using a variable makes the code easier to read.

```
Private Sub Form_Current()
    Dim WhereClause
    WhereClause = "Type = '" & [Type] & "'"
    If IsNull([Cost]) Or [Cost] = 0 Then
        CalcDiscount
    End If
    If IsNull([Installation]) Then
        CalcService
    Else
        If IsNull([ServiceUpdated]) Or _
        [ServiceUpdated] < _
        DLookup("[EnteredOn]", "Rates", WhereClause) Then
            CalcService
        End If
    End If
End Sub
```

The final modification is to make sure that the records in the Parts table receive a time-stamp as you update them. Typing **[ServiceUpdated] = Now** at the end of CalcService inserts the current date and time in the ServiceUpdated field, which ensures the accurate time-stamping of the records.

```
Sub CalcService()
    Dim RateInstall, Rate1Year, Rate3Year
    Select Case [Type]
        Case "Router", "DSU", "Server"
            RateInstall = DLookup("Install", "rates", _
            "Type = '" & [Type] & "'")
            Rate1Year = DLookup("[1 Year]", "rates", _
            "Type = '" & [Type] & "'")
            Rate3Year = DLookup("[3 Year]", "rates", _
            "Type = '" & [Type] & "'")
        Case Else
            RateInstall = Null
            Rate1Year = Null
            Rate3Year = Null
    End Select
```

```
[Installation] = RateInstall * ([List Price] - [Cost])
[1 Year Maintain]=[Installation] * (1 + Rate1Year)
[3 Year Maintain]=[Installation] * (1 + Rate3Year) * 3
'TimeStamp records
[ServiceUpdated] = Now
End Sub
```

> **Form: Calc 09**

Selecting time-stamped dates

The Now( ) function is quite handy because it stamps a very precise date and time into the time-stamp field. However, at some point you may want to go back and summarize or select by dates. For example, the Customers table has a time-stamp that records when each record is added to the table. The code required for this follows as part of the form's BeforeInsert event.

```
Private Sub Form_BeforeInsert(Cancel As Integer)
    Me.RecordCreated = Now
End Sub
```

> **Form: TimeStamp 01**

But suppose you wanted to count the number of customer records entered on each day. You might create a query such as the following example that counts records by grouping on the RecordCreated field.

```
SELECT RecordCreated, Count(CustomerID) As Count
FROM Customers
GROUP BY [RecordCreated]
ORDER BY [RecordCreated] DESC;
```

> **Query: Date Group 01**

But keep in mind that the RecordCreated field was not entered manually but inserted from the Now( ) function which includes the time portion of the of the time-stamp. The resulting data set looks like the following because each time-stamp is unique.

```
RecordCreated          Count
3/28/99 5:21:49 PM     1
3/27/99 9:32:49 PM     1
3/27/99 7:42:50 PM     1
3/27/99 9:08:50 AM     1
3/27/99 8:17:49 AM     1
3/25/99 11:06:50 PM    1
3/25/99 9:03:49 AM     1
3/25/99 1:23:49 AM     1
```

In order to better utilize the `RecordCreated` field for summary, you need to truncate the time portion of the date so that the each summary represents the aggregate for the date portion alone. This can be accomplished with the `DateValue()` function. This function is usually used to convert text strings into date values. If the argument is a date/time value, it returns only the date portion.

```
? DateValue(now())
3/29/99
```

The SQL statement in the following code applies the `DateValue` function to the problem of grouping so that the data set returned by the query counts all the records entered on the same day as a part of the same group.

```
SELECT DateValue(RecordCreated) AS EnteredOn,
Count(Customers.CustomerID) AS [Count]
FROM Customers
GROUP BY DateValue(RecordCreated)
ORDER BY DateValue(RecordCreated) DESC
```

Query: Date Group 02

On the other hand, many times you need to summarize dates into larger units, most commonly months, for summary purposes. Counting the number of customers entered in each month would be the type of summary frequently required by businesses. Once again the time-stamp field contains too much detail to get the desired groupings. The solution to this problem is the `Format()` function discussed in Chapter 3. This statement returns a string in the format `Mar-1999` from a time-stamp value:

```
? Format(Now(),"mmm-yyyy")
Mar-99
```

This next query uses format to limit the amount of information returned from the `RecordCreated` field to the month and year so that all the records entered for each month are summarized as a group.

```
SELECT Format(RecordCreated,"mmm-yy") AS EnteredOn,
Count(CustomerID) AS [Count]
FROM Customers
GROUP BY Format(RecordCreated,"mmm-yy")
ORDER BY First(RecordCreated) DESC;
```

Query: Date Group 03

Also take note that the correct sequencing of the groups was achieved. If the `ORDER BY` clause had used `Format(RecordCreated,"mmm-yy")` as the sort expression, the records would not have appeared in chronological order because the month abbreviations (Jan, Feb, Mar. . .) would have been sorted into alphabetical order. The solution was to use the expression `First(RecordCreated)` as the sort key. This expression selects the date of the first record in each group and use the chronological value of the date to sequence the groups. This works because all the orders in each group belong to the same month and year. Therefore it doesn't matter which date you pull out of that group to use as the sort key; all have the same month and year value, which is all you care about in this instance.

Entering Percentages

Most of the examples shown so far in this chapter involve the use of percentages. Percentages pose an interesting problem in entering data. If asked to enter a percentage, you have two possible choices: Enter the percentage as a whole number (for example, **17.5**) or enter the percentage as a decimal number (**.175**).

Which way is the right way to go? The answer depends on the assumptions you make at the time you design the database. Making sure that the people using your database are going to recognize or remember how to enter percentages into your forms or tables, however, is often quite a bit more difficult than simply choosing how to enter the values.

In using event procedures, you can circumvent this problem by realizing that people may enter percentages in either form. The code fragment in the following example shows how to deal with an entry made into the `Discount` field. The `If` statement checks the value the user enters into the field. If that value is greater than 1, the program assumes that the user entered the percentage as a whole number. In that case, the program is designed to convert the entry to a decimal value and inserts the value back into the field. If the entry is less than 1, the program assumes that the entry is in decimal format and needs no adjustment.

```
If [Discount] > 1 Then
   [Discount] = [Discount] / 100
End If
```

The following example shows this technique in context as part of the `AfterUpdate` event procedure for the `Discount` control:

```
Private Sub Discount_AfterUpdate()
   If [Discount] > 1 Then
      [Discount] = [Discount] / 100
   End If
   CalcDiscount
End Sub
```

ON THE CD

| Form: Check Entry |

Keep in mind that this technique isn't perfect. If, for example, someone enters a percentage less than 1 percent — such as .5 percent — the procedure doesn't convert .5 to .005 but leaves the value as .5, which is 50 percent.

Controlling Appearance with Visual Basic

In addition to performing calculations, you can use event procedures to alter the appearance of the form. In the inventory form discussed earlier in this chapter under "Isolating Business Rules," for example, no information appears in the Installation, 1 Year Maintain, and 3 Year Maintain fields for many of the items in the Parts table. On those records, the form displays empty text boxes.

Because these text boxes aren't meaningful for these records, the more sensible course is to make sure that those controls don't appear on records without data for those fields. You can hide a control by setting the control's Visible property to False. Conversely, you can make a hidden control visible again by setting the Visible property to True. The following example uses a Select Case structure to determine which set of controls is visible on the form, based on the value in the Type field.

Note that the name of the control that draws the box around the service controls is called Box15. The program includes this control as part of the group of controls that displays service information.

```
Private Sub Form_Current()
' existing code not shown
' hide unused controls
  Select Case [Type]
    Case "Router", "DSU", "Server"
        [Installation].Visible = True
        [1 Year Maintain].Visible = True
        [3 Year Maintain].Visible = True
        [Box15].Visible = True
    Case Else
        [Installation].Visible = False
        [1 Year Maintain].Visible = False
        [3 Year Maintain].Visible = False
        [Box15].Visible = False
  End Select
End Sub
```

> **Form: Hide Controls 01**

If you have trouble remembering the exact names of the controls and fields in the form as you enter code, you can open the Expression Builder window by right-clicking the module window and choosing Build from the shortcut menu.

Figure 4-10 shows the effect of the new section added to the Form_Current procedure. The entire Services section (four controls) remains hidden if the product type doesn't match one of the specified criteria. The display adjusts itself each time you move to a new record. When the type does match one of the specified types, the form returns to the full display, as shown in Figure 4-10.

Figure 4-10:
The
OnCurrent
procedure
hides some
controls
based on
the type
of product
being
displayed.

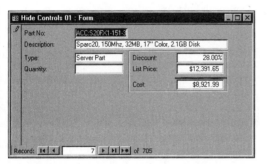

Using the Tag property

In the last example in the preceding section, your task was to change the value of a property — specifically, the Visible property for a group of controls. In that example, the only way to refer to the controls that you want to change is to specify by name each control belonging to the group.

Access controls have a special property called Tag that you can use to define a group of related controls. Tag is a special property, because Tag actually has no function at all. The purpose of Tag is to provide a means of defining a group of controls by giving all the controls the same value as in the Tag property. The Other tab of the Installation control's property sheet. The name *Service* appears in the Tag property. Table 4-3 lists the controls that form a group because their Tag properties all have the same value.

Table 4-3	Settings for the Tag Property
Control	*Tag Property*
Installation	Service
1 Year Maintain	Service
3 Year Maintain	Service
Box15	Service

What's the point of tagging controls? Using Tag enables you to write procedures that operate on just the members of that particular group of controls. The Tag property allows you to arbitrarily form a group by giving each control the same value in its Tag property. The following example hides all the controls on a form that display a Tag property value of *Service*. Take special notice of the following points in this example:

✔ **The Me object.** The Me object refers to the currently active Form or Report object. You can use Me to refer to any property, method, or collection within the form. The Me object can also serve as a prefix to any control or field in the current form. The following statement refers to the Installation control on the current form:

```
Me![Installation].Visible = True
```

In most cases, you don't need to specify the Me object, because Access 2000 assumes that any reference to a control or field in a form module refers to the Me object. The Me object is only available in a form or report module. Standard modules, that is, modules created from the Modules tab of the Database window cannot use the Me object.

✔ **The For Each structure.** You use this structure to enumerate all the controls on the form. This structure enables you to inspect the Tag property for each control and pick out those that belong to the Service group.

```
Dim C As Control
    For Each C In Me.Controls
        If C.Tag = "Service" Then
            C.Visible = False
        End If
    Next
```

Utilizing For Each...Next, you can develop a procedure that shows or hides the controls based on the Type of part being displayed. The program fragment shown in the following uses For Each to enumerate all the controls on a form. The program tests the Tag property of each control to determine which, if any, belong to the Service group.

```
Dim C As Control
    Select Case [Type]
        Case "Router", "DSU", "Server"
            For Each C In Me.Controls
                If C.Tag = "Service" Then
                    C.Visible = True
                End If
            Next
        Case Else
            For Each C In Me.Controls
                If C.Tag = "Service" Then
                    C.Visible = False
                End If
            Next
    End Select
```

> **Form: Hide Controls 02**

The primary advantage of using For Each to examine the Tag property of each control is that your code is no longer locked into a specific list of control names. You can easily include or exclude controls from the group simply by changing their Tag property instead of editing your code.

Dealing with controls as a group also eliminates errors that can arise if you fail to keep the hide and show control lists identical. In the previous example (Calc 11), the code required you to have two identical lists of controls entered under different Case statements. If the two lists were not identical, some controls would fail to hide or reappear when they were supposed to do so.

Passing parameters to a procedure

If you examine the statements included within the Case statements in the preceding section, you may notice that the code is almost identical in all the statements, with the exception that one case uses the False value and the other a True value. If you replace the True or False with a placeholder, ????, you find that you have a block of code that you can use to either show or hide a group of similarly tagged controls.

```
Sub GroupShow()
    For Each C In Me.Controls
        If C.Tag = "Service" Then
            C.Visible = ????
        End If
    Next
End Sub
```

But how can you avoid fixing the function of the code by specifying either True or False? The answer is to create a procedure that places a variable in the location where the True or False should go. In the following example, I insert the variable Show into the code in place of a specific True or False value.

```
Sub GroupShow()
    For Each C In Me.Controls
    Sub GroupShow()
        If C.Tag = "Service" Then
            C.Visible = Show
        End If
    Next
End Sub
```

If Show equals True, the GroupShow procedure shows the controls in the group. Conversely, if Show equals False, the procedure hides the controls. But how can you assign a value to a variable in a procedure called from another procedure? The rules that govern the scope of local variables prevents variables defined in one procedure from being available in any other procedure.

The solution lies in the capability of Visual Basic to *pass* parameters between procedures. When you pass a value, you send the a value defined in one procedure to another procedure that you are calling. A *parameter* is the value that the procedure passes to the procedure it is calling. You define parameters by placing a list of the parameters inside the ( ) that follows the procedure name in the Sub statement. The following example defines a parameter called Show that's required for the GroupShow procedure.

```
Sub GroupShow(Show)
    For Each C In Me.Controls
    Sub GroupShow()
        If C.Tag = "Service" Then
            C.Visible = Show
        End If
    Next
End Sub
```

If you want to execute the GroupShow procedure, you use a Call statement that specifies the name of the procedure to call and the value of the required parameter.

```
Call GroupShow True
```

The value that is passed to the GroupShow procedure is a True value. When the GroupShow procedure receives the value, the GroupShow procedure assigns the value to the variable name, Show, specified in the Sub statement. Within the GroupShow procedure, Show has the value of True.

You're not limited to passing a single parameter. The following example requires two parameters: GroupName and Show. You can use the procedure to show or hide and group of controls that share the same Tag property.

```
Sub GroupShow(GroupName, Show)
    For Each C In Me.Controls
    Sub GroupShow()
        If C.Tag =GroupName Then
            C.Visible = Show
        End If
    Next
End Sub
```

To execute the procedure, you enter the following statement in another procedure. Notice that you generally omit the optional keyword Call.

Be aware that the order of the parameters you write as a list must match the order of the variables in the Sub statement of the procedure you're calling. In this case, the group name comes first and the True/False value second.

```
GroupShow "Service", True
```

Access 2000 also enables you to specify arguments for user-defined procedures as *named arguments*. (Named arguments are introduced in Chapter 1.) The names of the arguments are the names specified in the Sub statement of the procedure you're calling. The following statement shows the use of named arguments. If you use the named argument form, the order of the parameters isn't important.

```
GroupShow Show:= True, GroupName:= "Service"
```

The following block of code shows how you can call the same procedure, GroupShow, to show or hide a group of controls:

```
Private Sub Form_Current()
'other statements not shown
Select Case [Type]
    Case "Router", "DSU", "Server"
        GroupShow GroupName:="Service", Show:=True
    Case Else
        GroupShow GroupName:="Service", Show:=False
    End Select
End Sub

Sub GroupShow(GroupName, Show)
    Dim C As Control
    For Each C In Me
        If C.Tag = GroupName Then
            C.Visible = Show
        End If
    Next
End Sub
```

Form: Hide Controls 03

Using Color

Graphical interfaces such as Windows provide many tools by which program designers can communicate with the person using the application that they have created. Among those tools is the ability to display items that appear on forms and in dialog boxes in many different colors. Color is a powerful tool because of the way the human mind and eye work. A change in color, especially a contrasting color, will be more quickly noted by a user looking at a screen than would a change in a number or text item.

Some situations cry out for a critical piece of information to stand out from the rest of the data on a form. As an example, suppose that you were selling a product, such as wine or other alcoholic beverage over the Internet. Currently such products are regulated not by the Federal government but by a laws that differ from state to state. If you have a list of customers, it is critical to recognize which live in states that allow direct shipment if alcoholic beverages and which forbid it by law. It might be useful to use color to indicate on the customer record which addresses were in open states and which were in closed states.

Color provides a means of accomplishing that goal. Access provides three ways to use color on a form:

- ✔ **Static color.** Static colors are colors that are assigned to the foreground or background of a form or a control on a form. The colors are part of the form's design and all the records displayed show the same colors. Static colors do not change based on the data in each record.

- ✔ **Current form colors.** You can alter the colors used for each record displayed on a form by inserting Visual Basic statements in the On_Current form event to change colors based on the values in each displayed record. Note that this method works correctly only when the form is displayed in the Single Form View. If the form is displayed in the Continuous Form View or in the Datasheet view, Access uses the current record's colors for all the records.

- ✔ **Conditional formatting**. Conditional formatting provides a means of linking the color of Text box and Combo box controls based on the data in the records. Conditional formatting works correctly for forms displayed in any view.

Note the difference between current form colors and conditional formatting. You can use current form colors to change the colors of any element on a form (not just text and combo boxes), but you can do so only in the Single Form View. Conditional formatting overcomes this limitation for multiple record form displays, but its formatting applies only to text and combo box controls.

Using On_Current to change colors

The On_Current event takes place each time the focus moves from one record to another on a form. If you view the form in the Single Form View mode, the On_Current event occurs once for each record that you display. In this mode, you can alter the colors assigned to one or more elements on the form to make the user immediately aware of critical information.

The form shown in Figure 4-11 changes the color of the City and State controls depending upon the state value. Because wine sales to California residents is not restricted, those records appear with black on white. All other states are displayed as white on red. Without actually reading the text, the user can tell which customers can receive wine and which can't.

Figure 4-11: The color of the City and State controls changes to reflect the location.

The following code example is inserted into the On_Current procedure of the form. The Form repaints each record when it displays so that the colors can adjust to reflect the customer's location.

```
Private Sub Form_Current()
    If Me.State <> "CA" Then
        With Me.State
            .ForeColor = vbWhite
            .BackColor = vbRed
            .FontBold = True
        End With
```

(continued)

(continued)

```
        With Me.City
            .ForeColor = vbWhite
            .BackColor = vbRed
            .FontBold = True
        End With
    Else
        With Me.State
            .ForeColor = vbBlack
            .BackColor = vbWhite
            .FontBold = False
        End With
        With Me.City
            .ForeColor = vbBlack
            .BackColor = vbWhite
            .FontBold = False
        End With
    End If
End Sub
```

| Form: Color 01 |

Performing a Lookup With SQL

The example in `Color 01` uses a very simple expression, State <>"CA", to determine the colors used when the record is displayed. But this accounts only for CA and treats the rest of the country as off limits. A better approach is to use a table that lists each state and includes a field that indicates whether or not sales can be made in those states. The `States` table included on the CD has such a field Yes/No type, called `IsOpen`, which indicates the legal status of that state.

In order to make use of this table to control form colors, you can use Visual Basic to perform a query that checks the current record's state against the States table. The first statement needed is one that creates a Recordset object variable. An *object variable* is a variable that you create to hold a specific type of object rather than simply holding a text or numeric value.

When you define StateStatus as a New Recordset, you create a container into which you can store the results of a SQL query. This is important because unlike the SQL queries you perform with the Query Grid, the result of the SQL query in a Visual Basic program creates no direct output to the screen. In this case, the purpose of the query is to retrieve a specific data item from a table and use it to determine the legal status of the customer whose record is being displayed in the form.

```
Dim StateStatus As New Recordset
```

After you create the variable `StateStatus`, it exists but is empty. The next task is to fill `StateStatus` with the results of SQL query. You can accomplish this with the `Open` method. To use the `Open` method, you must supply two pieces of information:

✔ **SQL statement.** The first argument is a SQL statement that defines that data you want to retrieve. Remember that SQL statements are text so that you can use various expressions to compose the statement in Visual Basic code. In this case the value displayed in the State control on the form is used as the criteria for the SQL statement.

✔ **Database connection.** You must supply a connection to the database upon which the SQL statement is processed. In the simplest case, you specify the name of the database you currently have open using the CurrentProject.Connection method.

If you have used previous versions of Access, you may notice that the code required to perform a SQL query in Visual Basic is simpler than the equivalent code required for Access 97. The reason is that the default database provider in Access 2000 is ADO (Active Data Objects) rather than DAO (Data Access Objects), which were the default provider in Access 97. CurrentProject.Connection in ADO is roughly the equivalent of CurrentDB in DAO. However, you can still use DAO in Access 2000 by adding a reference to DAO in Visual Basic. I discuss ADO and DAO in more detail in Chapter 5.

In the following example, the Open method executes the SQL query and stores the results in the StateStatus variable.

```
StateStatus.Open _
    "SELECT IsOpen FROM States " & _
    "WHERE State = '" & Me.State & "'", _
    CurrentProject.Connection
```

When you put these elements together, as shown in the next code example, you can then write an expression, Not StateStatus!IsOpen, that draws a field value from the recordset object and uses it as part of the Visual Basic code. The resulting form displays colors that are depend on the values stored in the States table. The user is informed, by means of highly visible color changes, of the legal status of each displayed customer.

```
Dim StateStatus As New Recordset
StateStatus.Open _
    "SELECT IsOpen FROM States " & _
    "WHERE State = '" & Me.State & "'", _
    CurrentProject.Connection
If Not StateStatus!IsOpen Then
    'statements ...
    'statements...
Endif
```

| **Form: Color 02** |

Handling exceptions when using SQL

One of the first and most critical lessons a programmer learns when she deploys an application is that the data actually entered into your carefully defined tables often includes things you never expected.

Take, as an example, the code used in Color 02, in which a SQL query is used to determine the status of a customer based on the value in the State field. That code includes a tacit assumption that each of the possible values in the State field can find a corresponding record in the States table. But is this a reliable assumption? Probably not. In fact, the sample Customers table contains Canadian addresses and even some records with blanks in the State field. Unless you take pains to tightly control all entries (see Chapters 5 and 6), you can have unexpected entries.

In many cases you simply can't control or guarantee the complete integrity of your source data. This means that every time you perform a SQL query to retrieve a value, you need to account for the possibility that the query may return an empty data set.

In Visual Basic you can check this possibility by using the Eof (end of file) property. If a query returns an empty recordset then the value of the Eof property is immediately set to True. Before you attempt to access any of the data in the State Status recordset, you should check to see if it is empty by checking the value of the Eof property.

```
If StateStatus.EOF Then
```

TECHNICAL STUFF

End of file? What file? Once again you encounter vestigial (I did occasionally go to class in college) terminology. The term "end of file" refers to a special value, usually ASCII character 26, called Ctrl+Z, used to mark the end of a data file. In BASIC, the first ASCII 26 encountered in a text file indicated the end and any program reading that file would stop at that point. Of course, in a relational database like Access, end of file refers to the last records in a data set but the old name still sticks around.

The revised code in the next example adds a section that immediately follows the opening of the recordset with code that checks for an empty recordset using the Eof property. In this case, the controls are changed to yellow indicating that the state entry cannot be used to determine the correct legal status of the customer record.

Note the use of the Exit Sub statement. This statement provides a means of terminating the procedure prior to the End Sub statement. The code entered in Color 02 assumed that a valid recordset would be available. The Exit Sub

statement is used to stop Visual Basic from running that section of the procedure when it turns out that the recordset is empty. Exit Sub provides an
emergency exit from the procedure when something unexpected occurs.

```
Dim StateStatus As New Recordset
StateStatus.Open _
    "SELECT IsOpen FROM States " & _
    "WHERE State = '" & Me.State & "'", _
    CurrentProject.Connection
If StateStatus.EOF Then
    With Me.State
        .ForeColor = vbBlack
        .BackColor = vbYellow
        .FontBold = True
    End With
    With Me.City
        .ForeColor = vbBlack
        .BackColor = vbYellow
        .FontBold = True
    End With
    Exit Sub
End If
If Not StateStatus!IsOpen Then
'remainder of the code...
```

Form: Color 03

As a general rule, you should include a routine to handle empty recordsets in
any procedure in which you rely on a recordset to return a critical data item.
While not explicitly an error handling routine (you don't use the On Error
Goto statement), you are avoiding an error that would occur if you tried to
access data, for example, If Not StateStatus!IsOpen, from an empty
recordset object.

Format Conditions

The On_Current approach to using colors works very well in most cases
where the form in question is going to be displayed in the single form display
mode, that is, when each screen represents one record.

It does not work properly when you display a form in the continuous or
datasheet display modes. In those cases, Access propagates any color
changes made to the control on the current record (the one with the focus)
to all the other records displays within the form or the datasheet. While the
colors will be accurate for the current record, they will be misleading for any
other records that are visible on the screen at the same time.

Microsoft has noted complaints from users about using colors in this situation and they have provided a method that allows color manipulation on
forms displayed in the continuous and datasheet modes (see Figure 4-12).

The feature is called Conditional Formatting, which you can implement by using the Conditional Formatting option on the Format menu in the Form Design mode. However, because this is a book about Access 2000 programming, I limit the discussion to how this feature works in Visual Basic. I won't explain how you can use this feature without programming.

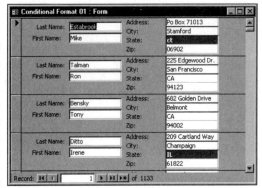

Figure 4-12:
Conditional
Formatting
allows color
changes to
continuous
form
displays.

Conditional Formatting is treated as a property of a control. This means that you can set the property when the form is opened and the conditional format will automatically take care of the details related to each record. Note that only text box and combo box controls can have a `FormatConditions` collection so that only these types of controls can have conditional formats.

This changes the programming task from something related to the `On_Current` event (which occurs each time a new record receives the focus) to the Form Load event, which takes place once when the form is loaded.

You create a conditional form using the `Add` method of the `FormatConditions` collection. To add a format condition you must specify three items:

✔ **Condition type.** Access supports three type of conditions. `acFieldValue` for evaluating the current control, `acFieldHasFocus` when the format should be used based on the control getting focus, and `acExpression` to enter an expression that involves data in other controls.

✔ **Operator.** A number or constant that indicates the type of comparison operator used to evaluate the condition.

✔ **Criteria expression.** A text string that contains the criteria (or a criterion expression) that controls the use of the conditional format.

The simplest form is `acFieldValue` type condition. This type of condition simply evaluates the current value of the control and invokes the formatting linked to that condition. The next example sets bold white on red as the format for the `State` control when the value of `State` is not equal (value 2) to CA.

```
With Me.State
    .FormatConditions.Add acFieldValue, 2, "'CA'"
    .FontBold = True
    .ForeColor = vbWhite
    .BackColor = vbRed
End With
```

> *Form: Conditional Format 01*

Take note of two points here. First, the criteria string must contain quotations. If you simply specify "CA", then Access treats CA as the name of another control on the form. To specify a literal value, you must embed the quotation marks within the string ("'CA'").

Second, it is not necessary to specify the "normal" color combination. The conditional formatting feature automatically resets the control to the colors assigned to the control in the form design. This simplifies the code required.

If you want to include more than one control in the formatting, you need to create a conditional format for each control. In the color examples, the goal is to have both the state and the city appear in the same conditional formatting. The upcoming code shows how two controls (State and City) can be synchronized to have the same formatting based on a condition.

The condition assigned to the City control is an expression-based condition because the data that determines its formatting is stored in a different control, State, than the one to which the formatting is being assigned. The expression in this case needs to specify the name of the control as well as the specific criteria. Remember that the second argument, in this case 2, indicates the not equal operator so that the condition applies when the State is not CA.

```
Dim FColor, BColor
FColor = vbWhite
BColor = vbRed
With Me.State
    .FormatConditions.Add acFieldValue, 2, "'CA'"
    .FontBold = True
    .ForeColor = FColor
    .BackColor = BColor
End With
With Me.City
    .FormatConditions.Add acExpression,2,"[State] = 'CA'"
    .FontBold = True
    .ForeColor = FColor
    .BackColor = BColor
End With
```

Form: Conditional Format 02

So far, so good. But recall that the goal is to have the criteria for the legal status utilize the States table rather than specific criteria like "CA". This gets a bit tricky because the Conditional Format feature is not designed to work with data in tables other than the one being displayed in the current form.

One solution is to create an unbound control, which in this case is called Status. You can assign Status a control source that contains a Dlookup() function that performs the lookup on the States table and returns a true or false value. Note that the Visible property of the control is set to False. This means that the value of the control is available to the conditional format feature but not displayed on the form.

```
Exp = "=DLookUp('IsOpen','States','State = ' & Chr(34) &
        [State] & Chr(34))"
With Me.Status
    .ControlSource = Exp
    .Visible = False
End With
```

After the formula is inserted into the Status control, the value of Status can be used to trigger the conditional formatting. The next example assigns identical conditional formats to all the controls that will indicate the legal status of the customer.

```
With Me.State
    .FormatConditions.Add acExpression, 2, "=[Status]"
    .FontBold = True
    .ForeColor = FColor
    .BackColor = BColor
End With
With Me.City
    .FormatConditions.Add acExpression, 2, "=[Status]"
    .FontBold = True
    .ForeColor = FColor
    .BackColor = BColor
End With
```

Form: Conditional Format 03

This approach allows you to have a multiple record form display controls with conditional formatting when the condition requires a reference to data in a lookup table such as States. The use of color in this way comes into play again in Chapter 5 when you use subforms to display records.

About colors in Visual Basic

Visual Basic includes 16 basic colors for which there are constants such as vbRed, vbWhite, and so on. If you want more colors, you can use the RGB() function. Windows uses a color system that blends red, green, and blue pigments to create color combinations. Each color has 256 (0 to 255) different intensities, where zero represent none of that color and 255 represents full intensity. The color combinations fall in a range from 0 to 16,777,215, which is the total number of different possible combinations of three 256 colors. (The number 16,777,216 is 2 raised to the 24th power.) The RGB() function allows you to select a color by entering a 0 to 255 value for the red, green, and blue components. For example, RGB(255,0,128) creates a reddish blue color because it specifies full red, no green, and half blue. If you want to set each pixel on the screen to any one of the 16,777,216 possible colors, you need to reserve 24 bits (three bytes) of memory for each pixel. A 24-bit color system is one with sufficient video memory available to allocate 24 bits for each pixel. If you're using a resolution of 640 x 480, you need about 0.9 MB of memory to display 24-bit color. Systems that don't support the full 16,777,216 possible colors simply substitute the closest color available if someone uses an unsupported combination.

Lookups

In the previous section, the States table was used to locate information about the legal status of a customer, based on their state location. Along the same lines, the SmartForms.MDB contains a table called ZipCodesUSA. This table contains a list of all the ZIP codes with the state and city in which the ZIP code belongs. If you were entering a new address into your database, you could save a lot of time and eliminate a whole bunch of errors if Access automatically fetched the corresponding city and state for the ZIP code you enter.

The first step is to write a procedure that checks to see if a given ZIP code appears in the ZipCodesUSA table. The function shown in the next example uses ADO to open a recordset of all the records in ZipCodesUSA that have the same ZIP code as the one entered into the Zip control. If the Eof property is true then the ZIP code on the form is not valid.

Note that in the IsValidZip function the If statement uses CheckZip.EOF instead of CheckZip.EOF = True. Visual Basic allows you to simplify an expression if all you want to do is determine if a given value is true or false. You do not have to add = True or = False to the expression. When Visual Basic encounters simply the name of a variable, field, or control with no comparison operator, it assumes you are checking for True or False. A value is considered False if it equals zero. If the value is anything other than zero, it is considered True. Keep in mind that -1 is a True value because it is not equal to zero.

```
Function IsNotValidZip()
    Dim CheckZip As New Recordset
    CheckZip.Open _
        "Select * from ZipCodesUSA Where zip = '" _
        & Me.Zip & "'", _
        CurrentProject.Connection
    If CheckZip.EOF Then
        MsgBox "The Zip Code " & Me.Zip & _
        " is not found in the zip code table.", _
        vbExclamation, "Zip Code Check"
    End If
End Function
```

You can call this function from the `BeforeUpdate` event of the `Zip` control. This ensures that each time a ZIP code is entered, its validity is checked.

```
Private Sub Zip_BeforeUpdate(Cancel As Integer)
    IsNotValidZip
End Sub
```

Form: Zip 01

Using the Cancel Parameter

You may have noticed that unlike the `AfterUpdate` event procedure, the `BeforeUpdate` event procedure contains a parameter called `Cancel`. The purpose of this parameter is to provide a means by which you can cancel the event. *Canceling* the event means that you return Access to the state it was in before it took the action that triggered the event, in this case the update of the `Zip` control.

```
Private Sub Zip_BeforeUpdate(Cancel As Integer)
```

Why would you want to cancel an event? Why not just use `AfterUpdate`? To understand the advantage that canceling an event provides, think about what happens when you enter an invalid ZIP code into the form `Zip 01`. Your program displays a message telling the user that they have entered an invalid ZIP code, but it does nothing to prevent the user from actually storing that invalid ZIP code in the database. In fact, as soon as the user click on the message the data is stored in the form and the cursor moves to the next item on the form exactly as if the entry was valid.

Canceling the procedure would stop Access from updating the control. The cursor would remain the control until the user entered a valid ZIP code.

You can terminate an event by setting the `Cancel` parameter equal to `True`. If `Cancel` is `False`, the event is not canceled and Access continues normally.

```
Cancel = True
```

In this case, whether or not an event should be canceled is determined by `IsNotValidZip` function. In Visual Basic, functions can return values. In this case, you would like the `IsNotValidZip` to evaluate as `True` (in order to cancel the update event) when an invalid zip code has been entered and `False` when a valid ZIP code is entered.

You can assign a value to the function by treating the name of the function as if it were a variable name. The statement `IsNotValidZip = True` would cause Visual Basic to return the `True` value for the function. That value could then be assigned to the `Cancel` parameter to cancel the update. The following code added to the `IsNotValidZip` function changes the function so that it now return a `True` or `False` value.

```
If CheckZip.EOF Then
    MsgBox "The Zip Code " & Me.Zip & _
    " is not found in the zip code table.", _
    vbExclamation, "Zip Code Check"
    IsNotValidZip = True
Else
    IsNotValidZip = False
End If
```

Now that the function returns a value, you can assign that value (`True` or `False`) to the `Cancel` parameter as shown in the following example. This means that the users will be either allowed or prevented from going on with their entry, based on the validity of the ZIP codes they enter.

```
Private Sub Zip_BeforeUpdate(Cancel As Integer)
    Cancel = IsNotValidZip()
End Sub
```

ON THE CD

Form: Zip 02

Now that we have handled the situation that occurs when an invalid ZIP code is entered, you can turn your attention to valid ZIP codes. In that case, you want to fill in the city and state for the user automatically. Remember that you have already performed one SQL query to locate the ZIP code in the ZIP code table. That means the recordset contains the information that you need to insert into `City` and `State` controls. This modification inserts those values in the case that a valid ZIP code has been entered:

```
    Else
        Me.City = CheckZip!LocalPostOffice
        Me.State = CheckZip!State
        IsNotValidZip = False
    End If
```

Form: Zip 03

You have now created a form that can catch typing errors before they get stored in the database, eliminate tedious typing, and improve accuracy. Not bad for 10 lines of code!

Chapter 5

Don't Type — Make Lists

● ●

In This Chapter

▶ Selection versus entry

▶ Self-referencing lists

▶ Linked list boxes

▶ Open a form from a list

▶ Miscellaneous techniques

● ●

*T*he theme of this chapter is simple — you're always better off picking from a list than typing something in. That's it! But don't let the simplicity of the theme make it seem trivial. One of the biggest differences between databases designed by people who can write Access 2000 programs and those designed by poor souls who cannot is the use of lists of all types to eliminate direct data entry. In this chapter you discover a number of ways to create user interfaces that eliminate typing, making your programs easier for people to use and less prone to errors.

Selection Versus Entry

In any database system, the most critical section of the application is *data acquisition* — or more simply, those segments in the program involving the input points for the data. PCs support any number of interesting ways to acquire data — from bar-code readers to downloads from other computer databases — but data acquisition's bread and butter still remains the keyboard, the mouse, and a user's hands.

Any programmer's most important task is to use those tools available in Access 2000 (including Visual Basic programming) to create a user interface that maximizes the chances for data to be entered quickly and accurately. One of the best ways to do this is to try to eliminate *direct data entry* — typing information into text boxes — by selecting data from lists of various types. While there is no way to eliminate all text entry, you can greatly reduce the amount of typing (and subsequently the number of typing errors) by taking advantage of the rich set of tools available to the Access 2000 programmer.

Database Folder: Chapter 5
Database File: Lists.mdb

To get ready to begin this chapter, open the database for Chapter 5, LISTS.MDB. After you open the database, click on the Forms tab to display a list of the forms discussed in this chapter. In addition, you may find other objects such as queries, modules, or tables, that are relevant to understanding the example. I specify these objects, when relevant, next to the On the CD icon.

Self-Referencing Lists

The first rule for making better entry forms is to eliminate, wherever possible, the user having to enter information that he or she can simply select. As an example, look at the form shown in Figure 5-1. This form displays text box controls that you use to display and enter data.

In theory, the data entered for the city, state, and ZIP code could be unique each time. But in many cases, that information may tend to repeat, which is especially true when the data entered comes from the same general geographic area.

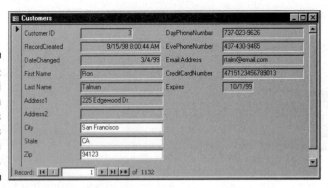

Figure 5-1:
A standard style form that uses text boxes for all data entry.

Form: Customer 01

One way to simplify the entry of these items is to create a self-referential combo box control. The term *self-referential* refers to the fact that the data source for the combo list box is not a separate lookup table, but actually the table itself. For example, imagine a table of customer names and addresses. In many cases, the names of the cities entered into the database repeat, sometimes quite frequently. If you wanted to save some typing and avoid spelling errors, you could create a combo box with a drop list that consists of a list of the city names already entered into the current table.

To illustrate, Figure 5-2 shows a form similar to the one in Figure 5-1. The only difference is that the controls displaying the `City`, `State`, and `Zip` fields were changed from a text boxes to a combo boxes.

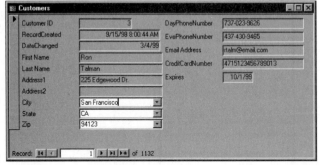

Figure 5-2:
Self-referential combo boxes are used for selecting City, State, and Zip.

The contents of the drop lists associated with the combo boxes are determined the `RowSourceType` and `RowSource` properties. The default `RowSourceType` is Table/Query. In addition to simply entering the name of a table or a query stored in the current database, you can assign a SQL statement to the `RowSource` property. The combo box drop list is the data set returned by the SQL statement.

In this case, the control's `RowSource` property needs to be a SQL query that retrieves a list of unique items from the table associated with the form. The statement takes the general form shown in the following code sample. The key element is the `DISTINCT` keyword. This keyword causes SQL to drop all the duplicate names from the list so that each city, state, or ZIP code appears only once in the list. In addition, you want to eliminate any null items from the list with `IS NOT NULL`. Of course you might assume none of your customer records to have missing ZIP codes or city names, but that seldom turns out to be the case.

```
SELECT DISTINCT field
FROM table
WHERE field IS NOT NULL;
```

The statement that follows applies this approach to the `City` field. An added benefit of using the `DISTINCT` keyword is that the items are automatically sorted in ascending order. Access sorts the records as part of the process used to determine which records contain duplicate entries.

```
SELECT DISTINCT city
FROM businesses
WHERE city IS NOT NULL;
```

The most common way to set the RowSource property is to use the form design mode to enter the SQL statement into the RowSource line of the control's property sheet. However, in this book I have chosen to set the RowSource properties of the controls by means of Visual Basic for three reasons:

- ✔ This is a book on programming, so the more programming code I show, the better the publisher likes it.

- ✔ When you are creating forms that use a number of SQL queries for list and combo box controls, assigning the SQL statements to the RowSource properties by means of Visual Basic code means that all the SQL involved with the form appears in one place. When the SQL statements are stored in the control's property sheets, you have to jump from control to control in order to read and edit the SQL.

- ✔ The remainder of this chapter involves using Visual Basic to dynamically alter the SQL statements that control the contents of various list and combo box controls. You might as well get started here.

If you click the builder icon (...) in the RowSource line of the control's property sheet, Access 2000 displays the query grid so that you can design a query without having to enter the SQL. When you close the query grid, Access inserts the equivalent SQL statement into the RowSource property line for you.

In order to set the initial RowSource properties of the controls on a form, you place your Visual Basic code in the Form_Load procedure. The Load event takes place every time a form is opened. It occurs before the form becomes visible on the screen, so any changes made to the form during this event determine how the form appears when it becomes visible on the screen.

In this case, the code consists of three statements that assign SQL statements to the three combo box controls shown in Figure 5-2. In each case, the drop list is populated with the unique values for the respective fields that have previously been entered into the Customers table.

```
Private Sub Form_Load()
    Me.City.RowSource = _
        "SELECT DISTINCT City FROM Customers " & _
        " WHERE city IS NOT NULL"
    Me.State.RowSource = _
        "SELECT DISTINCT State FROM Customers " & _
        " WHERE State IS NOT NULL"
    Me.Zip.RowSource = _
        "SELECT DISTINCT Zip FROM Customers " & _
        " WHERE Zip IS NOT NULL"
End Sub
```

Form: Customers 02

Updating a combo box list

Self-referential lists or combo box controls have one problem that may not be obvious when you first use the form. The problem is that the population of the lists is defined by the data set returned by the control's SQL statement. The population takes place the first time the user opens the drop list. But what if the user enters a new city, state, or ZIP code into the form? The new item will not appear on the list because it was added to the table after the contents of the lists were determined by the initial query. The result is that the list is out of sync with the contents of the table. This state continues until you close the form and then re-open it. When you reopen the form, Access performs the SQL queries again, picking up any additions made to the table during the previous session.

You can force a form to update all of its SQL-related properties by pressing Shift+F9, which is the Requery key. This updates all the SQL-related lists on the form. However, it also requeries the form's recordset, which causes Access to jump back to the first record. If you want to update the lists without jumping back to the first record, you must use the Visual Basic methods discussed in the following sections.

A better method is to design a form in which new items added during the current session are reflected in the lists automatically, avoiding the need to close and reopen the form. To illustrate how to accomplish this, I added a new control called Category to the Customer form, shown in Figure 5-3. The purpose of this field is to classify the customers. For example, you might classify them by their credit ratings, their sales regions, how they first heard about your company, and so on.

The important point about a category field is that you always want to display it in a list or combo list box control. Why? The purpose of a category is to create a group of records that can be selected and used at some later point. If you decide that you want to label some customers as "Big Spenders," then you want to make sure that you enter the exact same text (Big Spenders) each time so that you can correctly group them together later on. If you enter BigSpenders, Big Buyers, Big Sales, or Big Spendres, you end up losing some records when you attempt to select that group. The trick is to add each new category item to the list the first time it is entered — and then limit the entry to items on the list for all other records.

In this example, the Category control is linked to the Category01 field, which is a text type field. In the form's Load procedure, a SQL statement is assigned to the RowSource property of the combo box so that the list contains the distinct entries already contained in the category01 field.

In addition to the RowSource property, the code includes another setting, LimitToList, and sets the value as True. When the LimitToList property of a combo box control is True, Access allows the user to enter or select only items contained in the control's drop list. All other entries result in an error message. The user must select an item from the list or undo their entry.

```
Private Sub Form_Load()
    With Me.Category01
        .RowSource = _
        "SELECT DISTINCT Category01 FROM Customers " & _
        "WHERE Category01 IS NOT NULL"
        .LimitToList = True
    End With
End Sub
```

Note the use of the With...End With structure. This structure is a Visual Basic feature designed to make object-related code easier to enter and read. The With structure begins with the name of an object. You can then list methods and properties without having to write the full object reference. The preceding code that uses the With structure could be rewritten without With, as shown in the following code. Both examples have exactly the same meaning. The With structure is useful when you want to work with several properties or methods related to the same object.

```
Me.Category01.RowSource = _
        "SELECT DISTINCT Category01 FROM Customers " & _
        "WHERE Category01 IS NOT NULL"
Me.Category01.LimitToList = True
```

The LimitToList property does not directly address the problem of updating the combo box drop list each time a new item is added to the category01 field. In fact, it eliminates the possibility of making any new entries at all because it forces the user to enter or select something that is already on the list.

The solution to this problem involves controlling the NotInList event with a Visual Basic procedure. Each time the user attempts to add a new item to a combo box control that has its LimitToList property set to True, it generates the NotInList event.

The following code, entered for the Category01 NotInList procedure, changes the way that Access behaves when a user enters a new item into the combo box. In this case, the standard error message is suppressed, the user is allowed to enter a new item, and the drop list is updated to include the new item.

```
Private Sub Category01_NotInList(NewData As String, Response
            As Integer)
    Response = acDataErrAdded
    Me.Category01 = NewData
    DoCmd.RunCommand acCmdSaveRecord
End Sub
```

Despite the small size of the NotInList procedure, it contains a number of unusual elements that call for closer examination. First, the procedure has two parameters: NewData and Response.

- ✔ **NewData.** This parameter contains the newly entered value. Note that the control itself still retains the original value, if any, even though the screen may no longer show it. The control itself has not been updated at the point where the NotInList occurs.

- ✔ **Response.** This parameter determines the actions Access takes after the NotInList procedure has completed. The value assigned to this parameter during the NotInList procedure can be used to suppress the standard error message and/or cause Access to update the combo box drop list.

The first statement in the procedure assigns a value to the Response parameter. In this case, the constant acDataErrAdded is used. This value tells Access to suppress the standard error message that is usually displayed when a the user enters a value that is not on the list. It also causes Access to update the drop list for the combo box as soon as the NotInList procedure is complete.

```
Response = acDataErrAdded
```

Keep in mind that the `acDataErrAdded` setting cannot by itself ensure that no message will appear and that the list will be updated. When you use this setting, you must still perform actions within the `NotInList` procedure that eliminate need for the `NotInList` event. That is, you have to make sure the new entry is part of underlying table so that when the requery takes place, the newly entered value will appear on the drop list. If you were to end the `NotInList` procedure at this point, you would find that as soon as the procedure was over, Access would display the error message anyway.

The problem is solved by the next two statements. First, the `NewData` parameter actually changes the value of the control to the new entry. Recall that at the point when the `NotInList` procedure takes place, the actual value of the control has not been changed. It remains exactly as it was before the user made their entry. By using the following statement, you have forced Access to update the value of the combo box so that it matches the new value the user typed in.

```
Me.Category01 = NewData
```

The final step is to use the `acCmdSaveRecord` action. This is the Visual Basic equivalent of pressing Shift+Enter to save the editing changes made to the current record. This step is necessary because you must force Access to add the new value to the underlying table before it updates the combo box list. Remember that when you make edits to a record, the changes are not transferred to the table represented by the form until the entire record is saved.

```
DoCmd.RunCommand acCmdSaveRecord
```

When the procedure is complete, the `acDataErrAdded` causes Access to update the list. Because the new value has been saved to the underlying table, the updated list now contains the new entry. Because the new entry now matches an item on the updated list, the `NotInList` problem no longer exists.

Form: Customers 03

Using a lookup table

The self-referential list shown in `Customers 03` has two shortcomings. First, in order to add a new item to the list, the Visual Basic code saves the entire record. This eliminates the capability to undo the entire record, something you can do with normal edits. Second, when you begin entry into a blank table, the lists are always empty. Starting off with a set of values in the list prior to entry of any customer records might be useful.

Both of these problems can be overcome by using a lookup table. A *lookup table* is a table whose only purpose is to supply a list of values for combo box and list box controls. For example, suppose you created a table called CategoryList_Text that contained a single field called Item. Instead of using a self-referential SQL query to populate the Category list box, you can perform the query on the lookup table instead.

The first change needed when using the lookup table approach is to use a SQL statement in the RowSource property of the combo box that gets the list data from the lookup table rather than from the Customers table.

```
Private Sub Form_Load()
    With Me.Category01
        .RowSource = _
        "SELECT Item FROM CategoryList_Text"
        .LimitToList = True
    End With
End Sub
```

The NotInList procedure includes two new wrinkles. First, you add a message box that asks the users to confirm that they want to add a new item to the category list, as shown in Figure 5-4. This helps users who make typographical errors correct their mistakes rather than adding the misspelled (or differently spelled) item to the list.

Figure 5-4:
A message box asks for confirmation when a user enters a new item.

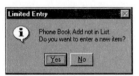

The code related to the message box uses Msgbox as a function rather than a statement. The function form of Msgbox does two things. First, it displays the message box shown in Figure 5-4. Second, it returns a value based on the specific button the user clicks in the message box. The buttons that appear in a message box are determined by the constants used in the second argument in the Msgbox function. In this case, vbYesNo adds a Yes and a No button to the box. The vbInformation sets the icon that appears in the box.

```
Dim DoYouMeanIt
DoYouMeanIt = MsgBox(StrConv(NewData, vbProperCase) & _
    " not in List." & _
    vbCrLf & "Do you want to enter a new item?", _
    vbInformation + vbYesNo, "Limited Entry")
```

When users click a button in the box, the value returned by the function is stored in the variable `DoYouMeanIt`. If they click the Yes button, the value is equal to the constant `vbYes`. If they click No, the value equals the constant `vbNo`. The next section of the procedure uses the value returned by the `Msgbox` function to determine whether the new item should be added.

If the user selects Yes, that is, `DoYouMeanIt = vbYes`, you need to execute code that updates the list to include the new entry. Keep in mind in this case the table that contains the list values is not the `Customers` table but the lookup table `CategoryList_Text`. You can use the ADO Recordset object to add a new item to that table. First, the `Dim` statement is used to define a Recordset type variable `ListItems`. The `Open` method activates the record-set. Note that two more arguments are added to the `Open` method; they are required when you want to modify the recordset. The `CursorType` deter-mines the level of control provided over the data in the recordset. The `LockType` parameter defines how records are treated when one user makes a change to the table. The settings used in the following code, `adOpenKeyset` and `adLockOptimistic`, allow for editing and adding records to the table specified in the data set. This is the same type of data access you get when you open a form bound to a table or a query.

```
Dim ListItems As New Recordset
ListItems.Open Source:="CategoryList_Text", _
    ActiveConnection:=CurrentProject.Connection, _
    CursorType:=adOpenKeyset, _
    LockType:=adLockOptimistic
```

The word *cursor* literally means move or movement. The `CursorType` para-meter refers to the SQL concept of a data cursor. Data cursors in SQL traditionally have defined limitations on accessing records in a data set. For example, a *forward-only* cursor in SQL allows you to access each record only once. You cannot go back and access a record a second time. On the other hand, a *dynamic cursor* allows you to move back and forth within the data set as many times as you like. The more flexibility you have in a cursor, the more resources the cursor consumes. When working with a simple Access data-base, the issue is not very critical.

To add a new record to a table through a ADO recordset object, you need to perform three operations.

- ✔ AddNew. This operation creates a new record entry for the specified table. Note that this operation does not save the new record. The sepa-rate `Update` method saves the record.

- ✔ Set Values. After you initiate the new record process with `AddNew`, you can assign the fields in the new record values.

- ✔ Update. This saves the new record as part of the table.

In this case, you want to store the `NewData` passed to the procedure from your form in the record you are adding to the lookup table.

```
ListItems.AddNew
ListItems!Item = NewData
ListItems.Update
```

After the new record has been added to the lookup table, you have eliminated the cause of the `NotInList` event. To complete the operation, you need to use the same strategy that you used in Customers 03 to assign the new value to the current combo box control — and then set Access to update the combo box list by setting the `Response` parameter of the `NotInList` procedure to `acDataErrContinue`.

```
Me.Category01 = NewData
Response = acDataErrAdded
```

What if the user had selected not to add the item to the list? In that case, all you need to do is set the `Response` parameter of the `NotInList` procedure to `acDataErrContinue`. This setting returns the user to the form without making any changes to the list. The assumption is that the user wants to pick an item from the original list rather than add a new item to that list.

```
Response = acDataErrContinue
```

This code shows all these elements combined into a single `NotInList` procedure.

```
Private Sub Category01_NotInList(NewData As String, _
    Response As Integer)
    Dim DoYouMeanIt
    DoYouMeanIt = MsgBox(StrConv(NewData, vbProperCase) _
        & " not in List." & _
        vbCrLf & "Do you want to enter a new item?", _
        vbInformation + vbYesNo, "Limited Entry")
    If DoYouMeanIt = vbYes Then
        Dim ListItems As New Recordset
        ListItems.Open Source:="CategoryList_Text", _
            ActiveConnection:=CurrentProject.Connection, _
            CursorType:=adOpenKeyset, _
            LockType:=adLockOptimistic
        ListItems.AddNew
        ListItems!Item = NewData
        ListItems.Update
        Me.Category01 = NewData
        Response = acDataErrAdded
    Else
        Response = acDataErrContinue
    End If
End Sub
```

Form: Customers 04

Using numeric links

The lookup table discussed in Customers 04 used text as the link between the customers and the lookup table. In general, you can more efficiently create links between tables based on unique numeric values (such as those generated by an AutoNumber field), especially when the numeric values are assigned as the primary key of the table. Access is able to search lookup tables much more quickly if the search is on a numeric primary key field rather than a text field.

The LookupCategory table included in the LISTS.MDB file is a standard lookup table that consists of two fields. The first, CategoryID is an Auto-Number field that is the primary key for the table. The second field is the Item field that contains the actual text that appears on the combo box drop list.

When you use this type of lookup table, each category is automatically assigned a numeric value when a new Item is added to the table. The Customers table information changes also. In Customer 04, a copy of the lookup table text was stored in the Customers table in the Category01 field. When you use a lookup table with a numeric ID for each category, all you need to store in the Customers table is the ID number of the category, not the text. Two advantages to this approach are as follows:

✔ **More efficient storage.** By storing the number of the category rather than the category text, you reduce the amount of space used because the entire database need contain only one copy of the category text, the one stored in the lookup table. All the other tables that use that item from the lookup table need only store the number of the item, which typically takes up much less memory and disk space.

✔ **Simple updates.** You can easily change the text related to a lookup item without having to modify all the related records. For example, suppose you assign the text Big Spenders as the text for category number 3. You assign 1,000 customers to category number 3 in the Customers table. What would you have to do in order to change the category text to "A1 Credit"? The answer is that you would need to make a single change in the lookup table. The 1,000 records linked to category number 3 in the lookup table would automatically show the new text for category number 3 the next time they were displayed. If you had used the text approach shown in Customers 04, you would have to perform a specific SQL query to modify all 1,000 records in the Customers table and update the category.

Hiding the ID Column

Although many sound reasons exist for using ID numbers as the links between tables, they do create a problem on forms. Figure 5-5 shows what happens on a form when the combo box control is bound to a number field rather than a text field. When the drop list is displayed, you can easily see the category ID numbers and the associated text. However, if you look at the box portion of the control, you can see that only the category ID number appears on the form (not the text) when the drop list is not open.

Figure 5-5:
The combo box displays the number value of the linked item.

Showing the ID number isn't a very useful display. Although it does serve as a link to the associated value in the lookup table, the user couldn't (or shouldn't) be expected to remember what text corresponds to that ID number. However, you can overcome this handicap.

The trick to using an ID as the link between tables is to hide the ID number from display in the combo box control. Look at the following code. Note the ColumnCount property is set to 2. This means that the list displayed in the combo box has two columns of data, as shown in Figure 5-5. However, the ColumnWidths property sets the width of the first column to zero. This has the effect of hiding the ID column and showing only the category text, both in the drop list and in the control itself (see Figure 5-6).

```
Private Sub Form_Load()
    With Me.category02
        .RowSource = _
        "SELECT * FROM LookupCategory ORDER BY Item"
        .LimitToList = True
        .ColumnCount = 2
        .BoundColumn = 1
        .ColumnWidths = "0; 1.2 in"
    End With
End Sub
```

Setting the first column to a width of zero causes the combo box to give the appearance of being a text control, even though the actual value stored in the field bound to the combo box control is an ID number. This simple trick allows you to get the benefits of linking by number without losing the benefit of displaying the category text on the form. Note that the `BoundColumn` control indicates which column in the drop list contains the value actually stored in the control. In this case, column 1 is the `CategoryID` column.

Figure 5-6:
A two-column list with one hidden column appears to be a one-column list.

You don't need to change the `NotInList` procedure used in Customers 04 to deal with numeric ID values. It works correctly with text or number links.

ON THE CD

Form: Customers 05

Linked List Boxes

The theme of this chapter is that using lists is one of the best ways to improve the look and feel of your forms. However, the usefulness of any list is limited by its size. For example, suppose you wanted to locate customers by geographical areas. You might want to do this if you knew of an event in a specific geographical location that you think your customer might be interested in attending.

You could simply create a combo box drop list with columns for state, city, last name, and first name. However, the Customers table included on the CD contains over 1,100 customers. Even at that size, scrolling through a list of customers is a tedious task.

On the other hand, to locate the customers you want to find, you probably don't need to look at all 1,100 names. For example, if you wanted to locate customers in the San Francisco Bay area, you would first select the state to get a list of cities in California — and then select San Francisco or Oakland from that list.

The idea is to break up the search into a series of lists organized in a hierarchy so that selection you make from the first list (state) then limits the second list (cities) to those that match the selection made in the first list. I call list box controls that function in this manner *linked lists*.

As a first example of linked lists, look at the form shown in Figure 5-7. This form contains two list boxes, one labeled `State`, the other `Cities`. The goal is to fill the `Cities` list with the names of cities from the state selected in the `State` list.

Figure 5-7:
The contents of the Cities list is controlled by the selection in the State list.

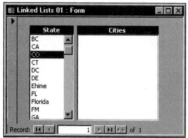

Unbound forms and controls

The form shown in Figure 5-7 is an *unbound form* that contains two *unbound controls*. This means that neither the form or its controls are directly connected to any of the tables in the database. None of the automatic data display features available in Access are utilized. Instead, the connection between the data in the tables and the controls on the form are defined totally with Visual Basic code. Taking this approach is necessary because you want to create controls whose data set changes each time the user clicks items already displayed.

The form contains two list boxes that are basically identical. But you are not going to treat them equally. The reason is that the information in one determines the information in the other. When you have linked lists, one of the lists is independent while the other is dependent. In this example, the `States` list is the independent list; the `Cities` list is dependent because its contents depend on the state selected in the `States` control.

As a rule, when the form is first loaded, only independent lists can be populated. Dependent lists are initially empty because at the time the form is first loaded, the user has yet to make a selection. The `Form_Load` populates the `States` control with a list of distinct states, all of them extracted from the `Customers` table.

```
Private Sub Form_Load()
    Me.List0.RowSource = _
    "SELECT DISTINCT State FROM Customers " & _
    "WHERE State IS NOT NULL"
End Sub
```

How and when does the `Cities` list get filled? The `Cities` list is filled each time the user names a selection from the `State` list. In Access, each time a new item is selected in a list box (with either the mouse or keyboard), the `Update` events for that control are triggered. In other words, the content of the `Cities` list is determined by the code entered into the `AfterUpdate` procedure of the `State` control.

That answers the "when" question. What about the how? As discussed throughout this chapter, lists can be filled by assigning SQL statements to the `RowSource` property of the control and using the `Requery` method to update the list. The challenge in this case is that the required SQL statement changes each time the user makes a different selection.

For example, if the user selects CO in the `State` list, the SQL statement for the cities list should be as follows:

```
SELECT city
FROM customers
WHERE state = "CO"
```

On the other hand, if a user selects CA as the state, the statement should read this way:

```
SELECT city
FROM customers
WHERE state = "CA"
```

You can see a pattern emerge. The only change in the SQL statement is the specific state name. If you revise the SQL statement so that Visual Basic inserts the text from the selection in the `State` list (control name `List0`) into the `RowSource` SQL statement for the `Cities` control (control name `List2`), then the two list boxes will always be synchronized.

```
SELECT city
FROM customers
WHERE state = Chr(34) & Me.List0 & Chr(34)
```

Note the `Chr(34)` functions insert quotation marks before and after the state text. If you were inserting a numeric value such as an ID number, they would not be needed.

The following `AfterUpdate` procedure applies this approach to the form shown in Figure 5-8. The result is that each time a new selection is made in the `State` list, a new `RowSource` SQL statement is assigned to the `Cities` control, limiting the cities displayed to the selected state.

```
Private Sub List0_AfterUpdate()
    With Me.List2
        .RowSource = _
        "SELECT DISTINCT city FROM Customers " & _
        "WHERE state = " & Chr(34) & Me.List0 & Chr(34)
        .Requery
    End With
    Me.Label5.Caption = Me.List2.ListCount&" cities in "& _
        Me.List0
End Sub
```

Note the use of the `ListCount` property in the procedure. `ListCount` returns the number of items currently displayed in a list box. This property is used to modify the label above the list box to show how many cities are displayed in the list box.

Figure 5-8:
The
selection in
States limits
the contents
of the Cities
list.

Form: Linked Lists 01

This technique is not linked to two lists. You can link as many lists as necessary in order to select the data you require. Figure 5-9 shows a third list box added to the form, labeled `Customers`. This list will be dynamically linked to the `Cities` list so that the customers displayed belong to the city selected from the `Cities` list.

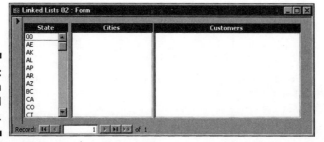

Figure 5-9:
A form with
three linked
lists.

To add another linked list, you need to write a procedure for the AfterUpdate event of the second control, in this case the Cities, that defines the RowSource of the third list, which in this case is a list of customers from the selected city and state. The SQL statement used for the RowSource includes the values in the other list box control as criteria in the WHERE clause.

```
Private Sub List2_AfterUpdate()
  With Me.List4
  .RowSource = "SELECT CustomerID, LastName, FirstName " & _
    "FROM Customers " & _
    "WHERE state = " & Chr(34) & Me.List0 & Chr(34) & _
    "AND City = " & Chr(34) & Me.List2 & Chr(34) & _
    "ORDER BY LastName, FirstName"
  .ColumnCount = 3
  .ColumnWidths = ".5 in;1 in;1 in;"
    .Requery
  End With
  Me.Label7.Caption = Me.List4.ListCount & _
    " customers in " & Me.List2 & ", " & _
    Me.List0
End Sub
```

The result is a form that has a series of lists that are linked together logically into a related set of selections. Figure 5-10 shows a list of customers defined by the selections made in the State and Cities lists.

Figure 5-10: The Customers list is limited by the selected state and city.

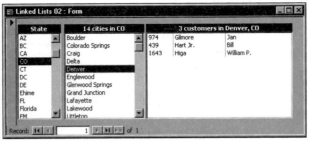

Form: Linked Lists 02

Composing a list

All the lists used in this chapter consist of data drawn directly from the fields in the specified tables. However, using the data as entered often creates list the are awkward to read. For example, the Customers table stores the first and last names in separate fields, and also uses a CustomerID field to ensure that customers who have the same name can be distinguished from one another. That is good database design. But when you display a list of customers for selection in a list box, simply listing these three fields in columns may not be the best way to present that information to the user.

Figure 5-11 shows an alternative to simply listing the data as entered into the customers table. The Customers list shows the names in the form *lastname, firstname*. Listing the names in this form creates a display that is easier to read because the entire name appears in a single column, not split across several columns.

Figure 5-11:
The
Customers
list displays
the names
using a
composed
column.

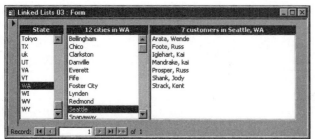

How can you display a column in the list box that does actually exist in the table used as the RowSource? The trick is to use the SQL statement assigned to the RowSource property to compose a column of data. The list box then displays this composed column as if it had been part of the original table.

The following SQL statement contains an expression that composes a new column by using a text expression to combine column data with literal text to create the desired *Lastname, Firstname* list.

```
SELECT  CustomerID, LastName & ', ' & FirstName
FROM Customers
```

The following code is a revised copy of the List2_AfterUpdate procedure that composes a column for display in the list box. Note that because the user probably doesn't need to see the CustomerID column, its width is set to zero (the ColumnWidths property) so it's hidden when the list is displayed.

```
Private Sub List2_AfterUpdate()
  With Me.List4
      .RowSource = "SELECT CustomerID, LastName & ', ' _
      & FirstName " & _
      "FROM Customers " & _
      "WHERE state = " & Chr(34) & Me.List0 & Chr(34) & _
      "AND City = " & Chr(34) & Me.List2 & Chr(34) & _
      "ORDER BY LastName, FirstName"
      .ColumnCount = 2
      .ColumnWidths = "0;2 in;"
      .Requery
  End With
  Me.Label7.Caption = Me.List4.ListCount & _
      " customers in " & Me.List2 & ", " & _
      Me.List0
End Sub
```

Form: Linked Lists 03

Composed columns can be useful in ways that you might not have expected. For example, if you were to add the customer's phone number to the expression used in the SQL statement, you would end up with a mini-Rolodex based on customer location (see Figure 5-12).

Figure 5-12: Adding phone numbers creates a mini-Rolodex based on customer location.

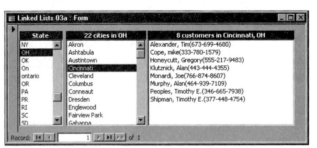

Form: Linked Lists 03a

Display results from a join

Keep in mind that the only limits on what you can display in the list box are the limits of SQL database queries. Imagine that you wanted to list the total amount of sales for each customer in the customers list along with the names, as shown in Figure 5-13. This may seem to pose a problem because sales information is stored in the `Orders` table, while name and address are stored in the `Customers` table.

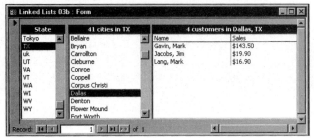

Figure 5-13:
Customer
sales totals
require a
join
between
two tables.

The answer is supplied through the magic of relational databases. Because the displayed information is the result of a SQL statement, you can perform a `JOIN` between the `Customers` and `Orders` tables to get the desired information and display it in the linked list box. See Chapter 3 for more information on `JOIN` syntax.

The key to any join is the `ON` clause, which indicates which fields in the joined tables indicate linked records. In this case, the `CustomerID` field links the orders to the customers. The basic `JOIN` is shown here:

```
SELECT *
FROM Customers INNER JOIN
ON Customers.CustomerID = Orders.CustomerID
```

However, in this case you do not want to list all the orders for each customer. Rather, you want to summarize the order totals and arrive at a total sales figure for each customer. The data set you want to retrieve contains one record for each customer — and a single total that summarizes all the sales made to that customer. To do this, you use the `GROUP BY` clause to summarize by customer, and then use a `SUM()` function to total all the orders from the `Orders` table.

```
SELECT lastname, Firstname, sum(ordertotal)
FROM Customers INNER JOIN
ON Customers.CustomerID = Orders.CustomerID
GROUP BY lastname, Firstname
```

Note that you only need to add the table name prefix to a field name if the same field name appears in more than one table. Because `OrderTotal` appears only in `Orders`, it does not need the prefix. `CustomerID`, which appears in both tables, does require a table name prefix so that SQL can tell which field to reference.

However, within the form into which you want to insert this SQL statement, you want to limit the list to a specific city and state. That means the statement must have a WHERE clause to limit the records included on any given list. When your SQL statement contains both a JOIN and a GROUP BY clause, the WHERE clause needs to follow the JOIN but precede the GROUP BY.

```
SELECT lastname, Firstname, sum(ordertotal)
FROM Customers INNER JOIN
ON Customers.CustomerID = Orders.CustomerID
WHERE state = 'CA' and city = 'antioch'
GROUP BY lastname, Firstname
```

The preceding statement serves as an outline for the Visual Basic code you need to add to the form. The SQL statement must be converted to a text expression that draws information from the other two list box controls on the form. The following code shows how to convert the preceding SQL example to operate inside the Visual Basic procedure that populates the list box.

```
Private Sub List2_AfterUpdate()
   With Me.List4
    .RowSource = _
    "SELECT Customers.CustomerID, " & _
    "lastname & ', ' & Firstname AS Name, " & _
    "Sum(Orders.OrderTotal) AS Sales   " & _
    "FROM Customers " & _
    "INNER JOIN Orders " & _
    "ON Customers.CustomerID = Orders.CustomerID " & _
    "WHERE Customers.State = '" & Me.List0 & _
    "' And Customers.City = '" & Me.List2 & _
    "' GROUP BY Customers.CustomerID, Customers.LastName," _
    "Customers.FirstName " & _
    "ORDER BY Customers.LastName, Customers.FirstName"
    .ColumnCount = 3
    .ColumnWidths = "0;1.5 in; .5 in"
    .ColumnHeads = True
    .Requery
   End With
   Me.Label7.Caption = Me.List4.ListCount & _
    " customers in " & Me.List2 & ", " & _
    Me.List0
End Sub
```

Note that in order to display the results of the joined SQL statement, a few of the list box settings have to change: ColumnCount is now 3, ColumnWidths is adjusted to display the totals, and the ColumnHeads property is set to True. When True, the ColumnHeads property adds column headings to the top of the list. When the column is a composed or calculated item, the name of the column is determined by the AS clause in the SQL statement. The AS clause gives you the capability to compose column headings for your lists that differ from the names of the fields in the table. In this case, the headings identify the meaning of the values displayed to the right of the names.

Form: Linked Lists 03b

Outer joins

Although the display shown in Figure 5-13 appears to provide the desired information, a potential problem lurks. If you were to open Linked List 03b and select CA as the State and Claremont as the City, you would see the display shown in Figure 5-14.

The screen shows something that at first doesn't seem to make sense — that is, no customers in the selected city and state. The reason this doesn't make sense: The city and states listed are those that have records in the Customers table for customers in those locations. If the table truly didn't contain any customers in that location, then the location shouldn't appear on the list in the first place.

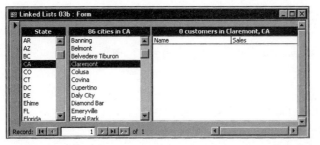

Figure 5-14: The join fails to list customers who have no orders.

The explanation for this apparent contradiction is related to exactly what an INNER join does. An INNER join includes only records that have matching values in both of the linked tables. In this example, it is possible to have customers listed in the Customers table who have never placed an order and therefore have no records in the Orders table matching their customer ID.

Because the State and City lists are not constrained by a JOIN clause to another table, they include *all* customers. The Customers list box is constrained by the JOIN so that it may have a smaller set of customers than the other lists.

The solution to this problem is to create an unbalanced join. In an *unbalanced join,* records are restricted in only one of the tables involved in the join. In this case, your goal would be to lift the constraint from the Customers table so that all customers, even those who have not made an order, would appear in the customer list.

In SQL terminology, this type of JOIN is called an OUTER join. You can choose from two types of outer joins, LEFT and RIGHT. The two types refer to which of the joined tables, the one on the left side or the right side of the JOIN clause, is meant to be unconstrained.

The following SQL statement returns an empty data set, not because of any SQL errors, but simply because no records in the Orders table matched the Customer ID field for customers in that location.

```
SELECT lastname, Firstname, sum(ordertotal)
FROM Customers INNER JOIN
ON Customers.CustomerID = Orders.CustomerID
WHERE state = 'CA' and city = 'Claremont'
GROUP BY lastname, Firstname
```

To lift the constraint from the Customers table, replace the word INNER with LEFT OUTER.

```
SELECT lastname, Firstname, sum(ordertotal)
FROM Customers LEFT OUTER JOIN
ON Customers.CustomerID = Orders.CustomerID
WHERE state = 'CA' and city = 'Claremont'
GROUP BY lastname, Firstname
```

This code shows the SQL statement embedded in the Visual Basic code for the AfterUpdate procedure of the List2 control:

```
.RowSource = _
    "SELECT Customers.CustomerID, " & _
    "lastname & ', ' & Firstname AS Name, " & _
    "Sum(Orders.OrderTotal) AS Sales  " & _
    "FROM Customers " & _
    "LEFT OUTER JOIN Orders " & _
    "ON Customers.CustomerID = Orders.CustomerID " & _
    "WHERE Customers.State = '" & Me.List0 & _
    "' And Customers.City = '" & Me.List2 & _
    "' GROUP BY Customers.CustomerID, Customers.LastName," _
    " Customers.FirstName " & _
    "ORDER BY Customers.LastName, Customers.FirstName"
```

The result, shown in Figure 5-15, displays all customers — regardless of whether they have made orders.

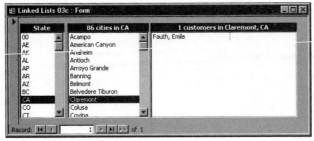

Figure 5-15:
The outer
join con-
strains only
one side of
the join.

Form: Linked Lists 03c

Nulls or zeros

In Figure 5-15, you may notice that the sales amount for customers who have
no actual sales in the Orders table appears as a blank. During an outer join,
any fields from the constrained table, in this case the Orders table, that do
not have any matches are returned as null values. They appear in the query
grid or list as blanks.

This style of display may be confusing; users may feel more secure if they see
a zero displayed rather than simply a blank. Access provides a function
called Nz(), which allows you to specify what character or value to return
if the specified field or expression is null. The following SQL statement uses
Nz(0) to insert a zero in each case where the expression sum(ordertotal)
returns a null.

```
SELECT lastname, Firstname, Nz(sum(ordertotal),0)
FROM Customers LEFT OUTER JOIN
ON Customers.CustomerID = Orders.CustomerID
WHERE state = 'CA' and city = 'Claremont'
GROUP BY lastname, Firstname
```

When placing the Nz() function into a list box, take into account one additional consideration. Back in Figure 5-13, notice that all the values are listed
use a currency format ($ with two decimal places). This is because the field
that is the source of the data is defined as a currency type field in the table
structure. If you use the Nz() function to define the column, Access will no
longer use the currency format automatically because the column is defined
by an expression rather than by a field or an SQL aggregate function such as
Sum(). This means that the values appear as unformatted numbers, for example, 143.5 instead of $143.50.

To specify currency formatting, you can use the Format() function. This SQL
example adds currency formatting to the column.

```
SELECT lastname,
Firstname, Format(Nz(sum(ordertotal),0),'currency')
FROM Customers LEFT OUTER JOIN
ON Customers.CustomerID = Orders.CustomerID
WHERE state = 'CA' and city = 'Claremont'
GROUP BY lastname, Firstname
```

> **Form: Linked Lists 03d**

Open a Form from a List

So far, so good. You have been able to create a form that contains a series of linked lists. The lists allow you to locate specific groups of customers by making a series of selections in different list boxes to narrow down the scope of the customer list.

Now what? In some cases, you may want to get more detailed information about one or more of the customers you have listed in the Customers box. Wouldn't it be nice if you could just double-click the name and pop open a customer form for that specific customer?

As it turns out, you can do just that with a relatively simple bit of Visual Basic code. Most form controls (with the exception of labels and buttons) support a double-click event — which is triggered whenever a user double-clicks on the control.

In addition, Access, through the DoCmd object I discuss in Chapter 1, provides the OpenForm method, which enables you to open a form through Visual Basic. This statement opens the Customer 03 form:

```
Docmd.Openform Formname:= "Customer 03"
```

However, simply opening the form is only part of the task. The goal is to open the form and display the customer information for the selected customer. One way to accomplish this is to specify a Where Condition parameter for the OpenForm method. The Where Condition is a text item that contains a SQL Where clause criterion, minus the word WHERE. The following statement opens the Customer 03 form but automatically restricts the form's record set to records where the CustomerID equals 567. Because each CustomerID is unique, the form is restricted to displaying that one record.

```
Docmd.Openform _
    Formname:= "Customer 03", _
    WhereCondition:= "CustomerID = 567"
```

But how do you determine the correct CustomerID in your linked list form where the selected customer can change at any moment? The answer lies in the hidden column in the `Customers` list box. Recall that column 1 contains the `CustomerID`, but it doesn't appear on the form because its column width is set to zero. What you need to keep in mind is that even though you can't see the `CustomerID`, it is still there and is available for use by your Visual Basic procedure.

The following example is the `DblClick` procedure for the `List4` (the `Customers` list box) control. It contains an `OpenForm` method that opens form Customer 03 when the user double-clicks the `List4` control (Figure 5-16). The `WhereCondition` parameter uses `List4` to complete the criteria.

```
Private Sub List4_DblClick(Cancel As Integer)
    DoCmd.OpenForm FormName:="Customers 03", _
        WhereCondition:="CustomerID = " & Me.List4
End Sub
```

With this addition, the linked list form becomes a means of accessing the customer records.

> **Form: Linked Lists 04**

Figure 5-16:
Double-
clicking a
customer
name in the
list box
opens
the corre-
sponding
customer
form.

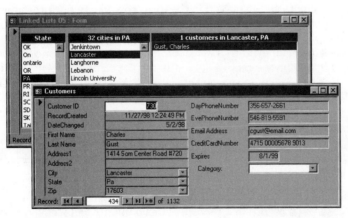

Navigation instead of filtering

The Linked Lists 04 form provided the user with the ability to use the names displayed in a list box to open another form that shows more information about that customer. This type of interface is often called a *drill-down* interface because the user moves from a very general selection down to a more and more detailed view.

The method used to open the form in Linked List 04 was the
WhereCondition parameter of OpenForm method. In effect, this parameter
automatically applies a filter to the form's normal record set, restricting the
form so that it displays only the record that matches the customer selected
in the other form.

In some cases, this approach may feel odd to the users because once they
see the customer form displayed, they find that they cannot move around in
the Customers form to other records. That's because the filter allows display
of only that one record.

A slightly different approach to this problem is to open the form in an unre-
stricted mode and then use navigation to locate the record of the selected
customer. You then need to add some Visual Basic code that searches for,
and displays, the customer whose name the user selected in the other form.
This means that the selected customer is the record initially displayed, but
the user is free to move to other records in the form as needed.

Searching within a form is usually accomplished through the use of the
RecordsetClone property of the form. When you open a form, Access automatically synchronizes the form's recordset with the controls displayed on
the form. That is what is meant by *binding* the form to a table or query. The
purpose of the RecordsetClone property is to provide Visual Basic with a
copy of the data set displayed in the form so you can perform operations on
the data without changing the record currently displayed on the form.

One thing you can do with a RecordsetClone is search for a specific record
without changing the record currently displayed on the form. You can use the
FindFirst property to search the RecordsetClone for a specific record.
The following code shows how to locate CustomerID 1007 in the
RecordsetClone.

```
Set Cust = Me.RecordsetClone
Cust.FindFirst "CustomerID = 1007"
```

After you have found the record you want in the RecordsetClone, you can
synchronize that form to the RecordsetClone using the Bookmark property.
In Access, each record in a recordset has a unique value called a *bookmark*.
The bookmark is not a value you can edit or display. You can, however, store
it in a variable or reference it in other Visual Basic statements.

The Bookmark property is the bookmark of the current record. Both the form
and the RecoredsetClone have separate bookmarks. The statement literally
sets the form's bookmark equal to the bookmark of RecordsetClone itself.
This synchronizes the records in the two data sets so the form now displays
the record located when the RecordsetClone was searched.

```
Me.BookMark = Cust.BookMark
```

You can apply this technique to the `Linked Lists` form. The following `DblClick` procedure opens the `Customer 03` form and then uses the `RecordsetClone` method to locate the `Customer` selected in the Linked Lists form. Note that when you use this method, the Customer 03 form is open to show the selected customer's record, but the form is not restricted to that record. You are free to move to any record in the `Customers` table.

```
Private Sub List4_DblClick(Cancel As Integer)
    Dim CustForm As Form
    Dim Cust As DAO.Recordset
    DoCmd.OpenForm FormName:="Customers 03"
    Set CustForm = Forms("Customers 03")
    Set Cust = CustForm.RecordsetClone
    Cust.FindFirst "CustomerID = " & Me.List4
    CustForm.Bookmark = CustForm.RecordsetClone.Bookmark
End Sub
```

In order to perform the `RecordsetClone` operation shown in the preceding code, you need to use a DAO `Recordset` variable, not an ADO `Recordset`. For information about using DAO in Access 2000, see the "References" section later in this chapter.

Also take note that both forms are open at the same time. You are free to go back to the `Linked Lists` form, make a new selection, and double-click the customer name to locate that customer in the `Customers` form. After a form has been opened, the `OpenForm` method will not open a second instance of the form. Instead, it will merely change the focus to the already-open instance of the form.

> **Form: Linked Lists 05**

Listing and opening orders

You can also use the techniques that link the lists with the customer information to fill lists and create links to other tables as well. The form shown in Figure 5-17 expands the previous `Linked Lists` form to include a fourth list box. This box displays details about the orders of a given customer. The `Orders` box is filled each time a customer is selected in the `Customers` list.

The `Orders` list box is populated by the `AfterUpdate` property of the `Customers` list (control name: `List4`). In this case, the SQL statement selects seven columns of data based on the `CustomerID` (as shown in the control `List4`). You can see that even an elaborate list such as the one displayed for orders can be populated by using the same basic approach.

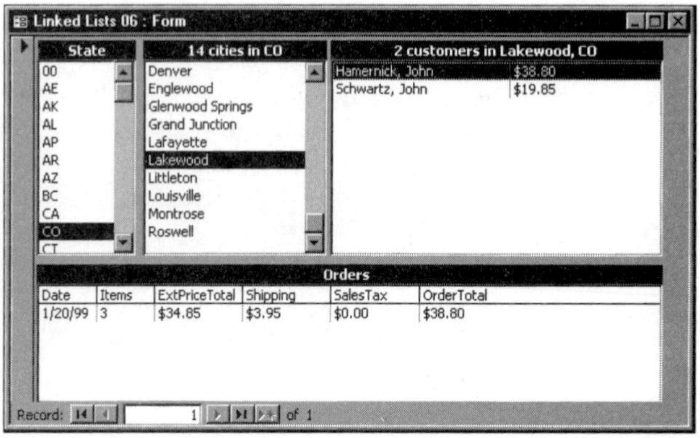

Figure 5-17: Order information is displayed whenever a customer name is clicked.

```
Private Sub List4_AfterUpdate()
   With Me.List8
    .RowSource = _
    "SELECT OrderID, DateValue([OrderDate]) AS [Date], " & _
    "Items, ExtPriceTotal, " & _
    "Shipping, SalesTax, " & _
    "OrderTotal " & _
    "FROM Orders WHERE CustomerID = " & Me.List4 & _
    " ORDER BY DateValue([OrderDate]) DESC"
    .ColumnCount = 7
    .ColumnHeads = True
    .ColumnWidths = "0;.5 in;.5 in;.75 in;" & _
        ".75 in;.75 in;.75 in"
    .Requery
   End With
End Sub
```

The Orders list is also a linking list; you can open an Order information form, Orders 01, by adding a DblClick procedure to the List8 control. That opens the Order 01 form and uses the RecordsetClone and Bookmark method of locating and displaying the order selected on the Linked Lists form.

```
Private Sub List8_DblClick(Cancel As Integer)
   Dim OrderForm As Form
   Dim Order As DAO.Recordset
   DoCmd.OpenForm FormName:="Orders 01"
   Set OrderForm = Forms("Orders 01")
   Set Order = OrderForm.RecordsetClone
   Order.FindFirst "OrderID = " & Me.List8
   OrderForm.Bookmark = OrderForm.RecordsetClone.Bookmark
End Sub
```

ON THE CD

| Form: Linked Lists 06 |

Miscellaneous Techniques

Before ending this chapter, I wanted to mention a couple of techniques that may help you when you construct your own linked-list-type forms.

Using Debug.Print

In this chapter, I use a variety of SQL statements embedded in Visual Basic code. When you convert a SQL statement, as you might enter it into a query window, into a text item that is part of a Visual Basic procedure, you may have trouble recognizing how that statement will ultimately function inside your procedure. In addition, in the query window, you can run the SQL statement and immediately see whether you have made any syntax errors (nor whether the data returned by the query meets your expectations). When you embed the SQL statement inside Visual Basic, the task of figuring out where you've gone wrong is not nearly so easy or simple.

Some of you might assume I just write out these SQL statements without error, straight from my superior brain. This is not the case, (at least not all time). I often use a trick with the `Debug.Print` statement to work out kinks in SQL statements (see Chapter 1 for more on the `Debug.Print` statement).

The `Debug.Print` statement displays information in the Immediate window. You can use this statement inside any Visual Basic procedure to send information to the Immediate window while a procedure is executing. After the procedure runs, you can display the Immediate window (Ctrl+G is the shortcut) and see the values used during the procedure.

In this case, you can output the text of the SQL statement used for the `RowSource` of the list box control by adding the statement `Debug.Print.RowSource` to the procedure.

```
With Me.List4
    .RowSource = _
    "SELECT Customers.CustomerID, " & _
    "lastname & ', ' & Firstname AS Name, " & _
    "Format(Nz(Sum(Orders.OrderTotal),0),'currency') AS Sales
        " & _
    "FROM Customers "
    ... statements
    Debug.Print .RowSource
    .ColumnCount = 3
    .ColumnWidths = "0;1.5 in; .5 in"
    .Requery
End With
```

When you open the Immediate window, you can see the actual SQL statement used by the application to populate the list box. This can often help you spot errors that you made in writing the procedure.

```
SELECT Customers.CustomerID, lastname & ', ' & Firstname AS
        Name, Format(Nz (Sum( Orders.OrderTotal ),0),'cur-
        rency') AS Sales  FROM Customers LEFT OUTER JOIN
        Orders ON Customers.CustomerID = Orders.CustomerID
        WHERE Customers.State = 'CA' And Customers.City =
        'Claremont' GROUP BY Customers.CustomerID,
        Customers.LastName, Customers.FirstName ORDER BY
        Customers.LastName, Customers.FirstName
```

If you can see what is wrong, you can copy the text from the Immediate window, paste it into a blank query window, and run the query to see why you are not getting the expected results.

Form: Linked Lists 05a

You can even eliminate the copy-and-paste operation by having Visual Basic directly write the SQL Text to a query and automatically open the query for you. The following function stores the SQLText passed as an argument to the query TestSQL, and then uses the OpenQuery method to display data set.

```
Function TestSQL(SQLText)
    CurrentDb.QueryDefs("TestSQL").SQL = SQLText
    DoCmd.OpenQuery "TestSQL"
End Function
```

Module: Functions, Procedure: TestSQL

You can automatically test the SQL statements as the procedure executes by inserting the statement TestSQL .RowSource into a procedure, as shown in this code snippet:

```
With Me.List4
    .RowSource = _
    "SELECT Customers.CustomerID, " & _
    "lastname & ', ' & Firstname AS Name, " & _
    "Format(Nz(Sum(Orders.OrderTotal),0),'currency') AS Sales
        " & _
    ... statements
    TestSQL .RowSource
    .ColumnCount = 3
    .ColumnWidths = "0;1.5 in; .5 in"
    .Requery
End With
```

Form: Linked Lists 05b

Right-aligned columns

You may have noticed that when you display numeric data in a list box, the data is always aligned on the left side of the column rather than the right. Access treats all the data displayed in list box columns as text — and therefore left-aligns all columns. To many people, this is a minor inconvenience, but you can approximate right-alignment of numbers by creating and using some special functions. They create the appearance of right-alignment by padding the column information with blank spaces.

For example, suppose you want to right align $34.50 in a column that is 15 characters wide. The first step is to count the number of characters in the text, in this case 6. That leaves 10 characters to make the total column width. To right-align the text, you would have to add 10 spaces to the front of the text.

The function PaddedCurrency performs this operation. The function requires two arguments: a numeric value and a number that indicates the size of the column.

The first step is to convert the numeric value to formatted text, using the Format function. For example, 34.5 would become $34.50. Next, use the String function to produce a set of spaces equal to the difference between the length of the formatted number and the size of the column. As an example, $34.50 contains 6 characters. If the column width is 15, that means the String function returns a block of 9 spaces. Note: Chr(32) is equal to a space. The spaces are then combined with the text to form the padded text, which is returned as the result of the function.

```
Function PaddedCurrency(Num, Size)
    Dim Pad, Fmt
    Fmt = Format(Num, "currency")
    Pad = String(Size - Len(Fmt), Chr(32))
    PaddedCurrency = Pad & Fmt
End Function
```

You can test how this function works by entering the following command into the Immediate window. The text returned is indented, due to the spaces padded onto the front of the number.

```
? PaddedCurrency(34.5,15)
    $134.50
```

The `PaddedWhole` function is a variation of the `PaddedCurrency` function with the difference being that the format used for the number is a whole number format.

```
Function PaddedWhole(Num, Size)
    Dim Pad, Fmt
    Fmt = Format(Num, "0")
    Pad = String(Size - Len(Fmt), Chr(32))
    PaddedWhole = Pad & Fmt
End Function
```

Module: Functions

You can apply these two functions to the problem of right-alignment of list-box data. The embedded SQL statement in the following Visual Basic procedure uses the `PaddedCurrency` and `PaddedWhole` functions to produce padded text that gives the appearance of being right aligned (see Figure 5-18).

```
Private Sub List4_AfterUpdate()
    With Me.List8
        .RowSource = _
        "SELECT OrderID, " & _
        "DateValue([OrderDate]) AS [Date]," & _
        "PaddedWhole(Items,13)AS Item," & _
        "PaddedCurrency(ExtPriceTotal,16) As Cost," & _
        "PaddedCurrency(Shipping,16) As Freight," & _
        "PaddedCurrency(SalesTax,16) AS Tax, " & _
        "PaddedCurrency(OrderTotal,16) AS Total " & _
        "FROM Orders WHERE CustomerID = " & Me.List4 & _
        " ORDER BY DateValue([OrderDate]) DESC"
        .ColumnCount = 7
        .ColumnHeads = True
        .ColumnWidths = "0;.5 in;.5 in;" & _
        "7.5 in;.75 in;.75 in;.75 in"
        .Requery
    End With
End Sub
```

Figure 5-18:
Numeric
data is right-
aligned in
list-box
columns.

Form: Linked Lists 07

References

In this chapter, you encounter two different types of `Recordset` objects: ADO
and DAO. Data Access Objects, a system developed by Microsoft, gave
Access 95 a uniform set of objects, properties, and methods you could use in
Visual Basic to manipulate ODBC databases (such as Access MDB, FoxPro,
and SQL Server). DAO was designed to work with relational databases built
by using standard SQL structures such as tables, views (queries), and fields
with strictly defined data types.

The following years saw a dramatic growth in interest in the Internet.
Microsoft shifted its entire corporate focus toward the Internet and Internet-
compatible products. One change was the development of ADO (ActiveX Data
Objects) as a replacement for DAO. The primary difference between DAO and
ADO is that DAO assumes the data source to be a traditional relational database. ADO is designed to accommodate non-relational as well as relational
databases within a single set of objects, properties, and methods. Instead of
assuming that data is organized in databases that contain tables and tables
that contain fields, ADO takes a more flexible approach by dealing with a
`Connection` object. In ADO, you establish a connection to a data source
(whether relational or non-relational).

Access 2000 supports the use of both ADO and DAO within Visual Basic. You
can use one or the other, or both, in a database. However, the default system
for Access 2000 is ADO. If you need to use DAO, as we did in this chapter
when I discussed the use of the `RecordsetClone` property, you must establish a reference to DAO.

Visual Basic allows you to integrate objects, methods, and properties from a variety of components by loading reference libraries. You can display or alter the references used in any Access 2000 database by doing the following:

1. **Select the Modules tab in the database window.**

2. **Open any existing module in the design mode, or open a new module.**

3. **Select the Tools⇨References command.**

   Access opens the Reference dialog box, shown in Figure 5-19. This box contains a list of all the object libraries of all types currently available on your system. Note that the list you see will vary with your system — various applications install different libraries. The checked boxes represent the currently loaded object libraries. Your Visual Basic program can contain references to any of the objects, methods, and properties included in any of the checked references.

   By default, Access 2000 includes Visual Basic for Applications, Microsoft Access 9.0, OLE Automation, and ActiveX Data Objects libraries. If you want to include other types of objects in your programs, you can select their object libraries by checking them. If you want to include DAO in your programs, you must add a reference to that library. If you do not do so, any code that contains reference to DAO objects such as `TableDefs` or `QueryDefs` produces an "object not found" error when you attempt to execute the code.

4. **Scroll down the list until you find Microsoft DAO 3.6 Library.**

5. **Check the box if it is not already checked.**

6. **Click OK.**

You can now use DAO references in your Visual Basic code. Office 2000 includes reference libraries for Office applications such as Excel, Word, and Outlook. To find out how to integrate these applications and their objects into Access programs using Visual Basic, see Chapter 11.

Figure 5-19:
The References dialog box allows you to add or remove object libraries from a given database.

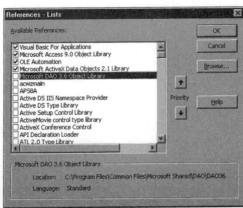

Keep these points in mind about references:

- ✔ References are part of the database so that once you add a reference, all the modules in that database can use it. References are stored as part of the MDB file. Each new database you create begins with the default set of references. If you use other libraries, you must select them each time you create a new database.

- ✔ If you move a database to a different computer, you may find that the new computer does not have all the same reference libraries.

- ✔ If you attempt to run a database on a computer that does not have all the references for which your database is configured, you may find that your database doesn't operate properly, even though none of the code you are executing involves the actual use of the libraries. For example, if you attempt to run a query that contains a `Format()` function, you may get an error saying that this function is not available in a query. The message is misleading; it is usually caused by a missing reference. You can check for missing references by opening any module and opening the References dialog box (refer to Figure 5-19). If a reference is missing, it appears on the list as checked but with the word `MISSING` in front of the name. Often, a missing reference (even one that you are not actively using) keeps Access from working with the other valid reference libraries such as Visual Basic. To fix the problem, uncheck the `MISSING` references and close the dialog box. Your code should execute properly.

- ✔ ADO and DAO use the same name for some objects. For example, the `Recordset` and `Field` objects appear in both reference libraries. By default, a `Recordset` or `Field` object is considered to be a ADO reference. If you want to use a DAO object, you must add DAO as a prefix. The following statement specifically defines RS as a DAO Recordset.

```
Dim Rs as DAO.Recordset
```

- ✔ If you only want to use DAO objects and not ADO, you can remove the ADO reference library by unchecking the reference in the References dialog box. You can then use DAO objects without the prefix because the ADO library isn't loaded.

Chapter 6

Data and Forms

∙ ∙

In This Chapter

▶ Linking to data sources

▶ Creating a schema table

▶ Setting up a workgroup

▶ SQL Server data sources

▶ Attaching a SQL Server table

∙ ∙

*T*he basis of any Access program is dual: the data sources and the forms in which those sources are displayed. In this chapter, you find out how to manipulate data sources using Visual Basic. In addition, you discover techniques for dealing with data sources from within forms.

> **Database Folder: Chapter 6**
> **Database File: FormsAndData.MDB**

To begin this chapter, open the database for Chapter 6, FormsAndData.MDB.

Linking to Data Sources

The simplest type of Access database is one in which all the elements of your program (tables, queries, forms, reports, and so on) are stored in a single file. This works perfectly well when you are creating databases for your personal use. However, when you build an application, your goal may be to create a program that is used by many different people to whom you distribute or (we can pray) sell your program.

Although it is possible to distribute a program as a single MDB file, you can run into a problem if you need to fix or update the program. The problem occurs because each of your users has already entered specific data into the tables that support your application. If you replace their existing MDB files with a new version of the program, you wipe out their data.

The traditional approach is to separate your Access objects into two different MDB files, as shown in Figure 6-1.

- ✔ **Program MDB.** This file contains all the elements of your program that the user will not change. This includes the queries, forms, reports, and Visual Basic code modules you create.
- ✔ **Data MDB.** This MDB is the one in which all user-specific information entered in tables is stored.

Figure 6-1: A program is typically divided between a program MDB and a data source MDB.

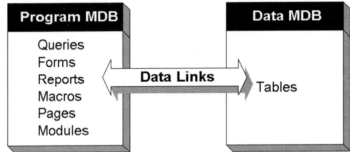

By dividing the program into these two parts, you can easily update an application by replacing the program MDB with a new version, while leaving the data MDB in place and unchanged.

Another advantage of separate data and program files is that you can locate the files on different computers within a network. For example, in order to improve performance, you might place a copy of your program MDB on the local hard drive of each user's computer, but have all the programs link to the same data MDB — located on a shared network drive. This approach speeds up the program because loading the graphic interface of the forms is usually the slowest part of an Access program. Note that you need to have all users join a workgroup if they are to share a common data MDB. I discuss setting up an Access workgroup (which is different from setting up a Windows workgroup) later in this chapter.

The key to this type of arrangement is the use of linked or attached tables. A *linked or attached table* is one that physically resides in a different MDB file but is accessible from your program MDB. In all regards, with the exception of modifying the structure, an attached table behaves like a table that is stored in the same MDB. This means that building and using forms and reports is exactly the same regardless of whether the tables involved are in the same database file — they can be linked tables.

One further note to keep in mind is that Access is not limited to linking to other Access files as data sources. Access, in conjunction with the ODBC system, can link to a variety of data sources, such as Dbase DBF files or SQL Server tables and views.

Accessing external databases

In Chapter 1, I introduce the concept of the CurrentDB object. CurrentDB represents the contents of the database in which you are currently working. So far, all examples in this book have utilized tables stored in the CurrentDB. However, the fact that you can have a CurrentDB implies that you can work with databases other than the current database. These databases are referred to as *external databases* — they physically reside in a file other than the one you are working on. Keep in mind that any MDB file you can locate on your network is a potential data source.

If you want to access the data in an MDB file that resides on a shared network drive, you must have full read/write permissions (as defined by your network administrator) to utilize the tables in that file. Access is not fully functional with read-only files.

The key to using tables stored in another Access *database* is the OpenDatabase method. This method allows you to create a *database object* through which you can gain access to the tables stored in Access databases other than the one in which you are writing your code.

The following procedure is a simple example of how you can get information from an external database. The Dim statement creates a variable that is defined as a database object. The Set command uses the OpenDatabase method to specify which MDB file the DBSource variable is connected to. After the connection is made, you can perform operations on the contents of the external data exactly as you would the current database. In this case, the message box displays a count of the number tables contained in the external database.

```
Sub Linking01()
    'counts tables in an external database
    Dim DBSource As Database
    Set DBSource = OpenDatabase("Datatables.mdb")
    MsgBox DBSource.TableDefs.Count
End Sub
```

The OpenDatabase() method requires the exact name of the file you want to access. You can include any valid path name, including network paths. The following example opens a file called WBase2.MDB located in a folder on server RKPNTSRV2.

```
Set DBSource = _
    OpenDatabase("\\rkpntsrv2\enotech\wbase2.mdb")
```

Keep in mind that the count returned by the `Count` method is the total
number of tables, including system tables, in the external database. For practical purposes, you are only interested in the user-defined tables stored in the
external database. `Linking02()` returns a count of the user-defined tables
only. This procedure takes advantage of the `For Each...Next` structure that
allows you to enumerate the members of a collection. In this case, the collection is the `TableDefs` collection of the external database.

The user-defined tables are located by checking the `Attributes` property of
the table definition. An `Attributes` value of zero means the table is a user-
defined table. Note that you must have two object variables, one a `Database`
and the other a `TableDef`, because you need to access both the database
and the table definitions within that database.

```
Sub Linking02()
    'count user defined tables in an external database
    Dim DBS As Database, Tbl As TableDef
    Dim TCount
    Set DBS = OpenDatabase("Datatables.mdb")
    For Each Tbl In DBS.TableDefs
        If Tbl.Attributes = 0 Then
            TCount = TCount + 1
        End If
    Next
    MsgBox TCount & " tables in " & DBS.Name
End Sub
```

`Linking03()` accesses the same data, but it returns a list of the table names
as well as the count. This is accomplished by using the `Name` property of the
table to build a text string, and variable name `TableList`, which accumulates
the list of names. The result of the procedure is shown in Figure 6-2.

```
Sub Linking03()
    'list user tables in an external database
    Dim DBS As Database
    Dim Tbl As TableDef
    Dim Tablelist, TCount
    Set DBS = OpenDatabase("Datatables.mdb")
    For Each Tbl In DBS.TableDefs
        If Tbl.Attributes = 0 Then
            TCount = TCount + 1
            Tablelist = Tablelist & Tbl.Name & vbCrLf
        End If
    Next
    MsgBox TCount & " tables in " & DBS.Name & vbCrLf & _
        Tablelist
End Sub
```

Figure 6-2:
A list of
tables
stored in an
external
database.

Module: DataAccess

Access 2000 can access tables stored in earlier versions, such as Access 97, Access 95, and Access 2.0 formats.

Attaching a table with Visual Basic

The previous procedures created a temporary channel of access to the external database in order to extract some information. The connection lasted only as long as the database object variables. When the procedure ended, the variables and the connection they represented were discarded.

In most applications, you use a set of externally stored tables for which you want to create a permanent connection because you use these tables for the forms and reports in your program. You can create these links using the File⇨Get External Data!⇨Link Tables menu command.

You can also do the same thing with Visual Basic. The key to performing this operation and a number of other operations that are related to external data is the *connection string* — a text item that contains information needed by Access to make a connection to an external data source. Although the current example uses an Access MDB as the data source, a connection string can be used to connect to a wide variety of data sources. The exact contents of a connection string vary depending upon the type of database you are connecting to. Connection strings use this general form:

```
"type;options;DATABASE=databasefile"
```

The simplest connection strings are those used for other Access MDB files because you do not have to specify the database type because the default is Access MDB. Note that the semicolon at the beginning of the string is required even though you do not have to fill in the database type when the file is an MDB.

```
";DATABASE=Datatables.mdb"
```

To attach an external table using Visual Basic, you must perform the following operations in your code:

- ✔ CreateTableDef. Using the current database object, define a TableDef variable. The name assigned to the variable is the name that appears in the tables list in the database window. Keep in mind that this name does not have to match the name of the table to which you are linking. For example, if you are linking to the Customers table in an external database, you might call the table Remote_Customers to indicate that it is an attached table.

- ✔ SourceTableName. Specify which table in the external database is the one that you want to link. Keep in mind that this name must match the name of a table in the external database.

- ✔ Connection. Specify the connection string that specifies the data source for the linked table.

- ✔ Append. Use the Append method of the current database's TableDefs collection to save the link as a permanent part of the current database.

The following procedure shows how to link the Customers table in Datatables.MDB to the current database.

```
Sub Linking04()
    'link a specific table in an external database
    Dim FrontDB As DAO.Database
    Dim Lnk As DAO.TableDef

    Set FrontDB = CurrentDb
    Set Lnk = FrontDB.CreateTableDef("Customers")
    Lnk.SourceTableName = "Customers"
    Lnk.Connect = ";DATABASE=Datatables.mdb"
    FrontDB.TableDefs.Append Lnk
End Sub
```

You may have noticed that the Dim statements in the procedure include the prefix DAO for object types such as Database and TableDef. As I mention in Chapter 5, Access 2000 contains two different data object libraries, ADO and DAO. ADO, the default, is used to extract data from a wide variety of sources but it does not support objects that manipulate the underlying data structures. If you want to write Visual Basic code that links, creates, or modifies not just the data in the tables but the table structures themselves, you must use DAO objects. In the FormsandData.MDB file, I have used the References dialog box to include both ADO and DAO object libraries. However, even though ADO and DAO work with different objects, they share some common object names. Both ADO and DAO have an object named Database, which even though they share the same name, they support a different set of methods and properties. If you simply say AS Database in a statement, Access uses the default object model, in this case ADO. Adding the prefix DAO to the object type ensures that the variable is defined as the correct object type.

You can check the results of this procedure by selecting the Tables tab in the database window. Access marks an attached Access table with an arrow icon.

You can reverse the process by unlinking the attached table, using the Delete method of the TableDefs collection. Keep in mind that the effect of the Delete method is quite different for an attached table from what it is for a table contained in the current database. When you delete an attached table, you are simply deleting the link from the current database. The table and its data, stored in the external file, are unaffected by this operation. You can re-establish the link without any loss of data. Conversely, if you apply the same Delete method to a table stored in the current database, the table is erased and you cannot recover the data.

This procedure removes the link to the Customers table that Linking04() created.

```
Sub Linking05()
    'unlink a specific table in an external database
    CurrentDb.TableDefs.Delete "Customers"
End Sub
```

If you look at the Tables tab of the database window, you may still see the table listed. This is not accurate — the link has been deleted. However, you need to force Access to refresh the display in order to get an accurate listing. You can force the change by clicking on any other tab and then clicking back to the Tables tab.

Passing values to a procedure

The code that attaches a table from an external database is almost always the same, with the exception of two names: the database file name and the table name. In Linking04() and Linking05(), the names were included in the code as literal text. This means that each time you execute the procedure, the exact same operation is performed. If you want to delete or attach a different table, you edit the Visual Basic code to include the new name.

A more efficient approach is to replace references to specific names with variables. Look at the following statement. The name of the new table definition is not actually specified. Instead the name of a variable, TableName, is inserted into the section of the statement that had previously been occupied by a specific name, such as "Customers".

```
Set Lnk = FrontDB.CreateTableDef(TableName)
```

The trick is to find a way to assign different names to the variables, such as `"Customers"`, `"Orders"`, or `"OrderDetails"`, outside" to the `TableName` variable, without having to modify the code.

The solution comes in the form of procedure parameters. A *parameter* is a value that a procedure uses to perform the operations coded into that procedure. The following statement executes the `Linking06` procedure and passes text values to the procedure. *Passing* a parameter means that you are feeding the procedure data that will be assigned to variables in that procedure, as shown in Figure 6-3.

```
Linking06 "Datatables.mdb","customers"
```

Figure 6-3:
Parameters
are passed
from one
statement
to a
procedure.

```
Linking06 "Datatables.mdb","customers"

Sub Linking06(DataBaseName, TableName)
    Dim FrontDB As DAO.Database
    Dim Lnk As DAO.TableDef
    Set FrontDB = CurrentDb
    Set Lnk = FrontDB.CreateTableDef(TableName)
    Lnk.SourceTableName = TableName
    Lnk.Connect = ";DATABASE=" & DataBaseName
    FrontDB.TableDefs.Append Lnk
End Sub
```

In order for a procedure to be able to use parameters, you must create parameter variables in the `Sub` or `Function` statement that begins a procedure. The following example defines two variables (`DataBaseName` and `TableName`) for the `Linking06` procedure.

```
Sub Linking06(DataBaseName, TableName)
```

One critical note: The number and order of the parameters in both statements must match exactly.

You can make sure that you have assigned the correct values to the correct parameters by using named arguments (see Chapter 1 for more details). When you create a procedure, the argument names are the variable names you place in the `Sub` or `Function` statements. For the `Linking06` procedure, the argument names are `DataBaseName` and `TableName`, respectively. The following statement illustrates the use of named arguments. In order to run `Linking06`, open the Immediate window (Ctrl+G) and enter this statement:

```
Linking06 DataBaseName:= "Datatables.mdb", _
    TableName:= "customers"
```

When completed, the procedure has attached the Customers table to the current database once again.

Using optional parameters

Now that you have created a generalized procedure for attaching tables in other Access MDB files, you can go a step further and create a procedure that adds or removes an attached table. In creating this procedure, think about these new concepts:

- **Switch parameter.** In the previous procedure, Linking06, the parameters passed to the procedure were values required by statements within the procedure. A switch parameter is used for a different purpose. A *switch parameter* is a value passed to a procedure in order to determine which action the procedure will execute. For example, if the procedure you create can either add or remove an attached table, you need to have a switch parameter to determine which action should be performed.

- **Select Case.** Use the Select Case structure to group one or more statements into blocks. Each block is associated with a specific value that might be assigned to a variable. When the procedure is executed, the block of code that is actually executed depends upon the value assigned to the variable that is associated with the Select Case statement.

  The diagram in Figure 6-4 shows how a Select Case structure works. The Select Case statement contains the name of a variable; in this case, it is a parameter variable called AddorDrop. Following the Select Case statement are several Case statements. Each Case is associated with a specific value, such as "Drop" or "Add". After each Case statement are one or more Visual Basic statements. The arrows in Figure 6-4 trace the flow of execution in the procedure. You can see that the execution follows different paths depending on the specific value assigned to the variable AddorDrop.

- **Optional parameters.** If you look at the following procedure, you can see that the two operations controlled by the Select Case structure do not require the same set of parameters. When you add a new attached table, the operation requires two parameters (DBName and TableName) and the operation that removes an attached table requires only the TableName parameter. Normally Visual Basic requires that the number of parameters listed in a statement that executes a procedure must match exactly the number of parameters list in the Sub or Function statement. You can use the Optional keyword to specify one or more parameters that are not required. In the example, the DBName parameter is designated as Optional. Visual Basic allows you to execute this procedure with two or three parameters. You must remember which option requires the optional parameter. If you attempt to attach a table without specifying the DBName, Visual Basic attempts to carry out the operation. However, the operation fails because it doesn't know which database to use as the data source.

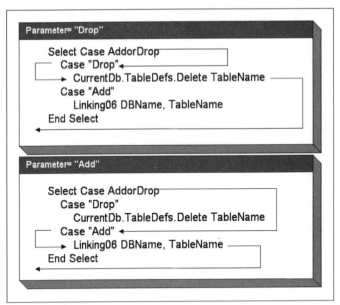

Figure 6-4:
A Select
Case struc-
ture
controls
which state-
ments are
executed
based on
the value of
a specified
expression.

```
Sub AddDropTable(AddorDrop, TableName, Optional DBName)
    'single operation to add or drop tables
    Select Case AddorDrop
        Case "Drop"
            CurrentDb.TableDefs.Delete TableName
        Case "Add"
            Linking06 DBName, TableName
    End Select
End Sub
```

Use the `AddorDrop` procedure to remove the link to the `Customers` table by entering the following statement into the Immediate window.

```
AddOrDrop "drop","Customers"
```

All optional parameters must be grouped together on the right side of any parameter list in a `Sub` or `Function` statement. This means that once you designate any parameter as `Optional`, all parameters listed after that one must also be `Optional`. Further, you must repeat the `Optional` keyword before each parameter; for example, `Sub Ex01(First, Last, Optional State, Optional Zip)`.

Linking an entire database

Up to this point, you needed to know the name of the table that you wanted to attach to the current database. But suppose you simply wanted to link all the user-defined tables in the data source to the current database. Can you do this automatically, without having to know the names of the tables in advance?

I already touched on the answer in this chapter in the Linking03 example. Recall that this procedure extracted a list of user tables in the specified database. You can then use the names extracted from the source database as the table names needed for linking tables.

The LinkAllTables procedure shown in the following code applies this concept. It uses two database objects. FronDB (for *front end*) is the current database into which you insert the links. BackDB (for *back end*) is the database that contains the source tables. The procedure then uses a For Each...Next structure to process the entire TableDefs collection. The Name property of the TableDef object is used to insert the current table name into the statements that perform the actual linking. The Attributes property is used to select only user-defined tables from the source database.

```
Sub LinkAllTables(DBName)
    'link all user tables in source database
    Dim FrontDB As DAO.Database, BackDB As DAO.Database
    Dim Tbl As DAO.TableDef, Lnk As DAO.TableDef

    Set FrontDB = CurrentDb
    Set BackDB = OpenDatabase(DBName)

    For Each Tbl In BackDB.TableDefs
        If Tbl.Attributes = 0 Then
            Set Lnk = FrontDB.CreateTableDef( _
                Name:=Tbl.Name)
            Lnk.SourceTableName = Tbl.Name
            Lnk.Connect = ";DATABASE=" & BackDB.Name
            FrontDB.TableDefs.Append Lnk
        End If
    Next
End Sub
```

Execute the procedure by entering the following statement into the Immediate window. Note that supplying the file extension .MDB with the database name isn't required because you are working with the default database type Access MDB.

```
linkalltables "datatables"
```

This procedure links all 11 tables contained in the DataTables database to the current database. You can check by looking at the Tables tab in the database window. Remember, you may need to force Access to refresh this window in order to see the newly linked tables.

Dropping all links

The opposite of linking a set of tables from an external source is to remove all of the external links. The following procedure scans the current database's TableDefs collection and deletes any attached tables. Note the use of the Attributes property to select only those tables that are attached tables while leaving system and local tables alone.

```
Sub DropAllLinks()
    Dim Lnk As DAO.TableDef
    For Each Lnk In CurrentDb.TableDefs
        If Lnk.Attributes = dbAttachedTable Then
            CurrentDb.TableDefs.Delete Lnk.Name
        End If
    Next
End Sub
```

How did I know the name of the built-in constant, dbAttachedTable, used to specify the value of the Attribute that indicated the table definition was an attached table? The Visual Basic editor supports a special window called the Object Browser, shown in Figure 6-5. You can open the Object Browser from any module window by choosing View➪Object Browser or using the F2 shortcut key.

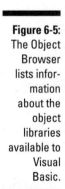

Figure 6-5:
The Object Browser lists information about the object libraries available to Visual Basic.

The Object Browser provides lists of objects, properties, methods, and constants included in all of the open object libraries. For example, to find the constant that specifies an attached table, perform the following steps:

1. **Open the Object Browser by pressing F2.**

   In the combo box located in the upper-left corner of the dialog box, open the drop list to select the library that corresponds to the object model you are working with.

2. **Select DAO from the combo box.**

   The Classes list now lists all the object classes in the DAO model. The first class in any library is `<globals>`. This class contains all the constants in the library listed alphabetically.

3. **Click `<globals>` and then click `dbAttachedTable`.**

   The gray box at the bottom of the window displays information about this constant (refer to Figure 6-5). The box tells you the decimal and hex value of the constant and displays a hyperlink to the group to which it belongs. In the case of `dbAttachedTable`, it belongs to the `TableDefAttributeEnum` class.

4. **Click on the green hyperlink `TableDefAttributeEnum`.**

The browser locates the `TableDefAttributeEnum` class in the Classes window and displays six names in the members window. The members list shows all of the constants that are related to table definition attributes.

You can use the browser to explore the object model. If you find an item you want to copy into your code, simply select it, press Ctrl+C to put it in memory, and then return to your code and press Ctrl+V to insert the name.

ON THE CD

> **Module: DataAccess**

Attaching tables with a form

You now have two procedures that are related to linking tables: `DropAll Links` and `LinkAllTables`. Figure 6-6 shows a format that lists all the MDB files in the current folder and allows you to select one of the names. When you press the button on the right side of the form, all the current links are dropped and new links are established to the tables in the selected database.

Using a loop

The list of files displayed in the form shown in Figure 6-6 raises a new programming challenge. In Chapter 5, all of the list boxes displayed are populated with data retrieved from database tables using a SQL statement to select the fields and records required. In this case, the contents of the list box reflect data about the files that exist in a disk folder. This information is not part of the Access database; nor is the Windows 95/98 folder system a relational database that can be queried using SQL.

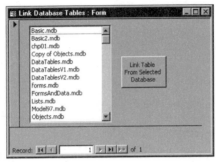

Figure 6-6:
You can
attach all of
the tables
from a
external
database.

In order to get the list of files shown in the form in Figure 6-6, you need to use some new techniques to first acquire information from the operating system about files and then populate a list box with data that is not accessible with a SQL query.

The solution to the first problem involves the use of the Visual Basic `Dir()` function. The `Dir()` is a bit of an odd hangover from Basic's past. The function operates in two distinct but related modes: *findfirst* and *findnext*. To operate `Dir()` in the findfirst mode, you include a Windows/DOS file specification as a parameter. Enter the following statement into the Immediate window.

```
? dir("*.mdb")
```

Visual Basic displays the name of the first file, if any, in the current folder that matches the file specification, for example, Basic.MDB. But what if more files match the specification? To get those names you execute the `Dir()` function in the findnext mode. This is done by using the function in another statement without a parameter.

```
? dir()
```

Visual Basic displays the next file that matches the specification assigned to the previous `Dir()` function that was entered in the findfirst mode. How can you tell when you have gotten to the end of the file list? The `Dir()` function executed in the findnext mode returns an empty text string if no more matching files are found. For example, the following statement is False if there are more files to list but True if you have reached the end of the list.

```
? dir() = ""
```

Keep in mind that the `Dir()` function returns the file names in the order in which they appear in the disk directory. This order is not alphabetical but random because Windows writes the names of the files using the first available entry space in the disk directory.

The Dir() function solves the problem of obtaining file names, but the way it operates poses a new programming problem. In order to obtain a full list of the desired file names, you must repeat the Dir() function over and over until it produces a blank result. You do not know in advance the number of files that will be retrieved. You can only repeat the operation and wait until you get a result that indicates that you can stop.

Visual Basic includes a structure that allows you to express exactly the logic I have just described. The structure uses two statements.

✔ **Do.** This statement marks the beginning of a block of one or more statements that need to be repeated. In the current example, you want to repeat the Dir() function to obtain a full list of files.

✔ **Loop.** This statement marks the turnaround point in your code for the block of statements you want to repeat. When the Loop statement is encountered, the flow of execution stops reading down your program code and recycles back to the location in the code where the Do statement is found creating a repeating loop.

You can use either the Do or Loop statements to specify the condition that determines if the loop should repeat. In order to facilitate the logic of looping, you can use special keywords with Do or Loop.

✔ **Until.** This operator continues the loop until the specified expression is True. The following statement continues looping until the variable Fname is equal to an empty text string.

```
Do Until FName = ""
```

✔ **While.** This operator continues the loop as long as the specified expression is true. As soon as it is False, the loop terminates. The following example continues the loop as long as the length — Len() function — of the file name is greater than zero. An empty text string would have a length of zero, making the expression False and stopping the loop.

```
Do While Len(FName) > 0
```

One issue is still unresolved: How do you get the names retrieved by the Dir() function into the list box control? The answer is supplied by the RowSourceType property of the list box control. The default value for this property is Table/Query, which means the list box expects a SQL statement as the RowSource. However, you can also set RowSourceType to "Value List", which allows the RowSource to be a text string that contains a list of items separated by semicolons. This example displays the two names in the list box control.

```
With Me.List0
    .RowSourceType = "Value List"
    .RowSource = "DataTables.MDB;DatatablesV1;"
End With
```

The procedure puts of all of these ideas together into a single working structure. Note the use of the loop, shown in Figure 6-7, to repeat the `Dir()` function as many times as necessary to obtain all the matching files. In this case, an `Until` operator is used to repeat the loop until the `Dir()` function returns an empty string. Appending each file named stored in `FName` to the `FList` variable and tacking on a semicolon creates the list of file names. When the loop is complete, `FList` contains the completed list for display in the list box.

```
Private Sub Form_Open(Cancel As Integer)
    Dim FName, FList
    FName = Dir("*.mdb")
    Do Until FName = ""
        FList = FList & FName & ";"
        FName = Dir()
    Loop
    With Me.List0
        .RowSourceType = "Value List"
        .RowSource = FList
    End With
End Sub
```

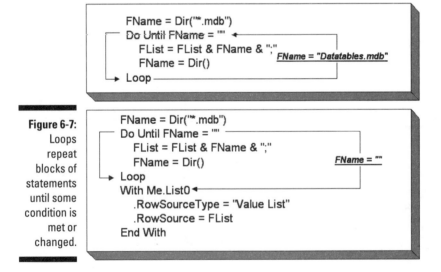

Figure 6-7:
Loops repeat blocks of statements until some condition is met or changed.

The code that actually attaches the tables from the selected data is rather lean. All you need to do is drop the old links and pass the name of the file selected in the list box to the `LinkAllTables` procedure.

```
Private Sub Command3_Click()
    DropAllLinks
    LinkAllTables DBName:=List0
End Sub
```

> **Form: Link Database Tables**

Refreshing links

In some cases, switching database sources is a matter of selecting a different copy of the same basic data source. For example, suppose you create an application that tracks sales. You may create one data source file for retail sales and a different copy of the data source for wholesale sales.

This means that all of the data sources to which you want to attach have the same set of tables but different data. If you wanted to switch your application from retail to wholesale operations, you could save some time by simply changing the connection string for the attached tables rather than dropping and adding all the attached tables.

The following procedure contained in the form Update Links uses the name of the database selected in the list box control to change the Connect property of the attached table. The Refreshlink method then alters the table's link to attach to the same source table in a different database file.

```
Private Sub Command3_Click()
    Dim T As DAO.TableDef
    For Each T In CurrentDb.TableDefs
        If T.Attributes = dbAttachedTable Then
            With T
                .Connect = ";DATABASE=" & Me.List0
                .RefreshLink
            End With
        End If
    Next
End Sub
```

> **Form: Update Links**

Creating a Schema Table

When you are creating a database application, the names of the tables and fields are key items of information. This is especially true if you are working with a set of tables you did not design. The list of tables and fields is called the database *schema*.

In Access 2000, you must open a table in the design mode to see a list of its fields. Browsing a list of all the fields in all the tables isn't easy. You can produce reports with the Documenter (Tools⇨Analyze⇨Documenter), but that only produces a printed report. What I like to work with is a table, usually called Schema, that lists all the fields in all the tables. However, manually entering all this information into a table would be tedious, difficult, and time consuming — three strikes already.

However, you don't need to do any of that manually. You can use the DAO objects to write a Visual Basic procedure that gathers all the required information about any database you select.

Creating the schema table

The first step is to create a table to hold the schema information. Although you can create this table manually through the Access 2000 interface, here are a couple reasons why you may want to write a procedure that creates a new table using Visual Basic.

- ✔ You can integrate table creation into your Visual Basic programs so that tables can be created on the fly whenever they are needed.
- ✔ You can create the new tables in the current database or in an external database.

The first step is to look at how a table is created with DAO. The key concept is the idea of collections and appending new elements into a collection. In this case, three objects and two collections are involved.

- ✔ Create a new `Field` and append it to the `Fields` collection of a `TableDef`.
- ✔ Create a new `TableDef` and append it to the `TableDefs` collection of a database.

In order to carry out these operations, you need to use to DAO methods.

- ✔ `CreateField`. This method creates a new field object. You must supply a name for the field and a type. The constants used for data types can be found in the Object Browser in the DAO library under `DataTypeEnum`. If the type is text, you must also supply a size. This statement creates a new text field.

```
Set F = T.CreateField("TableName", dbText, 30)
```

- ✔ `CreateTableDef`. This method creates a new DAO `TableDef` object.

```
Set T = DB.CreateTableDef("Schema")
```

Note that you cannot append a `TableDef` to the database until you have assigned it one or more fields. This means that when you write a program that creates a new table, you begin by creating the new `TableDef` object, but you must then add all the fields before you append it. The following procedure builds a table with the fields ID, `TableName`, `FieldName`, `FieldType`, `FieldSize`, and `FieldAttributes`.

```
Sub CreateSchemaTable(TableName)
    Dim DB As DAO.Database, T As DAO.TableDef, F As DAO.Field
    Set DB = CurrentDb
    Set T = DB.CreateTableDef(TableName)
    Set F = T.CreateField("ID", dbLong)
    F.Attributes = dbAutoIncrField 'autonumber field
    T.Fields.Append F
    Set F = T.CreateField("TableName", dbText, 30)
    T.Fields.Append F
    Set F = T.CreateField("FieldName", dbText, 30)
    T.Fields.Append F
    Set F = T.CreateField("FieldType", dbLong)
    T.Fields.Append F
    Set F = T.CreateField("FieldSize", dbLong)
    T.Fields.Append F
    Set F = T.CreateField("FieldAttributes", dbLong)
    T.Fields.Append F
    DB.TableDefs.Append T
End Sub
```

One additional feature occurs in the ID field, which is assigned the `dbAutoIncrField` attribute. This creates an `AutoNumber` field. Create a new schema table by entering the following statement into the Immediate window.

```
createschematable "Schema"
```

Load a database schema

Now that you have a table to hold the schema data, you need to fill it with the details of a database you need to analyze and work with. All of the information you need is stored in the DAO `TableDefs` and `Fields` collections of the database you want to analyze. However, the goal here is not merely to display this information (as you do in Chapter 2) but to write that information into a permanent structure — that is, into a database table where it can be accessed, reported, and even queried.

In order to add new data to a table in Visual Basic, you have to work with the following objects.

✔ RecordSet Object/OpenRecordSet. The OpenRecordset method creates a RecordSet object based on any table (local or attached) in the current database. Once it's created, you can use the RecordSet object to add new records, edit existing records, or delete records. These changes flow through to the tables associated with the RecordSet object. In Access 2000, you can open a RecordSet with a SQL statement or, if you want to access the entire table, simply specify the name of the table. The following two statements are equivalent.

```
Set STable = CurrentDb.OpenRecordset("Schema")
Set STable = CurrentDb.OpenRecordset(
"Select * From schema")
```

✔ AddNew. This RecordSet method adds a new record to the table.

✔ Fields. After you create a new record, you can assign values to the fields. The following three statements show alternative syntax for setting field values. The results are equivalent. In most cases, the ! syntax is the simplest to use.

```
STable.Fields(1) = "Smith"
STable.Fields("LastName") = "Smith"
STable!LastName = "Smith"
```

✔ Update. This statement completes the addition of a new record to a RecordSet object. After the update is issued, the data is permanently part of the table.

Note that these objects are the same in ADO as they are in DOA, although there are some differences in the exact way they operate. For example, in ADO you do not need to issue an explicit Update after each new record is added. ADO automatically updates the recordset as soon as another .AddNew method is executed. DAO requires an explicit Update or the new data is discarded. The following code is valid for ADO and DAO but produces different results. In ADO, the code adds two records while in DAO the first record is not saved because it was not explicitly updated to the recordset.

```
With STable
    .AddNew
    !LastName = "Smith"
    .AddNew
    !LastName = "Jones"
    .Update
End with
```

Performing a query in Visual Basic

When you are loading a new set of data into an existing table, you may want to delete all the existing records before loading a new schema. The best way to clear a table is to use a SQL DELETE query. You can perform a DELETE or UPDATE query directly from Visual Basic using the following elements.

✔ QueryDef **object/CreateQueryDef method.** The CreateQueryDef method creates a QueryDef object. This object is the Visual Basic equivalent of an Access query grid. If you do not name the QueryDef, it becomes a temporary query that you can use in your program (discarded when the program is over). This statement creates Q, a temporary QueryDef object.

```
Set Q = CurrentDb.CreateQueryDef("")
```

✔ **SQL.** The SQL property of a QueryDef object is used to assign a SQL statement to the query. The following example sets the SQL for the Q QueryDef object to delete all customers in the state of Florida.

```
Q.SQL = "DELETE FROM Customers WHERE state = 'FL'"
```

✔ **Execute.** When you assign a SQL statement to a QueryDef object, the statement is not immediately executed. In order to perform the query, you must issue an Execute method.

The following example shows how a simple DELETE query executes in Visual Basic. This one deletes all of the data in the Schema table.

```
Set Q = CurrentDb.CreateQueryDef("")
Q.SQL = "DELETE FROM schema"
Q.Execute
```

Loading schema from a form

The form shown in Figure 6-8 is the result of the concepts outlined in the previous sections. The user selects a database from the list box on the left and the schema for that database is loaded into the Schema table and then displayed in the list box on the right.

The key section of code used in the form is contained in the LoadSchema procedure stored in the DataAccess modules. The section contains two For Each...Next structures nested within each other. The outer structure processes all of the tables within the selected database using the TableDefs collection. The inner structure processes all of the fields in the current table using the Fields collection.

Figure 6-8:
Program
loads data
schema
from
selected
database
file.

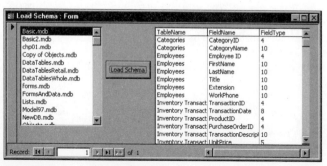

Inside of both is a `With` structure that adds a new record to the `STable` recordset. The attributes of the field object `Fld` are inserted into the fields in the `STable` recordset. When the loops finish, you have a complete map of the structure of the selected database.

```
For Each Tbl In BackDB.TableDefs
    If Tbl.Attributes = 0 Then
        For Each Fld In Tbl.Fields
            With STable
                .AddNew
                !TableName = Tbl.Name
                !FieldName = Fld.Name
                !FieldType = Fld.Type
                !FieldSize = Fld.Size
                !FieldAttributes = Fld.Attributes
                .Update
            End With
        Next Fld
    End If
Next Tbl
```

The `LoadSchema` procedure is integrated with the button on the form by adding the following code to the `Click` procedure of the button. This code executes the `LoadSchema` procedure for the database selected in the `List0` list box. After that is done, fields from the `Schema` table are selected for display in the list box on the right side of the form.

```
Private Sub Command3_Click()
    LoadSchema Me.List0, "schema"
    With Me.List6
        .RowSource = "Select TableName, FieldName, " & _
            "FieldType FROM schema"
        .ColumnHeads = True
        .ColumnCount = 3
    End With
End Sub
```

Form: Load Schema, Module: DataAccess

Writing a conversion function

If you look at the `FieldType` column displayed in the list box on the right side of the form in Figure 6-8, you notice that the data displayed. Figure 6-9 illustrates a better solution where actual descriptions of the field types replace the numbers.

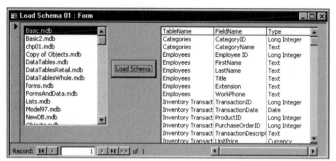

Access 2000 stores many of its values, such as field types and field attributes, as numeric values. When you display the numeric value for a data type, it is unlikely that you will know or remember what that value represents. In order to convert these arcane numbers into meaningful text, you need a conversion function. The following function is an example of a typical conversion function. It contains a `Select Case` structure that supplies a text description for each of the numeric values used by Access 2000 to indicate field type.

```
Function DataTypeName(TypeNumber)
    Select Case TypeNumber
        Case dbBoolean
            DataTypeName = "Yes/No"
        Case dbCurrency
            DataTypeName = "Currency"
        Case dbDate
            DataTypeName = "Date"
        Case dbDouble
            DataTypeName = "Double"
        Case dbLong
            DataTypeName = "Long Integer"
        Case dbMemo
            DataTypeName = "Memo"
        Case dbText
            DataTypeName = "Text"
    End Select
End Function
```

You can use these conversion functions in two ways:

✔ **At the point of output.** Converting data at the point of output means that you use the conversion function to convert the contents of numeric fields to text in any operation that displays the data. The following code shows a point of output conversion. The `DataTypeName()` function is used to convert the `FieldType` numeric data to text for the display in the list box control. Using the point of output method allows you to store the data in its original form — numeric, for example — but present the data in a text form. The main disadvantage of this method is that you must remember to convert the data each time you use it in a procedure or form.

```
Private Sub Command3_Click()
    LoadSchema Me.List0, "schema"
    With Me.List6
        .RowSource = "Select TableName, FieldName, " & _
            "DataTypeName(FieldType) AS Type FROM schema"
        .ColumnHeads = True
        .ColumnCount = 3
    End With
End Sub
```

Form: Load Schema 01, Module: DataAccess

✔ **At the point of input.** This approach converts the data before it is
stored in the table. The advantage of this method is that the conversion
takes place only once, when the data is first stored in the table. All subsequent uses of the data will simply reference the already converted
information so you don't need to remember to use a conversion function
in all your display operations. The disadvantage is that you must modify
the structure of the table to change fields from numeric to text. Further,
if you later want to use the data in the table to re-create the original
value — for example, use the schema to create a new table — you have
to create and use a second function that reverses the conversion by
translating text back to numbers.

The following code (LoadSchema01) performs point of input conversion.
Keep in mind that this change requires a modified schema table with a
text type field used for FieldType.

```
    For Each Tbl In BackDB.TableDefs
        If Tbl.Attributes = 0 Then
            For Each Fld In Tbl.Fields
                With STable
                    .AddNew
                    !TableName = Tbl.Name
                    !FieldName = Fld.Name
                    !FieldType = DataTypeName(Fld.Type)
                    !FieldSize = Fld.Size
                    !FieldAttributes = Fld.Attributes
                    .Update
                End With
            Next Fld
        End If
    Next Tbl
End Sub
```

**Form: Load Schema 02, Module: DataAccess, Procedure:
LoadSchema01**

Setting Up a Workgroup

If you plan to use Access 2000 databases on a network, you need to set up an Access workgroup. The workgroup manages multi-user access to a common data source and provides support for security features, such as password protection and selective permissions for database objects.

Keep in mind that an Access workgroup is not the same thing as a network workgroup. An Access workgroup consists of users who share the same MDW (Microsoft Database Workgroup) file. By default, the workgroup file is called SYSTEM.MDW. When Access 2000 is installed, a SYSTEM.MDW file is installed on the local hard drive of the computer. You can display the path of your workgroup file by entering the following statement into the Immediate window.

```
? systemdb
```

In order to set up a network workgroup, you need to create a SYSTEM.MDW on a network share. Then you need to have all of the users who want to work on a common data source join the workgroup. Joining a workgroup provides a commonly available point on the network for managing multi-user access to a common database.

You can join a workgroup on a permanent or temporary basis.

Joining a permanent workgroup

Joining a workgroup on a permanent basis makes sense when you have constant access to the shared network drive or folder where the SYSTEM.MDW is stored. Each time you start Access, it attempts to locate the SYSTEM.MDW file you have specified. If Access 2000 can't locate the file because of network access issues, then Access 2000 won't load.

For example, if you are using a laptop that is frequently used without a network connection, you probably don't want to permanently join a workgroup because most of the time your computer won't have access to the SYSTEM.MDW and you won't be able to use Access.

If you are working on a desktop computer attached at all times to the network, then you may want to join a permanent workgroup.

The program that sets your workgroup is called Wrkgadm.EXE, which is usually installed in the Office folder. Locate and double-click this file to launch the application, which displays the dialog box shown in Figure 6-10.

Figure 6-10:
The
Workgroup
Administra-
tor program.

If you are setting up a new workgroup, you must first create a new
SYSTEM.MDW file on the desired network share.

1. **Click the Create button.**

2. **Fill in your Name and Company name and create a workgroup ID.
   Click OK.**

3. **Use the Browse button to locate the network folder where you want to
   store the workgroup file. This can be the same folder as your shared
   database, but could be any shared folder.**

4. **Click OK twice. The program confirms the creation of the workgroup.
   Click OK and then click Exit.**

If you want to join an existing workgroup, run the Wrkgadm.EXE program and
do the following.

1. **Click the Join button.**

2. **Use the Browse button to locate the network folder containing the
   workgroup file. Click Open and then click OK.**

3. **When the program confirms that you have joined the workgroup,
   click OK and then click Exit.**

Joining a workgroup temporarily

If you do not have a permanent connection to the network folder that contains the workgroup SYSTEM.MDW, you may want to create a shortcut on
your desktop that you can run when you want to load Access 2000 with a specific workgroup file. The following is an example of the command line to
insert into a shortcut. This command uses the /wrkgrp switch to start
Access with a specific SYSTEM.MDW. In this example, the file is located on
drive J in the Enotech folder.

```
"C:\Program Files\Microsoft Office\Office\MSAccess.exe"
            /wrkgrp J:\enotech\system.mdw
```

SQL Server Data Sources

Microsoft SQL Server is a database service that runs on Windows NT servers. SQL Server is a relational database — data tables stored on a SQL Server can be accessed as attached tables from an Access 2000 database.

The primary difference between using an Access file as an external data source and using a SQL Server is that you do not directly access the files that SQL Server uses to store data. In fact, one of the main purposes of a SQL Server is to hide its file structure from network users. The SQL Server operates behind a wall of network security, which makes it much more difficult for unauthorized users to gain access to data than it is for them when the data is stored in an Access MDB file.

If you cannot specify the name of a file, how then do you attach a table stored in a SQL Server database? The answer is provided in the form of the ODBC (Open DataBase Connectivity) system, which is included with Office 2000. ODBC makes it possible to connect a wide variety of database sources to an Access database. In this case, I have narrowed the focus to SQL Server, but ODBC connects FoxPro, dBase, Oracle, and other non-Microsoft products to Access.

The key to ODBC connectivity is the DSN. DSN stands for Data Source Name. Defining a DSN consists of telling the ODBC system the details needed to establish a connection to a SQL Server. To create a DSN, you need to know the following:

- **Server name**. The name of the SQL Server. This is the name of the NT Server on which the SQL Server database service resides.

- **Database name.** The name of the database on the SQL Server that you want to access. One SQL Server can hold many databases.

- **Login/Password.** You can actually connect to a SQL Server without a login and password, but you won't be able to get any data or attach any tables. If you do not have a login and password, you need to see a database administrator who can provide you the access rights to the SQL Server.

You can create a DSN in two ways:

- **Control Panel.** The Windows Control Panel contains an applet installed by Office 2000 called ODBC Data Sources. This program provides a series of screens that help you create a DSN.

- `RegisterDatabase`. The `RegisterDatabase` method provides a tool in Visual Basic that creates a DSN. This method is functionally equivalent to using the ODBC applet.

The following procedure creates a new DSN on your system called MSAtoSQL using the RegisterDatabase method of the DBEngine object. The DBEngine object represents the Microsoft Jet Database program that runs as part of Access 2000.

The new DSN provides access to the Pubs database. The Pubs database is a sample database installed on all SQL Servers. If you have access to a SQL Server and you have permissions granted, you can duplicate the procedures in this section and get the same results.

Note that you must change the name of the server from RKPNTSR2 to the actual name of the SQL Server available to you. All the other settings stay the same.

```
Sub CreateDSN()
    Dim ServerName, DatabaseName, DSNName
    Dim ConnectionString

    'change to your server name
    ServerName = "rkpntsr2"

    DatabaseName = "pubs"
    DSNName = "MSAtoSQL"

    ConnectionString = _
        "Server=" & ServerName & vbCr & _
        "Database=" & DatabaseName & vbCr
    DBEngine.RegisterDatabase _
        dsn:=DSNName, _
        driver:="SQL Server", _
        silent:=True, _
        Attributes:=ConnectionString
End Sub
```

Create the DSN by entering the following statement into the Immediate window.

```
CreateDSN
```

After you establish the DSN, you can use it to connect to the tables in the Pubs database on the SQL Server.

| *Module: DataAccess* |

Connecting to a SQL Server database

One of the goals of the ODBC system is that any data source accessed through ODBC should have the same set of interface objects as any other DAO database. In practical terms, procedures written to work on a DAO source such as an Access MDB should work with another DAO database such as SQL Server. The only difference is the details of the command used to open the database. Other than that, all the other statements should operate without modification.

To test this theory, you can return to the first procedure written in this chapter. `Linking01` demonstrated that a Visual Basic procedure could perform operations, such as counting the number of tables in a database, on a data source that was external to the currently open database. The external database in this case was the Access database `Datatables.mdb`.

```
Sub Linking01()
    'counts tables in an external database
    Dim DBSource As Database
    Set DBSource = OpenDatabase("Datatables.mdb")
    MsgBox DBSource.TableDefs.Count
End Sub
```

If the concept of DAO working through ODBC is accurate, you should be able to execute the same procedure on a SQL Server database by simply changing the specific parameters used in the `OpenDatabase` method. In order to connect to an ODBC data source such as the SQL Server specified in the `MSAtoSQL` DSN, you need to use all four of the arguments supported by the `OpenDatabase` method. Keep in mind that there is no file name involved with a SQL Server. Instead, you are working through your DSN.

- ✔ **Name.** In this case, the name of the DSN through which you connect to the server.

- ✔ **Options.** This parameter is a constant from the DAO `DriverPromptEnum` class. By default, the ODBC applet automatically opens its user interface when an attempt is made to access an ODBC data source. The value `dbDriverNoPrompt` suppresses the applet and allows connection to an ODBC source directly through Visual Basic code.

- ✔ **ReadOnly.** Set to `True` if you want read-only access; False for read/write access.

- ✔ **Connection String.** Use this parameter to insert a connection string that includes any additional information needed to complete the connection. In this case, you need to include the login and password. In this book, I use the login *apd* with the password *dummies*. Substitute your actual login and password in place of these examples.

The following procedure is almost identical to Linking01 with the exception of the connection parameters. When you execute this procedure, it returns a count of the tables in the SQL Server Pubs database.

```
Sub LinkingSQL01()
    Dim DBSource As Database
    Set DBSource = OpenDatabase("MSAtoSQL", _
        dbDriverNoPrompt, False, _
        "ODBC;UID=apd;PWD=dummies")
    MsgBox DBSource.TableDefs.Count
End Sub
```

The next example is a copy of Linking03, the procedure that displays a list of the table in an external database. Once again, the only change needed to make this procedure work with a SQL Server source is to change the parameters used in the OpenDatabase method.

```
Sub LinkingSQL03()
    'list user tables in an external database
    Dim DBS As Database
    Dim Tbl As TableDef
    Dim Tablelist, TCount
    Set DBS = OpenDatabase("MSAtoSQL", _
        dbDriverNoPrompt, False, _
        "ODBC;UID=apd;PWD=dummies")
    For Each Tbl In DBS.TableDefs
        If Tbl.Attributes = 0 Then
            MsgBox Tbl.Name & " " & Tbl.Attributes
            TCount = TCount + 1
            Tablelist = Tablelist & Tbl.Name & vbCrLf
        End If
    Next
    MsgBox TCount & " tables in " & DBS.Name & vbCrLf & _
        Tablelist
End Sub
```

Module: DataAccess

Attaching a SQL Server Table

The form in Figure 6-11 is designed to display a list of the tables in a SQL Server database — in this example, the Pubs database available on all SQL Servers. The user can then attach any of the listed tables by selecting the table name and clicking the Attach SQL Server Table button. To confirm the attachment, the table is also opened in Access.

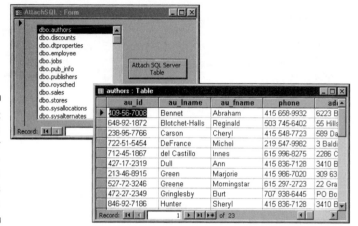

Figure 6-11:
Attached
SQL Server
table is dis-
played in
Access
2000.

What is interesting about the following procedures that are used to carry out the data-related operations in the Attach SQL Table form is not what new statements they contain, but the fact that they don't contain any new techniques. The FormLoad procedure extracts a list of tables from the SQL Server database and displays then in a list box control using the same "Value List" technique shown earlier in Figure 6-7.

```
Private Sub Form_Load()
    Dim DBS As Database
    Dim Tbl As TableDef
    Dim Tablelist
    Set DBS = OpenDatabase("MSAtoSQL", _
        dbDriverNoPrompt, False, _
        "ODBC;UID=apd;PWD=dummies")
    For Each Tbl In DBS.TableDefs
            Tablelist = Tablelist & Tbl.Name & ";"
    Next
    With Me.List0
        .RowSourceType = "Value List"
        .RowSource = Tablelist
    End With
End Sub
```

The following procedure attaches a selected SQL Server table to the current Access database. Once again, the technique is identical to that used to attach an external Access table. The only difference is the connection string assigned to the Connect property of the TableDef.

```
Private Sub Command2_Click()
    Dim Lnk As TableDef
    Set Lnk = CurrentDb.CreateTableDef(Mid(Me.List0, 5))
    Lnk.SourceTableName = Mid(Me.List0, 5)
    Lnk.Connect = "ODBC;DSN=MSAToSQL;UID=apd;PWD=dummies"
    CurrentDb.TableDefs.Append Lnk
    DoCmd.OpenTable Mid(Me.List0, 5)
End Sub
```

Many Access users view SQL Server as an alien creature with far greater powers than mere Access databases. While using SQL Server as a data source has many advantages, keep in mind that as a SQL-based relational database, SQL Server has far more in common with Access than it has differences with Access. In this chapter, you saw that you can easily transfer your knowledge of Access to SQL Server because both operate through the DAO interface. You can also access SQL Server through ADO also. You can find out more about both the similarities and differences between Access and SQL Server databases throughout the remainder of this book.

| Form: AttachSQL |

Part III
Controlling the Dialog

The 5th Wave   By Rich Tennant

"You know kids—you can't buy them just ANY database software."

In this part . . .

Windows users know that one of the most important and useful elements in the entire Windows system is the dialog box. It grabs the user's attention with options and choices that control what the user's system does.

Part III shows how Access creates its own forms that look and act like standard Windows dialog boxes.

Chapter 7

Making Your Own Dialog Boxes

· ·

In This Chapter

▶ Working with buttons

▶ New orders

▶ Forms as dialog boxes

▶ Forms and subforms

· ·

Forms are the basic building blocks of any application. In Chapter 6, you see how you can use your knowledge of SQL and Visual Basic to turn simple list box controls into powerful interactive elements for presenting complex data sets in an easy to view and use program interface.

In this chapter, you use those same skills to enhance the power and utility of other types of controls that you can use on a form. You also see how you can use forms as dialog boxes.

> **Database Folder: Chapter 7**
> **Database File: Dialog.MDB**

If you want to use the examples on the CD, open the database file Dialog.MDB and then click the Forms tab. This tab lists the forms I discuss in this chapter.

Working with Buttons

The most obvious purpose of a form in Access is to display data stored in a table and allow for basic keyboard editing of the data. However, beyond that simple function, forms provide an environment where you can monitor the user's interaction with the elements on the form and use Visual Basic to create procedures that can carry out tasks, from simple ones to highly complex ones, based on those interactions.

This approach to building applications is called *event-driven* programming. An event is simply some action the user takes, such as clicking a button, entering a new value, making a selection from a list, and so on.

The simplest type of interaction you can have on a form is clicking a command button control. In fact, command buttons are designed for exactly that purpose. They provide a visible object with which the users can interact to indicate that they want to perform some task.

As an example, look at the form shown in Figure 7-1, which displays data from a typical customer information table. As is often the case, each customer can have two addresses: a customer (billing) address and a shipping address. The form contains a tab control to separate the field for the two addresses.

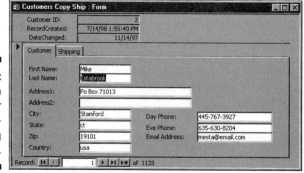

Figure 7-1:
A form with a customer and shipping address.

While (in theory) the billing and shipping address are not necessarily related, in practice you will often find they are the same or very close. To save time, most businesses simply entered "same" into the shipping address when the billing and shipping addresses were the same. A better solution is to place a button on the Shipping tab, as shown in Figure 7-2. Its purpose is to copy the billing address into the shipping address controls. This feature is useful even when the addresses are slightly different because most will share the same last name, city, state, and ZIP. You can copy the whole address and just edit the differences.

The code that copies the information is simply a series of statements that assign the value in one control, such as `LastName`, to another control, such as `ShipLastName`.

```
Sub CopyAddressToShipping()
    Me.ShipLastName = Me.LastName
    Me.ShipFirstName = Me.FirstName
    Me.ShipAddress1 = Me.Address1
```

```
      Me.ShipAddress2 = Me.Address2
      Me.ShipCity = Me.City
      Me.ShipZip = Me.Zip
      Me.ShipPhoneNumber = Me.DayPhoneNumber
End Sub
```

Figure 7-2:
A button
can be
designed to
copy the
billing
address into
the shipping
address
controls.

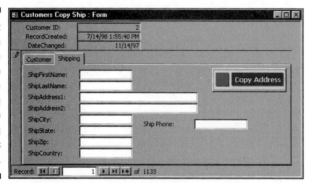

The button that appears on the Shipping tab, shown in Figure 7-2, calls the
CopyAddressToShipping procedure as part of the button's On Click event
procedure. This means that each time the button is clicked, the data in the
billing address controls is copied into the shipping address controls.

```
Private Sub Command27_Click()
    CopyAddressToShipping
End Sub
```

> **Form: Customers Copy Ship**

Using a map to copy

You may have noticed that the CopyAddressToShipping procedure shown
in the previous section did not include a statement that copied the contents
of the Country control into the ShipCountry control. How would you rectify
that omission? Your first instinct may be to modify the code to include
another statement that copies Country to ShipCountry.

What if you added Company and ShipCompany to the table? Then you would
also have to add a corresponding statement to the procedure.

In each case, a change in the specifics about which field is copied to which
other field requires you to alter the Visual Basic code. The copying of data
from one location to another is quite common in many applications. A different approach to this problem is to remove those details from your Visual

Basic code and create a generic procedure that is map-driven. A *map,* in this instance, is simply a list of the field pairs involved in the copy process. Table 7-1 lists the field pairs involved in the billing-to-shipping example.

Table 7-1	A Map of How to Copy a Billing Address to a Shipping Address
Source	*Target*
FirstName	ShipFirstName
LastName	ShipLastName
Address1	ShipAddress1
Address2	ShipAddress2
City	ShipCity
State	ShipState
Zip	ShipZip
Country	ShipCountry

When you observe Table 7-1, what comes to your mind? The lists look like a data table. The table is the map for your procedure to follow in performing the copy operation. The idea is to write a procedure that looks at a data table like the one in Table 7-1 and proceeds to copy data from FirstName to ShipFirstName, LastName to ShipLastName, and so on.

How would this work? First, an important point to keep in mind is that there are three ways to refer to a control on a form by name:

```
Me.ShipLastName = Me.LastName
Me!ShipLastName = Me!LastName
Me("ShipLastName") = Me("LastName")
```

The most intriguing form is the last one because the name of the control is specified as a text string. If you can use a text string to specify the name of the control, you can also use a variable or object property that evaluates to a text string as well. The following code shows two variables (SourceFieldName and TargetFieldName) used to indirectly refer to the ShipLastName and LastName controls.

```
SourceFieldName ="ShipLastName"
TargetFieldName ="LastName"
Me(SourceFieldName ) = Me(TargetFieldName)
```

You can use this approach to copy data between any pair of controls by assigning their names to the variables. Note that in this code and the following code the last statement, the one that actually copies the value from one control to another, is identical.

```
SourceFieldName ="Address1"
TargetFieldName ="ShipAddress1"
Me(SourceFieldName ) = Me(TargetFieldName)
```

Suppose now that instead of getting the text from the variables SourceFieldName and TargetFieldName, you use the SourceFieldName and TargetFieldName fields in a recordset named Map to supply the names of the source and target fields. This would greatly simplify the code. The following statement uses names drawn from fields in a table to specify controls involved in the copy operation.

```
Me(Map!SourceFieldName) = Me(Map!TargetFieldName)
```

Creating a map table

In order to use a map, you must create and populate a Map table. Table 7-2 shows the typical structure of a Map table. You can use the fields in this table to specify which fields to copy to which other fields as part of a given operation. The Task field enables you to specify which task a given set of records is related to. For example, you can call this task CopyToShipping. The Task field enables you to store multiple mapping tasks in a single table.

Table 7-2	Structure of a Map Table (Map_ShipTo)	
Name	*Type*	*Size*
ID	Long Integer	4
Task	Text	30
SourceTableName	Text	30
SourceFieldName	Text	30
TargetTableName	Text	30
TargetFieldName	Text	30

In this example, the fields to be copied all come from the same table. However, later in this chapter you see that mapping can take place between different tables. In order to accommodate that type of mapping, the SourceTableName and TargetTableName fields are included in the table. Figure 7-3 shows the data stored in the table Map_ShipTo. The data is essentially the information listed in Table 7-2 placed into a table structure.

Figure 7-3:
A mapping
table shows
the pairing
of source
and target
fields.

	ID	Task	SourceTable	SourceFieldNan	TargetTableNa	TargetFieldName
	11	CopyToShipping	customers	FirstName	customers	ShipFirstName
	12	CopyToShipping	customers	LastName	customers	ShipLastName
	14	CopyToShipping	customers	Address1	customers	ShipAddress1
	15	CopyToShipping	customers	Address2	customers	ShipAddress2
	16	CopyToShipping	customers	City	customers	ShipCity
▶	17	CopyToShipping	customers	State	customers	ShipState
	18	CopyToShipping	customers	Zip	customers	ShipZip
	19	CopyToShipping	customers	Country	customers	ShipCountry
	28	CopyToShipping	customers	DayPhoneNumbe	customers	ShipPhoneNumber
*	(Number)					

Map_ShipTo : Table

Record: 6 of 9

After you have a mapping table, you can write a procedure that uses the pair-
ings contained in the mapping table to perform the copy operation. The
following procedure, used in the Customers Copy Ship Map form, uses the
Map_ShipTo table as the source for the names of the fields to be copied. The
procedure first creates a recordset that extracts the data from the Map table.
Then a Do...Loop structure processes each pair of names contained in the
recordset.

```
Private Sub Command27_Click()
    Dim Map As New Recordset
    Map.Open "SELECT * FROM Map_ShipTo " & _
        "WHERE TargetFieldName is not null", _
        CurrentProject.Connection
    Do Until Map.EOF
        Me(Map!TargetFieldName) = Me(Map!SourceFieldName)
        Map.MoveNext
    Loop
End Sub
```

Form: Customers Copy Ship vMap, Table: Map_ShipTo

Well, that was a lot of work and abstract thinking just to copy a couple of
values from one field to another. Why bother? For two primary reasons:

✔ Using a mapping table makes it easier to add or remove field pairs from
the operation. If you modify the form to include other fields, such as
Company and ShipToCompany, you won't have to change any of your
code. Simply add the new pairing to the Map table and the same procedure includes the new pair in the copying process.

✔ Because the values that control the mapping operation are stored in a
table, not in Visual Basic code, users can easily customize the process
by editing the Map table. You can easily create a form with combo boxes
that lists the names of the fields (in order to make it easier to revise) by
taking advantage of the *Field List* RowSourceType option available on
combo box controls. The following code sets the drop lists of two
combo boxes so that they list the fields in the Customers table as their
possible values.

```
Private Sub Form_Load()
    With Me.SourceFieldName
        .RowSourceType = "Field List"
        .RowSource = "Customers"
    End With
    With Me.TargetFieldName
        .RowSourceType = "Field List"
        .RowSource = "Customers"
    End With
End Sub
```

> **Form: Edit Map_ShiptTo**

No editing controls

Another feature that appears in the `Customers Copy Ship` forms is a procedure used to set one or more controls on the form so that they are displayed
but can be edited. I have a habit of showing read-only controls by setting three
properties: `Enabled = False`, `Locked = True`, and `BackColor = gray`.
Although you can set all these properties in the Design mode, I find it annoying to have to set or unset three settings just to get the desired control set. In
particular, selecting the color required a few extra clicks to select the color
from the color picker dialog box.

Instead I take advantage of the `Tag` property. Each of the controls on the form
that I want to appear as read-only (for example, the `CustomerID` field, which
is an autonumber, or the `DateCreated` field, which is automatically time-
stamped when the record is created) have a `Tag` property of *NoEdit*. The `Tag`
property has no function in Access 2000. It exists for just this purpose — that
is, to tag certain controls so that they can be treated as a group.

The following procedure searches the `Controls` collection of the form and
sets the three attributes I use for read-only on all of the controls marked with
the tag *NoEdit*.

```
Sub SetNoEditControls()
    Dim C As Control
    For Each C In Me.Controls
        If C.Tag = "NoEdit" Then
            With C
                .Enabled = False
                .Locked = True
                .BackColor = RGB(192, 192, 192)
            End With
        End If
    Next
End Sub
```

You can place a statement in the Form_Load procedure that executes the SetNoEditControls each time the form is loaded.

```
Private Sub Form_Load()
    SetNoEditControls
End Sub
```

> **Form: Customers Copy Ship**

Manipulating controls from a module

Of course, SetNoEditControls is such a useful procedure that you may want to use it in a number of your forms. Instead of copying the code into each new form, you can store the code in a stand-alone module rather than in the form's code module. Code in a standard module is available to all forms in the same database.

However, after you place the code in a module, you have to account for the fact that the Me object, which refers to the current form, no longer exists because a module is not associated with any particular form.

The following procedure is almost identical to SetNoEditControls(). The only change is that instead of working with the Me object, the procedure requires a Form as a parameter. The variable Frm has all of the properties, methods, and collections that the Me object has because they are both Form objects.

```
Sub SetReadOnlyControls(Frm As Form)
    Dim C As Control
    For Each C In m.CoFrntrols
        If C.Tag = "NoEdit" Then
            With C
                .Enabled = False
                .Locked = True
                .BackColor = RGB(192, 192, 192)
            End With
        End If
    Next
End Sub
```

You can use the procedure with any form by passing the Me object of the form to the procedure. You can use the following procedure with any form in the database to set the controls tagged as NoEdit to a specific format. All the forms utilize the same procedure, SetReadOnlyControls, rather than having a separate procedure stored in each form.

```
Private Sub Form_Load()
    SetReadOnlyControls Me
End Sub
```

> **Form: Customers Copy Ship vMap, Module: Operations**

Another benefit of this approach is that you can easily modify the specific attributes of the NoEdit controls without having to modify the design of any of the forms. For example, suppose you decide that NoEdit controls should not have a line around the control. If you had not used the approach outlined here, you would have to go back to each form and modify either the code or, worse yet, the properties of the controls, assuming you remember all of the forms and controls involved.

But when you control the appearance by means of a procedure in a module, you can make a single change in one location and have the effect automatically propagated throughout your application. The following code fragment taken from SetReadOnlyControls() suppresses the outline on all controls tagged as NoEdit.

```
With C
    .Enabled = False
    .Locked = True
    .BackColor = RGB(192, 192, 192)
    .BorderStyle = 0
    .BorderColor = 0
    .SpecialEffect = 0
End With
```

Keep in mind that not only does this technique save time, it also gives your application a more professional look because all of the forms use the same appearance settings. Achieving this professional look is time consuming when you have to manually modify the properties of dozen of controls on dozen of forms each time you change your mind about the visual style of your application.

New Orders

When you design a database application, you often focus on the data contents of the application rather than on the way that work actually takes place. For example, a sales database has customers, orders, and order details as its primary tables. You would therefore create tables to hold the data and forms to allow the user to enter data.

But to build an application, you need to go beyond that outline and ask questions about how your application can support the way in which people actually work. For example, how do users create new orders?

One answer is to open a form that displays the fields in the Orders table and let the user enter data. But that solution doesn't take into account the fact that creating an order is a different process if the customer is an existing customer rather than a new customer. Taking the first case, filling out an order for an existing customer means that you would want to start out not with a blank order screen, but with an order screen containing information from their customer record such as billing address, shipping address, or perhaps even credit card information. In other words, a new order is seldom the same as a blank order. As an example, the following list contains the tasks your database must perform when creating a new order for an existing customer:

- ✔ Locate the customer in the database.
- ✔ Select to create a new order for that customer.
- ✔ Copy information from the customer table into the new order.
- ✔ Display the new order in a form so that the user can fill in details.

Copy or link? Why copy the customer information into the order record? Why not simply link the order to the customer record and avoid having to save the address information again in another table? In theory, linking is the preferred approach. But in reality, you find that individual orders may vary — in terms such as the address or credit card number — from the data on file in the Customer table. By copying the data from the Customer table, you allow for things such as gift orders where the shipping address is different from the normal shipping address.

Using dialogs to locate records

The new order process has several dimensions, with each posing some programming challenges. The first task in creating a new order is to determine if the customer already exists in your database and, if so, locating their customer record. In most cases, the key to locating the desired customer record is searching for a last name. In Figure 7-4, the form shows the LastName control displayed using the *shadow* special effect. In this application, that effect indicates that double-clicking on that control initiates a search on that field.

The search consists of three distinct operations, each of which you must perform as part of your search procedure.

- ✔ Get the users to input part or all of the names they are looking for.
- ✔ Search the Customers table for any matching records.
- ✔ Display the matching record in the form.

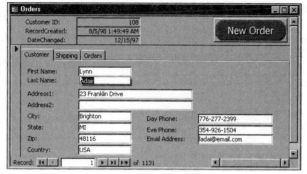

Input boxes

The simplest way to get the user to enter a single item of information is the
Inputbox() function, which I discuss briefly in Chapter 2. When you include
the function in a statement, it displays a box into which the user can make a
single text input. The value input is assigned to a variable. The following
statement stores the user's input in a variable called Locate.

```
Locate = InputBox("Search for last name:", "Search")
```

In order to make the search as flexible as possible, the user's input is treated
as a partial criteria by using a Like operator. For example, if the user enters
Smith as the search criterion, the following statement is used to locate matching records.

```
LastName Like "Smith*"
```

How is this criterion used to locate records? The technique is the same one
used in Chapter 5 (the form Linked Lists 05) in which the FindFirst
method is applied to the RecordSetClone of the form. Recall that the
RecordSetClone is a duplicate of the recordset displayed in the form. You
can search the clone for a record and force it to be displayed in the form by
setting the Form's bookmark property to the bookmark of the clone.

The following procedure, executed when the user double-clicks the LastName
control, applies this approach to the problem of locating a customer by last
name. First, an input box is displayed so that the user can enter the name for
which they want to search. A clone is made of the form's recordset and the
FindFirst method is applied in order to locate the first match, if any, in the
recordset. The bookmark properties are used to change the form's displayed
record to match the record located in the clone. In the case where no match
is found (the clone's NoMatch property is True), a message box is displayed
telling the user that the search failed to locate a match.

```
Private Sub LastName_DblClick(Cancel As Integer)
    Dim Locate, rs As DAO.Recordset
    Locate = InputBox("Search for last name:", "Search")
    Set rs = Me.RecordsetClone
    rs.FindFirst "LastName like '" & Locate & "*'"
    If rs.NoMatch Then
        MsgBox "No Matches. Cannot locate a name like the one
            entered."
    Else
        Me.Bookmark = rs.Bookmark
    End If
End Sub
```

The recordset produced by the `RecordSetClone` method of the `Form` object is inherently a DAO object. You must define your recordset object as a `DAO.Recordset` in order to use the bookmark properties to change the displayed record.

> **Form: Customers Find 01**

Dealing with multiple matches

The procedure used in `Customers Find 01` to locate a customer works well if only a single customer in the database matches the criterion entered by the user, or if no matches exist. The procedure, however, doesn't deal with the case where more than one record matches the criterion.

In the previous find procedure, the search was performed on the clone of the form's recordset. A slightly different approach is to use the user's criterion to generate a separate recordset object that includes all of the customers matching the criterion. This approach results in three possible outcomes:

✔ **Recordset.EOF is True.** This condition indicates that no matches for the specified criterion were found. Action: Display a message box confirming no matching records.

✔ **Recordset RecordCount is 1.** This condition indicates only one matching record was found. Action: Display the matching record in the form.

✔ **Recordset RecordCount is more than 1.** Action: Display a message indicating the number of matches and then display the first matching record in the form.

The first step is to generate the recordset object. You can use either ADO or DAO to create this object. Because ADO is the default, I used an ADO recordset object. The following statement shows that an ADO recordset can be defined from the user's input stored in the variable `LocateName`. Confusingly, ADO uses a different syntax with the `Like` operator than DAO. In DAO, and in Access queries, * is the wildcard operator. ADO uses % instead of * for the same function. Use of % is consistent with most client/sever databases such as SQL Server and Sybase.

```
rs.Open "SELECT CustomerID FROM Customers WHERE " & _
    " lastname like '" & LocateName & "%'", _
    CurrentProject.Connection, adOpenKeyset, adLockOptimistic
```

The following procedure implements the three different cases outlined earlier in this section. Note that the procedure uses both ADO and DAO recordsets. The ADO recordset is used to determine the number of matching records. The DAO recordset, defined by the `RecordsetClone` property, is used to display the first matching record when one or more matches occur. Figure 7-5 shows the message box that is displayed when more than one record matches the entered criterion.

```
Sub MatchingRecords(LocateName)
    Dim rs As New Recordset, FrmRs As DAO.Recordset
    'ADO uses % for wildcard
    rs.Open "SELECT CustomerID FROM Customers WHERE " & _
        " lastname like '" & LocateName & "%'", _
        CurrentProject.Connection, adOpenKeyset, _
    adLockOptimistic
    If rs.EOF Then 'no match - display message
        MsgBox "No Matches. Cannot locate a name like the one
            entered."
    Else
        rs.MoveLast
        If rs.RecordCount > 1 Then 'if more than 1 match
            MsgBox "There are " & rs.RecordCount & _
                " customers that match " & LocateName & "."
        End If
        '1 or more matches - display first matching record
        'DAO use * for wildcard
        Set FrmRs = Me.RecordsetClone
        FrmRs.FindFirst " lastname like '" & LocateName &
            "*'"
        Me.Bookmark = FrmRs.Bookmark
    End If
End Sub
```

Form: Customers Find 02

Forms as Dialog Boxes

The message box shown in Figure 7-5 informs the user that multiple possible matches exist for the entered criterion. But it does not provide a mechanism by which the user can select which of the matching records they want to use. This cannot be done using the Msgbox function because its interface (one message and one to three buttons) is too limited. What is needed is a display that shows a detailed list of customers and allows the user to make a selection from that list. The selection results in the display of the selected customer's data in the current form.

In Access 2000, only a form object possesses the attributes required. This means that as part of your procedure, you need to include code that does the following:

- Displays an input box so the user can enter the search criteria.
- Creates a recordset that contains all matching records.
- If more than one matching record exists, opens a form that displays a list of matching customers.
- Allows the user to make a selection from a list.
- Uses that selection to change the active record in the customer form to show the data for the selected customer.

The programming challenge, in this case, is that you cannot write a single procedure that controls the entire process. When a procedure opens an input box or message box, Access 2000 pauses execution of the procedure until the user closes the box. That is not the case when a procedure opens a form. After opening a form, Access 2000 immediately continues executing the remaining statements in the procedure without regard to the state of the previously opened form. In some cases, this behavior fits your design goals. However, when you want to use a form to obtain user input that affects subsequent actions, then you have a problem.

The solution is to divide the code among the various forms involved in the operation. In the example outlined earlier in this section, the Customer form can only contain the code for the first three steps. After the second form is opened, the code that performs steps four and five must be executed from that form, not the Customer form.

Access 2000 does not directly support the use of user-designed dialog boxes beyond the InputBox() and MsgBox() functions. You can use forms to simulate the behavior of a dialog box, but you need to keep in mind that Access 2000 can't tell the difference between a data form, such as the Customers form, and a dialog box form, such as the one proposed here. You create the illusion that you are opening a dialog box by the code you distribute among the forms.

The following procedure substitutes the Msgbox() function with a DoCmd.OpenForm statement that opens a form called DLG_PickName. Note that after this statement is executed, there are no more statements in this procedure that are executed. That is because after the DLG_PickName form is open, the code that completes the task must be executed from that form, not the Customers form.

```
Sub MatchingRecords(LocateName)
   Dim rs As New Recordset, FrmRs As DAO.Recordset
   'ADO uses % for wildcard
   rs.Open "SELECT CustomerID FROM Customers WHERE " & _
   " lastname like '" & LocateName & "%'", _
   CurrentProject.Connection, adOpenKeyset, _
   adLockOptimistic
   If rs.EOF Then
     MsgBox "No Matches. Cannot locate a name like " & _
     LocateName & "."
   Else
   rs.MoveLast
    If rs.RecordCount > 1 Then
       'OPEN FORM ======================================
       DoCmd.OpenForm _
       FormName:="Dlg_PickName", _
       OpenArgs:="lastname like '" & LocateName & "*'"
     Else '======================================
       Set FrmRs = Me.RecordsetClone
       FrmRs.FindFirst "lastname like '" & LocateName & "*'"
       Me.Bookmark = FrmRs.Bookmark
    End If
  End If
End Sub
```

The OpenArgs property

You now know that you must use a form to display the list of matching names so that the user can make a selection. However, the list of names displayed in DLG_PickName is related to the user-entered criterion in the InputBox displayed by the procedure running in the Customers form.

What is needed is a mechanism by which data from the MatchingRecords procedure can be passed to the procedures running in the DLG_PickName form. Access 2000 provides a special form property called *OpenArgs* (opening arguments) that is designed for exactly this purpose. It allows you to pass a text item to the code module of a form when you issue the OpenForm statement. The following statement, taken from MatchingRecords, assigns the text lastname like '" & LocateName & "*' to the OpenArgs property of the form.

```
DoCmd.OpenForm _
FormName:="Dlg_PickName", _
OpenArgs:="lastname like '" & LocateName & "*'"
```

Assigning a value to OpenArgs does not in itself have any effect on the form that is opened. However, the value assigned to OpenArgs is available to any procedure that executes with the form. For example, the following statement displays the text assigned to the OpenArgs property of the current form.

```
Msgbox Me.OpenArgs
```

In this example, the purpose of the OpenArgs text is to define the criterion to use to control which names to display. The following code populates the list box shown in Figure 7-6. The OpenArgs property is used to define the WHERE clause of the SQL statement used for the RowSource of the list box. The result is that the names shown in the DLG_PickName form are linked to the search criterion entered into the Customers form. Note that the city and state are displayed to help the user distinguish between identical names should they occur.

```
With Names
    .RowSource = "SELECT customerid, " & _
        "lastname & ', ' & firstname AS Name, " & _
        "City & ', ' & State As Location" & _
        " FROM Customers WHERE " & Me.OpenArgs
    .ColumnCount = 3
    .ColumnWidths = "0;1.5 in;1.5;"
    .ColumnHeads = True
    .Requery
End With
```

Dlg_PickName : Form	
Name	Location
Smith, Alice	New York, NY
Smith, Charles	Stillwater, OK
Smith, David	Waterbury, VT
Smith, Glenn	Fairbanks, AK
Smith, Jeff	Studio City, CA
Smith, Jerry	Trumbull, CT
Smith, Jim	Forest Hill, MD
Smith, Michael	Spring Grove, IL
Smith, michael	Natick, MA
Smith, Paul	Cleveland, OH
Smith, Robert	Bisbee, , AZ
Smith, Steve	Tarrytown, NY
Smith, Suzy	Irvine, CA
Smith, Tina	Mckee, KY
Smith, Tony	Floral Park, CA

Figure 7-6:
The form
used as a
dialog box
displays the
list of
matching
names.

Now that you have a list of the desired names displayed, you need to find
a way to connect the user's selection — a double-click in the list box
control — with the Customers form. Your goal is to use the selection to
change the displayed record in the other form. How can this be done?

The answer is to use a `Form` object variable. The following code defines the
variable F as a `Form`. You can then assign that variable all the properties,
methods, and collections of a specific open form. In this case, the `Customers`
form (specifically `Customers Find 03`) is assigned to the variable.

```
Dim F As Form
Set F = Forms![Customers Find 03]
```

Keep in mind that you can only assign a form to a `Form` object variable if the
form is currently open.

Assigning the form to a `Form` object variable gives you a sort of *remote control* over the form itself. You can issue the same statements using the `Form`
object variable F as you would if you used the `Me` object. In the following
double-click procedure, two forms are actually controlled: F controls
`Customers Find 03` and `Me` controls `DLG_PickName`. Because both forms
are available to the procedure, you can write statements that use elements of
both forms. In this case, the value of the selection in the list box is used to
search the clone recordset of the `Customers` form and use the bookmark
property to display that record in the `Customers` form.

```
Private Sub Names_DblClick(Cancel As Integer)
    Dim F As Form, R As DAO.Recordset
    Set F = Forms![Customers Find 03]
    Set R = F.RecordsetClone
    R.FindFirst "CustomerID = " & Me.Names
    F.Bookmark = R.Bookmark
    DoCmd.Close acForm, Me.Name
End Sub
```

Note the final statement, DoCmd.Close, closes the current form, Me.Name. This means that when the user makes a selection from the list, the dialog box form is automatically removed from the screen.

One other small issue is the formatting of a form used as a dialog box. In most cases, you'll want to turn off the navigation button and record selector display because the dialog box form is not connected to a recordset. This can be done by inserting the following statements in the Form_Load procedure.

```
With Me
    .NavigationButtons = False
    .RecordSelectors = False
End With
```

> **Form: Customers Find 03, DLG_PickName**

Using a modal form

As mentioned previously, Access 2000 does not distinguish between data-oriented forms and dialog box forms. To Access, all of the forms are the same. In the previous example, the user could open the DLG_PickName form and then click back to the Customer form without making a selection. Access 2000 normally allows you to have as many forms open as memory resources allow, and you can move freely between the forms using the mouse, the key-board (Ctrl+F6 cycles the focus among the open forms), or the Window menu.

If you want to force the user to deal with a specific form before you allow then to select any of the other open forms, you can open the form as a modal form. A *modal form* is one that maintains the focus until it is closed. If the user tries to select a different form, Access sounds a beep and ignores the attempt. The only way to continue is to close the modal form.

You can designate a form as modal in two ways:

- ✔ In the design mode, you can set the Modal property to Yes.
- ✔ You can use the WindowMode parameters of the OpenForm method to open the form as modal.

You cannot set the Modal property through Visual Basic while the form is open because a form must be designated as modal or non-modal before you open it.

The following code shows the additional argument, WindowMode, used to open the form Dlg_PickName 01 as modal. Note that the constant used to indicate modal operation is acDialog. This forces the user to deal with the dialog box form before returning to the Customers form.

```
FormName:="Dlg_PickName 01", _
    OpenArgs:="lastname like '" & LocateName & "*'", _
    WindowMode:=acDialog
```

> **Form: Customers Find 04, DLG_PickName**

Preparing a new record

You now have a method of effectively locating the desired customer. The next step in the new order process is to *prepare* the new record. Rather than simply opening a blank order form, it makes sense to populate the new record with information that is already known about the customer and the order. In this example, you want to copy the billing address, shipping address and credit card information from the customer's record into the new order because that is the starting point for all new orders.

Note that in the application being described in this chapter, you can't create a new order until you have first created a customer record. This helps ensure that every new order is linked to a customer record.

Preparation of a new record can be done by hard-coding details of the field to the field copying process in your Visual Basic code, as shown here:

```
Orders!ShipLast = Customers!ShipLastName
Orders!ShipFirst = Customers!ShipFirstName
```

As I discuss earlier in this chapter, you can handle operations of this sort more easily by using a mapping table, such as the one used to copy the billing address to the shipping address.

Making a map table

You can save some time in setting up a mapping table by using some Visual Basic to first create the mapping table and then filling in the source field names automatically.

The `CreateMapTable` procedure in the `WorkingForms` module creates a new map table. You can create a new map table by entering a statement such as the following one into the immediate window. In this case, that table has already been created in the example database.

```
CreateMapTable "NewOrder_Map"
```

> ### Module: WorkingForms, Procedure: CreateMapTable

You also use Visual Basic to populate the table with a list of fields. For example, if you want to copy data from the Customers table into the Orders, you can create records for all the fields in the Customers table using the AddSchemeToMap procedure. The following example fills in the NewOrder_Map table with one record for each field in the Customers table. This table has already been created in the example database.

```
AddSchemeToMap TaskName:="NewOrder", _
    SourceName:="Customers", _
    MapName:="NewOrder_Map"
```

> ### Module: WorkingForms, Procedure: AddSchemeToMap

Figure 7-7 shows a form, EditNewOrder_Map, in which the links between the Customers and the Orders tables are defined. Because the table is already populated with the fields from the Customers table, all you need to do is select the field in the Orders table into which to copy the Customers information. Any fields that don't have a target field designed will simply be skipped.

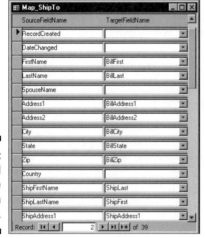

Figure 7-7:
A form used
to fill in the
mappings in
a map table.

> ### Form: EditNewOrder_Map

Keep in mind that using a mapping table to define which data is copied by a specific operation makes it much easier to add or remove items from the process because no changes need to be made to the Visual Basic code.

The final step is to write a procedure that performs the initial population of the new order record before it is displayed for editing. This procedure is assigned to the Click procedure of the New Order button placed on the Customers form. In this case, you need to work with three different record-sets as the same time:

- ✔ The customers record contained in the Customers table.
- ✔ The Orders table in which you add a new record.
- ✔ The Map_Customers table that contains the data that control which fields from Customers are copied to which fields in Orders.

The code begins by defining three recordset variables that correspond to the three recordsets you need to work with. Also, a variable NewOrderID is used to capture the autonumber generated when the new order is added to Orders table. That ID is used to specify which order to show when the Orders form is opened at the end of the procedure.

```
Private Sub Command27_Click()
    Dim Cust As DAO.Recordset
    Dim Ord As DAO.Recordset
    Dim Map As DAO.Recordset
    Dim NewOrderID
```

The next task is to create the actual recordsets by assigning the recordset variables their SQL statements. The Cust recordset is defined by the CustomerID displayed in the current form. The Ord recordset is simply the entire Orders table. Finally, the Map recordset consists of all the matched source and target items listed under the task NewOrder in the NewOrder_Map table.

```
Set Cust = CurrentDb.OpenRecordset( _
    "SELECT * FROM Customers " & _
    "WHERE CustomerID = " & Me.CustomerID)
Set Ord = CurrentDb.OpenRecordset( _
    "SELECT * FROM Orders")
Set Map = CurrentDb.OpenRecordset( _
    "SELECT * FROM NewOrder_Map " & _
    "WHERE Task = 'NewOrder' AND TargetFieldName is not
            null")
```

After you create the recordsets, you can perform operations using those recordsets. In this case, you begin by adding a new record to the Ord record-set by using the AddNew method. The order date is immediately inserted by using the Date function to insert the system date. Note that if you use Now instead of Date, you get a date *and* time stamp. In many cases, that is more detail than you need, so you use Date instead of Now.

```
Ord.AddNew
Ord!OrderDate = Date ' use Now for timestamp
```

The next section of the procedure uses the mapping table to transfer values from the `Customers` table to the new order record. Here you can see how using a mapping table greatly simplifies the code. The following loop handles all of the copying with only a few statements because the details are stored in the mapping table where they are easier to read and modify, if necessary.

```
Do Until Map.EOF
    Ord(Map!TargetFieldName) = Cust(Map!SourceFieldName)
    Map.MoveNext
Loop
```

Before the addition of the new record is completed with the `Update` method, the `OrderID` is stored in the variable `NewOrderID`. Why? The answer involves how a DAO recordset behaves after a new record has been added. Following the start of a new record, triggered by the `AddNew` method, the new record is the current record. Any reference to a field in the recordset refers to the new record being added. However, when you use the `Update` method to complete the addition process by saving the record, the current record becomes the first record in the data set, not the new record you have just added. For that reason, it is necessary to store a copy of the new record's `OrderID` in a variable before the `Update` method is applied. Using the value in the variable you can locate the new record by selecting for that `OrderID`.

```
NewOrderID = Ord!OrderID
Ord.Update
```

When you are working with an ADO recordset, the behavior is different. After an `Update`, the current record is the newly added record.

The final step is to use the order number stored in `NewOrderID` to open the `OrderForm` form and display the newly created order.

```
DoCmd.OpenForm _
    FormName:="OrderForm 01", _
    WhereCondition:="Orderid = " & NewOrderID
```

Figure 7-8 shows the results of clicking on the New Order button in the `Customers` form. A new order is displayed in the `Order` form that has the same address information as the displayed customer, indicating that the map-based copying process has correctly set up a new order.

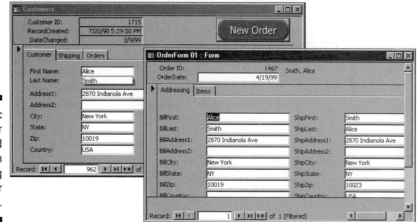

Figure 7-8:
A new order
created
from an
existing
customer
record.

Form: Customers New Orders, Order Form 01

Chapter 8

Using Functions to Fill Lists

> *Database Folder: Chapter 8*
> *Database File: Classes.MDB*

*T*o begin this chapter, load the database for Chapter 8, Classes.MDB. When the database is open, click on the Forms tab. This is where you can find the forms discussed in this chapter.

Throughout this book you have worked with the objects, methods, properties, and collections that are provided as part of Access 2000. Most of the procedures you have worked with in this book use Visual Basic to manipulate these objects in order to automate one task or another. The object models work well because they provide an organized framework into which all the hundreds of methods, properties, and collections can be organized. In addition to using Visual Basic to manipulate the objects provided with Access 2000, you can use Visual Basic to define your own objects, properties, methods, and collections. In this chapter, you take advantage of this capacity in order to organize complicated operations, such as importing and exporting data between Access and other software systems.

Communicating with Other Systems

Access 2000 is a powerful application, but it can't do everything. In many cases in business, the data in your database will need to be updated to include information provided from other sources. On the other hand, you will often need to provide Access data to other applications for special processing.

Any order processing system may need to deal with the payment process and the order fulfillment process. In today's highly computerized and electronically connected business environment, many order processing–related activities can be performed on PCs and PC networks.

For example, several popular systems are available that enable you to perform credit card operations directly from your PC. You can also perform shipping-related tasks by using PC software from the major shipping companies.

The key issue is that these external systems are not linked to a common data source. Each application uses its own data format, which is related to the task they perform. For example, software that performs credit card verification needs information about the credit card account and the charge you want to place against that account. It is not, however, the least bit interested in the order details, the breakdown of shipping and sales tax, and other information. On the shipping side, the carrier needs shipping address information only. Data related to how the order was paid for and who the order is billed to aren't relevant. Only your application is concerned with storing and organizing all the various data items that relate to the entire order process.

The goal of this chapter is to look at the tools provided in Access 2000 that enable an Access database application to exchange information with other systems on a regular basis.

Writing Text Files

Even after nearly 20 years of PC development, most applications that store data do so in a *proprietary* structure — that is, a data file format that is unique to that specific application. However, because data exchange between programs is often a requirement, most applications will allow data to be imported or exported in a text format. Two basic types of text formats are used for data exchange, shown in Figure 8-1.

> ✔ **Delimited.** A delimited text file, shown in the top of Figure 8-1, marks the end of each field by inserting a specific character, usually a comma. The end of each record is marked by a carriage return/linefeed (vbCrLf). In addition, text items are often enclosed in quotation marks.

✔ **Fixed length.** A fixed-length text file, shown at the bottom of Figure 8-1, does not use any special characters to separate the fields. Instead, each field is written using a fixed number of characters. If the field is smaller than the fixed column width, the text is padded with spaces. The end of each record is marked with a carriage return/linefeed (vbCrLf).

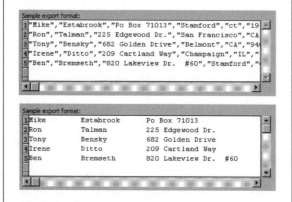

Figure 8-1:
Examples of delimited and fixed-length text formats.

The most universally accepted format is a comma-delimited file (called CSV) because it requires the least configuration on the part of the application reading the file. When you load a comma-delimited text file, the importing application can begin reading data with no special setup. Each time the application encounters a comma or a CR/LF, it knows that it has reached the end of a field or record, respectively.

A fixed-length file requires some preparation on the part of the importing application. Before you can load the data, you must specify the column widths so that the importing application knows when a field ends. Otherwise, the importing application reads the entire record as a single field. Many applications can read and write both fixed-length and comma-delimited formats. In this chapter, the focus is on writing delimited files.

Access 2000 provides an import/export wizard, which is automatically activated when you use the File⇨Get External Data⇨Import or the File⇨Export commands and you select Text File as the file type.

Creating text files with Visual Basic

In general, Visual Basic itself does not include a database function. Rather, it uses the objects provided by Access 2000, SQL Server, or some other ODBC data source to store and retrieve data. In each instance where data access is required, an object — such as a DAO Recordset object — is required.

There is one exception. Visual Basic as it exists in Access 2000 is the latest in a long line of BASIC languages whose lineage goes back farther than the creation of the PC. Built into those early versions of BASIC was the ability to read and write basic text files, such as the delimited and fixed length files. Visual Basic still retains this ability, and it can be quite a useful tool, despite all the sophisticated database interfaces available in Access 2000.

The text file abilities of Visual Basic are contained in a set of five statements listed here:

- ✔ Open #. Establishes a connection to a text file or creates a new text file and opens a connection to it. The statement also assigns a file number to the connection. All subsequent statements that interact with the same file do so by using the file number assigned in the Open # statement. You can use the full path name of the file you want to create to place the file in a location other than the current default folder.

- ✔ Write #. Sends one or more items to the text file. All items are automatically formatted as comma delimited data.

- ✔ Print #. Sends data to a text file without any formatting. This statement allows you to model your text file when the standard comma-delimited format is not appropriate.

- ✔ Input #. Reads in a single data item — in effect, one field — from a text file.

- ✔ Close #. This statement close the file and terminates the link between your procedure and the data file.

All these statements share the # as a common characteristic. The # refers to the file number assigned to the file in the Open statement. The file number has a similar function to a Connection object in that it identifies the file that is being accessed.

The following procedure shows a simple method of writing data to a text file, TextFile01.TXT. First, the Open statement connects a file name with a file number. When you specify For Output, a new file is created. If the file already exists, it is automatically overwritten with a new file of the same name. The Write statements send data to the file. Each statement appends new data onto the file until the Close statement saves the file and breaks the connection.

```
Sub WriteText01()
    Open "TextFile01.txt" For Output As #1
    Write #1, "Access Programming for Dummies"
    Write #1, "Text File Example"
    Close #1
End Sub
```

If you want to add data to an existing text file rather than replacing it, use the keywords For Append in place of For Output in the Open # statement.

> **Module: FileOperations**
> **Procedure: WriteText01**

Recall that you can run a procedure in a module by placing your cursor any-where in the module and pressing F5.

To read data from a file, you begin by opening the file with the `For Input` keywords in the `Open` statement. Note that you cannot directly access the data in the text file. You must first create a variable, such as `txtData`, and use the `Input` statement to load one field from the text file into that variable. Once in the variable, you can use data by using the variable in subsequent statements. In this case, the data is displayed in a message box, as shown in Figure 8-2. Note that Visual Basic automatically strips off the delimiters and field and record separators when it loads data from the file with the `Input #` statement so that only the text is stored in the variable.

```
Sub ReadText01()
    Dim txtData
    Open "TextFile01.txt" For Input As #1
    Do Until EOF(1)
        Input #1, txtData
        MsgBox txtData
    Loop
    Close #1
End Sub
```

Figure 8-2:
Data loaded from a text file and displayed in a message box.

> **Module: FileOperations**
> **Procedure: ReadText01**

Reading data from a text file is similar to reading data from a recordset object, but keep in mind these very significant differences:

✔ Because text file operations preceded the development objects in Visual Basic, the file connections don't have properties or methods. Instead of using the Eof property to determine the end of the file, you use the EOF() function. You use the file number as the argument for the function. The value of the function is associated with the Input # statement. When Input # cannot locate any more fields in the file, it sets the EOF() function to True.

✔ There is no MoveNext property. Each time a field is read with the Input # statement, Visual Basic moves to the next field, if any, in the text file.

✔ Data is extracted from the text file in a forward-only direction. You cannot move backwards in the file.

You can randomly read and write data in a text file — similar to the way that you can randomly move through a recordset object — by using the keywords Random or Binary with the Open # statement and the Get and Put statements. In most cases, where random access is required, you're better off importing the text into an Access table and using ADO or DAO objects to access the data.

You can find on the CD the procedures WriteText02 and ReadTest02, which illustrate the use of the Print # statement to write a text file.

> **Module: FileOperations**
> **Procedure: WriteText01**

Exporting a recordset

You can combine Access objects along with text file operations to perform operations such as exporting or importing data. You can create a text file from any recordset by using the text file statements discussed in the previous section.

The following procedure opens a recordset, ExpNames, and then writes the data to a text file called *CustNames.TXT*.

```
Sub ExportRSDeli01()
    Dim ExpNames As New Recordset
    ExpNames.Open _
        "SELECT firstname, lastname, address1, city, state,
            zip " & _
        " FROM Customers ORDER BY LastName", _
        CurrentProject.Connection

    Open "CustNames.txt" For Output As #1
    Do Until ExpNames.EOF
        Write #1, _
            ExpNames!FirstName, _
            ExpNames!LastName, _
            ExpNames!City, _
            ExpNames!Zip
        ExpNames.MoveNext
    Loop
    Close #1
End Sub
```

The Write # statement enables you to write one or more data items with a single statement. All the items in the list are written as fields within a single record as shown here:

```
"Lynn","Adair","Brighton","48116"
"James","Adams","Lompoc","93436"
"Dennis","Adams","Lebanon","17042"
"Pamala","Adams","Oak Forest","60452-4013"
"Ronald","Adams","San Francisco","94123"
```

> **Module: FileOperations**
> **Procedure: ExportRSDeli01**

You can use the approach shown in ExportRSDeli01 to create a procedure that exports the contents of any recordset. The following procedure requires two parameters. The first is the name of the text file to be created, and the second is a recordset object that contains the data to be exported.

```
Sub ExportRSDeli02(FName, R As Recordset)
    Dim FileNumber
    Dim Kounter
    FileNumber = FreeFile
    Open FName For Output As #FileNumber
    Do Until R.EOF
        For Kounter = 0 To R.Fields.Count - 2
            Write #FileNumber, R(Kounter);
        Next
        Write #FileNumber, R(R.Fields.Count - 1)
        R.MoveNext
    Loop
    Close #FileNumber
End Sub
```

The procedure includes some techniques associated with the text file statements.

- ✔ FreeFile. This function is used to automatically generate a file number to use with the text file statements. Because Visual Basic allows you to open multiple text files at one time, the FreeFile statement avoids possible conflicts among open files.

- ✔ In this case, you do not know in advance the number of fields included in the recordset. The Fields.Count property of the recordset is used to determine the number of fields. Keep in mind that in the Fields collection, the first field is zero so that the last field is R.Fields.Count – 1.

- ✔ Normally, the Write # statement starts a new record each time it is used. However, in this case you want to have consecutive Write # statements add fields to the current record until the last field in the recordset has been added to the record. Placing a semicolon at the end of the Write # statement suppresses the start of a new record and causes the text to be added to the same record.

- ✔ The last field in each record, R.Fields.Count – 1, is treated differently than the other fields because it marks the end of a record. The Write # statement used to export the last field does not have a semicolon. This tells Visual Basic to add the CR/LF to mark the end of a record.

The following procedure defines a recordset by drawing data from the Orders table. The data is exported to a file called Example2.TXT by using the ExportRSDeli02 procedure to perform the text file operations.

```
Sub WriteRS02()
    Dim ExpNames As New Recordset
    ExpNames.Open _
        "SELECT ShipLast & ', ' & ShipFirst, " & _
        " OrderDate, OrderTotal " & _
        " FROM Orders ORDER BY OrderID DESC", _
        CurrentProject.Connection
    ExportRSDeli02 "Example2.txt", ExpNames
End Sub
```

Module: FileOperations
Procedure: ExportRSDeli02, WriteRS02

The result is a file that contains data as shown here:

```
"Bremseth, Arthur",#1999-03-09 20:35:27#,"42.8"
"Miller, Ray",#1999-03-09 18:49:03#,"14.9"
"Inbar, Susan",#1999-03-09 18:41:05#,"41.8"
"Rosenberg, justin",#1999-03-09 13:39:54#,"44.8"
"Tocher-grogan, Stephen",#1999-03-09#,"65.75"
```

Note that when Visual Basic writes values taken from Access 2000 date fields, it writes them in a special format, such as #1999-03-09 20:35:27#. Most applications can't recognize this as a date. When you are exporting data from date fields, define the date format in the recordset by using a `Format` function as shown in this example.

```
ExpNames.Open _
    "SELECT ShipLast & ', ' & ShipFirst, " & _
    "Format(OrderDate,'short date') , OrderTotal " & _
    " FROM Orders ORDER BY OrderID DESC", _
```

The result is a text file that contains dates in the usual m/d/yy format.

```
"Bremseth, Arthur","3/9/99","42.8"
"Miller, Ray","3/9/99","14.9"
"Inbar, Susan","3/9/99","41.8"
"Rosenberg, justin","3/9/99","44.8"
"Tocher-grogan, Stephen","3/9/99","65.75"
```

> **Module: FileOperations**
> **Procedure: ExportRSDeli02, WriteRS02a**

Dealing with nulls

Another special case is the way Visual Basic deals with null values that occur in an Access 2000 recordset. Visual Basic inserts the text #Null# in the text when a null is encountered. For example, most of the records in the `Customers` table have a null for the `Address2` field. If you export a recordset containing that field, you get a result like the following text.

```
"Estabrook","Po Box 71013",#NULL#,"19101"
"Talman","225 Edgewood Dr.",#NULL#,"94123"
"Bensky","682 Golden Drive",#NULL#,"94002"
"Ditto","209 Cartland Way",#NULL#,"61822"
"Bremseth","820 Lakeview Dr.  #60",#NULL#,"06902"
```

The #Null# symbol won't be understood by most applications. In order to avoid having your file peppered with #Null# symbols, you have to alter the export procedure to replace the #Null# symbols with a null string, "", a value which is generally understood to be a placeholder for a missing item in a text file. The following procedure eliminates the #Null# symbols from the exported data.

```
Do Until R.EOF
    For Kounter = 0 To R.Fields.Count - 2
        If IsNull(R(Kounter)) Then
            Write #FileNumber, "";
        Else
            Write #FileNumber, R(Kounter);
        End If
    Next
    If Not IsNull(R(R.Fields.Count - 1)) Then
        Write #FileNumber, R(R.Fields.Count - 1)
    End If
    R.MoveNext
Loop
```

> **Module: FileOperations**
> **Procedure: ExportRSDeli03, WriteRS03**

Importing Data

The following data represents a text file, NewNames.TXT, which contains the names of customers that need to be added to the Customers table in your database application. The data in this file is not organized in the same way as the data in the Customers table. The name is not divided into first and last; nor is the city, state, and zip information separated. In addition, the phone number's format is different from the one used in the Customers table.

```
"Walter Lafish","1400 Main Street","Walnut Creek, CA
        94553","(925) 377-3737"
"Nancy Davolio","507 - 20th Ave.","Seattle, WA 98122","(504)
        555-9857"
"Andrew Fuller","908 W. Capital Way","Tacoma, WA
        98401","(504) 555-9482"
"Janet Leverling","722 Moss Bay Blvd.","Kirkland, WA
        98033","(504) 555-3412"
"Margaret Peacock","4110 Old Redmond Rd.","Redmond, WA
        98052","(504) 555-8122"
```

This procedure reads in the data stored in the NewNames.TXT file.

```
Sub ImportNames()
    Dim FileNumber, txtImport
    FileNumber = FreeFile
    Open "NewNames.txt" For Input As #FileNumber
    Do Until EOF(FileNumber)
        Input #FileNumber, txtImport
        Debug.Print txtImport
    Loop
End Sub
```

ON THE CD

> **Module: FileOperations**
> **Procedure: ImportNames**

The mechanics of loading the data from a text file is a relatively simple matter, as illustrated by the previous procedure. But that is not the same thing as actually getting the data inserted into the appropriate fields in a new Customer record. That is because the structure used in the text file to organize the information is different from the structure used in the Customers table.

In order to insert the data, you need to transform the data read from the text file into values that match the structure of the Customers table. This means that the importing process requires a translation layer that transforms the data loaded from the text file into data compatible with the database's structure.

One way to approach this problem is to think of the incoming data as an object that has two sets of properties, input properties and output properties, as listed in Table 8-1. The input properties correspond to the data that will be loaded from the text file. The output properties correspond to the field data you need to enter when you add a new record to the Customers table.

Table 8-1	The Properties of a Name Import Object
Input Properties	*Output Properties*
FullName	FirstName
Street	LastName
CSZ	Address1
Phone(old format)	City
	State
	Zip
	Phone(new format)

If Access included such an object with these properties, you could use it to write some fairly simple code to perform the task of converting the input data to the required field data. The following example uses an object called ImportCust. If you assign the FullName property *Andrew Fuller,* you can then use the LastName and FirstName properties to store those items in the corresponding fields in the Customers table.

```
ImportCust.FullName = "Andrew Fuller"
Customers!FirstName = ImportCust.FirstName
Customers!LastName = ImportCust.LastName
```

But hold on now. Access doesn't have any such ImportCust object. I just made that up. Too bad, isn't it? It would be nice to have objects in the database that corresponded to the specific types of requirements of your data. As it turns out, Visual Basic includes a set of features that enables you to do just that — create your own custom-designed object with properties that you design.

Class modules

In Visual Basic, custom-designed objects are created with Class modules. Each Class module you create defines one object and all its properties and methods. To see how Visual Basic classes work, create a new Class module.

1. **In the database window, select the Modules tab.**

2. **Instead of clicking the New button, choose Insert⇨Class Module.**

Access 2000 opens a new module window in the Visual Basic editor. A Class module looks just like any other Access module. What makes the difference is the types of procedures that you add to the module and the way that they work together as a single unit.

Defining a new property

In ordinary modules, the procedures are either Function or Sub procedures. Class modules can also have these procedures. But in addition, Class modules use Property procedures. There are two basic types of Property procedures.

- ✔ **Property Let**. A Let procedure defines the value of a class property.
- ✔ **Property Get**. A Get procedure is used to return the current value, if any, of a class property.

In order to facilitate creating Property procedures, Visual Basic provides the Add Procedure command.

1. **Choose Insert⇨Procedure.**

   Access 2000 displays the Add Procedure dialog box shown in Figure 8-3.

Figure 8-3:
Data loaded
from a text
file and dis-
played in a
message
box.

2. **In the Name box, enter** FullName.

3. **Click the Property radio button.**

4. **Click OK.**

Access inserts the two procedures shown here:

```
Public Property Get FullName() As Variant

End Property

Public Property Let FullName(ByVal vNewValue As Variant)

End Property
```

How Property procedures work

The code inserted by the Add Procedure dialog box is merely an outline of
the code that is required to create a working Property procedure. You need
to fill in the details in order to get a working user-defined property.

It is important to understand that Property procedures do not function in
isolation. They can be understood only as elements that work together within
a class module. That is in sharp contrast to a standard module in which Sub
or Function procedures operate independently from one another. The fact
that two functions are stored in the same standard module does not imply
that they work together in any way.

On the other hand, a user-defined property requires at least three different
elements stored in the same class module to work together.

✔ **Property Let.** A Let procedure provides a means by which a value can
be assigned to a property. This procedure makes it possible to write a
statement such as the following one that assigns the name Andrew
Fuller to the FullName property.

```
UserObject.FullName = "Andrew Fuller"
```

✔ **Property Get.** A `Get` procedure provides a means of extracting a value from a property of a user-defined object. The following statement displays in a message box the last value, if any, assigned to the `FullName` property.

```
Msgbox UserObject.FullName
```

✔ **Memory Variable.** User-defined properties require that data entered into a `Let` procedure be available to the corresponding `Get` procedure. Normally any data stored in a procedure is discarded when the `End` statement is encountered. In order to create a bridge between the procedures that operate in the same `Class` module, it is necessary to create a *module-level* variable. Module-level variables are created when a `Dim` statement is used in the declarations section of the module. The declarations section refers to any code that appears at the top of the module before the first procedure. If a variable is defined in this section, it becomes available to all the procedures in the module.

The following code illustrates what you need to create the simplest possible property. Two procedures, a `Let` and a `Get`, are related to the `FullName` property. In the declarations section, the variable `vFullName` is defined.

```
Option Compare Database
Option Explicit
Dim vFullName

Public Property Get FullName() As Variant
    FullName = vFullName
End Property

Public Property Let FullName(ByVal vNewValue As Variant)
    vFullName = vNewValue
End Property
```

If you look at the diagram in Figure 8-4, you can see how these elements work together to create a property. When a value is assigned to the property (the `Let` phase), the value is passed as the parameter `vNewValue`, which is in turn assigned to the `vFullName` variable. The `Get` phase reverses the process. When a statement in another module wants to get the `FullName`, the class module passes the current value of the variable `vFullName` to the `Property Get FullName` procedure, which returns that value to the statement that requested the data.

This seems like an awful lot of work just to store and retrieve a value, such as `Andrew Fuller`. If you are patient, you can see by the end of the chapter what a useful tool this can become.

In order to use this simple class module that you created, you need to save the class module. This is another difference between standard and class modules, because you don't have to save standard modules before you execute them.

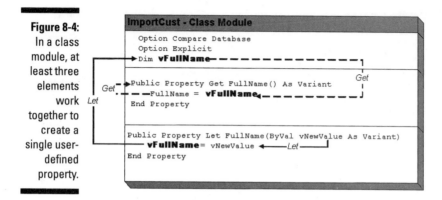

Figure 8-4:
In a class module, at least three elements work together to create a single user-defined property.

```
ImportCust - Class Module
    Option Compare Database
    Option Explicit
    Dim vFullName
    Public Property Get FullName() As Variant
        FullName = vFullName
    End Property

    Public Property Let FullName(ByVal vNewValue As Variant)
        vFullName = vNewValue
    End Property
```

1. **Choose File⇨Save.**

   The Save As dialog box appears.

2. **Enter the name of the class module:** ImportCust.

3. **Click OK.**

You need to understand that the name you give to the class module becomes the name of the object you have created.

Module: CustImport01

Please note that in order to allow you to follow along with the commands listed for creating a class module, the class module on the CD has the name ImportCust01 so that it wouldn't conflict with the example you just saved, CustImport. In the code that follows, I refer to the class modules provided on the CD — for example, CustImport01, CustImport02, and so on.

Accessing a user-defined object

After you have created a class module, the new object type defined by that class module automatically becomes part of the object library available to any procedure in the database. In order to use the newly defined object, you must create an *instance* of that object. The following statement creates a new instance of the ImportCust01 object.

```
Dim Cust1 as New ImportCust01
```

To get a feel for how this works, you can create a simple procedure that uses the new object you created with the ImportCust01 class module.

1. **Open a new standard module by selecting the Module tab in the database window and clicking New.**

2. **Create a new procedure by typing** `Sub UserClass01()` **and then press Enter.**

3. **In the module window, type** `Dim Cust1 As New Imp`.

   Note that Access displays the object list box as you are typing. In the box, you see the names of the class modules, such as `ImportCust01`, list along with the standard object names.

4. **Complete the entry by clicking** `ImportCust01` **in the object list and then press Enter.**

5. **In the module window, type** `Cust1.`.

   As soon as you type the period, Access automatically displays the property and method list for the current object, as shown in Figure 8-5. Because the object you are working with, `Cust1`, is an instance of your user-defined object type `ImportCust01`, the property lists consists of the one property you have defined for that class, `FullName`. Access treats your user-defined object and properties as part of the overall object model of the active database.

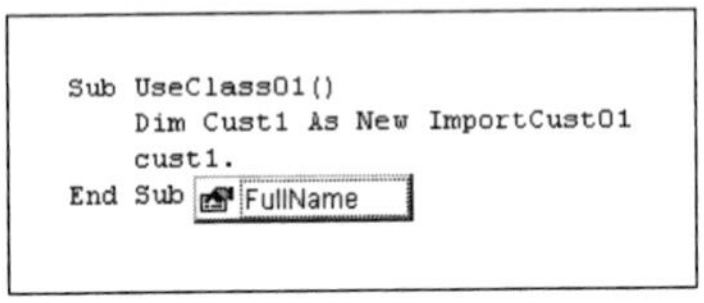

Figure 8-5:
In a class module, at least three elements work together to create a single user-defined property.

```
Sub UseClass01()
    Dim Cust1 As New ImportCust01
    cust1.
End Sub  [ ] FullName
```

6. **Complete the object reference by selecting** `FullName` **from the list.**

7. **Type** `= "Andrew Fuller"` **and press Enter.**

8. **Type** `MsgBox Cust1.FullName`.

You have now created the following procedure. When you execute the procedure, a message box is displayed showing the name `Andrew Fuller`. This is not a very significant operation, but it does demonstrate that you can assign a value to an object property and retrieve it from that object property. This is the basis for all user-defined objects.

```
Sub UserClass01()
    Dim Cust1 As New ImportCust01
    Cust1.FullName = "Andrew Fuller"
    MsgBox Cust1.FullName
End Sub
```

Multiple instances

Visual Basic treats user-defined objects in the same manner that it treats standard objects. This means that you can create multiple instances of the same object within a procedure. The following example creates two instances of the ImportCust object, Cust1 and Cust2. Both instances have the same set of properties, but each can be assigned a different values. The procedure returns two names in the message box.

```
Sub UserClass02()
    Dim Cust1 As New ImportCust01
    Dim Cust2 As New ImportCust01
    Cust1.FullName = "Andrew Fuller"
    Cust2.FullName = "Walter LaFish"
    MsgBox Cust1.FullName & vbCrLf & _
        Cust2.FullName
End Sub
```

Derived properties

A *derived* property is one whose value is not directly assigned but derived from other values. In this example, the first and last names can be derived from the value of the FullName property. The following code illustrates how the derived properties, LastName and FirstName can be added to the class module. The derived properties require only a Property Get procedure to return the derived value. Because these properties are never directly assigned, you don't need to have Property Let procedures associated with them.

```
Dim vFullName, vLastName, VFirstName
...
Public Property Get LastName() As Variant
    LastName = Mid(vFullName, _
            InStr(vFullName, " ") + 1)
End Property
Public Property Get FirstName() As Variant
    FirstName = Mid(vFullName, 1, _
            InStr(vFullName, " ") - 1)
End Property
```

The statements that derive the FirstName and LastName from the FullName utilize two built-in Visual Basic functions.

✔ Mid(text, start, length). This function provides a means of selecting part of a text string by specifying the starting position and the length of the text you want to return. The first example selects the first six characters in the name in order to return the first name. The second example starts at the eighth character and returns the remainder of the text because no length value is specified.

```
Mid("Walter Lafish",1,6) equals "Walter"
Mid("Walter Lafish",8) equals "Lafish"
```

✔ Instr(text,findtext). This function returns a value that indicates the location of a character within a text string. The following example locates the first space character in the name and returns its position, that is, the seventh character.

```
Instr("Walter Lafish"," ") equals 7
```

The Property procedures combine the two functions in order to separate the first and last names. The Instr() function locates the first space in the text; for example, the seventh character. That means the first name consists of all the characters from the beginning (1) to just before the space (7 – 1 = 6). The last name starts at the character after the space (7+1 = 8).

Of course, this system isn't perfect. It assumes that full names have one, and only one, space. If a name contains multiple spaces, you don't have an obvious way to make the procedure separate the first and last names.

Your new object, defined by the ImportCust02 class module, now has both input and derived properties. The following procedure shows how to use the new object to extract separate first and last names from the Fullname input.

```
Sub UserClass03()
    Dim Cust As New ImportCust02
    Cust.FullName = "Walter Lafish"
    Debug.Print Cust.LastName, Cust.FirstName
End Sub
```

Note that when properties are listed in the quick info displays box, you cannot tell which properties are derived, because all properties are listed with the same icon. However, if you attempt to assign a value to a property for which you have not created a Property Let procedure, you get an error when you run the code.

> **Module: CustImport02, UsingClasses**
> **Procedure: UserClass03**

The next step is to expand the properties in the class module to handle all the inputs and outputs required to convert the text file addresses to the appropriate fields for the Customers table. The following code shows the derived property formulas added to the class module to transform the CSZ and Phone inputs into data compatible with the Customers table.

```
Public Property Get City() As Variant
    City = Mid(vCSZ, 1, _
              InStr(vCSZ, ",") - 1)
End Property
Public Property Get State() As Variant
    State = Mid(vCSZ, _
    InStr(vCSZ, ",") + 2, 2)
End Property
Public Property Get Zip() As Variant
    Zip = Mid(vCSZ, _
    InStr(vCSZ, ",") + 5)
End Property
Public Property Get Phone() As Variant
    Phone = Mid(vPhone, 2, 3) & "-" & _
        Mid(vPhone, 7)
End Property
```

Module: CustImport03

You now have a class module that has all the properties described in Table 8-1. The additional properties are reflected in the properties and methods list (see Figure 8-6). This is a very significant aspect of user-defined objects. When you write procedures that utilize user-defined objects, the code begins to reflect the business process terminology that you have built into the class module. Your code begins to look less like generic Visual Basic and more like the application you are building.

Figure 8-6:
The
properties
and
methods
box lists all
the
properties
defined in
the class
module.

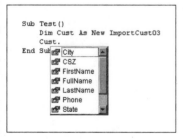

The following procedure tests the effectiveness of the class module. The procedure creates an instance of the `ImportCust03` class called `Cust`. Values are assigned to the input properties and the derived properties are output to the Immediate window by means of the `Debug.Print` method.

```
Sub UserClass04()
    Dim Cust As New ImportCust03
    Cust.FullName = "Walter Lafish"
    Cust.Street = "1400 Main Street"
    Cust.CSZ = "Walnut Creek, CA 94553"
    Cust.Phone = "(925) 377-3737"
    Debug.Print _
        "First= " & Cust.FirstName, _
        "Last= " & Cust.LastName, _
        "Street = " & Cust.Street, _
        "City= " & Cust.City, _
        "State= " & Cust.State, _
        "Zip= " & Cust.Zip, _
        "Phone= " & Cust.Phone
End Sub
```

ON THE CD

> **Module: UsingClasses**
> **Procedure:UserClass04**

The next step is to connect the class module with the techniques discussed in the beginning of the chapter for accessing a text file. The following procedure opens the text file NewNames.TXT and loads the data from that file into an instance of the `ImportCust03` object class. It requires four `Input #` statements to assign values to each of the input properties of the `Cust` object. When that has been done, you can use the derived properties — for example, `City` or `State` — to display data in the Immediate window.

```
Sub ImportNamesToClasses()
    Dim FileNumber, txtImport
    Dim Cust As New ImportCust03
    FileNumber = FreeFile
    Open "NewNames.txt" For Input As #FileNumber
    Do Until EOF(FileNumber)
        Input #FileNumber, txtImport
            Cust.FullName = txtImport
        Input #FileNumber, txtImport
            Cust.Street = txtImport
        Input #FileNumber, txtImport
            Cust.CSZ = txtImport
        Input #FileNumber, txtImport
            Cust.Phone = txtImport
    Debug.Print _
        "First= " & Cust.FirstName, _
        "Last= " & Cust.LastName, _
        "Street = " & Cust.Street, _
        "City= " & Cust.City, _
        "State= " & Cust.State, _
```

```
            "Zip= " & Cust.Zip, _
            "Phone= " & Cust.Phone
            Set Cust = Nothing
        Loop
End Sub
```

One important feature to note is the statement `Set Cust = Nothing`, which precedes the `Loop` statement. Keep in mind that all the data displayed by this procedure is loaded into a single instance of the user-defined object, `Cust`. The `Set Cust = Nothing` statement is used to ensure that the `Cust` object begins each iteration of the loop with a blank set of properties. Because each property in the object is assigned a new value in the procedure, this statement is not necessary in this case. However, in cases where a property may not be assigned a value each and every time, `Set Object = Nothing` eliminates the possibility of data from the previous iteration being carried forward into the next loop.

> **Module: UsingClasses**
> **Procedure:ImportNamesToClasses**

User-Defined Collections

At this point, you have created an object that handles the transformation of the text file inputs into a series of outputs compatible with the Customers table. Each `ImportCust03` corresponds to one of the new customer names included in the text file.

But what about the text file as a whole? The text file is actually a collection of one or more new customer records. If your goal is to import a series of new customer records, then you may want to create a user-defined object that corresponds to the entire group of new customers. If you look at the text file in object model terms, each record in the text file is a customer object. The entire file is a collection of one or more customer objects. You might call this object an `ImportBatch` because it represents all the records that are imported in a single operation.

Visual Basic allows you to create user-defined objects that are collections of other objects, either built-in or user-defined. The following statement creates a new collection type object.

```
Dim NewNames As New Collection
```

After you have a collection object, you can add any type of object to the collection using the `Add` method. Visual Basic doesn't care what type of object you add. It can be a built-in object like a `Recordset` or a `Field` or an object defined by a class module. The following statement adds an object to a collection.

```
NewNames.Add = Cust
```

You can refer to objects in a collection by number where 1 is the first object added to the collection.

```
NewNames(1)
```

You also have the option to process all the objects in a collection using a For Each statement.

```
For Each Cust in NewNames
```

The following code defines a new class of user-defined objects called ImportBatch. The purpose of this object is to act as a repository for all the new customers that are imported.

```
Option Compare Database
Option Explicit
Dim vNewNames As New Collection
Public Property Set AddName(ByVal vNewValue As ImportCust03)
    vNewNames.Add vNewValue
End Property
Public Property Get NameCount()
    NameCount = vNewNames.Count
End Property
Public Property Get NewNames() As Collection
    Set NewNames = vNewNames
End Property
```

Note several points about how this class is constructed. The ImportCust03 class dealt with only properties that consisted of single values. The ImportBatch class includes more complex objects. For example, the AddName property adds a new object to the collection. In this case, each object is an ImportCust03 object, not merely a text or numeric value. The data type specified by the As keyword must correspond to the type of object that should be added to the collection.

```
Public Property Set AddName(ByVal vNewValue As _
    ImportCust03)
```

The NewNames property is used to return the entire collection of ImportCust03 objects so that the batch can be processed with a structure like a For Each loop. When a property simply returns a text or numeric value, you don't need to use the As keyword. In this case, As is needed to allow the property procedure to return the collection object. Further, the assignment statement in the procedure must be a Set statement. Visual Basic requires that when the item being assigned is an object (not a text or numeric value) that Set be used.

```
Public Property Get NewNames() As Collection
    Set NewNames = vNewNames
End Property
```

The following procedure utilizes both of the user-defined objects. The
ImportCust03 object is used to load customer data from the text file in an
organized unit. Each instance of the Cust object is added to an instance of
the ImportBatch collection.

```
Dim FileNumber, txtImport
Dim Upload As New ImportBatch
Dim Cust As New ImportCust03
FileNumber = FreeFile
Open "NewNames.txt" For Input As #FileNumber
Do Until EOF(FileNumber)
    Input #FileNumber, txtImport
        Cust.FullName = txtImport
    Input #FileNumber, txtImport
        Cust.Street = txtImport
    Input #FileNumber, txtImport
        Cust.CSZ = txtImport
    Input #FileNumber, txtImport
        Cust.Phone = txtImport
    Set Upload.AddName = Cust
    Set Cust = Nothing
Loop
```

At the end of the loop there exists a collection object called Upload that contains a series of ImportCust03 objects. The NameCount property enables
you to obtain a count of the number of ImportCust03 objects currently in
the collection.

```
MsgBox Upload.NameCount
```

The NewNames property returns the collection object. This enables you to
use a For Each...Next structure to process each of the members of the
collection.

```
For Each Cust In Upload.NewNames
    MsgBox Cust.LastName
Next
```

> ***Module: ImportCust03, ImportBatch, UsingClasses***
> ***Procedure: ImportNamesToCollection***

Chapter 9

Printing, Reports, and Output

• •

In This Chapter

▶ Calculating report headings

▶ Numbering records

▶ Summary tables on reports

▶ Multiple selections

▶ Fast form letters

▶ E-mail, HTML, and other output

• •

*I*n this chapter, I move into the wonderful world of printing, reports, and output. Without these three, you don't get the most out of programming with Access (and you'll soon find out why).

> **Database Folder: Chapter 9**
> **Database File: Reporting.mdb**

To begin this chapter, load the database for Chapter 9, Reporting.MDB. Click the Forms tab in the database window. The forms I discuss in this chapter appear in that file.

Controlling Reports

Reporting remains one of the strongest features in Access 2000. Many developers, including myself, like to use Access to develop applications in large part because of its report features. But to make truly effective use of reports, you need to be able to control the reporting process. For example, most reports dealing with sales have a time element involved. Users typically like to be able to select a range of dates and then produce a report for that specific date range.

The basic tool for controlling reports through Visual Basic is the `DoCmd.OpenReport` method. The following statement prints a report named `Basic Sales List`.

```
DoCmd.OpenReport "Basic Sales List"
```

Like the `DoCmd.OpenForm` method, `OpenReport` accepts a `WhereCondition` parameter. This parameter is a text string that can function as a SQL `WHERE` clause to select records for the report. The following example prints the report and restricts the recordset to records whose date is 1/1/99.

```
DoCmd.OpenReport "Basic Sales List",,"Date = #1/1/99#"
```

Keep in mind that the expression used with the `WhereCondition` parameter is a SQL expression. This enables you to use SQL operators such as `Like` or `Between...And` along with Visual Basic operators and functions. When formatting a date range, the `Between...And` operator provides the simplest way to include the dates.

```
DoCmd.OpenReport "Basic Sales List",, _
    "Date Between #1/1/99# And #12/31/99#"
```

One way to control reports is to use Access 2000 forms as dialog boxes. Figure 9-1 shows a simple form whose purpose is to print a report called `Basic Sales List`. The two text boxes on the report allow the user to enter a starting and ending date. The idea is to use those dates to set a date range limit on the data displayed in the report.

Figure 9-1:
A simple form used to control the date range of a report.

The basic technique is shown in the following procedure. The dates entered into the form are used to compose a `WHERE` clause expression, which is passed to the report as the `WhereCondition` parameter of the `OpenReport` method.

```
Private Sub Command0_Click()
    Dim ReportName
    ReportName = "Basic Sales List"
    DoCmd.OpenReport _
        ReportName:=ReportName, _
        view:=acViewPreview, _
        WhereCondition:="Date Between #" & _
            Me.StartDate & "# AND #" & _
            Me.EndDate & "#"
End Sub
```

> **Form: Report Dialog 01**

Filling in dates

The form shown in Figure 9-1 provides the basic outline of a form that you can use to control a report. The critical entry is the dates placed into the two entry boxes, which form the basis of the criteria that controls the recordset used by the report.

Instead of leaving the dates blank when a user opens the form, you can improve the functionality of the form by filling in the dates with some default values.

For example, you may want to insert dates that represent the actual range of dates found in the source table in this case — the Orders table.

The following procedure uses an ADO recordset to query the Orders table to return the actual range of dates. The Min() and Max() aggregate functions return lowest and highest values from the OrderDate field. The values are then inserted into the StartDate and EndDate controls.

```
Private Sub Form_Load()
    Dim DateRange As New Recordset
    DateRange.Open _
        "SELECT Min(DateValue(OrderDate)) as SDate," & _
        "Max(DateValue(OrderDate)) as EDate " & _
        "FROM Orders", _
        CurrentProject.Connection
    Me.StartDate = DateRange!Sdate
    Me.EndDate = DateRange!edate
End Sub
```

> **Form: Report Dialog 02**

Building a date information class

The date range default values used in the previous section are useful in that they provide the user with information about the range of possible dates for which this database contains data. If you think about the way that businesses or organizations work, you can think of other date ranges that are potentially more meaningful as possible default values.

For example, companies commonly report sales information on a monthly basis. In order to print a monthly sales report, you would need to enter the first and last days of the month for which you want to print the report. Although the first day of the month is easy to remember, the last day of a given month is a bit harder. Due to the vagaries of the solar system and human history, we have a calendar whose month lengths represent an arbitrary series of values that you need to memorize. As simple as this task may seem, I am not ashamed to admit I often have to start saying "Thirty days hath . . ." in order to fill in the correct date value. Things get worse if I want to do weekly date ranges.

One solution is to let the computer do the work and provide these key dates automatically. For example, the following list of items provides the dates needed for monthly or weekly reporting.

- ✔ FirstofMonth. The first day of the current month.
- ✔ LastofMonth. The last day of the current month.
- ✔ FirstofBizWeek. The Monday of the current week.
- ✔ LastofBizWeek. The Friday of the current week.

There are several ways to approach this problem in Visual Basic. You could use Visual Basic to create a series of user-defined functions, each of which returns one of the date values.

However, a better approach is to think of the dates described earlier as properties possessed by a specific date. If you start with any given date you might ask, "What is the first day of the month that contains that date? What is the last day of the month that contains that date? What are the Monday and Friday dates of the week that contains that date?"

What all these dates have in common is that they are derived by performing a calculation based on a single date that is the starting point. Visual Basic class modules provide a structure that is ideal for expressing this type of relationship. Imagine that you create an object called DateInfo that has properties such as FirstofBizWeek and LastofBizWeek. Anytime you need to get information about a weekly or monthly date range, you can create an instance of a DateInfo object and use the properties to obtain the exact dates needed.

The upcoming code is a Property Get procedure, FirstofMonth, that calculates the first day of the month for any date defined by the vInitDate variable. The procedure uses three calendar-related functions built into Visual Basic.

- ✔ Month(date). This function returns a numeric value equal to the month portion of a date.

✔ Year(date). This function returns a numeric value equal to the year portion of a date.

✔ DateSerial(YearNumber, MonthNumber,DayNumber). This function returns a date based on numeric values for year, month, and day.

The procedure uses the current month and year values and inserts 1 as the day to calculate the first day of the month.

```
Public Property Get FirstofMonth() As Variant
    FirstofMonth = DateSerial(Year(vInitDate), _
        Month(vInitDate), 1)
End Property
```

Calculating the last day of a given month is a bit trickier. The calculation requires the use of an additional Visual Basic function called DateAdd(). DateAdd allows you to add or subtract units of time from a given date. The units are specified by codes such as "mm" for month, "ww" for week, or "yyyy" for year.

The Property Get LastofMonth procedure calculates the last day of the current month by first calculating the first day of the month in the same manner as the FirstofMonth procedure. DateAdd is then used to incre ment that date by one month, which returns the first day of the next month. Finally, subtracting one day from that date provides the last day of the current month.

```
Public Property Get LastofMonth() As Variant
    LastofMonth = DateAdd("m", 1, _
                  DateSerial(Year(vInitDate), _
                  Month(vInitDate), 1)) _
                  - 1
End Property
```

You can perform day-based date calculations without using any date functions. Adding or subtracting numbers from a date value treats each day as having a value of 1. For example, Date() -1 returns yesterday's date. Date() + 7 adds seven days to the current date. If you use a decimal number, the decimal is treated as a percentage of a day. Date() + 1.75 returns the date for tomorrow plus the time 6:00 PM.

The weekly date values are calculated using the Visual Basic function WeekDay(). WeekDay returns values 0 to 6, corresponding to the days of the week starting with Sunday (0) to Saturday (6).

```
Public Property Get LastofBizWeek() As Variant
    LastofBizWeek = vInitDate + (6 - Weekday(vInitDate))
End Property

Public Property Get FirstofBizWeek() As Variant
    FirstofBizWeek = vInitDate - (Weekday(vInitDate) - 2)
End Property
```

Because all the date calculations are based on a date stored in a variable called vInitDate, defining that value is a significant part of the class module. The following property procedures enable you to retrieve and set the vInitDate property so that you can use the DateInfo object to get dates, such as LastOfMonth, relative to any date you define as vInitDate.

```
Public Property Get InitDate() As Variant
    InitDate = vInitDate
End Property
Public Property Let InitDate(ByVal vNewValue As Variant)
    vInitDate = vNewValue
End Property
```

The Initialize event

Every class module supports two events: Initialize, which occurs each time a new instance of the object is created, and Terminate, which occurs each time an instance of the object is discarded.

The Initialize event provides a mechanism for setting default values for an object class. For example, you may want to set the vInitDate value to the current system date by default. The following example uses the Class_Initialize procedure to set the default value for vInitDate.

```
Dim vInitDate
Private Sub Class_Initialize()
    vInitDate = Date
End Sub
```

Increment methods

The properties defined in the DateInfo class return key dates that are calculated in relation to the vInitDate value. In addition to properties, a class can have methods also. A method is some action that a class can perform. For example, it may be useful to provide methods in the DateInfo class that automatically increment the vInitDate forward or backward a month or a week at a time. These methods allow you to start with a given date and then move the DateInfo class backward or forward in time in specific increments.

You can create class methods by adding Sub or Function procedures to the class module. The following Sub procedures each modify the value of vInitDate by adding or subtracting a week or month date unit.

```
Sub NextMonth()
    vInitDate = DateAdd("m", 1, vInitDate)
End Sub
Sub PreviousMonth()
    vInitDate = DateAdd("m", -1, vInitDate)
End Sub
Sub NextWeek()
    vInitDate = DateAdd("ww", 1, vInitDate)
End Sub
Sub PreviousWeek()
    vInitDate = DateAdd("ww", -1, vInitDate)
End Sub
```

Using the DateInfo class

Now that you have the `DateInfo` class available, you can use it to supply
date Information to any procedure. Suppose that you wanted to set the
default date range for a report to the current month. The `StartDate` control
would be equal to the `FirstofMonth` property and the `EndDate` control
would be equal to the `LastofMonth` property.

The following `Form_Load` procedure provides the desired dates using only
three statements by using a `DateInfo` class. The `Dim` statement is used to
create a new instance of the `DateInfo` object. Recall that because the
`DateInfo` class contains a `Class_Initialize` procedure, the object is automatically assigned a `vInitDate` value equal to the current date. The
procedure then inserts the `FirstofMonth` and `LastofMonth` properties into
the corresponding controls.

```
Private Sub Form_Load()
    Dim Dt As New DateInfo
    Me.StartDate = Dt.FirstofMonth
    Me.EndDate = Dt.LastofMonth
    With Me
        .NavigationButtons = False
        .ScrollBars = 0
        .RecordSelectors = False
        .DividingLines = False
    End With
End Sub
```

Form: Report Dialog 03

Incrementing date ranges

In the previous example, the DateInfo class was used to set the default dates for the dialog box to a date range for the current month. But the DateInfo class provides the ability to do much more than that. As an example, look at the form shown in Figure 9-2. In this form, two arrow buttons are placed above the date range. The up and down arrows increase or decrease the value of the date range by one month each time a user clicks them. These arrow buttons enable users to easily select whatever month they desire as the report range without actually having to enter the dates manually.

Figure 9-2:
Arrow
buttons
used to
increment
the date
range.

The coding required to modify the form to perform this new task is relatively minor because the details related to the date calculations are stored in the class module. All that is needed in the form's module are statements that use the PreviousMonth and NextMonth methods of the DateInfo object.

Object lifetime

However, before you deal with the code that executes these methods, an important but subtle change needs to be made to the form. The change involves the location of the statement that creates the instance of the DateInfo object.

In the previous example (Report Dialog 03), the Dim statement shown in the following code was placed into the Form_Load procedure. Creating an instance of the object inside of a procedure means that the object will continue to exist only while that procedure is executing. As soon as the Form_Load procedure is finished, the Dt object will be discarded.

```
Private Sub Form_Load()
    Dim Dt As New DateInfo
    statements...
End Sub
```

The length of time that a variable (either a standard or an object variable) exists within an application is called the *lifetime* of the variable. The capability of a variable to retain its value is called the *scope*. Visual Basic recognizes four different combinations of lifetime and scope.

✔ **Procedure-level.** If the `Dim` statement appears inside a procedure, the variable exists and retains its value for only the duration of the procedure. Its scope and lifetime are limited to that procedure.

✔ **Module-level.** If you place the `Dim` statement in the `Declarations` section of the module (the area before the first procedure), the variable is available to all the procedures in the module and it retains its value throughout the module. The lifetime and scope of a module-level variable cover all the procedures in that module.

✔ **Public.** If you use the keyword `Public` in place of `Dim`, the variable becomes available to any procedure in any module in the application and the value is retained throughout the application. These variables have the same scope and lifetime as the application of which they are a part.

✔ **Static.** If you use the keyword `Static` in place of `Dim` within a procedure, the variable's value is retained after the procedure ends. Its lifetime is limited to the procedure, but its scope is on the module level. This means that Visual Basic retains the last value assigned to the variable, even after the procedure ends, and it is available the next time the procedure is executed. However, only the procedure that created the variable can use it.

In this case, you want to make the `DateInfo` object available to the entire module so that the arrow button procedures are working with the same `DateInfo` object that was used to set the default values for the text box controls. The `Dim` statement is moved from the `Form_Load` procedure to the declarations section of the form's Visual Basic module.

```
Option Compare Database
Option Explicit
Dim Dt As New DateInfo
Private Sub Form_Load()
    Me.StartDate = Dt.FirstofMonth
    Me.EndDate = Dt.LastofMonth
    With Me
        .NavigationButtons = False
        .ScrollBars = 0
        .RecordSelectors = False
        .DividingLines = False
    End With
End Sub
```

The `Dt` variable is not available to all the procedures in the form. The following two procedures are assigned to the `Click` event procedures of the Down and Up buttons, respectively. They each modify the value of the `Dt` object by applying either the `PreviousMonth` or `NextMonth` methods to the `Dt` object. The new start and end date values are inserted into the text box controls.

```
Private Sub Down_Click()
    Dt.PreviousMonth
    Me.StartDate = Dt.FirstofMonth
    Me.EndDate = Dt.LastofMonth
End Sub

Private Sub Up_Click()
    Dt.NextMonth
    Me.StartDate = Dt.FirstofMonth
    Me.EndDate = Dt.LastofMonth
End Sub
```

Using the buttons, users can quickly select a range of dates for any month they desire.

> *Form: Report Dialog 04*

Using different time increments

Recall that the DateInfo object supports date changes on a weekly as well as a monthly basis. The form shown in Figure 9-3 enables the user to select either monthly or weekly date range changes.

Figure 9-3:
The form
can change
date ranges
on a weekly
or monthly
basis.

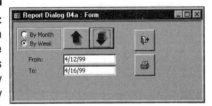

In order to implement two different date increments, a frame control with two buttons is added to the form. The frame control returns a numeric value that corresponds to the selected button. In this example, the frame control is called Increment. The Monthly button returns 1, and the Weekly button returns 2.

The following procedures use the frame control to select which methods and properties of the DateInfo object Dt are applied to the form. This provides the user with the option to change the dates in weekly or monthly increments.

```
Private Sub Down_Click()
    If Me.Increment = 1 Then
        Dt.PreviousMonth
        Me.StartDate = Dt.FirstofMonth
        Me.EndDate = Dt.LastofMonth
    Else
        Dt.PreviousWeek
        Me.StartDate = Dt.FirstofBizWeek
        Me.EndDate = Dt.LastofBizWeek
    End If
End Sub

Private Sub Up_Click()
    If Me.Increment = 1 Then
        Dt.NextMonth
        Me.StartDate = Dt.FirstofMonth
        Me.EndDate = Dt.LastofMonth
    Else
        Dt.NextWeek
        Me.StartDate = Dt.FirstofBizWeek
        Me.EndDate = Dt.LastofBizWeek
    End If
End Sub
```

Form: Report Dialog 04a

Preventing empty reports

When you limit the recordset of a report by dates, you can't guarantee that the selected range actually contains any data. You may find that when you print the report, you get #ERROR marks on the report because the recordset of the report is empty.

Although this output doesn't do any harm, you may want to avoid this situation in the first place by using Visual Basic to determine if valid records exist for the selected date range prior to printing the report.

Figure 9-4 shows a form in which the print button is disabled because no records in the table match the displayed dates. In addition, the title bar of the dialog box shows that 0 records exist for the selected dates.

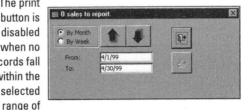

How can the form determine in advance whether the report will be empty or include data? You can obtain the answer by defining a recordset variable that uses the date range displayed on the form as its criterion. Because you apply the same date-range criterion to the report, the recordset's contents will exactly match the recordset of the report.

The following procedure called CountSales creates a recordset variable, R, that queries the Orders table for records that fall within the displayed date range and returns a count of the records.

```
Sub CountSales()
    Dim R As New Recordset
    R.Open "SELECT count(*) FROM Orders " & _
        "WHERE datevalue(orderdate) Between #" & _
        Me.StartDate & "# AND #" & _
        Me.EndDate & "#", _
        CurrentProject.Connection
    Me.Command0.Enabled = R(0)
    Me.Caption = R(0) & " sales to report."
End Sub
```

One point to note is the way in which the value of the Enabled property of the print button (Command0) is set with a single statement. If you look at the following code, you can see that the value returned by the recordset, R(0), is evaluated by an If statement. If the value is zero, the button's enabled property is set to False; that is, the button is disabled. If the value is not zero, it is enabled.

```
If R(0) = 0 Then
    Me.Command0.Enabled = False
Else
    Me.Command0.Enabled = True
Endif
```

However, you may recall from earlier in the book that a value of zero is equivalent to a `False` value and that any value that is not zero is the same as a `True` value. This means that `True` and `False` in this case directly correspond to the numeric value returned by the recordset. You can simplify the code to a single statement like this one:

```
Me.Command0.Enabled = R(0)
```

You need to insert the `CountSales` procedure into the form's module in any procedure that changes the date range, such as the `Form_Load` procedure.

```
Private Sub Form_Load()
    Me.StartDate = Dt.FirstofMonth
    Me.EndDate = Dt.LastofMonth
    CountSales
    With Me
        .NavigationButtons = False
        .ScrollBars = 0
        .RecordSelectors = False
        .DividingLines = False
    End With
End Sub
```

In addition to `Form_Load`, the `Down_Click`, `Up_Click`, `EndDate_AfterUpdate`, and `StartDate_AfterUpdate` procedures should call the `CountSales` procedure in order to ensure that the count is updated each time the dates are altered.

Form: Report Dialog 05

Defining range options

In the previous examples, the user could enter or insert a date range for a report. Another approach would be to anticipate the date ranges that would typically be used with a given report and generate a list of available periods from which the user can make a selection.

For example, suppose that a sales report is printed on a monthly basis. You can summarize in a list of monthly periods the date ranges for which reports could be printed, as shown in Figure 9-5.

You can obtain the list shown in Figure 9-5 by performing a query on the `Orders` table that groups the orders by the financial period. Keep in mind that the `OrderDate` field contains full date/time values. If you want to group by financial period, you must convert the dates to month and year periods. One way to accomplish this is by using the `Format()` function to change the dates into period names — such as July 1998, August 1998, and so on — as shown in the following code expression.

Figure 9-5:
A list box
displays the
financial
periods for
which a
report can
be printed.

```
Format([OrderDate],'mmmm yyyy')AS Period
```

Keep in mind that although the text produced by the `Format` function creates the correct monthly grouping, the groups won't be in the correct chronological order because the names of the months are alphabetized by the month name.

The solution is to include a field in the recordset that does contain date values that can then be used with the `Order By` clause to sort the recordset chronologically. In this case, the following expression is used. It uses the `First()` function to return a date/time value from the `OrderDate` fields. The `DateValue()` is used to truncate any time value stored along with the date.

```
First(DateValue(OrderDate)) AS InitDate
```

Which date is selected by `First()`? The answer in this case is that it doesn't matter. The orders are already being grouped by period. Any date within that period that is selected will have the desired month and year value, and that is all you need to get the records sorted chronologically.

The following procedure summarizes the `Orders` table into the list shown in Figure 9-5. The `DESC` keyword specifies descending sort order so that the most recent financial period appears at the top of the list. As a bonus, the query counts the number of orders in each period. Also, notice that the `InitDate` column is given a zero width so that it does not appear on the form. You do, however, need to have that date available because you can use that value to calculate the start and end dates for the report.

```
Private Sub Form_Load()
    Dim SQLText
    SQLText = "SELECT Format([OrderDate],'mmmm yyyy') AS
            Period," & _
    "Count(OrderID) AS Sales," & _
    "First(DateValue(OrderDate)) AS InitDate " & _
    "FROM Orders " & _
    "GROUP BY Format([OrderDate],'mmmm yyyy') " & _
    "ORDER BY First(Orders.OrderDate) DESC"
    With Me.FiscalPeriods
```

```
            .RowSource = SQLText
            .ColumnCount = 3
            .ColumnWidths = "1 in;.5 in;0"
            .ColumnHeads = True
        End With
    End Sub
```

The following procedure shows how the user's selection from the financial period list is converted into an actual date range. Again, the procedure utilizes the DateInfo class to calculate the precise dates required to print the report. The `DateInfo` object's `InitDate` property is assigned the date in column 2 (the hidden column) from the `List` property. Once assigned, the `DateInfo` object can return the required `FirstOfMonth` and `LastofMonth` dates, which are passed to the report.

```
Private Sub Command0_Click()
    Dim ReportName, Dt As New DateInfo
    ReportName = "Basic Sales List"
    Dt.InitDate = Me.FiscalPeriods.Column(2)
    DoCmd.OpenReport _
        ReportName:=ReportName, _
        view:=acViewPreview, _
        WhereCondition:="Date Between #" & _
            Dt.FirstofMonth & "# AND #" & _
            Dt.LastofMonth & "#"
End Sub
```

| Form: Report Dialog 06 |

Preview or print?

The default operational mode for the `OpenReport` method is to send the report directly to the printer. A more useful method, however, is to include a set of option buttons that enables the user to send output either to the screen preview display or directly to the printer, as you can see in Figure 9-6.

By default, Access 2000 assigns consecutive values to the buttons added to a frame control such as the one shown in Figure 9-6. In that case, the top button, `TogglePreview`, would be 1 and the second, `TogglePrint`, would be assigned the value of 2. The following procedure uses the value of the frame control, called `OutputMode`, to determine which constant, `acViewPreview` or `acViewNormal`, is passed to the `OpenReport` method.

Figure 9-6:
Option buttons enable the user to control the output mode of the report.

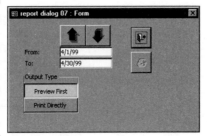

```
Private Sub Command0_Click()
    Dim ReportName
    Dim SendTo
    Select Case Me.OutputMode
        Case 1
            SendTo = acViewPreview
        Case 2
            SendTo = acViewNormal
    End Select
    ReportName = "Basic Sales List"
    DoCmd.OpenReport _
        ReportName:=ReportName, _
        view:=SendTo, _
        WhereCondition:="Date Between #" & _
            Me.StartDate & "# AND #" & _
            Me.EndDate & "#"
End Sub
```

> **Form: Report Dialog 07**

Although nothing is wrong with that code, it might seem a bit convoluted if you recall that each of the constants used in Visual Basic actually stands for a numeric value. The values of the constants used with the `OpenReport` method's View argument are listed in Table 9-1.

Table 9-1	OpenReport View Argument Values	
Value	**Constant**	**Meaning**
0	acViewNormal	Send directly to printer
1	acViewDesign	Open in the design mode
2	acViewPreview	Display the print preview window

In order to figure out the actual numeric value of a built-in constant, you can enter a command such as ? acViewNormal in the Immediate window, which prints the result. An even better method is to open the Object Browser (press F2 in an open module window) and search for the constant you want to locate. To search, enter the text in the second combo box in the upper-left corner of the form and click the binocular icon. Click on the constant name and the actual value, Const acViewNormal = 0, appears in the gray area at the bottom of the window. It also shows you the group to which this constant belongs, in green. Click the group to see a list of all constants in that group.

If you look at the Case structure used to determine the output mode with the number rather than the constants, you can see that you are really involved in swapping one number for another. For example, if the control value is 1, then the output mode value should be 2.

```
Select Case Me.OutputMode
    Case 1
        SendTo = 2
    Case 2
        SendTo = 0
End Select
```

You can simplify the code by assigning the constant values directly to the button to which they correspond. The following three statements set the values and the default for the frame control. The values of the buttons now have the numeric values that correspond to their function.

```
Private Sub Form_Load()
    Me.TogglePreview.OptionValue = acViewPreview
    Me.TogglePrint.OptionValue = acViewNormal
    Me.OutputMode = acViewPreview
End Sub
```

In the procedure that prints the report, you can eliminate the Select Case structure and simply insert the value of the frame control, Me.OutputMode, directly into the OpenReport method as the output mode parameter.

```
Private Sub Command0_Click()
    Dim ReportName
    ReportName = "Basic Sales List"
    DoCmd.OpenReport _
        ReportName:=ReportName, _
        view:=Me.OutputMode, _
        WhereCondition:="Date Between #" & _
            Me.StartDate & "# AND #" & _
            Me.EndDate & "#"
End Sub
```

Form: Report Dialog 07a

Choosing the Report

You can use a single dialog box to control more than one report. The form in Figure 9-7 contains a frame control that lists two reports from which the user can select.

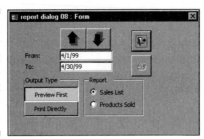

To accommodate additional reports, a `Select Case` structure is added to the procedure that prints the report. Note that the `Case` structure defines two values. The first is the name of the report to be printed. The second is the name of the field in the corresponding data set that contains the dates that will be selected. In this case, you can see that the two reports use different records sources and that the date field is different in each case.

```
Private Sub Command0_Click()
    Dim ReportName, DateFieldName
    Select Case Me.PickReport
        Case 1
            ReportName = "Basic Sales List"
            DateFieldName = "Date"
        Case 2
            DateFieldName = "FiscalPeriod"
            ReportName = "Basic Product List"
    End Select
    DoCmd.OpenReport _
        ReportName:=ReportName, _
        view:=Me.OutputMode, _
        wherecondition:=DateFieldName & " Between #" & _
            Me.StartDate & "# AND #" & _
            Me.EndDate & "#"
End Sub
```

Form: Report Dialog 08

Showing the Parameters on the Report

One problem that occurs when you control the content of a form from a dialog box is that nothing prints on the form to indicate the range of dates for which the report was produced. Because you don't know in advance what dates will be selected, you can't add the date range to the report's design.

Figure 9-8 shows a report that displays the dates entered in the dialog box that controls the recordset of the report. Now, anyone reading the report will know the original date range that was used to produce the report.

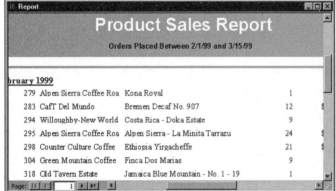

Figure 9-8:
The
selected
date range
appears on
the form.

This effect was achieved by using Visual Basic inside the report form itself. Like forms, reports can have code modules as well. The event model of the report is much simpler than a form because no user interaction takes place with controls and sections of a report. Reports have three basic events:

- ✔ **Format.** This event occurs the first time Access 2000 formats a section of the report. Formatting involves the layout of the controls in that section.

- ✔ **Retreat.** The retreat event occurs when Access 2000 is forced to return to an already formatted section and make adjustments.

- ✔ **Print.** This event occurs after the format has been completed. This is when the data is filled into the controls on each page to produce the final image.

In this case, you want to use the Print event of the Report Header because that is where the DateRangeLabel control is located. The procedure creates a form variable that refers to the dialog box form used to initiate the printing of the report. In effect, the report is looking back at the dialog box that triggered the report to see the exact set of dates used in the dialog box. A second copy of the date range is inserted into the control GrandTotalLabel, which is placed in the Report footer.

```
Private Sub ReportHeader_Print(Cancel As Integer, PrintCount
        As Integer)
    Dim F As Form
    Set F = Forms![Report Dialog 09]
    Me.DateRangeLabel.Caption = _
        "Orders Placed Between " & F!StartDate & _
        " and " & F!EndDate
    With Me.GrandTotalLabel
        .Caption = "Totals for " & F!StartDate & _
        " and " & F!EndDate
    End With
End Sub
```

Keep in mind that you cannot reliably calculate the date range from the data
in the report. For example, if you select the date range 3/1/99 to 3/31/99, you
may find that the range of dates in the recordset that falls within those dates
is smaller than the full month — for example, 3/3/99 to 3/28/99. If you were to
calculate a date range by selecting the Min([OrderDate]) and
Max([OrderDate]) values of the Reports recordset, you would find that
people reading the report may wonder why the full month (3/1/99 to 3/31/99)
isn't represented on the report. For this reason, using the actual dates
entered in the dialog box more accurately represents the meaning of the
report. If there are no orders for 3/1/99 to 3/2/99, that fact is clear if the selection date range appears on the report.

The report also contains another handy feature that you can implement in
the reports code module, which is alternating bands of gray printed in the
details section. This produces a report that is a bit easier to read when you
have a large number of details on each page. The code requires a procedure
level variable, LineKounter, to keep track of the lines printed throughout
the report.

```
Option Compare Database
Option Explicit
Dim LineKounter
Private Sub Detail_Format(Cancel As Integer, FormatCount As
            Integer)
    LineKounter = LineKounter + 1
    If LineKounter Mod 2 Then
        Me.Detail.BackColor = RGB(192, 192, 192)
    Else
        Me.Detail.BackColor = vbWhite
    End If
End Sub
```

> **Form: Report Dialog 09**
> **Reports: Basic Sales List 01, Basic product List 01**

Print Multiple Selections

Not all reports are column-type reports. For example, you can use a report to print an invoice. In that case, you would want to print one invoice for each order.

A handy way to select orders for invoice printing is in batches. Figure 9-9 shows a form that displays all the orders not marked as paid (PaymentVerified = False). In this example, the list box is set for multiple selection. *Multiple selection* means that the user can highlight one or more items in the list, in contrast to the normal selection mode in which only one item at a time can be selected. Access 2000 has two options for the Multi Select property.

✔ **Simple.** Each mouse click toggles the item between selected and unselected status.

✔ **Extended.** This method of selecting items is similar to what you use in Windows 95/98 lists: In making extended selections, you use the Shift and Ctrl keys in combination with the mouse to select items.

In this case, the simple Multi Select option has been used.

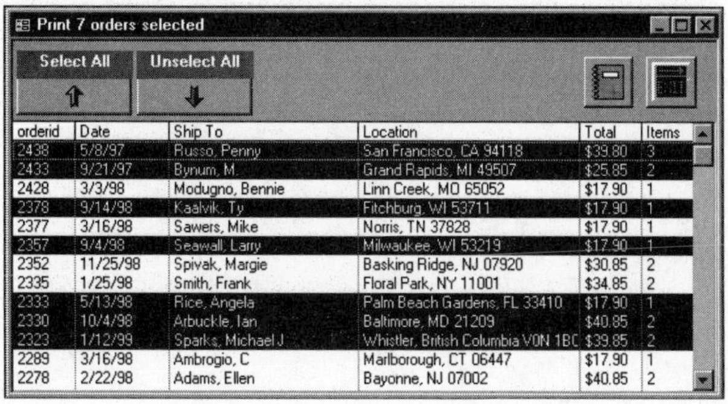

Figure 9-9: A form that enables you to make multiple selections of names from one list.

A list box with Multi Select activated is a type of collection in which item the list has an ItemData value and a Selected value. The following statement prints the value from the first row in the list box. The data printed belongs to the bound column, which is by default the first column.

```
Debug.Print Me.UnverifiedOrders.ItemData(0)
```

Keep in mind that the collection of items in a list box is a zero-based collection, which means that the last item is ListCount -1. The following statement displays the last item in the list.

```
Debug.Print Me.UnverifiedOrders.ItemData( _
Me.UnverifiedOrders.ListCount - 1)
```

If the `ColumnHeads` property of a list box is `True`, then the first row with data is row 1. Row 0 is occupied by the column headings.

When a list box has `Multi Select` activated, the `ItemsSelected` collection contains all the rows that are currently selected. The following statement prints the current number of items selected.

```
Debug.Print Me.UnverifiedOrders.ItemsSelected.Count
```

In addition to having the user make selections with the mouse or keyboard, you can perform operations that automatically select or unselect one or more rows in the list box. The form shown in Figure 9-9 has two buttons that affect the selection. The Select All button applies selection to all the rows in the list box by executing the following procedure. The procedure scans the collection and sets the `Selected` property to `True`. When the procedure is done, all the items on the screen appear selected. The Unselect All button executes the same code with the exception that a `False` value is assigned to each item, removing the highlight from the screen.

```
Function SelectAllOrders()
    Dim I, K
    For I = 1 To Me.UnverifiedOrders.ListCount - 1
            Me.UnverifiedOrders.Selected(I) = True
    Next
    UpdateCount
End Function
```

The `UpdateCount` procedure displays the current number of selected items in the title bar of the form.

```
Sub UpdateCount()
    Me.Caption = "Print " & _
    Me.UnverifiedOrders.ItemsSelected.Count & " orders
            selected"
End Sub
```

The ultimate purpose of this dialog box is to print an invoice for each of the selected orders. Users can — by their selections — define batches of orders for which they want to print invoices. The following procedure uses a `For...Each` loop to process all the members of the `ItemsSelected` collection, which represents the currently selected rows in the list box. The procedure prints a copy of the Invoice report for each selected item using the `OrderID` contained in the list box as the `WhereCondition` parameter of the `OpenReport` method.

```
Private Sub PrintButton_Click()
    Dim OID, RC
    For Each OID In Me.UnverifiedOrders.ItemsSelected
        RC = SysCmd(acSysCmdSetStatus, _
            "Printing Invoice for order #" & _
            Me.UnverifiedOrders.Column(0, OID) & _
            " " & Me.UnverifiedOrders.Column(2, OID))
        DoCmd.OpenReport _
            ReportName:="Invoice", _
            view:=acViewNormal, _
            wherecondition:="Orderid = " &
            Me.UnverifiedOrders.Column(0, OID)
    Next
    RC = SysCmd(acSysCmdClearStatus)
End Sub
```

The procedure contains some new techniques.

- ✔ SysCmd( ). This function is used to display text on the status bar at the bottom of the Access 2000 application window. This display helps the user keep track of the printing process by showing which orders are being printed.

- ✔ Column(col,row). This property allows you to extract any value, even in a hidden column, contained in a list box control by specifying its column and row position.

Note that the technique illustrated in the procedure works only if you send the reports directly to the printer. You cannot use the preview mode to process a series of reports. If you try to do so, only the first selected report will be displayed.

> **Form: Report Dialog 10**
> **Reports: Invoice**

Fast Form Letters

The primary purpose of Access 2000 reports is to output information in row and column reports. If you want to send form letters — a document that uses paragraph-oriented text — you typically use a paragraph-oriented application, such as Microsoft Word, to take advantage of its merge functions to interact with Access 2000 data. I discuss these techniques in Chapter 11.

You can, however, also use Visual Basic to automatically generate simple paragraph-style form letters directly from an Access 2000 form. This process is a lot faster than merging with Word, and the results print much faster.

The form letter report form contains a single, large label control. If you enter large amounts of text into a label control, Access 2000 automatically wraps the text to the next line, just as a text editor or word processing program does. You can even start new lines by pressing the Shift+Enter combination as you're typing within the control.

In addition to the text, the control contains some special text items that you insert where you want to enter information from a table or a form. You enter these special items, called *tokens*, by using a distinct format, as shown in the following example. The token is simply a word or phrase that you later replace with data from a form or a record. In this case, you enclose the tokens in [**] to differentiate them from the normal text. The [**] have no special meaning. This pattern simply is unlikely to appear in normal text.

```
[*name*]
```

The tokens represent items that you need to fill in with data from some other source. The goal is to print a form letter for the record that appears in the form after you click the a button. The Members form contains a Send Dues Letter button that triggers the printing of this report.

The Replace function

The key to this form letter technique is a function created in Visual Basic called Replace(). The purpose of this function is to locate a token within a block of text and replace the token with some other text. The first line in the procedure for the Replace() function lists three arguments, as shown in the following example and described in the following list:

```
Function Replace (Block, Token, ReplaceText)
```

- ✔ Block. The Block argument is the overall block of text that you're modifying. In the current example, the block is all the text within a Label control on a report. You can reference this text by using the Caption property.

- ✔ Token. This argument is a text value that indicates the portion of the block that you're changing. In this example the tokens are items such as [*Name*] or [*Dues*]. The text of the tokens doesn't matter. The only function of these tokens is to mark the locations in the text where you intend to insert various replacement values. I have chosen [* and *] since those character combinations rarely appear in normal text.

- ✔ ReplaceText. This argument is the information you intend to insert into the block. In the current example, the form letter report obtains this information from the Access form that is displayed before you print the form letter.

How does this procedure accomplish the goal of inserting text into some location within the block of text? The technique is fairly simple. First, you divide the block of text into the following two parts:

- ✔ Front. This part contains all the text from the beginning to the location of the token.

- ✔ Back. This part contains all the text starting after the token and continuing to the end of the block.

The two parts, Front and Back, combine with ReplaceText in between to create the new block of text.

The first step in the process is to calculate the locations of the token within the text. You accomplish this task with the aid of the InStr function. This function locates the first occurrence of one item (Token) with another (Block). Notice that you must subtract 1 from the InStr() value so that the value doesn't include the first character in the token itself, as follows:

```
StartToken = InStr(Block, Token) - 1
```

You then use StartToken to calculate where the end section of the text begins by adding the length of the token, Len (Token), plus 1, as follows:

```
EndToken = StartToken + Len(Token) + 1
```

After you calculate these two values, you can break the text into the two parts — the text before and the text after the token — by using the Left() and Mid() functions, as shown in the following example. Left() starts with the first character in the block and ends at the character indicated by the StartToken value. Mid() begins at EndToken and includes the remainder of the block.

```
Front = Left(Block, StartToken)
Back = Mid(Block, EndToken)
```

You reassemble the pieces in the final statement, as shown in the following example. You insert the ReplaceText between the two parts. Notice that setting the reassembled text to the variable Replace (the name of the function) causes the function to return the modified text as its value.

```
Replace = Front & ReplaceText & Back
```

The entire Replace procedure is shown in the following example:

```
Function Replace (Block, Token, ReplaceText)
    StartToken = InStr(Block, Token) - 1
    EndToken = StartToken + Len(Token) + 1
    Front = Left(Block, StartToken)
    Back = Mid(Block, EndToken)
    Replace = Front & ReplaceText & Back
End Function
```

You can put the Replace function in a procedure that specifies how to replace tokens in the report's Label control with actual text from the controls displayed on the form. In this example, a function called FillInForm() links together the tokens in the report and the data in the form. The following procedure uses two objects: FillIn is the form that contains the information you need to fill out the form letter, and Template is the label control on the report that contains the form letter with the tokens you need to replace.

```
Sub FillInForm(FillIn As Form, Template As Control)
```

The rest of the procedure is simply a matter of executing one Replace() function for each token. To insert the correct date into the letter, for example, you replace the [*Today*] token with the value of the Date function as illustrated by the following code fragment:

```
With Template
    .Caption = Replace( _
    Block:=Template.Caption, _
    Token:="[*Today*]", _
    ReplaceText:=Format(Date, "mmmm dd, yyyy"))
```

In some cases, you replace the token with an expression. You replace the [*CSZ*] token, for example, with an expression that combines the city, state, and ZIP code fields as illustrated in the following code:

```
.Caption = Replace( _
    Block:=Template.Caption, _
    Token:="[*CSZ*]", _
    ReplaceText:=FillIn![City] & "," _
    & FillIn![State] & " " & FillIn!Zip)
```

The [*Salutation*] token doesn't correspond to a field because you enter the contact's first and last names into a single field. For this token, you use an expression that picks out the portion of the contact name from the first part of the contact field, as follows:

```
.Caption = Replace( _
    Block:=Template.Caption, _
    Token:="[*Salutation*]", _
    ReplaceText:=Left(FillIn![Contact], _
    InStr(FillIn![Contact], " ") - 1))
```

You, connection between the report and the form is created by entering a call to the `FillInForm` procedure from within the Visual Basic module of the report. The call is made from the `Detail_Format` event procedure of the `Form Letter Report` report form, shown next. The procedure specifies the source of the data — in this case, the `Members` form — and the control to format (the `FormLetter` label control).

```
Private Sub Detail_Format(Cancel As Integer,_
FormatCount As Integer)
    FillInForm Forms![Members], Me![FormLetter]
End Sub
```

In the form, you assign the following procedure to the Send Dues Letter button, which opens the form letter. The `FillInForm` procedure fills the form letter with the data appearing on the form.

```
Private Sub Command16_Click()
DoCmd.OpenReport ReportName:= "Form Letter Report", _
    view:=acViewPreview
End Sub
```

The result is that you can print a simple form letter, shown in Figure 9-10, including data that Access 2000 inserts into paragraph text, simply by clicking the Send Dues Letter button in the form. You have no recordset to manipulate in this case because the procedures are what fill in the report, which isn't bound to any recordset. Because you don't save as part of the report any changes that the Visual Basic procedures make to the control, you can use the same form over and over again to print any number of reminder letters. Printing the form letter doesn't destroy the tokens.

Figure 9-10:
A form that enables you to make multiple selections of names from one list.

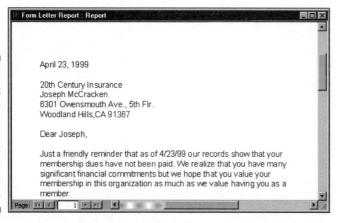

Form Letter Report : Report

April 23, 1999

20th Century Insurance
Joseph McCracken
6301 Owensmouth Ave., 5th Flr.
Woodland Hills, CA 91367

Dear Joseph,

Just a friendly reminder that as of 4/23/99 our records show that your membership dues have not been paid. We realize that you have many significant financial commitments but we hope that you value your membership in this organization as much as we value having you as a member.

Form: Members
Report: Form Letter Report
Module: Report Functions
Procedure: Replace, FillInForm

Part IV
Active Controls and Objects

The 5th Wave   By Rich Tennant

"She just found out she'd rather be a programmer than a fairy princess, but she doesn't want to give up the wardrobe."

In this part . . .

Access and its Microsoft Office partners have more in common that being in the same box. Microsoft technology ties all of the Office suite components together with each other and the BackOffice suite of network applications.

This technology is called ActiveX. Whatever you call it, Part IV explains how to take advantage of ActiveX features.

Chapter 10

Active Server Pages

● ●

In This Chapter

▶ Relating the Web to databases

▶ Exploring ASP and VBScript

▶ Examining databases and ASP

▶ Working with Active Server Page forms

▶ Dealing with no matches

▶ Inserting new data

● ●

*A*ccess was originally designed to serve the needs of individual users and local workgroups who needed a database that combines ease of use with the capability to be expanded into a finished database application. The dramatic growth of the Internet and internet technologies has opened up a new arena for Access and Access databases which can serve as database sources for Web-based applications. In this chapter you will learn how Access can be integrated with the Web in order to build applications available through a local intranet or even the global Internet.

> **Database Folder: Various ASP Files**

Live examples

The CD included with this book contains copies of all the files discussed in this chapter. However, you can't run these examples unless you have access to a Web server, such as Microsoft Personal Web Server or NT IIS. If you don't have access to a Web server, you can try any of the examples directly on the Internet by accessing my Web site. Simply enter the URL listed in the book and you can see the results in your Web browser. The URLs are also contained in the file URL.TXT to save you the time of typing them in.

How the Web Relates to Databases

Well, I guess that I'm supposed to define what the Web is for those readers who have been locked in a closet for the last decade or so. Everyone knows what the Web is, right? However, in the spirit of the . . .*For Dummies* series, here I go.

The Web is a list of folders. Hey, wait a minute, pal! That's too simple, you say. I have a computer with lots of folders and I'm not part of the Web, am I? No, not unless you take the additional steps of becoming part of a larger network of computers and enabling file sharing on your computer.

I'm not just making this up. If you have file sharing enabled on your computer and you dial up your Internet service provider (ISP), you expose files in any of those shared folders to anyone else on the Web. By definition, your computer is now a server on the Web, and your files can be accessed through the Web network of which your computer is now a part. That's why most ISPs warn their users not to dial up if they have file sharing enabled.

The Web is simply all the folders on all the computers that people have made available for the public to access. When you use the Web, you enter a name, called a URL, which is simply the name of a computer that has one or more folders open to the public. The following URL is the name of a folder on a computer that contains copies of the files discussed in this chapter. I have placed them there so that anyone who wants to access them can do so.

```
www.wbase2.com/cgi-bin/apdexamples
```

But the preceding URL doesn't look like the kind of folder that you would enter on a Windows local area network. The reason is that Windows uses a different style of naming convention to specify the name of the computer. The following path name shows the name of the same folder as it may be entered into a Windows application.

```
\\RKPNT\WebSite\cgi-bin\apdexamples
```

The only difference is the convention used for the name of the server. A server is any computer that provides information — that is, a service — to other computers. In a Windows network, \\ indicates the name of a server. On Internet networks, the *domain* name, www.wbase2.com, refers to a server.

Note that a single network can allow both types of names. For example, if you work on a Windows NT network, you could add Internet services to the network and give domain names to the various servers. In that case, you would have two ways to refer to the same resources. In Office 2000, the File Open/Save dialog boxes enable you to use Window names or select Internet-style names.

Web servers

One additional difference between Windows and Internet server names is that the Internet names specify the type of service you want to access as well as the location. The two most popular Internet services are as follows:

✔ **WWW.** The World Wide Web service is designed for publishing documents to anyone who wants to get access to them. When you access a WWW service, you're not challenged for a password or other ID. Instead, the service immediately supplies you with the requested information, which appears in your browser window. If you don't specify what document on the server you want to see, the Web service returns the document that has been designed as the default document. The Web service on a given server doesn't attempt to limit the number of people accessing the documents it provides. The computer attempts to service as many people at the same time as it can. Web services are designated by the prefix `http`:

```
http:\\domainname/folder/document
```

✔ **FTP.** File Transfer Protocol is a publishing service used to copy files rather than display them. FTP typically requires some sort of login and identification. The FTP service is limited to a specific number of users at one time; after that maximum is reached, no new users can gain access until one of the current users logs off. FTP services are designated by the prefix `ftp`:

```
ftp:\\domainname/folder/document
```

Static and Dynamic HTML

The Web was originally conceived a publishing service. If you wanted to publish information on the Web, you created a document, using HTML, and placed the document into a folder accessible via the Web. If you wanted to alter the document, you edited the HTML and saved the revised document into the Web folder. Documents prepared in this manner are called *static* documents because you can change them only by actually editing the HTML code stored in the document.

As the Web grew in importance, the capability to simply publish static documents was too limiting. Dynamic HTML documents can contain programming code that allows the content of the document to change depending on various conditions. Unlike static HTML documents that look the same every time they are displayed, the content of Dynamic HTML documents can change based on logical programming statements (such as an `If...Then` statement) embedded within the document.

VBScript and JavaScript are programming languages that you can integrate with HTML in order to create dynamic Web documents. In this chapter, you discover how to use VBScript to access databases through Web pages.

ASP and VBScript

At the heart of any Active Server Page is VBScript. *VBScript* is a scaled-down version of Visual Basic. When you include VBScript in an Active Server Page, the statements are interpreted and executed by the Internet server and the results are returned on the Web page. This means that you can use your knowledge of Visual Basic to create Web pages that include code.

To see how this works, you can begin with a very simple Visual Basic operation and see how that operation could be included in a Web page.

HTML tags

HTML (HyperText Markup Language) is kind of like a programming language that allows for the insertion of *tags* (or instructions) along with the text. When your Web browser reads the document, it interprets the tags and presents the text per those instructions. For example, look at the following HTML code:

```
Access <I>Programming</I> For <B>Dummies</B>
```

In this example, the `<I>...</I>` tags make the text within them italic, and the `<B>...</B>` tags make the text bold. These tags work in pairs; the first tag — `<I>` — represents the beginning of the instruction and the same tag with / inserted at the beginning — `</I>` — indicates the end of an instruction.

What do these instructions mean? The answer depends on what program you use to view the HTML document. If the application is Notepad, a basic text editor, the text looks exactly like the preceding example, in which the tags appear in the text. If the program is a Web browser like Netscape or Internet Explorer, the result looks like the following example, in which the tags are not displayed but you can see the formatting that the tags impose:

Access *Programming* For **Dummies**

One important difference exists between writing HTML code and Visual Basic code. In Visual Basic, data is stored in tables and code is stored in modules. When you write HTML, you mix your code (the HTML tags) right in with the data (the text you want to display). If you look at the preceding simple HTML code fragment, you can see that as the HTML document gets more complex, it will become very hard to read, edit, and revise. For that reason, most Web pages are created in programs that hide the raw HTML code from the users and give them a word-processor or page-layout style interface that shows the page as it would appear in the browser. Microsoft FrontPage is an example of an application that helps you create Web pages without requiring you to deal with the HTML code.

However, in this chapter, you deal directly with the raw HTML. The reason is that (unlike Visual Basic) you insert VBScript directly into the HTML document along with standard HTML codes and Web page text. It's messy to look at, but that's what you have to deal with if you want to create Active Server Pages. Brace yourself and go ahead.

The world's simplest Web page

If you open any HTML document, you see a plethora of HTML tags filling up most of the document. This is especially true if you use a program like FrontPage to create the document, because FrontPage sticks in a lot of special-use tags that most users won't even know are there.

However, you can make a Web page that works with only a few tags. The following HTML code is the simplest possible Web page that you can create. It begins with the <HTML> tag that tells the browser that this is an HTML document. The <BODY> tag marks the section of the HTML code that specifies what should appear in the browser window. In this case, it's a single text phrase, World's Simplest Web Page. To complete the document, ending tags correspond to the <BODY> and <HTML> tags.

```
<HTML>
<BODY>
World's Simplest Web Page
</BODY>
</HTML>
```

That's all you need. The following URL displays the document in your browser, as shown in Figure 10-1. Not very dramatic, but it works.

```
www.wbase2.com/cgi-bin/apdexamples/verysimple.asp
```

Figure 10-1:
World's sim-
plest Web
page.

The world's simplest VBScript Web page

HTML is limited to creating static Web documents. A static HTML document appears exactly the same way every time it loads into a Web browser. You can use VBScript to add programming code — similar to Visual Basic code — to HTML documents. When the document loads into a browser, the VBScript elements execute and the results appear along with the rest of the document.

VBScript enables you to create Web documents that change depending on what results the code included with the document produces. The following code is a simple Visual Basic statement that you could enter into any module or the Immediate window in Access 2000. The statement uses the Date() function to return the current date.

```
Debug.Print Date()
```

The following code shows how you can use VBScript to insert the date into a Web document. Note that the VBScript statement is enclosed in <%...%> tags. These tags indicate the beginning and end of a block of VBScript. Also note that you don't need to specify where to send the output of the state-ment. Simply entering =date() implies that the resulting text should be inserted into the document at the same location where the VBScript state-ment is located.

```
<HTML>
<BODY>
<% =date() %>
</BODY>
</HTML>
```

You can see the results at the following URL. When you load the document into your browser, the Web server processes the VBScript statement and inserts the current date in place of the code.

```
www.wbase2.com/cgi-bin/apdexamples/barebones1.asp
```

 If you're placing documents with VBScript on your own Web server, such as the Microsoft Personal Web Server, you must turn on the Execute property for the folder that contains the ASP documents in order to have the Web server run the VBScript. If your documents load without error but don't show the VBScript results, you probably didn't turn on the Execute property for that folder.

VBScript functions

Like Visual Basic, VBScript supports special functions that are built into the language. For example, if in Visual Basic you want to display the current date in the long format, you use the following (Format) function:

```
Debug.Print Format(Date(),"long date")
```

In this case, the code that you use in VBScript is similar to, but not exactly like, the preceding Visual Basic code. Recall that VBScript is a scaled-down version of Visual Basic, so not all the features of Visual Basic are available in VBScript. In this case, VBScript doesn't support the Visual Basic Format() function. Instead, VBScript has functions for different types of formats:

- ✔ FormatDateTime()
- ✔ FormatCurrency()
- ✔ FormatNumber()
- ✔ FormatPercent()

The following example displays the long format of the current date in the browser window.

```
<HTML>
<BODY>
<% = FormatDateTime(date(),vblongdate) %>
</BODY>
</HTML>
```

To see what this page looks like, check out the following URL:

```
www.wbase2.com/cgi-bin/apdexamples/barebones2.asp
```

HTML and VBScript

So far, the two VBScript examples contained only VBScript. However, the power of VBScript comes into play when you combine standard static HTML code with dynamic VBScript code. The following example combines standard HTML with VBScript. Note that the <B> tags bracket the VBScript code, which means that whatever text is inserted for the script appears in bold in the browser window.

```
<HTML>
<BODY>
Today's date is <B><% = FormatDateTime(date(),vblongdate)
        %></B>
</BODY>
</HTML>
```

To see what this page looks like, check out the following URL:

```
www.wbase2.com/cgi-bin/apdexamples/barebones3.asp
```

Figure 10-2 shows the results of the code. The Web server evaluates the VBScript and inserts the current date, in the long date format, into the document in place of the VBScript. Because the script was enclosed in <B> tags, the date is shown in bold.

Figure 10-2:
VBScript
inserts the
current date
and time
into the
Web page.

Programming structures in VBScript

In addition to simple statements that insert data into an HTML document, VBScript enables you to take advantage of programming structures, such as If...Then, For...Next, and Do...Loop.

The following code uses a For...Next loop to print a series of dates at one-month intervals using the current date as the starting point.

```
For kounter = 1 to 6
    Debug.Print kounter, DateAdd("m",kounter,Date())
Next
```

To perform the same operation in an Web page, you need to embed the parts of a For...Next structure into the HTML code of the page. The following code shows the VBScript equivalent of the preceding Visual Basic code.

```
<HTML>
<BODY>
<% For kounter = 1 to 6 %>
<P><% =kounter %>. <% =DateAdd("m",kounter,Date()) %></P>
<% Next %>
</BODY>
</HTML>
```

Here are several points to consider when you look at the code:

- ✔ The elements of the For...Next structure aren't entered in a single VBScript tag. Instead, each component is placed inside a separate VBScript tag. Between the tags, other HTML and VBScript elements are inserted.

- ✔ VBScript supports standard variables as does Visual Basic. In the example, the variable kounter is assigned values by the For...Next structure. The VBScript expression =kounter inserts the value of the variable into the Web document.

- ✔ VBScript supports the Visual Basic DateAdd function so that you can perform chronological calculations in a Web document.

- ✔ In order to place each date on a separate line, the HTML paragraph tags, <P> and </P>, are added.

You can see the results of the VBScript For...Next structure in the following URL, as shown in Figure 10-3:

```
www.wbase2.com/cgi-bin/apdexamples/barebones4.asp
```

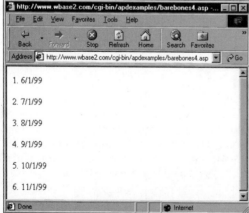

Figure 10-3:
A For...Next loop in a Web page generates a series of lines of information.

If you compare Figure 10-3 to the HTML/VBScript code, you may notice something very interesting: The output contains more lines of information than the code used to generate it. This is the opposite of static HTML, in which the amount of HTML stored in the Web page directly corresponds to the data displayed in the browser. VBScript provides a means of using structures like loops to process a large amount of information with a small number of instructions.

Server-side scripting

Both Netscape and Internet Explorer enable you to view the source HTML of any document loaded into the browser. For example, if you have the barebones4.ASP document loaded in Internet Explorer, you can choose View⇨Source to display the HTML version of the document in a Notepad window.

However, when you do this, what you see is not the HTML code that was stored in barebones4.ASP but an HTML version of the specific data that is displayed in the browser. Instead of the VBScript code, you see the dates that resulted from this code.

Why don't you see the VBScript? The answer is related to the concept of server-side scripting. To put it another way, what exactly happens when you request a document that contains VBScript from a Web server?

When you request an Active Server Page that contains VBScript, the Web server doesn't immediately send you the document requested by the browser. Instead, the server scans the contents of document looking for VBScript code. The code is then passed to a program running as part of the Web server that executes the VBScript statements and merges any output from those statements with the static HTML portion of the Web document. After the two elements have merged, the Web server sends that page back to the browser requesting the page.

The reason you don't see the VBScript in the source display is that the VBScript code is never sent to the Web browser. All the statements are executed on the server side of the operation.

Databases and ASP

So far, the VBScript examples have been interesting because they show how you can enhance Web documents with programming statements. But they haven't been all that useful. The real power of Active Server Pages is revealed when you use VBScript to access database information stored in data sources such as Access .MDB files or SQL Server databases.

Microsoft's Internet Information Server supports the ADO database model, which means that you can write VBScript code to manipulate ADO objects within a Web page, using many of the same techniques shown earlier in this book.

Server-side DSN

Because the Web was originally designed to publish static documents, no direct connection exists between a Web page and a data source, such as an Access .MDB file or a SQL Server database. The key to bridging this gap in Active Server Pages is the use of a server-side ODBC data source — for example, a DSN.

Suppose that you have a database file, MSAData.MDB, stored on a Web server. Your goal is to allow users to access the data in this file by loading Active Server Pages into their Web browser. Using this approach to get data from an Access database solves the several problems related to proving database information to a broad range of potential users:

- ✔ **Non-Access Users.** Normally, only users who have Access 2000 can access the data stored in .MDB files. Active Server Pages allow these users to get information from the Access 2000 database through their Web browsers, avoiding the necessity of installing copies of Access 2000 on every desktop.

- ✔ **Remote Users.** Users who travel to other locations can access data through the global Internet when they're not connected to their organizations' internal networks. This solution is simpler, cheaper, and often more reliable than supporting remote dial-in to a private network.

- ✔ **Virtual Client/Server.** When an Access database is queried through an Active Server Page, it functions more like a client/server database: The results of the query are determined by the Web server and only the results are transmitted back to the browser requesting the information.

The diagram in Figure 10-4 outlines the process. First, the user requests an Active Server Page that contains VBScript. The VBScript on that page contains a database query and the name of a ODBC data source. In this chapter, the DSN is called APD (Access Programming For Dummies).

When the Web server executes the code, it searches the ODBC data sources on the server to determine the actual database used by the ODBC DSN. In the example, APD is an Access MDB data source that is linked to the file MSAData.MDB, which resides in a location that the Web server can access. The Web server passes the SQL query to ODBC, which directs it to the data source.

When the query has been processed, the resulting data set is then passed back to ODBC to the Web server, which inserts the data into the Active Server Page and merges it with the standard HTML in the page. The result is a Web page that displays database information based on SQL queries.

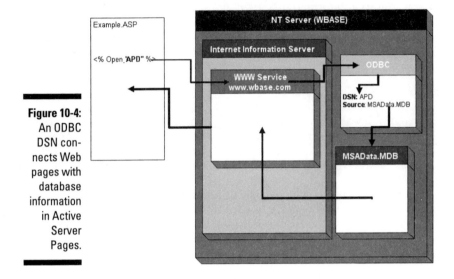

Figure 10-4:
An ODBC
DSN con-
nects Web
pages with
database
information
in Active
Server
Pages.

You must keep in mind that the ODBC technique is a sever-based solution and it requires modifications to the Web server. Remember:

- ✔ The DSN must be set up on the computer that acts as the Web server. Active Server Pages can't use the DSNs that exist on users' computers, if any. If you're setting up an Active Server Page application on your organization's Web site, you need to have the network administrator set up the DSN directly on the actual Web server. You can't do this remotely. After you set up the DSN, you can remotely do all the other steps needed to complete the application.

- ✔ The database associated with the DSN doesn't have to reside on the Web server. The only requirement is that the database file or SQL Server being specified can be located by the Web server.

ADO recordsets in VBScript

The basic tool for adding database data to a Web page is the use of ADO recordsets created by VBScript and embedded in a Web page. For the most part, the VBScript statements used to create and manipulate ADO recordsets are almost identical to the corresponding statements in Visual Basic, with one major exception. The exception concerns how you create the connection and recordset objects.

The object models available to VBScript are provided by the Web server — for example, IIS or PWS (Personal Web Server). To create a specific object, you use the CreateObject method of the server. The following statement uses `CreateObject` to define `Cnt` as an ADO connection. Note that ADO is referenced as `ADODB` in VBScript.

```
Set Cnt = Server.CreateObject("ADODB.Connection")
```

After you create a connection object, you can use the `Open` method to specify the DSN that the connection will use to access the actual data source. Once again, keep in mind that the DSN being referenced is a DSN defined on the Web server. The following statement specifies the APD ODBC DSN as the data source for this connection. Because the data source is an Access database that isn't password-protected, the name of the DSN is all that's needed.

```
Cnt.Open "APD"
```

You can also use the Server object to create a recordset object, as follows:

```
Set Cust = Server.CreateObject("ADODB.Recordset")
```

You can then use the `Open` method of the recordset object to define the data set using a SQL query. In this case, the query counts the total number of records in the customers table.

```
Cust.Open "SELECT Count(*) As CustCount FROM Customers", Cnt
    %>
```

After you define a recordset, you can insert the data from that recordset into the HTML document by referencing the fields in the recordset either by name or field number. Recall that the `Fields` collection is zero-based, so the first field is zero. The following two VBScript statements are equivalent because they both insert the value returned by the query into the Web page.

```
<% =Cust("CustCount")
<% =Cust(0)
```

The following Active Server Page example produces the results shown in Figure 10-5. In this case, the query accesses the MSAData.MDB file stored on the Web server and returns the count of the customers table to the Web page. Note that in this system the actual data source, in this case the MSAData.MDB file, is not explicitly referenced. The reference in the code is to the DSN, APD. Keep in mind that with a DSN on the Web server that connects to the MSAData.MDB file, the Active Server Page can't retrieve the data.

```
<HTML>
<BODY>
<% Set Cnt = Server.CreateObject("ADODB.Connection")
   Set Cust = Server.CreateObject("ADODB.Recordset")
   Cnt.Open "APD"
   Cust.Open "SELECT Count(*) As CustCount FROM Customers",
           Cnt %>
The Customer table contains <% =Cust("CustCount") %> cus-
           tomers.
</BODY>
</HTML>
```

Figure 10-5:
The server
object
allows ADO
queries to
be
processed
as part of an
Active
Server
Page.

To check out this example on the Web, go to the following URL:

```
www.wbase2.com/cgi-bin/apdexamples/ADO1.asp
```

Processing multiple records

The query executed through the Active Server Page in the previous example returns a single row. However, a query executed against a data source may quite possibly return any number of rows. For example, suppose you want to get a count of customers summarized by state. Such a query would return, perhaps, 50 or more rows.

How do you code your Active Server Page to handle a multi-row recordset? The answer is that you use the same basic technique as in Visual Basic — that is, create a Do...Loop. The following VBScript shows how to code a Do...Loop structure in VBScript. If you examine the VBScript, you see that it contains the same statements that you use in Visual Basic to process the contents of a recordset object. The only difference is that the ADO statements are mixed in with the HTML tags in order to place the database information on the page displayed in the Web browser.

```
<% Do Until Cust.Eof %>
<P><I><% =Cust(0) %></I> <B><% =Cust(1) %></B></P>
<% Cust.MoveNext
Loop %>
```

Note that in this example, references to fields in the ADO recordset are made by field number rather than by field name. You can use either method in VBScript. For the full contents of the ADO2.ASP file, examine this code:

```
<HTML>
<BODY>
<% Set Cnt = Server.CreateObject("ADODB.Connection")
   Set Cust = Server.CreateObject("ADODB.Recordset")
   Cnt.Open "APD"
   Cust.Open "SELECT State, Count(*) As CustCount FROM
           Customers WHERE State is not Null GROUP BY State",
           Cnt %>
<P>Customer Count By State</P>
<% Do Until Cust.Eof %>
<P><I><% =Cust(0) %></I> <B><% =Cust(1) %></B></P>
<% Cust.MoveNext
   Loop %>
</BODY>
</HTML>
```

To see this example on the Web, check out this URL:

```
www.wbase2.com/cgi-bin/apdexamples/ADO2.asp
```

Displaying data sets in tables

The previous example displays the data drawn from the database as a series of paragraphs. A more common (and pleasing-to-the-eye) approach is to display the data in a table. HTML tables require three types of tags: `<TABLE>`, `<TR>`, and `<TD>`. In addition, the `<TABLE>` tag supports properties that define the appearance of the table.

- `<TABLE>, </TABLE>`: These tags mark the start and end of a table within a document. One document can have multiple tables.

- `<TABLE border=X>`: A numeric value sets the width of the outside border drawn around the table.

✔ `<TABLE cellpadding=X>`: A numeric value sets the distance between the text in the table cells and the cell borders.

✔ `<TABLE cellspacing=X>`: A numeric value sets the space that separates the cells inside the table.

✔ `<TABLE width=X>`: This variable is usually a percentage that sets the horizontal width of the table. For example, a table with a 50% width means that the table expands to ½ the width of the browser display. Note that if you change the width of the browser window, the table adjusts to maintain a 50% ratio. If you enter a number — for example, 125 — rather than a percentage, the table width is fixed at that size, regardless of the browser window width.

✔ `<TR>, </TR>`: These tags begin and end a table row.

✔ `<TD>, </TD>`: These tags mark the contents of a cell on a table row.

To display a recordset in an HTML table, you need to integrate your VBScript with the HTML table tags. The first step is to start the table with a `<TABLE>` tag. This tag lists the table property settings — border, width, and so on.

```
<TABLE border = 2 cellpadding = 2 cellspacing = 1 width =
        "75%">
```

To add a row to the table, you start with a `<TR>` tag. Following that tag comes one or more sets of `<TD>...</TD>` tags. Each one of these tags adds a column to the current row of the table. When the last column has been added, the `</TR>` tag ends the row.

The following code defines a single row with two columns. The additional lines and indents are designed to help make the HTML code easier to read. Keep in mind that the spacing doesn't affect the display produced by the HTML code.

```
<TR>
      <TD>State</TD>
      <TD>Count of Customers</TD>
</TR>
```

Embedding the data contained in the recordset within the table follows a similar pattern. First, use VBScript to start a `Do...Loop`. The purpose of this loop is to write one row in the table for each record in the recordset. This means that between the `Do` statement and the `MoveNext` method, the HTML code that defines one row should be inserted. You can see that the `<TR>...</TR>` tags fall between the `Do` and `MoveNext` statements so that one row is produced for each record. Each field reference is enclosed in `<TD>` tags

so that each data item is placed into a separate cell on the table row. The
</TABLE> tag appears after the Loop statement. Figure 10-6 shows the result-
ing Web page, in which the data is displayed in a table format.

```
<% Do Until Cust.Eof %>
<TR>
    <TD><% =Cust(0) %></TD>
    <TD><% =Cust(1) %></TD>
</TR>
<% Cust.MoveNext
    Loop %>
</TABLE>
```

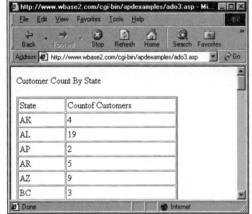

Figure 10-6:
The record-
set data is
inserted into
an HTML
table.

To see what this looks like on the Web, check out this URL:

```
www.wbase2.com/cgi-bin/apdexamples/AD03.asp
```

Conditional logic

One of the primary tools in Visual Basic is the If...Then structure, which
provides a means of building conditional logic into your Visual Basic code. If
statements provide a means by which alternative sets of statements can be
executed based on some logical expression.

For example, suppose that in the Web page you want to highlight states with
more than ten customers in bold. You know that bold text in HTML is created
by inserting <B>...</B> tags around the text you want to appear in bold.
The trick is to use VBScript to control which cells in the table display bold
text — and which do not — by using the value of the customer count to control the insertion of the <B> tags.

In the following code, VBScript `If...Then` statements are inserted after the `Cust(1)` field. The condition, `Cust(1) >= 10`, determines whether the `<B>` tag should be inserted into the Web page. Note that the `End If` statement is a separate VBScript tag. The VBScript tags bracket the `<B>...</B>` tags. This has the effect of having the logic expression in VBScript control the HTML formatting.

```
<% Do Until Cust.Eof %>
<TR>
    <TD><% =Cust(0) %></TD>
    <TD>
      <% IF cust(1) >= 10 Then %>
        <B>
      <% End If %>
      <% =Cust(1) %>
      <% IF cust(1) >= 10 Then %>
        </B>
      <% End If %>
    </TD>
</TR>
<% Cust.MoveNext
    Loop %>
```

Because bold requires two tags, you must use a second `If` statement to control the insertion of the `</B>`, which marks the end of the bold text. Figure 10-7 shows values of 10 or greater as bold text.

Figure 10-7: VBScript If statements control bold formatting based on the number of customers.

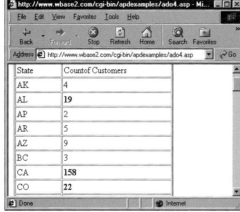

State	Countof Customers
AK	4
AL	**19**
AP	2
AR	5
AZ	9
BC	3
CA	**158**
CO	**22**

To see this example on the Web, go to the following URL:

```
www.wbase2.com/cgi-bin/apdexamples/AD04.asp
```

Using colors conditionally

You can change the background color of a cell based on its value. For example, values ten or over can have a yellow background and the others a silver background. You can set the color of a cell by using the `bgcolor` property of the `<TR>` tag. The following tag sets the background color of the cell to silver.

```
<TD bgcolor = silver>
```

The following code changes the color of the table cell in response to the value returned by the `CountofCustomers` field. Note that this code turns out to be simpler than the previous example because changing the color requires only one tag, but setting bold text requires two. Figure 10-8 shows what occurs when you load ADO5.ASP. The VBScript within the document causes the background color of the cells to vary according to the value contained in that cell.

```
<% Do Until Cust.Eof %>
<TR>
    <TD><% =Cust(0) %></TD>
    <% IF cust(1) >= 10 Then %>
        <TD bgcolor=yellow>
    <% else %>
        <TD bgcolor=silver>
    <% End If %>
    </TD>
</TR>
<% Cust.MoveNext
    loop %>
```

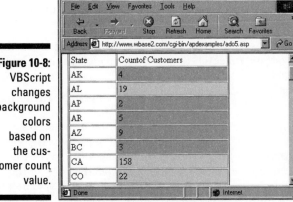

Figure 10-8: VBScript changes background colors based on the customer count value.

To see this sample on the Web, check out this URL:

```
www.wbase2.com/cgi-bin/apdexamples/ADO5.asp
```

Active Server Page Forms

All the Active Server Pages described up to this point execute queries that are included in the ASP file. In the previous examples, each ASP includes a query that summarizes all the records in the Customers table.

But suppose you want to create an ASP that returns information about one customer at a time. You may, for example, enter a Customer ID into a Web page and want the ASP to retrieve information related to that customer.

Getting user input

To create ASPs that retrieve data based on user input, you need to add a new element to the document's HTML code. That element is the <FORM> tag and its related tags. The following list of tags work together to create a interactive display on an HTML page into which a user can enter information.

- ✔ <FORM>...</FORM>: These tags define an area in an HTML document that contains places where the user can input information. A form can contain one or more <INPUT> tags.

- ✔ <FORM method/FORM action>: These properties of the form determine how the user input made in the Web document should be treated. The examples in this book all use the Post method to send the user input to another ASP file. The file is specified by the action property.

- ✔ <INPUT>: An <INPUT> tag is roughly equivalent to a control on a form. The tag creates a text box, list, or button on an HTML form.

- ✔ <INPUT type>: This property defines the type of entry element that appears on the form.

- ✔ <INPUT name>: This property assigns the input a name. You can use the input name to refer to the data entered into the form element in a similar manner to the way that you can use control names in Visual Basic.

- ✔ <INPUT size>: This property sets the width of the control on the form.

The simplest possible form you can create in a Web document requires a <FORM> tag and a minimum of two <INPUT>tags. The first tag begins the form and defines what should happen after the user submits the form. In the following code, the Post method is the HTML command to send a copy of the data entered into the form to some location. The Action property specifies the location, in this case another ASP document called GetData1.ASP.

```
<FORM Method="Post" Action = "GetData1.asp">
```

The interactive elements on the form are defined by `<INPUT>` tags. Each `<INPUT>` tag places a single text box, list, or button on the form. The simplest form element is a text box into which users can type anything they desire. The following HTML code places a text box on the form. The text box is assigned the name `cid`, which refers to the data entered into the box by the user.

```
<P>Enter the Customer ID: <INPUT type="text" Name="cid" size
    = 25></P>
```

The final required element in the form is the Submit button. In this case, `Submit` refers to a special type of button. When this button is clicked, the method and action specified in the `<FORM>` tag are executed. On most forms, the Submit button shows `Submit` as the caption. This is not a requirement. What makes a button a `Submit` button is that the `type` property is set to `Submit`. The caption that appears on the screen is controlled by the `value` property, which you can set to anything you want to display. So long as the `Type` is `Submit`, the button performs the submit function when clicked.

```
<P><INPUT type="Submit" value="Retrieve" name="submit">
```

These three items create the form shown in Figure 10-9.

Figure 10-9:
A simple
entry form
created
using the
HTML
`<FORM>`
and
`<INPUT>`
tags.

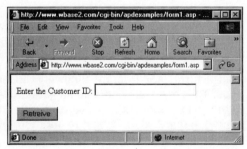

To check this example out on the Web, go to this URL:

```
www.wbase2.com/cgi-bin/apdexamples/form1.asp
```

Responding to user input

The form created in the previous section takes care of the input part of the data retrieval process. The actual retrieval of the data is performed by a different ASP — that is, the ASP specified in the `action` property of the form. In this case, that page is called GetData.ASP.

The key problem is how to make GetData.ASP deal with the data, in this case the Customer ID number, entered in a different document. The answer is that the Web server acts as a bridge between the document that contains the form and the document specified in the action property of the form. When the Post method is performed, all the data entered into the form document is copied to the memory of the Web server and stored in an object called Form. This means that when the user clicks the Submit button, all the entries are posted to the Form object of the Web server, from which another ASP document can retrieve them.

The Form object is contained within the Web server's Request object. The Request object stores a number of different items of information about the current user's interaction with the Web site. In this case, you're interested in data stored within the Form object, specifically the value the user entered in the cid text box. The following statement retrieves that value from the Request.Form object maintained by the Web server.

```
Request.Form("cid")
```

The following example shows how an ASP can retrieve data from the Request.Form object that was entered into a form. The items in the Form object are referenced by the names assigned in the HTML form. In this example, the entry made in the cid INPUT tag is extracted from the Web server by referencing the name "cid" in the Form object.

```
<HTML>
<BODY>
You enter <% =Request.Form("cid") %> in the previous page.
</BODY>
</HTML>
```

To test this operation, load the form1.ASP from the following URL and enter a number — for example, 1000. The responding document, getdata1.ASP, displays the value entered in the form document (see Figure 10-10). This proves that you can pass data entered in one ASP document to another ASP document for further processing.

```
www.wbase2.com/cgi-bin/apdexamples/form1.asp
www.wbase2.com/cgi-bin/apdexamples/getdata1.asp
```

Figure 10-10:
The Response. Form object provides user input to an ASP.

Defining a recordset by user input

The previous example showed that values can pass from the form in one ASP document to another ASP document by means of the server's `Report.Form` object. The question remains as to how you can use that value to define a recordset. In this case, you want to retrieve information stored in the `Customers` table about the customer that matches the ID number entered in the form.

The solution is to use the form values to compose a SQL statement that retrieves the requested data. Look at the following SQL statement. It retrieves data for customer 1000.

```
"SELECT * FROM Customers WHERE CustomerID = 1000"
```

You can use the `Request.Form` object to replace the actual value, 1000, with whatever value the user places into the HTML form, shown as follows.

```
"SELECT * FROM Customers WHERE CustomerID = " & _
  Request.Form("cid")
```

The following VBScript uses this approach to define a recordset, `Cust`, based on the `cid` value entered into an HTML form. The code first defines a SQL statement by combing literal text with the data retrieved from the `Form` object. That text, stored in the variable SQLText, is then used to define the ADO recordset.

```
<% SQLText = _
   "SELECT Firstname & ' ' & Lastname As Name," & _
   "dayphonenumber As Day, evephonenumber as Evening," & _
   "EmailAddress as Email FROM Customers " & _
   "WHERE CustomerID = " & Request.Form("cid")
  Set Cnt = Server.CreateObject("ADODB.Connection")
  Set Cust = Server.CreateObject("ADODB.Recordset")
  Cnt.Open "APD"
  Cust.Open SQLText, Cnt
%>
```

After VBScript generates the requested data set, the next step is to display the information on the form. The following code shows a general technique for displaying any record in a table. A `For...Each` loop is used to loop through the Fields collection of the recordset. The first column displays the name of the field, `Col.Name`. The second column is the contents of the field, `Col.Value`. This code displays any single record because the `Fields` collection adjusts to match the contents of the recordset. Note that the field names are the names as defined by the `As` keyword in the SQL statement, which allows you to give the displayed fields any name you like. You don't have to use the field name as defined in the underlying database table.

```
<TABLE <TABLE border = 2 cellpadding = 2 cellspacing = 1
          width = "75%">
  <% For Each Col in Cust.Fields %>
  <TR>
      <TD><% =Col.Name %></TD>
      <TD><% =Col.Value %></TD>
  </TR>
  <% Next %>
</TABLE>
```

To test this code, load Form2.ASP from the Web site and enter 1000 as the Customer ID. The result is shown in Figure 10-11.

```
www.wbase2.com/cgi-bin/apdexamples/form2.asp
www.wbase2.com/cgi-bin/apdexamples/getdata2.asp
```

Figure 10-11:
Customer
data
retrieved
based on
user input.

 If you want to perform more tests on the forms available on the Web site, you can check out the contents of the database by looking at the data in the copy of the database, MSAData.MDB, included on the CD.

Dealing with No Matches

What happens if the user makes an entry and no data in the database matches that value? In the previous example, the result is an empty recordset and a VBScript error because VBScript can't display data from an empty recordset.

You can prevent this problem by using the same technique I discuss earlier in this book for handling the problem in Visual Basic — that is, testing the EoF property of the recordset before you attempt to access any data. The following code uses an If structure in VBScript to deal with a potential empty recordset.

```
<% If Cust.eof Then %>
    Customer <% =Request.Form("cid") %> not found.
<% Else %>
<TABLE <TABLE border = 2 cellpadding = 2 cellspacing = 1
          width = "75%">
    <% For Each Col in Cust.Fields %>
    <TR>
        <TD><% =Col.Name %></TD>
        <TD><% =Col.Value %></TD>
    </TR>
    <% Next %>
    </TABLE>
<% End If %>
```

To test this code, load Form3.ASP from the Web site and enter **5000** as the
Customer ID. The responding document returns a message indicating that
the value cannot be found in the database.

```
www.wbase2.com/cgi-bin/apdexamples/form3.asp
www.wbase2.com/cgi-bin/apdexamples/getdata3.asp
```

Displaying related records

You can use VBScript to create and display multiple recordsets within a
single Web document. For example, suppose that along with the customer
information retrieved by the document, you also wanted to list the orders
placed by that customer.

The following code shows a second recordset created in the Web document.
This recordset uses the cid value to select records from the Orders table.

```
<H2>Orders</H2>
    <% SQLText = "SELECT OrderID, OrderDate, " & _
      "ShipFirst & ' ' & ShipLast As ShipTo, " & _
      "OrderTotal, Items " & _
      "FROM Orders " & _
      "WHERE CustomerID = " & Request.Form("cid")
    Set Orders = Server.CreateObject("ADODB.RecordSet")
    Orders.Open SQLText, Cnt %>
```

In this case, the recordset returned may have one or more records. The following code illustrates a general method for displaying a recordset as a table,
in which each column represents a field and each row represents the data
from one record.

The following code works in two sections. The first section uses a For Each
loop to write the column headings using the Name property of each of the
fields in the recordset. The second section begins with a Do loop that

processes each of the records in the Orders recordset. With the Do loop is a For Each loop that creates one column for each field in the recordset and inserts the field value into the cell. Keep in mind that the you can use the example to display any recordset because no specific field names are mentioned in the code. Instead, the code is driven by the contents of the Fields collection, which can vary with each recordset.

```
<TABLE <TABLE border = 2 cellpadding = 2 cellspacing = 1
         width = "75%">
<TR>
<% For Each Col in Orders.Fields %>
   <TD><% =Col.Name %></TD>
<% Next %>
</TR>
<% Do Until Orders.Eof %>
   <TR>
   <% For Each Col in Orders.Fields %>
   <TD><% =Col.Value %></TD>
   <% Next %>
   </TR>
   <% Orders.MoveNext %>
<% Loop %>
```

To test this code, load Form4.ASP from the Web site and enter 1000 as the Customer ID. Figure 10-12 shows the data that is retrieved.

```
www.wbase2.com/cgi-bin/apdexamples/form4.asp
www.wbase2.com/cgi-bin/apdexamples/getdata4.asp
```

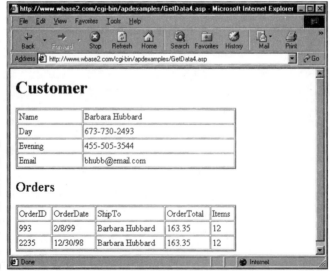

Figure 10-12: Order data retrieved along with the customer record.

Inserting New Data

You can use Active Server Pages to add new records to a table as well as extract existing records. As with data retrieval, the process uses two forms:

✔ The first ASP is a form that enables the user to enter the data they want into the database.

✔ The second document uses VBScript and ADO to insert those values into a new record in the appropriate database table.

The example is the form pictured in Figure 10-13. This form stores data in a table called ReaderLog. Because the sample form is available on the Web, you can actually enter records into the database. Feel free to enter as many records as you like.

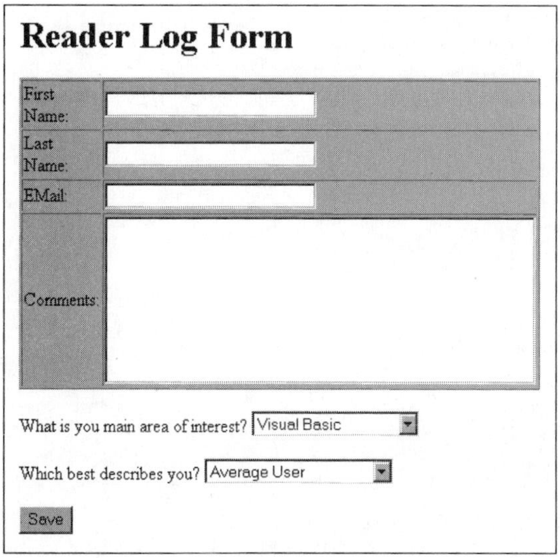

Reader Log Form

First Name:

Last Name:

EMail:

Comments:

What is you main area of interest? Visual Basic

Which best describes you? Average User

Save

Figure 10-13: HTML form enables the user to fill out data to be stored in a database.

www.wbase2.com/cgi-bin/apdexamples/logform.asp

The code for the form is shown next. No VBScript is needed in this document because the form can be handled by standard HTML. The form specifies the SaveLog.ASP file as the document that handles the data entered in this form.

```
<HTML>
<BODY>
<H1>Reader Log Form</H1>
<FORM Method="post" Action="SaveLog.ASP">
<TABLE bgColor=silver border=1 cellPadding=1 cellSpacing=1
          width="75%">
  <TR>
    <TD>First Name: </TD>
    <TD><INPUT name=First size=25></TD>
  </TR>
  <TR>
    <TD>Last Name: </TD>
    <TD><INPUT name=Last size=25></TD>
  </TR>
  <TR>
    <TD>EMail: </TD>
    <TD><INPUT name=Email size=25></TD>
  </TR>
  <TR>
    <TD>Comments: </TD>
    <TD><INPUT name=Comment size=25
      style="HEIGHT: 1.5in; WIDTH: 4in"></TD>
  </TR>
</TABLE>
 <P>What is you main area of interest?
  <SELECT name=Interest>
    <OPTION>Visual Basic</OPTION>
    <OPTION>SQL Server</OPTION>
    <OPTION>Active Server Pages</OPTION>
  </SELECT></P>
 <P>Which best describes you?
    <SELECT name=ReaderType>
      <OPTION>Average User</OPTION>
      <OPTION>Power User</OPTION>
      <OPTION>In House Developer</OPTION>
      <OPTION>Professional Developer</OPTION>
      <OPTION>MIS Director</OPTION>
      <OPTION>Dazed and Confused</OPTION>
    </SELECT></P>
 <INPUT type="submit" value="Save" name=submit1>
</FORM>
</BODY>
</HTML>
```

The only new element in the form is the use of the SELECT tag to create list boxes.

- ✔ `<SELECT>`...`</SELECT>`: This tag defines a drop list. The only required property is the Name of the list.

- ✔ `<OPTION>`...`</OPTION>`: The SELECT tags are followed by one or more OPTION tags. The OPTION tags provide the choices for the list box.

When the form is submitted, the text of the item visible in the select boxes is passed to the Form object as the value of the item.

Adding new records

After the user submits the form that contains the data to be stored, the ASP document referenced in the Action method has the task of using ADO to add that data to a new record in the underlying database.

In this example, the ReaderLog entry needs to be stored in the ReaderLog table in the MSAData.MDB file available to the Web server. The following VBScript creates a recordset object for that table, using ADO. Only one addition is made to this technique: the two additional parameters included with the Open method of the RLog recordset object. These values correspond to the CursorType and LockType arguments of the Open method. The value 1 is the equivalent of the adOpenKeyset constant and 3 corresponds to adLockOptimistic. When you were simply reading the data from the data source, you didn't need these arguments. However, in this case you plan to modify the contents of the database. This requires that you define a cursor type and lock type that are compatible with the operation you intend to perform.

```
Set Cnt = Server.CreateObject("ADODB.Connection")
Set RLog = Server.CreateObject("ADODB.Recordset")
Cnt.Open "APD"
RLog.Open "SELECT * FROM ReaderLog",Cnt,1,3
```

After you open the recordset, you can use the AddNew method to add a new record. In this case, the source of the new data is the entries made by the user in the HTML form. You can retrieve the form's data using the Request.Form object maintained by the Web server. The following code inserts the user entry into the new record. Note that the EntryDate field is not populated from the Form object. Instead, the current date and time are inserted by calling the VBScript function Now.

```
Rlog.AddNew
Rlog.Fields("EntryDate") = Now()
Rlog.Fields("FirstName") = Request.Form("First")
Rlog.Fields("LastName") = Request.Form("Last")
Rlog.Fields("Email") = Request.Form("EMail")
Rlog.Fields("Comment") = Request.Form("Comment")
Rlog.Fields("Interest") = Request.Form("Interest")
Rlog.Fields("ReaderType") = Request.Form("ReaderType")
Rlog.Update
```

The full code for the SaveLog.ASP document is shown next. The document displays the name of the user adding the record to confirm that it has been saved. Figure 10-14 shows the text displayed by the SaveLog.ASP, which confirms that the data has been saved in a record.

```
<HTML>
<BODY>
<%
  Set Cnt = Server.CreateObject("ADODB.Connection")
  Set RLog = Server.CreateObject("ADODB.Recordset")
  Cnt.Open "APD"
  RLog.Open "SELECT * FROM ReaderLog",Cnt,1,3
  Rlog.AddNew
  Rlog.Fields("EntryDate") = Now()
  Rlog.Fields("FirstName") = Request.Form("First")
  Rlog.Fields("LastName") = Request.Form("Last")
  Rlog.Fields("Email") = Request.Form("EMail")
  Rlog.Fields("Comment") = Request.Form("Comment")
  Rlog.Fields("Interest") = Request.Form("Interest")
  Rlog.Fields("ReaderType") = Request.Form("ReaderType")
  Rlog.Update
%>
<H1>Reader Log Entry Saved</H1>
<H2>From: <% =Request.Form("First") & " " &
           Request.Form("Last") %></H2>
<H1>Thank you!</H1>
</BODY>
</HTML>
```

Go to these URLs to see what the results look like:

```
www.wbase2.com/cgi-bin/apdexamples/LogForm.asp
www.wbase2.com/cgi-bin/apdexamples/SaveLog.asp
```

As an enhancement, you might want to display a copy of the entire user entry to show exactly what was stored in the record. You can do so by using the same VBScript code used in form3.ASP. The code displays the field names and the field contents of the current record in a given recordset. In ADO, when you add a new record to a recordset, the new record is the current record after you perform the Update method. In this case, the active recordset, Rlog, has the newly added record as its current record. All you need to do is display the items in the recordset. When you fill out the form in LogForm1.ASP, the ASP displays a copy of your entry, similar to Figure 10-15.

Figure 10-14: The display confirms that the record has been saved.

> **http://www.wbase2.com/cgi-bin/apdexamples/SaveLog.ASP - ...**
> File Edit View Go Favorites Help
> Address http://www.wbase2.com/cgi-bin/apdexamples/SaveLog.ASP
>
> # Reader Log Entry Saved
>
> **From: Walter Lafish**
>
> # Thank you!

Here's the code:

```
<TABLE <TABLE border = 2 cellpadding = 2 cellspacing = 1
        width = "75%">
  <% For Each Col in RLog.Fields %>
  <TR>
      <TD><% =Col.Name %></TD>
      <TD><% =Col.Value %></TD>
  </TR>
  <% Next %>
</TABLE>
```

Here's where to see its results:

```
www.wbase2.com/cgi-bin/apdexamples/LogForm1.asp
www.wbase2.com/cgi-bin/apdexamples/SaveLog1.asp
```

Depending upon where you are located, the time stamp on the record may look incorrect. Keep in mind that the time stamp is generated by the Web server, which in this case is in the Eastern U.S. time zone. Users in other time zones will see the time as out of sync with their local time.

Using SQL Server with ASP

Access .MDB files provide a handy way to add database resources to a Web server. However, here are several reasons why you might consider using a SQL Server as the data source.

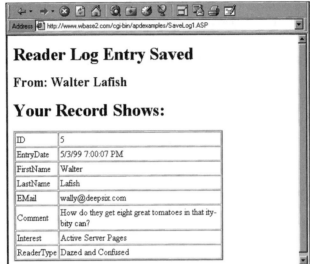

Figure 10-15:
The form displays the entire contents of the new record.

- SQL Server is capable of handling larger databases (and processing requests from a large number of users) without creating significant delays in returning the data to the requesting applications.

- SQL Server provides a more robust security environment.

- SQL Server supports programs called *stored procedures,* which can perform large database operations at a high rate of speed. SQL Server stored procedures provide powerful server-side tools for performing data operations that are too large or complex to be handled by VBScript. Note that SQL Server stored procedures are written in the Transact SQL language, which is not related directly to Visual Basic or VBScript.

In terms of ASP coding, there isn't much difference between using Access or SQL Server. In these examples, only two changes have to be made.

- **DSN:** In order to connect to a SQL Server, an ODBC DSN must be created on the computer that is running the Web service. The DSN must connect to the SQL Server where the database resides that contains data to support the ASPs. The SQL Server referenced does not have to reside on the same computer as the Web service. The DSN can connect to any SQL Server available to the computer running the Web service. Further, keep in mind that if the SQL Server is separate from the Web server, you don't need to define an ODBC DSN on that machine. Only the Web server requires the DSN.

✔ **Connection string:** The connection string used with a SQL Server is a bit more elaborate than the one used with a simple Access .MDB file. The basic parameters required with SQL Server are shown in the following code: the name of the database in which the desired table (or tables) are stored, the name of the ODBC DSN that connects to the SQL Server, and the user's name and password.

```
"DATABASE=;DSN=;UID=;PWD=;"
```

The following code is contained in the ASP SaveLogSQL.ASP. It saves an entry made into the form displayed by SaveLogSQL.ASP into a table on a SQL Server available over the Internet. As you can see from this example, identical code is used to perform the same operation on an Access .MDB file. That is the value of using ADO and ODBC to handle communication with data sources: ADO and ODBC present a common interface for all supported data sources. Put more simply, you can use the same code to perform similar tasks, regardless of the specific data source you are working with.

You can test out this script by loading the logformsql.ASP document and filling out the form.

```
<%
   Set Cnt = Server.CreateObject("ADODB.Connection")
   Set RLog = Server.CreateObject("ADODB.Recordset")
   Cnt.Open
            "DATABASE=SC1ADB;DSN=wbasenet;UID=UC1ADB3;PWD=xxxx
            xxxx;"
   RLog.Open "SELECT * FROM ReaderLog",Cnt,1,3
   Rlog.AddNew
   Rlog.Fields("EntryDate") = Now()
   Rlog.Fields("FirstName") = Request.Form("First")
   Rlog.Fields("LastName") = Request.Form("Last")
   Rlog.Fields("Email") = Request.Form("EMail")
   Rlog.Fields("Comment") = Request.Form("Comment")
   Rlog.Fields("Interest") = Request.Form("Interest")
   Rlog.Fields("ReaderType") = Request.Form("ReaderType")
   Rlog.Update
%>
```

Here's where to see the results:

```
www.wbase2.com/cgi-bin/apdexamples/LogFormSQL.asp
www.wbase2.com/cgi-bin/apdexamples/SaveLogSQL.asp
```

Chapter 11

ActiveX

- -

- -

*I*s ActiveX something new? The answer is . . . both yes and no. This ambiguous response results from the turmoil in the computer industry that the rapid emergence of Internet technologies has caused. Although applications such as word processing or spreadsheets don't directly concern the Internet itself, the Net can provide a common method of communication among users of different types of computers and software.

Having a common means of communication doesn't do much good if the stuff you're communicating comes in a variety of incompatible formats. (The concept's a bit like being able to place a phone call to any country in the world but not necessarily being able to understand the language of the person on the other end.) You have the communications link but no meaningful communication. ActiveX is the key.

On a larger scale, COM (Common Object Model) and DCOM (Distributed Common Object Model) refer to technologies that help define how objects can be exchanged among applications that run across local area networks and larger networks, including the global Internet. This chapter focuses on using objects within the Office 2000 suite.

> ***Database Folder: Chapter 10***
> ***Database File: ActiveX.MDB***

To begin, load the database for Chapter 11, ActiveX.MDB. Click the Forms tab to display a list of the forms that I discuss in this chapter.

About Names

In this book, I use the term *ActiveX* to refer to the technology that Microsoft uses to exchange objects among applications in its Front and Back Office application suites. Microsoft has long been interested in technologies that allow information to flow between applications. The first try at making Windows programs work together was called *DDE* (Dynamic Data Exchange). With this technology, you could pass data between two Windows applications running at the same time. It was kind of like an automatic clipboard function in which the data was automatically pasted into the target application. DDE could also execute macro commands if they were supported by the other application.

The primary disadvantage of DDE was that, after the data was exchanged, it became part of the receiving application. For example, if you sent Excel spreadsheet data to a Word document, the data entered Word as text. You couldn't recalculate the information because it was no longer part of the Excel spreadsheet. Now it was merely Word text and you could only edit it, not recalculate it.

Microsoft's next upgrade was called *OLE* (Object Linking and Embedding). This technology allowed data from one application to be integrated into another application while still maintaining the data's connection to the original application. For example, you could link or embed an Excel spreadsheet in a Word document. You would double-click the area in the Word document that contained the spreadsheet and Excel would automatically take control of the data and perform any of its normal functions, such as recalculating, without your having to close Word.

In OLE, the program receiving the data — for example, Word getting an Excel spreadsheet — was called the *OLE client*. The program providing and servicing the data was the *OLE server*.

With the growth of the Internet and the need for applications that could exchange data over large networks, Microsoft expanded OLE to become ActiveX. Thus, ActiveX is both new and old, depending on what part you work with. The older OLE terminology is built right into Access 2000. Unfortunately, you can find no easy way to stay consistent in the use of the terms *OLE* and *ActiveX*. If you stick with OLE, some folks may accuse you of using an obsolete technology. If you refer to ActiveX, other people may wonder why you store ActiveX stuff in OLE fields and controls. In this book, I use *ActiveX* and *OLE* interchangeably. I use *OLE* only if the term appears in a property sheet or a VBA statement.

Working with ActiveX

Most of the Access 2000 programming techniques you read about in this book involve the use of VBA to manipulate the methods and properties that the various objects in the Access 2000 model support.

But Microsoft designed its object model to encompass more than a single application and the set of objects that application supports. The goal of the object model is to break down the barriers between applications so that objects from different applications can interact to form integrated applications. VBA is designed to work not only with Access 2000 objects but also with objects that other applications provide, including those in the Office 2000 suite (such as Internet Explorer, Excel 2000, PowerPoint 2000, Word 2000, and Outlook 2000), plus other network applications (such as Exchange, SQL Server, and Internet Server II).

Microsoft uses the name *ActiveX* to represent a set of technologies that enable objects of different types to interact in a common structure. Access 2000 can integrate objects that you create in other applications with its set of database objects. This integration takes three forms:

- **ActiveX applications.** An ActiveX component is a program that can function as either a stand-alone application or an ActiveX object server. You can use Word 2000, for example, as a stand-alone word processing program or to provide word processing services to another application, such as Access 2000, that can function as an ActiveX controller. If you use Word 2000 as an ActiveX server, your Access 2000 VBA program sends commands directly to Word 2000 as if Word 2000 were a part of the Access 2000 system. All Microsoft Office 2000 applications are ActiveX components.

- **ActiveX controls.** An ActiveX control is similar to an ActiveX component in that the control is a separate application that provides Access 2000 with special objects that would not normally be part of the Access 2000 object model. Controls, however, can't function as stand-alone programs. You can use them only within the context of some other Access 2000 object, such as a form. For example, Microsoft supplies Access 2000 with an ActiveX Calendar control, which builds in a calendar display that you can use in Access 2000 forms to provide a perpetual calendar.

- **ActiveX components.** A number of ActiveX technologies consist of object libraries that provide information or execute operations but have no obvious visual components. For example, when you install Internet Explorer, a set of scripting components is also installed along with it. The scripting components are used by Internet Explorer, but they can also be used by other applications. One useful component is the `FileSystemObject` that provides an object interface to the drives, folders, and files that you can use in place of Visual Basic functions and statements, such as `Dir( )` or `ChDir`.

An ActiveX application, control, or component consists of one or more executable files (.EXE, .DLL, or .OCX) that contain the code that implements the ActiveX function. When a program uses ActiveX, it loads the data from the appropriate file as part of its overall execution. The trick in ActiveX programming is to write code that can run as part of an existing application. For this system to work, the writer of the ActiveX program must follow a clearly defined set of rules that determine how ActiveX components should interact with the host application. You can use Visual Basic 6.0 or Visual C++ 6.0 to write ActiveX components that work with programs like Access 2000.

This chapter looks at examples of all three types of ActiveX features.

ActiveX controls

In Access 2000, *controls* are objects that you place on a form to provide a way to display information and a way for the user to enter information. Access 2000 provides a set of 11 native controls that are part of the standard set of on-screen objects in Access 2000: check box, combo box, command button, frame, image, label, list box, option button, tab strip, text box, and toggle button.

In addition to the native controls, which appear in the Design mode toolbox, Access 2000 enables you to insert ActiveX controls into a form. An *ActiveX control* is a type of plug-in control that adds a new way for users to view or enter information. Keep in mind that you're not limited to using ActiveX controls with Access 2000. Other applications that support ActiveX can also use these controls, including Visual Basic, Excel 2000, or Internet Explorer.

One example is an ActiveX calendar control that comes with Access 2000 and as part of the Microsoft Office 2000 Premium package. The Calendar control provides users with an easy-to-recognize way of displaying or entering date information.

The Calendar control isn't part of the default installation package for Office 2000. If you don't have the Calendar control installed on your system, you have to run the Office 2000 Setup program and select to Add the Calendar control to your Office installation.

To insert a Calendar control into a form, follow these steps:

1. **Open a new or existing form in the Design mode.**

2. **Choose Insert⇨ActiveX Control from the menu bar.**

   This action opens the Insert ActiveX Control dialog box. This dialog box lists the names of each ActiveX control you have installed on your system. Because ActiveX controls work with more than one application, you may find that your system lists controls installed by other applications (such as Visual Basic). The list shown in Figure 11-1 probably won't match the list on your system. Be aware that some of the controls listed in this dialog box may be designed for Visual Basic only and won't work correctly with Access 2000. Also, some controls are demos and can't be used unless you get a license from the manufacturer.

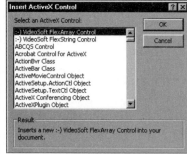

Figure 11-1:
The dialog box lists all the ActiveX controls installed in the system.

3. **Scroll down the list and select Calendar Control 9.0.**

4. **Click OK.**

Access 2000 inserts the control into the form, as shown in Figure 11-2.

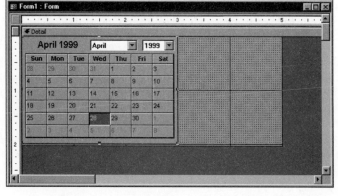

Figure 11-2:
The Calendar control inserted in a form in the Design mode.

ActiveX control properties

Native Access 2000 controls, such as a combo box or command button controls, display all their properties in the tabs of the property sheet window. ActiveX controls, however, have the following two levels of properties:

✔ **ActiveX container properties.** These properties represent the standard set of Access 2000 properties that appear in the property sheet window of every ActiveX control, such as Name, Height, Width, Visible, and Enabled.

✔ **ActiveX control-specific properties.** These properties relate specifically to the ActiveX control. The Calendar control, for example, has a property called FirstDay that determines which day of the week appears in the leftmost column of the calendar. By default, this property is set to Sunday.

You can also access the property list for an ActiveX control by right-clicking the control and choosing the name of the control (for example, Calendar Object) from the shortcut menu that appears. Then choose Properties to open a dialog box containing settings for the control's properties, as shown in Figure 11-3. In addition to the properties they list, most dialog boxes include a Help button. This Help button is important, because the Help files that come with the control store information about the methods and use of the control. Clicking the Help button opens the Help file for the control. Typically, you discover how to integrate the control into your form from this Help file.

Keep in mind that an ActiveX control actually consists of two distinct structures. Each structure has its own set of properties and contains one of the following:

✔ **The ActiveX container.** Each ActiveX control added to a form is placed into a generic container called an *OLE Object Frame*. Access 2000 uses the same frame no matter what type of object you're going to insert into the form. Each OLE Object Frame has a set of properties that relate to the container but have nothing specifically to do with the object inside, such as a Calendar. For example, if you move the control to another location in the form, you have altered a property of the OLE Object Frame, not the ActiveX object contained within it. The programming code for the OLE Object Frame is contained within Access 2000.

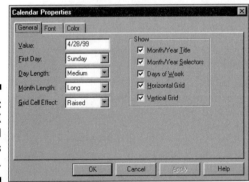

Figure 11-3:
ActiveX
control
properties
dialog box.

✔ **The ActiveX object.** The actual ActiveX component is called the *object*. The object actually consists of the .EXE, .DLL, or .OCX file that contains the programming code that implements the ActiveX object. For example, the Calendar control code is stored in the file MSCAL.OCX. When the ActiveX control is activated, the code in this file executes as if it were part of Access 2000. The rules that govern ActiveX programming ensure that the control functions seamlessly, as if it were a built-in part of the containing program.

The Calendar control

The Calendar control provides an interactive object that looks like a calendar on-screen. The object enables users to select dates by working with a visual display that looks like a paper calendar. The value of the Calendar control is always the date of the button on the control that is selected. This means that you can use the Calendar control to select dates rather than have the user make an entry.

The Calendar control also supports special methods. For example, the NextMonth and PreviousMonth methods change the current date of the calendar control to those dates based on the currently selected date. This is the same date calculation performed by the DateAdd( ) function in Visual Basic.

Early binding

Before you look at operations involving the Calendar control, you need to be aware of some special issues involved in writing code that refers to an ActiveX control. The form pictured in Figure 11-4 contains a command button labeled *NextMonth*. This button executes the NextMonth method of the Call Calendar control. The following statement performs this operation.

```
Me.Call.NextMonth
```

Figure 11-4: The Calendar control inserted into a form.

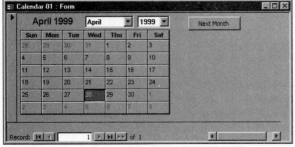

However, if you actually enter this statement into a Visual Basic module, you notice that Visual Basic doesn't list the `NextMonth` method as part of the properties and methods list for the `Calendar` control. This is because Access 2000 doesn't identify the specific object type of the ActiveX control. Instead, Access 2000 identifies the ActiveX control as generic and displays only the standard set of properties and method that belong to all ActiveX controls. Unfortunately, this means that you must know in advance what properties and methods are supported by the `Calendar` control because Visual Basic doesn't provide lists or quick information displays to aid you in coding the statements. Ironically, it's probably more important to have the control-specific properties and methods listed for ActiveX controls than it is for native controls because ActiveX controls probably include properties and methods with which you're not familiar.

You can overcome this shortcoming. The method is called *early binding* of an object, which means that you identify to Visual Basic the specific type of object that is contained in the ActiveX control in the Design mode. This allows Visual Basic to retrieve the specific properties and methods supported by the object in the ActiveX control. In other words, when you use early binding, the Visual Basic editor knows the object type at the time you are writing the code, which allows Visual Basic to display lists of options and check your syntax as you write. If you do not use early binding, Visual Basic must wait until you attempt to run the code to discover whether you have used the proper property and method names.

The following code is an example of early binding. First, an object variable is defined as the specific object type of the ActiveX control that you want to manipulate. The object list, displayed when you type the keyword **As**, includes the `Calendar` object type because a `Calendar` control is in the current form.

The trick comes in the second statement in which the `Object` method of the control that contains the Calendar — for example, `Call` is assigned to the `Calendar` object variable `vCal`. The *v* distinguishes the variable from the control. When you reference `vCal` in your code, Access 2000 can now display a list of the object-specific properties and methods along with a Quick Info display related to the ActiveX object, as shown in Figure 11-5.

```
Dim vCal As Calendar
Set vCal = Me.Call.Object
vCal.NextMonth
```

Form: Calendar 01

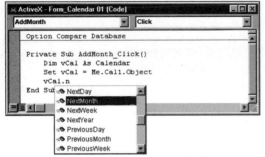

Figure 11-5:
Early bind-
ing allows
Access 2000
to display
the object-
specific list
of proper-
ties and
methods.

Using the Calendar control

Figure 11-6 shows a `Calendar` control used to report order information for a
selected date. Each time the user clicks on the `Calendar` control, the form
changes so that the sales and sales totals for that day appear.

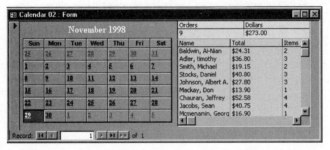

Figure 11-6:
Data dis-
plays based
on the
selection in
the
Calendar
control.

Form: Calendar 02

The following procedure uses the current value of the `Calendar` control to
define the `RowSource` property for the two list boxes that appear on the right
side of the form shown in Figure 11-6.

```
Sub CalcSales()
 Dim WClause
 WClause = "WHERE DateValue(OrderDate) = #" & Me.Cal1 & "#"
 With Me.DailySalesSummary
  .RowSource = "SELECT Count(*) As Orders, " & _
   " Sum(OrderTotal) AS Dollars " & _
    "FROM Orders " & WClause
```

(continued)

(continued)

```
   .ColumnCount = 2
   .ColumnHeads = True
  End With
 With Me.DailySalesList
   .RowSource = "Select billlast & ', ' & billfirst" & _
     "As Name, OrderTotal as Total, Items " & _
     "FROM Orders " & WClause
   .ColumnCount = 3
   .ColumnHeads = True
  End With
End Sub
```

The procedure is then linked to the `AfterUpdate` event of the `Calendar` control to ensure that the values change each time the date in the calendar changes.

```
Private Sub Call_AfterUpdate()
    CalcSales
End Sub
```

Creating a pop-up calendar

The `Calendar` control is an easy and intuitive way for users to select date values. However, the `Calendar` control uses up a lot of valuable screen real estate. If you used a `Calendar` control in place of a text box for each date that you needed to select, the form would probably be crowded.

A better solution appears in Figure 11-7, which shows a form (the `Report Dialog 01` from Chapter 9) that requires a starting and ending date entry to print a report. Instead of having the user type in the date, a second form containing a `Calendar` control pops up when the user double-clicks in the date box. After the user makes a selection from the pop-up calendar, the date is inserted into the control and the calendar form closes. Using this approach gives you the best of both worlds.

The key to this technique is the use of the `OpenArgs` property. When you want to coordinate operations between two forms, you must split the code between the two forms and use the `OpenArgs` property to pass data to the form that is being opened. (For a refresher on coordinating operations between two forms, see Chapter 9.)

In this case, the critical data that needs to be passed to the form that displays the `Calendar` control is the name of the form and control into which the date should be inserted. Keep in mind that your goal is to insert into a text box control in one form the date selected on a `Calendar` control on another form. If you pass the form and control names to the calendar form, those names can be used to insert the date back into the desired control.

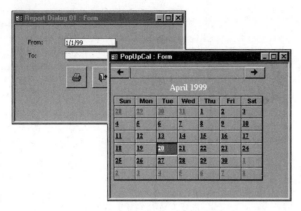

Figure 11-7:
Use a
Calendar
control in a
pop-up form
to insert a
date into a
control on
another
form.

The following procedures contain a single statement that uses the `OpenForm` method to display the popup calendar form. In order to determine which control on the form should have a date inserted into it, you need to specify two pieces of information: the active form's name and the active control's name. Unfortunately, the `OpenArgs` property is limited to a single text string. The solution is to create a single text string that can easily be divided into two parts. The expression below combines the form name (`Me.Name`) with the control name (`Me.ActiveControl.Name`).

```
Me.Name & "/" & Me.ActiveControl.Name
```

The names are separated by a / character. When you double-click either of the date text boxes, the popup calendar form opens and the name of the form and control are passed as a single text string in the `OpenArgs` property.

```
Private Sub EndDate_DblClick(Cancel As Integer)
    DoCmd.OpenForm FormName:="PopUpCal", _
        OpenArgs:=Me.Name & "/" & Me.ActiveControl.Name
End Sub

Private Sub StartDate_DblClick(Cancel As Integer)
    DoCmd.OpenForm FormName:="PopUpCal", _
        OpenArgs:=Me.Name & "/" & Me.ActiveControl.Name
End Sub
```

The code that inserts the date into the text box control is contained in the `PopUpCal` form. The procedure is assigned to the double-click event of the `Calendar` control. The user can double-click on a date and have that date inserted into the text box in the other form.

The procedure first breaks down the OpenArgs text into a FName (form name) portion and a CName (control name) portion by locating the / within the string and taking the text on either side of that character respectively. The FName text is used as the identifier in the Forms collection. In turn, the CName text identifies the control that the user double-clicked at the beginning of the process. The value of the Calendar control is then assigned to the control. The last statement closes the calendar form, which returns the focus to the original form.

```
Private Sub Call_DblClick()
    Dim vF As Form
    Dim vC As Control
    Dim FName, CName
    FName = Mid(Me.OpenArgs, 1, InStr(OpenArgs, "/") - 1)
    CName = Mid(Me.OpenArgs, InStr(OpenArgs, "/") + 1)
    Set vF = Forms(FName)
    Set vC = vF(CName)
    vC = Me.Call
    DoCmd.Close acForm, Me.Name
End Sub
```

Note that you can use this popup calendar with any text box control on any form. Simply insert the statement that opens the pop-up calendar in the double-click procedure of any text box control.

> **Forms: PopUpCal, Report Dialog 01**

The MS Chart control

Another control that is included with Office 2000 and works as part of Access 2000 is the MS Chart control. This is the control that is inserted in a form or a report when you either use the Insert⇨Chart command in the Design mode or use the Form or Report Chart Wizards, which invoke the built-in Access 2000 chart designer.

Figure 11-8 shows a format that contains a chart original created with the chart designer but modified and controlled by Visual Basic code. In this example, Visual Basic is used to change both the data set, which the chart graphs, and the appearance options of the chart, such as the chart type, the text of the chart titles, and the colors used in various aspects of the chart.

Changing the data set

In the example form shown in Figure 11-8, the data displayed on the chart is a summary of the number of orders placed on each day for a specified range of dates. The goal is to allow the user to change the date range (starting and ending dates) and have the chart inside the form update to display only the selected range of dates. In this example, the dates that appear on the form are stored in unbound controls called SDate and EDate.

Figure 11-8:
Use Visual
Basic to
alter the
data and
appearance
of charts
displayed in
an MS Chart
control.

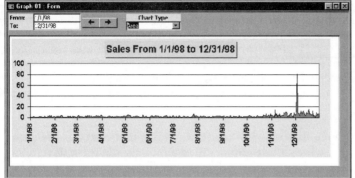

Figure 11-8:
Use Visual Basic to alter the data and appearance of charts displayed in an MS Chart control.

The data source of an MS Chart control is refined by the SQL statement assigned to the control's rowsource. In order to change the data displayed in the form, you need to modify the SQL statement in the RowSource property and then use the Requery method to update the chart. The procedure below uses the current values of the SDate and EDate controls to alter the RowSource statement so that the chart's contents reflect the currently entered date range.

```
Sub ChangeChartData()
    With Me.Graph1
        .RowSource = "SELECT DateValue(Orderdate), " & _
            "Count(OrderId) As Orders FROM Orders " & _
            "WHERE DateValue(OrderDate) Between #" & Me.SDate
            & _
            "# AND #" & Me.EDate & "# GROUP BY
            DateValue(OrderDate)"
        .Requery
    End With
    ChangeChartTitle
End Sub
```

The previous procedure also executes ChangeChart Title, a procedure I discuss in the next section.

Chart title

Note that the RowSource property belongs to ActiveX container control. In this case, you don't have to use the ActiveX control's Object property, because the MS Chart control automatically links with the RowSource property of the ActiveX container control.

On the other hand, any properties that are concerned with the details of the charts appearance must be accessed through the Object property of the ActiveX container control in which the chart displays. For example, when you change the date range of the data displayed in the chart, you probably would like to reflect the change in the chart title. This doesn't happen automatically when you change the rowsource because the text of the chart title isn't linked to the RowSource property. To have the title reflect the rowsource, you must create a Visual Basic procedure that coordinates the two properties.

In order to write Visual Basic code that modifies the appearance, in contrast to the RowSource, of an MS Chart ActiveX control, you need to add the Chart library to your references. Here's how:

1. **Open the code module for the form that contains the chart by using the View⇨Code command available in the form design mode.**

2. **Choose Tool⇨References from the menu.**

3. **Scroll down the list until you locate Microsoft Graph 9.0 Object Library.**

4. **Check the box next to that library and click OK.**

You can now include code in the form's module that controls the chart object on the form. Keep in mind that after you add a reference to a library to any module in a database, that library is available to all other modules. If you add more charts to the same database, the library is already available to use in your Visual Basic code.

After you reference the library, you can create a Chart type object variable using a statement like the following one. This variable isn't required because you can access the properties of the chart through the control's Object property. However, as discussed in the previous section about the Calendar control, creating the variable provides early binding, which means Access 2000 displays lists of properties, methods, constants, and quick info for the chart object. Because charts have a large number of parts and you probably don't work with an object as often as a recordset, having these lists appear is a great help in writing code related to changing the appearance of the chart.

```
Dim G As Chart
Set G = Me.Graph1.Object
```

The following procedure changes the text of the title to reflect the current values in the SDate and EDate controls. In addition, the procedure sets the color for the text and for the background area on the chart where the title appears.

```
Sub ChangeChartTitle()
    Dim G As Chart
    Set G = Me.Graph1.Object
    With G.ChartTitle
        .Text = "Sales From " & Me.SDate & _
            " to " & Me.EDate
```

```
            .Font.Color = vbBlue
            .Shadow = True
            .Interior.Color = RGB(192, 240, 255)
        End With
End Sub
```

The result is that the chart's title accurately reflects the date range of the rowsource because the ChangeChartData procedure (which alters the rowsource) also executes ChangeChartTitle so that both changes always take place together.

Changing chart type

The MS Chart control can display the data defined in the RowSource property in a wide variety of chart types, such as line, area, column, and so on. In addition, you can choose 3-D style variations of the basic types. The chart shown in Figure 11-8 contains a combo box control (ChangeChart), which provides the user with six options for the chart type. The following code, assigned to the AfterUpdate procedure of the ChangeChart control, modifies the ChartType property of the MS Chart control based on the user's selection. In addition, the color of the plot area background is set to gray for 3-D charts and white for standard charts.

```
Private Sub ChangeChart_AfterUpdate()
    Dim Cht As Chart
    Set Cht = Me.Graph1.Object
    Cht.ChartArea.Interior.Color = vbPaleYellow
    Select Case Me.ChangeChart
        Case "Line"
            Cht.ChartType = xlLine
            Cht.PlotArea.Interior.Color = vbWhite
        Case "3D Line"
            Cht.ChartType = xl3DLine
            Cht.PlotArea.Interior.Color = vbSilver
        Case "Column"
            Cht.ChartType = xl3DBarClustered
            Cht.PlotArea.Interior.Color = vbWhite
        Case "3D Column"
            Cht.ChartType = xl3DColumnClustered
            Cht.PlotArea.Interior.Color = vbSilver
        Case "Area"
            Cht.ChartType = xlArea
            Cht.PlotArea.Interior.Color = vbWhite
        Case "3D Area"
            Cht.ChartType = xl3DArea
            Cht.PlotArea.Interior.Color = vbSilver
    End Select
End Sub
```

Note that this procedure also uses early binding to create a `Chart` type object variable. This is very useful in this case when you enter statements that involve the `ChartType` property, which supports 70 different values (each with its own constant name).

ON THE CD

> **Forms: Graph 01**

Automation

Another facet of ActiveX technology is called Automation. *Automation* takes place when Visual Basic code running in one application is used to control operations in another application. For example, you can write code in Access 2000 that takes control of Excel and creates worksheets, enters data, applies formats, and even writes formulas.

An application that allows itself to be controlled by Visual Basic code running in a different application is called an *Automation server*. If the code is written in Access 2000 and it controls Excel 2000, then Excel 2000 is the Automation server because it provides Access with spreadsheet services.

Controlling Excel 2000

You can come up with many uses for ActiveX Automation between Excel 2000 and Access 2000. One of the most common uses is exporting the results of an Access query to an Excel spreadsheet. Why bother? Isn't this feature already in Access 2000?

The answer is yes. But keep in mind that in many cases, simply exporting the query grid doesn't produce the type of worksheet that users want to work with. However, Automation does provide a number of abilities not supported when you import or export data between applications. In the case of Access 2000 data being sent to an Excel 2000 spreadsheet:

- ✔ You can control which cells on the spreadsheet are filled with data, which enables you to skip a row between the column headings and the first line of data.

- ✔ You can apply formatting to the cells.

- ✔ You can add extra columns, such as column and row totals, that don't appear on a query grid.

- ✔ You can write formulas into the Excel cells instead of simply inserting a value. This means that you can create a worksheet that users can use for modeling, which is set to automatically recalculate totals rather than simply write in column totals that don't recalculate when changes are made to the worksheet.

In order to write Visual Basic code that interacts with Excel, you need to add to your references the Excel library. Here's how:

1. **Open the code module for the form that contains the chart by using the View⇨Code command available in the form design mode.**

2. **Choose Tool⇨References from the menu.**

3. **Scroll down the list until you locate Microsoft Excel 9.0 Object Library.**

4. **Check the box next to that library and click OK.**

Creating a new workbook

All operations that involve Excel 2000 require that you create an Excel application object. The following statement is the Automation equivalent of loading Excel 2000.

```
Dim Ex As New Excel.Application
```

However, one significant difference exists. Unlike opening Excel 2000 from the Start menu, when you open it as an Automation server, Excel doesn't immediately create a new workbook. The application object is equivalent to opening Excel while closing all the open workbooks.

To perform worksheet operations in Excel 2000, you must first add a workbook by using the Add method of the Excel application object. This is the Automation equivalent of choosing the File⇨New command on the Excel 2000 menu bar.

```
Set WrkBk = Ex.Workbooks.Add
```

When you create the workbook, you create a default set of worksheets (usually set at 3) that you can begin working with immediately. In object terminology this means that you begin with a Worksheets collection that contains three worksheet objects. In the following example, a new workbook is created and the value of 100 is inserted into cell A1. In the Excel model, all cells are Range type objects.

```
Sub XLS1()
    Dim Ex As New Excel.Application
    Dim WrkBk As Excel.Workbook
    Set WrkBk = Ex.Workbooks.Add
    WrkBk.Worksheets(1).Range("A1") = 100
    Ex.Visible = True
End Sub
```

One unusual aspect of Automation is related to the last statement in the procedure, which sets the `Visible` property of the Excel 2000 application to `True`. Why? As it turns out, when you create an Excel Automation object, nothing appears on-screen. The Excel Automation object is in memory and it can be manipulated — but it won't appear on-screen until you explicitly instruct Excel to show itself. After you do this, you can see that the Visual Basic code has written the value `100` into cell `A1` of worksheet 1.

> **Module: XLS Operations, Procedure: XLS1**

Changing cells

The primary reason for controlling Excel is to write data and formulas into the worksheet cells. To take advantage of early binding, you want to create a variable that is an Excel `Range` object:

```
Dim Rng As Excel.Range
```

The following procedure writes the current date into cell A1 of an Excel worksheet. In addition to merely inserting the date, the procedure also applies formatting to the cell.

```
Sub XLS2()
    Dim Ex As New Excel.Application
    Dim WrkBk As Excel.Workbook
    Dim Wks As Excel.Worksheet
    Dim Rng As Excel.Range

    Set WrkBk = Ex.Workbooks.Add
    Set Wks = WrkBk.Worksheets(1)
    Wks.Name = "Example"

    Set Rng = Wks.Cells(1, 1)
    With Rng
        .Value = Date
        .NumberFormat = "mmmm dd yyyy"
        With .Font
            .Bold = True
            .Color = vbBlue
            .Size = 11
        End With
    End With
    Set Rng = Wks.UserRange.Columns
    Rng.Autofit
    Ex.Visible = True
End Sub
```

You should note a few items in the previous procedure:

- ✔ `Cells( )`. The `Cells` method enables you to refer to any cell in an Excel worksheet by its row and column number. This means that A1 refers to Cells(1,1) and C4 refers to Cells(4,3). Using numeric values is often simpler than dealing with letter combinations because you can easily add and subtract numeric values.

- ✔ `UserRange`. This property returns a range that includes all the cells in the worksheet that have actually been used.

- ✔ `Columns`. This property returns a range that consists of all the columns in a given range, which is equivalent to highlighting a range of columns when you want to use the `AutoFit` command.

- ✔ `AutoFit`. This property applies the `AutoFit` operation to the selected range of columns. Note that you can only apply this method if the range object contains a column, not a cell, range.

The following statements automatically adjust column widths across the specified worksheet:

```
Set Rng = Wks.UserRange.Columns
Rng.Autofit
```

> **Module: XLS Operations, Procedure: XLS2**

Writing a recordset to a worksheet

You can now apply these Automation fundamentals to the task of creating a worksheet based on the content of some recordset. As an example, the record-set object is the following cross tabulation query. The `TRANSFORM` keyword is supported in Access 2000 SQL in order to create cross tab outputs. The goal in this case is to use the cross tab recordset to populate an Excel worksheet.

```
Rs.Open "TRANSFORM Sum(ExtPrice) AS Sales " & _
    " SELECT SKU FROM Orders INNER JOIN " & _
    "OrderDetails ON Orders.OrderID = OrderDetails.OrderLink
        " & _
    " GROUP BY SKU PIVOT Format([OrderDate],'yyyy mm')", _
    CurrentProject.Connection
```

Using the Excel application object, you create the workbook into which you're going to write the data. You then assign the range object — for example, Rng — to the cell that is the starting point for the data.

```
Set WrkBk = Ex.Workbooks.Add
Set Wks = WrkBk.Worksheets(1)
'Start At
Set Rng = Wks.Cells(1, 1)
```

Column headings

You can write column headings by using the Name property of the fields in the recordset. You can use the Fields collection of the recordset to automatically write the field names across the starting row of the worksheet. The key to this section of the procedure is the Offset method. The Offset method enables you to define a cell range based on its position relative to an existing cell range.

```
range.Offset(number of rows, number of columns)
```

The following statement uses the Offset method to change the cell defined by Rng to the next cell on the same row. If the current value of Rng is A1 — that is, row 1, column 1 — the Offset method adds 0 to the row value and 1 to the column value. The result is that the range changes from A1 to B1 (row 1, column 2).

```
Set Rng = Rng.Offset(0, 1)
```

Because the Offset method is always relative to the specified range, you can work your way across or down a group of cells by repeating the statement each time you want to move on to the next cell. The following procedure inserts the Offset method inside a For...Each loop. The result is that each field name is placed one column over from the previous column.

```
'Column Headings
For Each Col In Rs.Fields
    With Rng
        .Value = Col.Name
        .Font.Bold = True
    End With
    Set Rng = Rng.Offset(0, 1)
Next
```

You can also use the Offset method to write the recordset data into a series of rows and columns. The following code shows how this is accomplished. You begin by locating the first cell to work with. In this case, select C1, which allows a blank row, row 2, between the headings and the data. The recordset is looped so that all the records are processed.

For each row, a For...Each loop writes the field information across the row using the Offset method to move to the next column. The Type property of the field determines which cells should have numeric formatting. In this case, numeric formatting is applied when the field is a currency type field. At the end of each set of fields, another Offset method is used. This time its purpose is to increment the row value by 1 and reset the column value back to that of the first column.

```
'Start Data At
Set Rng = Wks.Cells(3, 1)
'Write Data
Do Until Rs.EOF
    For Each Col In Rs.Fields
        With Rng
            .Value = Col.Value
            If Col.Type = adCurrency Then
                .NumberFormat = "#,###.00"
            End If
        End With
        Set Rng = Rng.Offset(0, 1)
    Next
    Rs.MoveNext
    Set Rng = Wks.Cells(Rng.Row + 1, 1)
Loop
```

When all the rows have been written, the AutoFit method is applied to the worksheet to ensure that all the cells display their contents.

```
Set Rng = Wks.UsedRange.Columns
Rng.AutoFit
Ex.Visible = True
```

ON THE CD

Module: XLS Operations, Procedure: XLS3

Adding rows and columns with Sum formulas

One of the advantages of creating worksheets with Automation is that you can write cell formulas as well as store values in cells. When you perform a cross-tabulation query in Access 2000, the program doesn't generate any additional columns or rows for row or column totals. However, having these summary formulas on a worksheet when you have to do a cross-tabulation is common.

You can take care of this problem by using Visual Basic to write cell formulas. The following statement writes the formula =Sum(A1:A25) into the range Rng. Keep in mind that when you write formulas with Automation, Excel recalculates those formulas in the same manner as it would any formula entered manually by a user, which means that you can use Automation to create worksheet models in contrast to merely importing data.

```
Rng.Formula = "=Sum(A1:A25)"
```

Suppose that you want to end each row in the worksheet with a formula that sums the values in the row. The trick is to figure out the column letters involved — for example, B3:K3. In this case, you can assume that column B contains the first value because the recordset begins with a single text field.

But what about the ending column? That's going to vary with the data in the table. You can use the Column property to figure out the column value of the currently defined range. The expression below would return the numeric value of the ranges column.

```
Rng.Column
```

But Excel requires a column letter rather than a column number. The following function converts an Excel column number to the appropriate column letter. The Chr( ) function changes a number to a letter by adding 64 to the value because ASCII code 65 is the letter A. So if the column number is 1, then 64+1 = 65, or column A. Excel worksheets can have up to 255 columns; you need to account for 2 Letter columns. The Int( ) and Mod( ) functions perform calculations using the value 26 (because there are 26 letters in the alphabet) to figure out separate values for the two column letters.

The math is a little tricky here, so an example may help. Suppose that you want to refer to column 113 on a worksheet. If you were to open Excel and count 113 columns, you would end up at DI. But how to calculate that location? Begin with the first letter, D. Because that letter changes every 26 columns, you would calculate 113/26 = 4.34. Because D is the fourth letter in the alphabet, the first letter of the column reference is D (64+4 in the ASCII code.) The Mod( ) returns the remained, 113 Mod 26 = 9. Because the ninth letter in the alphabet is I, column 113 is column DI.

```
Function ColumnLetter(ColNumber)
    Dim Letter1, Letter2
    If ColNumber < 27 Then
        ColumnLetter = Chr(64 + ColNumber)
    Else
        Letter1 = Chr(Int(ColNumber / 26) + 64)
        Letter2 = Chr((ColNumber Mod 26) + 64)
        ColumnLetter = Letter1 & Letter2
    End If
End Function
```

The following code applies the ColumnLetter function to the problem of calculating the column reference for the formula. This additional code adds a Sum formula at the end of each row.

```
    ...
    Next
    'Row Total
    Rng.Formula = "=Sum(B" & Rng.Row & ":" & _
        ColumnLetter(Rng.Column - 1) & _
        Rng.Row & ")"

    Rs.MoveNext
    Set Rng = Wks.Cells(Rng.Row + 1, 1)
Loop
    ...
```

In order to produce column Sum formulas, add the following code to the end of the procedure. The row is incremented by 2, leaving a blank line, and a formula is written that sums all the rows in the column. The ColumnLetter figures out the letter that corresponds to the column.

```
Set Rng = Wks.Cells(Rng.Row + 2, 1)
For Each Col In Rs.Fields
    If Col.Type = adCurrency Then
        Rng.Formula = "=Sum(" & ColumnLetter(Rng.Column) & _
            "3:" & ColumnLetter(Rng.Column) & _
            Rng.Row - 1 & ")"
    End If
    Set Rng = Rng.Offset(0, 1)
Next
```

One final formula writes a grand total by summing all the row sums.

```
Rng.Formula = "=Sum(" & ColumnLetter(Rng.Column) & _
    "3:" & ColumnLetter(Rng.Column) & _
    Rng.Row - 1 & ")"
```

> **Module: XLS Operations, Procedure: XLS4**

Sending e-mail

Access 2000 includes the Send To command on the File menu that enables you to send Access objects, such as tables, as attachments to e-mail messages. This function is available through Visual Basic by means of the SendObject method of the DoCmd object.

You can use the SendObject method to write an e-mail message with no attachment at all, which means that you can write a Visual Basic procedure that sends e-mail messages directly from Access 2000. There are two advantages to using Visual Basic to generate e-mail.

- ✔ You can compose an e-mail message based on the data in your database. For example, you can notify a customer that an order has been shipped or back-ordered.

- ✔ You can send the same message to a list of recipients by using e-mail addresses that you have stored in your database.

Sending a message

The following procedure is contained in a form called SendMessage. This form contains information from the Orders table plus the e-mail address of the customer. The procedure composes a text message based on the data on the form and then uses the SendObject method to insert the message into a new e-mail. The e-mail goes the address in the emailAddress field.

```
Private Sub Command32_Click()
    Dim MessText
    MessText = Me.BillFirst & "," & vbCrLf & _
        "Order Shipping Confirmation" & vbCrLf & _
        "Order #" & Me.OrderID & _
        " on " & Me.OrderDate & vbCrLf & _
        "Shipped to:" & vbCrLf & _
        Me.ShipFirst & " " & Me.ShipLast & vbCrLf & _
        Me.ShipAddress1 & vbCrLf & _
        Me.City & ", " & Me.ShipState & " " & Me.ShipZip

    DoCmd.SendObject _
        ObjectType:=acSendNoObject, _
        To:=Me.EmailAddress, _
        Subject:="Order Confirmation", _
        MessageText:=MessText, _
        EditMessage:=True
End Sub
```

⬛ *Form: SendMessage*

Sending to a list

Another handy way to use `SendObject` is to create an e-mail address list based on customer information that you have stored in a table. Figure 11-9 shows a form that selects customers based on particular criteria. In this case, the customers are selected by entering **WA** as the billing state and clicking the Search button.

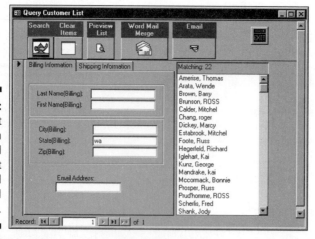

Figure 11-9:
SendObject
creates an
e-mail
address list
for all
selected
customers.

The Email button is linked to the following procedure. This procedure defines a recordset that contains the emailaddress field for all the selected customers. The procedure loops through the recordset and appends each address plus a semicolon to the AddressList variable. This operation creates a semicolon-separated list of e-mail addresses that is compatible with Outlook's addressing scheme. The AddressList is then inserted into the To parameter of the SendObject method. The result is that you have a new e-mail message that is automatically addressed to the selected list of customers.

```
Private Sub EMail_Click()
    Dim MList As New Recordset, AddressList
    MList.Open "SELECT emailaddress FROM Customers " & _
        BuiltWhereString() & " ORDER BY Lastname, firstname"
        _
        , CurrentProject.Connection
    Do Until MList.EOF
        If Not IsNull(MList(0)) Then
            AddressList = AddressList & MList(0) & ";"
        End If
        MList.MoveNext
    Loop
    DoCmd.SendObject ObjectType:=acSendNoObject, _
        To:=AddressList, EditMessage:=True
End Sub
```

| Form: Email |

Word 2000

Word 2000 can also operate as an Automation server, which means that you can use Access 2000 Visual Basic procedures to control word-processing tasks that take advantage of all the features in Word 2000.

In Word, the basic unit of operation is the Document object. In the following procedure, Wrd refers to the Word 2000 application. Doc is defined as a new Document opened in Word. To add text to the document, the InsertAfter method is used to insert text in the Contents object. InsertAfter refers to where the text is inserted relative to the current cursor location. As with Excel, Word doesn't become visible unless you specifically set the Visible property of the application to True.

```
Sub MakeDoc1()
    Dim Wrd As New Word.Application
    Dim Doc As Word.Document
    Set Doc = Wrd.Documents.Add
    Doc.Content.InsertAfter "This is an example."
    Wrd.Visible = True
End Sub
```

A more useful routine is one that inserts the contents of a recordset into a Word document as a table. This routine is roughly the Word 2000 equivalent of the Excel 2000 procedures discussed earlier in this chapter that copied a recordset to an Excel worksheet. The procedure begins by creating a new Word document and an Access recordset.

```
Sub MakeDoc2()
    Dim R As New Recordset, F As Field
    Dim Wrd As New Word.Application
    Dim Doc As Word.Document
    Set Doc = Wrd.Documents.Add
    R.Open "Select LastName, FirstName FROM Customers " & _
        "WHERE state = 'CA' ORDER BY LastName", _
        CurrentProject.Connection
```

You can create a new table in a Word document by using the Add method of the Tables collection. Note that, in this case, the Fields collection determines the number of columns in the table so that the table columns automatically match the recordset fields. Note that the table is given a single row. Word automatically adds rows to the table as you insert the text. Also, notice that the text is inserted using the TypeText method of the application's Selection object. This method duplicates manual entry from the keyboard so that Word responds to the text as if it had been entered from the keyboard. The MoveRight method advances the cursor to the next cell after each entry.

```
Doc.Content.Tables.Add Doc.Content, 1, R.Fields.Count
```

The next loop writes the field names into the first row:

```
For Each F In R.Fields
    Wrd.Selection.TypeText F.Name
    Wrd.Selection.MoveRight unit:=wdCell, Count:=1
Next
```

The next section loops through the recordset and inserts the value of each field in one of the columns in the table:

```
Do Until R.EOF
    With Wrd.Selection
        For Each F In R.Fields
            .TypeText R!LastName
            .MoveRight unit:=wdCell, Count:=1
        Next
    End With
    R.MoveNext
Loop
```

When the table is filled, the AutoFormat method is applied to the table to quickly format the headings, borders and text:

```
Doc.Tables(1).AutoFormat _
    Format:=wdTableFormatSimple3
Wrd.Visible = True
```

You can change the contents of the table by simply altering the recordset assigned to R. Because the code uses the Fields collection to determine the number and order of the columns, the data in the table matches the column in the SELECT statement used to define the recordset.

> **Module: WordOperations, Procedure: MakeDoc2**

Mail Merge

The form in Figure 11-9 also contains a button labeled Word Mail Merge. This button is attached to a procedure that uses the list of customers to create a Word mail merge document.

When the user clicks the button, the procedure creates a new blank Word document and then links that document to the customer records selected in the form. Figure 11-10 shows the result of this procedure. The Word document is linked to the customers that appear in the form. You can use the Insert Merge Field in Word to insert Access data into your form letter.

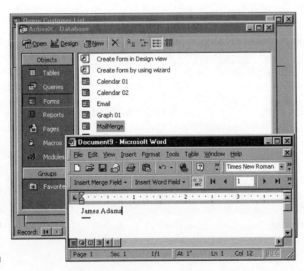

Figure 11-10: A mail merge document is linked automatically to a selected list of customers.

The following procedure that creates this link uses automation to control Word. The MailMerge statements are Word 2000 Visual Basic methods, not Access 2000 methods.

```
Sub StartMM(WC)
    Dim Wrd As New Word.Application
    Dim MM As Word.Document
    Dim Source
    Source = CurrentDb.Name
    Set MM = Wrd.Documents.Add
    MM.MailMerge.MainDocumentType = wdFormLetters
    MM.MailMerge.OpenDataSource Name:=Source, _
        ConfirmConversions:=False, _
        ReadOnly:=False, _
        LinkToSource:=True, _
        AddToRecentFiles:=False, _
        Revert:=False, _
        Format:=wdOpenFormatAuto, _
        Connection:="TABLE Customers", _
        SQLStatement:= _
            "SELECT * FROM [Customers] WHERE " & WC & _
            " ORDER BY LastName, FirstName", _
            SQLStatement1:=""
    MM.MailMerge.EditMainDocument
    Wrd.Visible = True
End Sub
```

Module: WordOperations, Form: MailMerge

Outlook

Outlook contains a number of data sources, such as calendars, to-do lists, contacts, and mailboxes. However, unlike Access, Outlook data sources are not relational database sources, which means that you can't interact with the data by using SQL statements. Instead, you must use techniques that are specific to the structure of the Outlook elements. While I don't have enough space in this book to fully discuss Outlook programming, you may find it useful to see how you can work with the elements in Outlook from Access using Visual Basic.

Calendar

You can add appointments to your Outlook calendar based on information stored in your Access tables and inserted by Visual Basic code attached to Access for objects.

For example, suppose that you want to be able to insert appointments into your calendar while you look at the customer's record in Access. The appointment shown in Figure 11-11 was created by the next procedure, which is attached to a button on the Customers form.

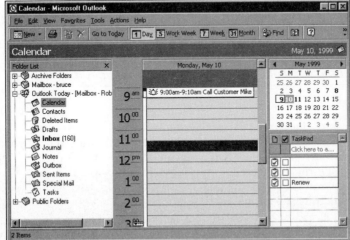

Figure 11-11:
Outlook
appointment
scheduled
directly from
an Access
2000 form.

The key to the procedure is the AppointmentItem object. To add a new appointment, you use the OLCreateItem method of the Outlook application object. You then assign the AppointmentItem the appropriate values for Start (the date and time), Duration, Subject and Body. The Save method adds the new appointment to your calendar.

In this procedure, the CID value passes to the procedure from the Customers form so that the appointment is scheduled for the displayed customer. An input box displays so that you can enter the date and time of the appointment. The default date and time is tomorrow at 9:00 AM.

```
Sub MakeAppointment(CID)
    Dim Cust As New Recordset
    Dim OL As New Outlook.Application
    Dim Apt As Outlook.AppointmentItem
    Dim AptDateTime
    AptDateTime = InputBox("Appointment Time:", , Date + 1 &
            " 9:00 AM")
    Cust.Open _
        "SELECT * FROM Customers WHERE CustomerID = " & CID, _
        CurrentProject.Connection
    Set Apt = OL.CreateItem(olAppointmentItem)
```

(continued)

(continued)

```
    With Apt
        .Start = AptDateTime
        .Duration = 10
        .Subject = "Call Customer " & Cust!FirstName & _
            " " & Cust!LastName
        .Body = Cust!FirstName & " " & Cust!LastName & _
            "Phone: " & Cust!DayPhoneNumber
        .Save
    End With
End Sub
```

| Module: OutlookOperations, Form: MakeAppointment |

Mail

You can perform most e-mail operations by using the `SendObject` method of the `DoCmd` object in Access 2000. However, if you want to read your mail as part of an Access application, you can do so using Automation. Figure 11-12 shows a form that searches your inbox for messages that match (in any part) the text you enter into the box on the left. In this case, the name `Tony` was entered; the list returned on the right reflects the contents of the inbox.

Figure 11-12: Outlook appointment scheduled directly from an Access 2000 form.

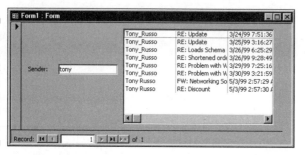

The basic technique for reading the inbox is shown below. In this case, the `MBox` variable is assigned as the default inbox folder for the Outlook client on the current system. The `For...Each` loop reads all the messages in the inbox and displays information from the messages — such as the date received, the sender name, and the subject. You could request the body text or a count of the number of attachments, if any, for each message.

```
Sub ReadMail1()
    Dim OL As New Outlook.Application
    Dim Ns As Outlook.NameSpace
    Dim MBox As Outlook.MAPIFolder
```

```
      Dim Msg As Outlook.MailItem

      Set Ns = OL.GetNamespace("MAPI")
      Set MBox = Ns.GetDefaultFolder(olFolderInbox)

      For Each Msg In MBox.Items
          Debug.Print Msg.SenderName, Msg.Subject, _
              Msg.ReminderTime
      Next
  End Sub
```

The technique is applied to search for senders whose names contain a specified text phrase by the following procedure, which you can find in the
ReadMail form.

```
Private Sub Text2_AfterUpdate()
    Dim MsgList, Sender
    Dim OL As New Outlook.Application
    Dim Ns As Outlook.NameSpace
    Dim MBox As Outlook.MAPIFolder
    Dim Msg As Outlook.MailItem

    Set Ns = OL.GetNamespace("MAPI")
    Set MBox = Ns.GetDefaultFolder(olFolderInbox)

    For Each Msg In MBox.Items
        If InStr(Msg.SenderName, Me.Text2) > 0 Then
            MsgList = MsgList & _
            Msg.SenderName & ";" & _
            Msg.Subject & ";" & _
            Msg.ReceivedTime & ";"
        End If
    Next
    With Me.List0
        .RowSourceType = "Value List"
        .RowSource = MsgList
End Sub  .Requery
    End With
```

> **Module: OutlookOperations, Form: ReadMail**

Part V
The Part of Tens

In this part . . .

Part V features my favorite programming tips in ten easy steps. Enjoy!

Chapter 12

Top Ten Programming Tips

● ●

● ●

> *Database Folder: Chapter 10*
> *Database File: TopTen.MDB*

I spend a lot of time writing programming code and I find that I often encounter the same problems in different applications. Here are my top ten favorite little procedures that I use over and over again.

Dollars

Unlike Excel 2000, Access 2000 doesn't have a rounding function that you can use to convert arithmetic values to values rounded to a specific number of decimal places. In many cases where you may not expect extra decimal places, you can find them. For example, suppose you're working with a currency type field called `SalesTax` and you stored a value in that field using the statement below.

```
Rs!SalesTax = 25 * .0675
```

If you look at the field in the table grid display, you see $1.69 as the value. But if you displayed the value in a message box, you would see that the value stored in the field is actually 1.6875. I created this simple function called `Dollars` to make sure that the calculated values I store in various fields don't contain extra decimal places. Use it when you perform multiplication or division.

```
Function Dollars(vValue)
    Dollars = Val(Format(vValue, "0.00"))
End Function

Rs!SalesTax = Dollars(25 * .0675)
Msgbox SalesTax
 1.69
```

NumbersOnly

In many instances, the data stored in a field is a number sequence, such as a phone number, credit card number, or Social Security number. While input masks can help in entering values consistently, if your system acquires data from other sources (for example, a Web site), you may find that these number sequences are entered in a variety of ways. For example, you may get phone numbers in any of the formats below:

```
415 555-1212
(415)-555-1212
415.555.1212
415 555 1212
(415)555-1212
```

I wrote the following `NumbersOnly` function to strip out all the non-number characters from these sequences. This method not only helps make your data more consistent, but it provides the correct format for credit card processing or sending phone numbers to UPS and FedEx shipping systems, which don't want delimited phone numbers.

```
Function NumbersOnly(T)
    Dim K, Result
    If IsNull(T) Then
        NumbersOnly = Null
        Exit Function
    End If
    For K = 1 To Len(T)
        If Asc(Mid(T, K, 1)) >= 48 _
            And Asc(Mid(T, K, 1)) <= 57 Then
            Result = Result & Mid(T, K, 1)
```

```
        End If
    Next
    If Len(Result) = 0 Then
        NumbersOnly = Null
    Else
        NumbersOnly = Result
    End If
End Function
```

PhoneNumber

After you strip out the unwanted characters from a number sequence, you can then add the specific formatting style you want to use with your system. I created the PhoneNumber function to reformat any phone numbers acquired in an application to a standard phone number form. In this case, I choose the (aaa)eee-nnnn format. Note that this function uses the NumbersOnly function to strip out any non-number characters.

```
Function PhoneNumber(T)
    Dim PNumber, Ac, Ext, Num
    If IsNull(T) Then
        PhoneNumber = Null
        Exit Function
    End If
    PNumber = Left(NumbersOnly(T), 10)
    Ac = Left(PNumber, 3)
    Num = Right(PNumber, 4)
    Ext = Mid(PNumber, 4, 3)
    PhoneNumber = "(" & Ac & ")" & Ext & "-" & Num
End Function
```

Example:

```
? PhoneNumber("(415)-555.1212")
(415)555-1212
```

CleanText

Another variation on the NumbersOnly theme is the CleanText function. I wrote this function to strip out all non-number and letter characters from text. This function drops any characters like *, #, !, -, _, and so on. It also deletes nonvisible characters, such as CR/LF, which can appear in text acquired from external sources such as Web sites.

```
Function CleanText(T)
    Dim K, Result, Code
    If IsNull(T) Then
        CleanText = Null
        Exit Function
    End If
    For K = 1 To Len(T)
        Select Case Asc(Mid(T, K, 1))
            Case 48 To 57, 65 To 65 + 26, 97 To 97 + 26
            Result = Result & Mid(T, K, 1)
        End Select
    Next
    If Len(Result) = 0 Then
        CleanText = Null
    Else
        CleanText = Result
    End If
End Function
```

Example:

```
? CleanText("AXR-666 990")
AXR666990
```

Entering Percents

When you ask a user to enter a percentage, you always run the risk of some confusion as to whether or not the entry should be a decimal value (for example, .0675) or a percentage (for example, 6.75). You can place as many warnings as you like on the screen, but chances are some users may enter the values the wrong way. I created the Pct( ) function to deal with the problem as it occurs. The function converts any values of 1 or greater to decimal values but lets decimal values be entered without change.

```
Function Pct(vValue)
    If vValue >= 1 Then
        Pct = vValue / 100
    Else
        Pct = vValue
    End If
End Function
```

When you have a percentage field displayed on a form, add the following statement to the AfterUpdate property. This ensures that no matter which style the user chooses for entry, the value stored in the field is always a decimal value.

```
Private Sub Percentage_AfterUpdate()
    Me.Percentage = Pct(Me.Percentage)
End Sub
```

IsEmail Address

While building an application for giving and grading tests over the Internet, I noticed that the e-mail addresses entered were frequently not complete. For example, America Online (AOL) users tend not to realize that their Internet domain is aol.com and not simply aol. I wrote this function to determine whether the text entered looks like a valid e-mail address so that I could avoid having my application send mail to addresses that don't work.

```
Function InterNetSMPT(S)
    Dim HasAt, HasDomain, Host, Server
    If InStr(S, "@") > 0 Then
        HasAt = True
        Server = Mid(S, InStr(S, "@") + 1)
        If InStr(Server, ".") = 0 Then
            InterNetSMPT = False
            Exit Function
        End If
    Else
        InterNetSMPT = False
        Exit Function
    End If
    InterNetSMPT = True
End Function
```

IsNotNull

Visual Basic provides the IsNull( ) function to test for nulls. However, I found that most of the time I was testing for Not Null. For example, if I want to send e-mail in a procedure, I'd send mail only if the e-mail address isn't a null. I found quite often that I was writing code that looked like the example below, which always felt awkward to me.

```
If Not IsNull(Cust!EmailAddress) Then
    DoCmd.sendObject ...
Endif
```

I wrote the IsNotNull function in order to have a way to make the code read closer to its meaning.

```
Function IsNotNull(DataItem) As Boolean
    If IsNull(DataItem) Then
        IsNotNull = False
    Else
        IsNotNull = True
    End If
End Function
```

I can write the same procedure using the IsNotNull function, which to my mind makes reading code easier.

```
If IsNotNull(Cust!EmailAddress) Then
    DoCmd.sendObject ...
Endif
```

Replace/Remove Text

Often, I find the need to perform the equivalent of a search-and-replace operation on a text string. In these cases, I want to remove all instances of a character or phrase from a larger text string. In others, I want to replace one item with another. In both cases, I want to deal with all instances of the specified items within the source text with a single operation.

I created the RemoveText and ReplaceText functions, to give me this ability.

```
Function RemoveText(Source As String, TextToRemove As String)
    Dim A, B, C, PStart, Pend
    Do Until InStr(Source, TextToRemove) = 0
        If InStr(Source, TextToRemove) > 0 Then
            PStart = InStr(Source, TextToRemove)
            Pend = PStart + Len(TextToRemove) - 1
            Source = Mid(Source, 1, PStart - 1) & Mid(Source,
            Pend + 1)
        End If
    Loop
    RemoveText = Source
End Function
```

```
Function ReplaceText(Source As String, _
    TextToRemove As String, TextToInsert As String)
    Dim A, B, C, PStart, Pend
    Do Until InStr(Source, TextToRemove) = 0
```

```
        If InStr(Source, TextToRemove) > 0 Then
            PStart = InStr(Source, TextToRemove)
            Pend = PStart + Len(TextToRemove) - 1
            Source = Mid(Source, 1, PStart - 1) &
            TextToInsert & Mid(Source, Pend + 1)
        End If
    Loop
    ReplaceText = Source
End Function
```

Example:

```
? ReplaceText("ABC/132/456","/","-")
ABC-132-456
? RemoveText("ABC/132/456","/")
ABC132456
```

Get Parameters

As you build applications, you will find that different users or different installations will need to change certain key values. For example, in each installation, you may need to specify the location of files, directories from which to read or write data for import or export functions, and so on.

One way to handle these key values in Access 2000 is to create a `Parameters` table. The table would have a column for the `Parameter name` and another for the `StringValue` associated with that parameter.

The `GetParameter` function in your code would fetch the value of a specific parameter from the `Parameters` table.

```
Function GetParameter(ParameterName)
    GetParameter = DLookup("StringValue", _
    "Parameters", "Parameter = '" & ParameterName & "'")
End Function
```

The statement below displays the company code stored in the `Parameters` table.

```
? GetParameter("CompanyCode")
```

While this method works perfectly well, I personally have a problem remembering the exact names that I give the various parameters when an application becomes large and complex. If Access could automatically list the parameter names when I write the code, life would be a whole lot easier.

You can accomplish this by using the data in the Parameters table to write the code for a class module, which I call AppParameters. The procedure below deletes and then rewrites a series of Get Property procedures, one for each record in the Parameters table.

```
Sub CreateParametersClass()
    Dim M As Module, R As New Recordset
    Set M = Modules("AppParameters")
    M.DeleteLines 1, M.CountOfLines
    R.Open "Select * FROM [Parameters]",
        CurrentProject.Connection, _
        adOpenKeyset, adLockOptimistic
    Do Until R.EOF
        M.InsertText "Public Property Get " & _
            R!Parameter & "() As Variant"
        M.InsertText vbTab & R!Parameter & " = " & _
            Chr(34) & R!StringValue & Chr(34)
        M.InsertText "End Property"
        R.MoveNext
    Loop
End Sub
```

The procedure produces Property procedures, such as the one below, for each record in the Parameters table.

```
Public Property Get CompanyCode() As Variant
    CompanyCode = "Krummy Vineyards"
End Property
```

After the class is created, you can write code like what appears below. In this instance, I can get the company code by selecting the CompanyCode property of the PM (Application Parameters) object. This function makes coding applications with a large number of parameters much easier.

```
Dim Pm as New AppParameters
Msgbox Pm.CompanyCode
```

Note that you need to remember to re-run the CreateParametersClass() each time you edit, append, or delete from the Parameters table in order to keep the class module up to date.

Design Tools

One of the jobs I like least about building applications is laying out forms and reports. An experienced programmer has to spend the same amount of time moving boxes around a form or report as anyone else does.

To get the job done faster, I created a set of functions that work in the design mode for forms and reports. The code is contained in the `CodeTools` module. The functions are linked to macros on the AutoKeys macro.

I find that these operations greatly help in form and report layouts. They're also easier to use because they're keyboard shortcuts, which don't require menu selection.

Use the following shortcut commands for size and alignment of form and report controls.

✔ **Ctrl+Shift+C.** Copies the settings for the highlighted control into memory. You can then select another control and use the following key combinations to set properties for that control, which helps you quickly size and align the control.

✔ **Ctrl+Shift+V.** Sets the control width to match the copied control.

✔ **Ctrl+Shift+L.** Sets the `Left` property of the selected control to match the copied control. The two controls are now aligned vertically.

✔ **Ctrl+Shift+N.** Sets the `Left` property of the selected control so that it aligns on the right side of the copied control. The selected control in now aligned next to the copied control.

✔ **Ctrl+Shift+E.** Sets the `Top` property of the selected control to match the top property of the copied control. The two controls are now aligned horizontally.

✔ **Ctrl+Shift+H.** Sets the `Height` property of the selected control to match the height of the copied control.

These commands become useful because you can quickly execute several setting in rapid succession. For example, if you use Ctrl+Shift+C to copy the setting of one control and then select another control, you can hold down Shift+Ctrl and press V and then L to have the selected control match the size and left position of the copied control.

You can use two additional shortcuts to write formulas into text boxes that are copies of other text boxes.

✔ **Ctrl+Shift+I.** This function converts a reference to a field to a formula that displays the field name as shown below. When you lay out a report, you have text boxes in the detail section that display the contents of the fields on the form. However, you also need to have column headings in the Page Header section that correspond to these fields. One quick way to get these headings is to simply copy the row of field text boxes from the detail section to the Page Header section. The text boxes are easy to align because they exactly match the fields in the detail section. To convert the field references to labels, place the cursor on the Control Source line of the each control's property sheet and press Ctrl+Shift+I. This converts the field reference to a label formula. Move to the next text box and repeat Ctrl+Shift+I until you convert all of them to label formulas.

```
OrderTotal changes to ="OrderTotal"
```

✔ **Ctrl+Shift+S.** This command converts a field reference to a Sum formula. The idea is similar to the technique used to convert references to labels. In this case, you can copy the fields that need to be totaled from the details section to the group and/or report footer section. Place the cursor on the Control Source line of the each control's property sheet and press Ctrl+Shift+S to create the sum formula. Repeat the operation for each control that needs to be totaled.

```
OrderTotal changes to =Sum(OrderTotal)
```

Module: Code Tools, Macro: AutoKeys

Part VI
Appendix

The 5th Wave   By Rich Tennant

ONE DAY IT REALLY HIT BERTHA JUST HOW OBSESSED HER HUSBAND HAD BECOME WITH HIS COMPUTER.

In this part . . .

Part VI tells you all about the helpful CD-ROM included with this book. Look here for everything from system requirements to setup instructions.

Appendix

About the CD

● ●

*T*he CD included with this book contains all of the programming examples discussed in this book, including programming code, forms, reports, and tables. There is one folder for each chapter in the book.

You cannot use Access MDB files if they are marked as read-only. If you do not want to use the Access Database Installer provided on the CD and you use Windows to copy the MDB files from the CD to your hard drive, you must remove the read-only attribute from the file. To remove the read-only attribute from a copied file, select the file in the My Computer window and press Alt+Enter to open the Properties dialog box. Uncheck the box marked Read-Only and click OK. You can now open the file with Access 2000. Note that this operation is automatically performed by the Access Database Installer.

System Requirements

In order to use the CD, your system must have the following basic requirements:

- ✔ A PC with a 486 or faster processor.
- ✔ Microsoft Windows 95 or later.
- ✔ At least 16MB of total RAM installed on your computer. For best performance, we recommend that Windows 95-equipped PCs have at least 32MB of RAM installed.
- ✔ At least 40MB of hard drive space available to install all the software from this CD. (You'll need less space if you don't install every program.)
- ✔ A CD-ROM drive — double-speed (2x) or faster.
- ✔ Recommended: A monitor capable of displaying at least 256 colors or grayscale.
- ✔ Recommended: A modem with a speed of at least 56K.

Also, examples in this book that deal with Web-based applications can be run directly from my Web site, www.wbase2.com, so you can see how the programs work live, on the Internet.

If you need more information on the basics, check out *PCs For Dummies,* 6th Edition, by Dan Gookin, *Windows 95 For Dummies,* 2nd Edition, or *Windows 98 For Dummies,* both by Andy Rathbone (all published by IDG Books Worldwide, Inc.).

Using the CD

1. **Open the My Computer window and double-click the drive that contains the CD supplied with this book.**

2. **Find the file called Chapzip.exe and double-click that file.**

3. **Follow the instructions in the Setup program.**

   When you have completed the Setup program, you will find a new item on your Start menu's Programs menu: Access Programming. This menu contains an icon entitled Access Database Installer. This program will allow you to install some or all of the database. Start the Access Database Installer and select the chapters you want to install. That is all there is to it.

If You've Got Problems (Of the CD Kind)

The two likeliest problems are that you don't have enough memory (RAM) for the programs you want to use or you have other programs running that are affecting the installation or running of a program. If you get error messages like `Not enough memory` or `Setup cannot continue,` try one or more of these methods and then try using the software again:

- ✔ Turn off any antivirus software that you have on your computer. Installers sometimes mimic virus activity and may make your computer incorrectly believe that it is being infected by a virus.

- ✔ Close all running programs. The more programs you're running, the less memory is available to other programs. Installers also typically update files and programs. So if you keep other programs running, installation may not work properly.

- ✔ Have your local computer store add more RAM to your computer. This is, admittedly, a drastic and somewhat expensive step. However, if you have a Windows 95 PC, adding more memory can really help the speed of your computer and allow more programs to run at the same time.

If you still have trouble with installing the items from the CD, please call the Hungry Minds Customer Care phone number: 800-762-2974 (outside the U.S.: 317-572-3993).

Index

● *T* ●

Wiley Publishing, Inc.
End-User License Agreement

READ THIS. You should carefully read these terms and conditions before opening the software packet(s) included with this book "Book". This is a license agreement "Agreement" between you and Wiley Publishing, Inc. "WPI". By opening the accompanying software packet(s), you acknowledge that you have read and accept the following terms and conditions. If you do not agree and do not want to be bound by such terms and conditions, promptly return the Book and the unopened software packet(s) to the place you obtained them for a full refund.

1. **License Grant.** WPI grants to you (either an individual or entity) a nonexclusive license to use one copy of the enclosed software program(s) (collectively, the "Software" solely for your own personal or business purposes on a single computer (whether a standard computer or a workstation component of a multi-user network). The Software is in use on a computer when it is loaded into temporary memory (RAM) or installed into permanent memory (hard disk, CD-ROM, or other storage device). WPI reserves all rights not expressly granted herein.

2. **Ownership.** WPI is the owner of all right, title, and interest, including copyright, in and to the compilation of the Software recorded on the disk(s) or CD-ROM "Software Media". Copyright to the individual programs recorded on the Software Media is owned by the author or other authorized copyright owner of each program. Ownership of the Software and all proprietary rights relating thereto remain with WPI and its licensers.

3. **Restrictions On Use and Transfer.**

   (a) You may only (i) make one copy of the Software for backup or archival purposes, or (ii) transfer the Software to a single hard disk, provided that you keep the original for backup or archival purposes. You may not (i) rent or lease the Software, (ii) copy or reproduce the Software through a LAN or other network system or through any computer subscriber system or bulletin- board system, or (iii) modify, adapt, or create derivative works based on the Software.

   (b) You may not reverse engineer, decompile, or disassemble the Software. You may transfer the Software and user documentation on a permanent basis, provided that the transferee agrees to accept the terms and conditions of this Agreement and you retain no copies. If the Software is an update or has been updated, any transfer must include the most recent update and all prior versions.

4. **Restrictions on Use of Individual Programs.** You must follow the individual requirements and restrictions detailed for each individual program in the "About the CD" appendix of this Book. These limitations are also contained in the individual license agreements recorded on the Software Media. These limitations may include a requirement that after using the program for a specified period of time, the user must pay a registration fee or discontinue use. By opening the Software packet(s), you will be agreeing to abide by the licenses and restrictions for these individual programs that are detailed in the "About the CD" appendix and on the Software Media. None of the material on this Software Media or listed in this Book may ever be redistributed, in original or modified form, for commercial purposes.

FOR DUMMIES®

The easy way to get more done and have more fun

PERSONAL FINANCE

0-7645-5231-7

0-7645-2431-3

0-7645-5331-3

Also available:

Estate Planning For Dummies
(0-7645-5501-4)

401(k)s For Dummies
(0-7645-5468-9)

Frugal Living For Dummies
(0-7645-5403-4)

Microsoft Money "X" For Dummies
(0-7645-1689-2)

Mutual Funds For Dummies
(0-7645-5329-1)

Personal Bankruptcy For Dummies
(0-7645-5498-0)

Quicken "X" For Dummies
(0-7645-1666-3)

Stock Investing For Dummies
(0-7645-5411-5)

Taxes For Dummies 2003
(0-7645-5475-1)

BUSINESS & CAREERS

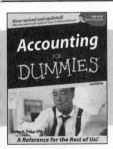

0-7645-5314-3

0-7645-5307-0

0-7645-5471-9

Also available:

Business Plans Kit For Dummies
(0-7645-5365-8)

Consulting For Dummies
(0-7645-5034-9)

Cool Careers For Dummies
(0-7645-5345-3)

Human Resources Kit For Dummies
(0-7645-5131-0)

Managing For Dummies
(1-5688-4858-7)

QuickBooks All-in-One Desk Reference For Dummies
(0-7645-1963-8)

Selling For Dummies
(0-7645-5363-1)

Small Business Kit For Dummies
(0-7645-5093-4)

Starting an eBay Business For Dummies
(0-7645-1547-0)

HEALTH, SPORTS & FITNESS

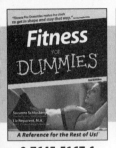

0-7645-5167-1

0-7645-5146-9

0-7645-5154-X

Also available:

Controlling Cholesterol For Dummies
(0-7645-5440-9)

Dieting For Dummies
(0-7645-5126-4)

High Blood Pressure For Dummies
(0-7645-5424-7)

Martial Arts For Dummies
(0-7645-5358-5)

Menopause For Dummies
(0-7645-5458-1)

Nutrition For Dummies
(0-7645-5180-9)

Power Yoga For Dummies
(0-7645-5342-9)

Thyroid For Dummies
(0-7645-5385-2)

Weight Training For Dummies
(0-7645-5168-X)

Yoga For Dummies
(0-7645-5117-5)

Available wherever books are sold.
Go to www.dummies.com or call 1-877-762-2974 to order direct.

FOR DUMMIES®

A world of resources to help you grow

HOME, GARDEN & HOBBIES

0-7645-5295-3

0-7645-5130-2

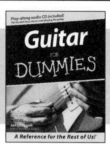

0-7645-5106-X

Also available:

Auto Repair For Dummies
(0-7645-5089-6)

Chess For Dummies
(0-7645-5003-9)

Home Maintenance For Dummies
(0-7645-5215-5)

Organizing For Dummies
(0-7645-5300-3)

Piano For Dummies
(0-7645-5105-1)

Poker For Dummies
(0-7645-5232-5)

Quilting For Dummies
(0-7645-5118-3)

Rock Guitar For Dummies
(0-7645-5356-9)

Roses For Dummies
(0-7645-5202-3)

Sewing For Dummies
(0-7645-5137-X)

FOOD & WINE

0-7645-5250-3

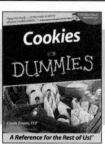

0-7645-5390-9

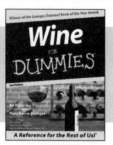

0-7645-5114-0

Also available:

Bartending For Dummies
(0-7645-5051-9)

Chinese Cooking For Dummies
(0-7645-5247-3)

Christmas Cooking For Dummies
(0-7645-5407-7)

Diabetes Cookbook For Dummies
(0-7645-5230-9)

Grilling For Dummies
(0-7645-5076-4)

Low-Fat Cooking For Dummies
(0-7645-5035-7)

Slow Cookers For Dummies
(0-7645-5240-6)

TRAVEL

0-7645-5453-0

0-7645-5438-7

0-7645-5448-4

Also available:

America's National Parks For Dummies
(0-7645-6204-5)

Caribbean For Dummies
(0-7645-5445-X)

Cruise Vacations For Dummies 2003
(0-7645-5459-X)

Europe For Dummies
(0-7645-5456-5)

Ireland For Dummies
(0-7645-6199-5)

France For Dummies
(0-7645-6292-4)

London For Dummies
(0-7645-5416-6)

Mexico's Beach Resorts For Dummies
(0-7645-6262-2)

Paris For Dummies
(0-7645-5494-8)

RV Vacations For Dummies
(0-7645-5443-3)

Walt Disney World & Orlando For Dummies
(0-7645-5444-1)

FOR DUMMIES®

Plain-English solutions for everyday challenges

  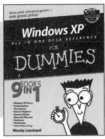

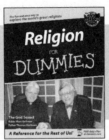

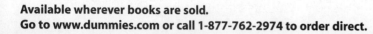

Notes

Notes